Come Thirsty
Traveling Light
Next Door Savior

Come Thirsty
Traveling Light
Next Door Savior

Max Lucado

Thomas Nelson
Since 1798

NASHVILLE DALLAS MEXICO CITY RIO DE JANEIRO BEIJING

Published in Nashville, Tennessee, by Thomas Nelson. Thomas Nelson is a registered trademark of Thomas Nelson, Inc.

Thomas Nelson, Inc., titles may be purchased in bulk for educational, business, fund-raising, or sales promotional use. For information, please e-mail SpecialMarkets@ThomasNelson.com.

ISBN 978-0-8499-2103-2

Printed in the United States of America
08 09 10 11 12 QW 5 4 3 2 1

Contents

Come Thirsty

PART FOUR
Receive His Love

Traveling Light

Next Door Savior

PART TWO
No Place He Won't Go

COME THIRSTY

MAX
LUCADO

Published in Nashville, Tennessee, by Thomas Nelson. Thomas Nelson is a registered trademark of Thomas Nelson, Inc.

Thomas Nelson, Inc., titles may be purchased in bulk for educational, business, fund-raising, or sales promotional use. For information, please e-mail SpecialMarkets@ThomasNelson.com.

Library of Congress Cataloging-in-Publication Data

Lucado, Max.
Come thirsty / by Max Lucado.
p. cm.
Includes bibliographical references.
ISBN 978-0-8499-1761-5 (hc)
ISBN 978-0-8499-1404-1 (sc)
ISBN 978-0-8499-9130-1 (ie)
1. Christian life. I. Title.
BV4501.3.L812 2004
248.4—dc22 2004007737

ANDREA,

your mom and I proudly dedicate this book to you

on your eighteenth birthday.

Tell me, where have the years gone?

If I knew, I'd gladly reclaim and relive each one of them.

We love you, dear daughter.

May your smile never fade and your faith ever deepen.

Foreword

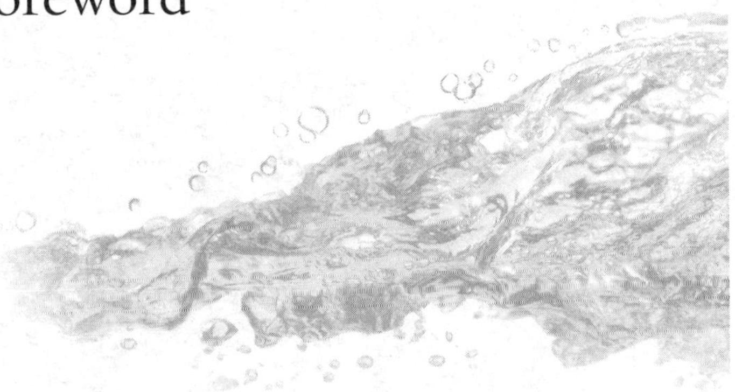

We all know what it is like to be thirsty—both physically and spiritually. That longing to quench your dry mouth can be powerful. But a dry heart—that's unbearable. You need refreshment, and you need it now. If your heart has become a little crusty, if your spirit is dry, if your heart is parched, you've come to the right place. In the pages of this book, Max leads us to the *w-e-l-l* that God provides for us. And, just as importantly, Max shows us how to receive from God *all* that He longs to give us.

It is often difficult for us to receive. But Max helps us grasp that, more than anything, God wants us to receive, to come thirsty and drink deeply from the living water available to each of us.

I have learned so much from Max Lucado. For years his books have been a consistent source of inspiration to me. And his friendship is something that I will always treasure. I have had the privilege of being ministered to one-on-one by Max, and I have had the wonderful opportunity to watch as he ministers—just as effectively—to an arena of fifteen thousand people.

My prayer for you, the reader, is that your soul is ministered to and refreshed through this wonderful book.

— Michael W. Smith

Acknowledgments

They prodded, applauded, extolled, and cajoled. These friends made the book a book. And to them I offer great gratitude.

Jim Barker—the God-seeking golf professional. You sowed these seeds while trying to fix my swing. At least the seeds bore fruit.

Liz Heaney and Karen Hill—If dentists had your skill, we'd have wider smiles and less pain. Great editing!

Carol Bartley—You did it again. We applaud your patient addiction to detail and precision.

Thanks to Hank Hanegraaff for generously giving your time and your insights.

David Moberg and Thomas Nelson—You make me feel like a middle-schooler playing on an NBA squad!

The Oak Hills leadership and church family—celebrating our greatest year yet!

Susan Perry—Look up the word *servant* in the dictionary and see your picture. For your gracious service, thank you.

Jennifer McKinney—We appreciate your service almost as much as your smile.

Margaret Mechinus—Your skill at organization matches my proclivity toward chaos. Thanks for ensuring that at least my bookshelves make sense.

Charles Prince—true sage and dear friend. Thanks for the research.

Steve Halliday—Thanks to you, readers once again have another great discussion guide.

Andrew Cooley and the UpWords staff—a home-run-hitting team!

Steve and Cheryl Green—Denalyn and I regard you as permanent partners and dearest friends.

Michael W. Smith—Here's to many great moments together, and we're just getting started.

Jenna, Andrea, and Sara—The galaxy is missing three stars. Thanks to you, the whole world is brighter, especially mine.

My wife, Denalyn—Who would give a Renoir to a hillbilly? The Hope diamond to a pawnshop? Entrust a Lamborghini to a ten-year-old? I guess God would. For he gave you to me. And I'm still amazed.

And God—For your endless aquifer of grace, I thank you.

If you are thirsty, come!
If you want life-giving water,
come and take it.
It's free!

—Rev. 22:17 CEV

Each of us is now a part of his resurrection body,
refreshed and sustained at one fountain—
his Spirit—where we all come to drink.

—I Cor. 12:13 MSG

Meagan

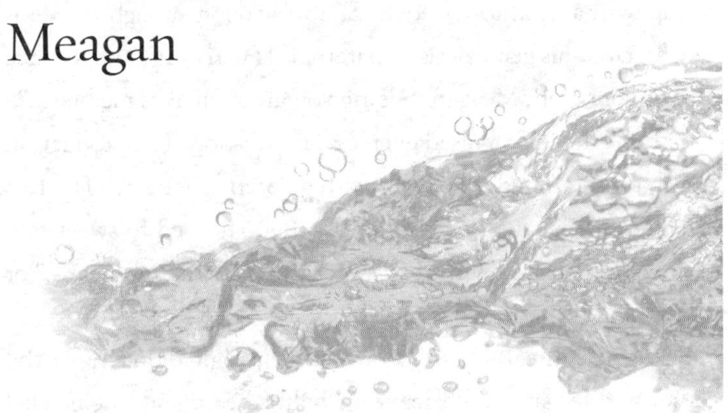

Bentley Bishop stepped out of the elevator into a buzz of activity, all directed at him. The first voice was the urgent one of Eric, his producer.

"Mr. Bishop, I've been trying to reach you for the last two hours." Eric simmered with nervous energy. He stood a couple of inches over five feet in a wrinkled suit, loose tie, and the same scuffed loafers he'd worn for the last year. Though he was barely thirty, his hairline had retreated halfway and appeared on pace to soon evacuate the dome. His fashion turned no heads. But his media savvy did.

Eric read society like a radar screen. Departing fads, incoming trends, who teens followed, what executives ate—Eric knew the culture. As a result, he knew talk shows. He knew the hot topics, the best guests, and Bentley Bishop knew his show was in good hands with Eric. Even if he was prone to panic.

"I never carry a phone on the golf course, Eric. You know that."

"Didn't the pro shop tell you I'd called?"

"They did." By now the makeup artist was tying a bib around Bishop's neck. "Did I get some sun today, honey?" he asked, sizing her up with a head-to-toe look. She was young enough to be his daughter, but his glance wasn't paternal. "Then again, the red face may be your fault, Meagan. Seeing you always makes me blush."

Bishop's flirting repulsed everyone but Bishop. The production crew had seen him do the same with a dozen other girls. The two receptionists cut their eyes at each other. He used to sweet-talk them. Now he toyed with the "sweet thing in the tight jeans," or so they had heard him describe her.

Eric would fire Meagan in a heartbeat, but didn't have the authority. Meagan would leave in half a heartbeat, but needed the money.

"Mr. Bishop." Eric scowled, looking at his watch. "We've got a problem."

From down the hall came the announcement. "Fifteen minutes to air."

"Oops." Bishop winked, untying the makeup bib. "Looks like we'll have to finish this later, babe."

Meagan powdered his cheek one final time and forced a smile.

"Dr. Allsup canceled," Eric inserted as the two headed for the studio.

"What?"

"Weather. He called from O'Hare."

"The Midwest is having weather problems?"

"Apparently Chicago is."

The two stopped in the middle of the hallway, and for the first time, Bishop gave Eric his full attention. He loomed over his producer by a full foot, his mane of thick white hair making him look even taller. Everyone in America, it seemed, recognized that square jaw and those caterpillar eyebrows. Twenty years of nightly interviews had elevated him to billboard status.

"What's our topic?" he asked.

"Surviving stress."

"Appropriate. Did you phone some fill-ins?"

"I did."

"Dr. Varner?"

"Sick."

"Dr. Chambers?"

"Out of town."

"What about those two guys we had last month who wrote that breathing book?"

"*Breathe Right, Live Right.* One has a cold. The other didn't call back."

"Then we're stuck with the rabbi."

"He's out too."

"Rabbi Cohen? He's never out. He's been subbing for ten years."

"Fifteen. His sister died and he's in Topeka."

"So where does that leave us? Doing a remote? I don't like remotes." By now Bishop's voice was beginning to boom and Eric's face to redden. The ninth-floor hallway of the Burbank Plaza Building was silent—busy, but silent. No one envied Eric.

"No remote, Mr. Bishop. The system is down."

"What?"

"Lightning from last night's storm."

"Did we have a storm last night?" Bishop asked everyone in hearing distance.

Eric shrugged. "I had us hooked up with the president's physician, then discovered the technical problems. No outside feeds."

The smile had long since vanished from Bishop's face. "No guests. No feeds. Why didn't you call me?"

Eric knew better than to answer honestly.

"Studio audience?"

"Packed. They came to see Dr. Allsup."

"So what do we do?" Bishop demanded.

"Ten minutes!" came a voice.

"We have a guest," Eric explained, slowly turning toward the studio door. "He's already in makeup."

"Where did you find him?"

"I think he found us." By now they were walking fast. "He sent me an e-mail an hour ago."

"How did he get your e-mail address?"

"I don't know. Nor do I know how he found out about our situation, but he did." Eric pulled a piece of paper from his jacket side pocket. "He told me he's sorry about Varner, Chambers, the Chicago weather, and last night's lightning. But he didn't like the breathing book anyway. And, knowing our plight, he volunteered to do the show."

"That's crazy." Eric opened the door. Bishop entered, never losing eye contact with Eric. "You let him in?"

"Actually, he sort of let himself in. But I called around. He's causing quite a stir, mainly in smaller markets. Teaches ethics at a junior college near Birmingham. Some religious leaders are concerned, but the rank and file like him. He lectures at colleges, popular on the banquet circuit. Talks a lot about finding peace in your soul."

By now Bishop was stepping toward the set. "I could use some peace. Hope this guy's good. What's his name?"

"Jesse. Jesse Carpenter."

"Never heard of him. Let's give him fifteen minutes. For the last half of the program, rerun the highlight show."

"But we did that last week."

"People forget. Go to makeup and check on this Carpenter fellow."

Meagan could see both her face and Jesse's in the mirror. She would later describe him as nice looking but not heart stopping. He wore a brown, elbow-patched corduroy coat, khaki slacks, and an acceptable but forgettable tie. A straight part separated his hair on the side, giving it a just-cut look. Meagan tied the apron around his neck and began with polite chitchat. His smile required no coaxing.

"First time on the show?"

"Yes."

"First time to the West Coast?"

"You might say that."

Meagan dabbed base powder on his cheeks, then stopped. He was staring at her. "Is this required?" he asked. He wasn't enjoying the drill.

"Keeps the glare down," she explained.

As she powdered, Jesse closed his eyes, then opened them and looked at her, saying nothing.

Meagan wondered about him. When men stared at her, she knew what they wanted. He's probably the same. She stepped behind the chair and sprayed his hair. He closed his eyes again. She looked at herself, curious what he might think of her—tattooed rose on her neck, jet-black hair and fingernails. T-shirt tied tight in the back, leaving her stomach exposed. A far cry from her role as a majorette in the high-school band. Her older brother, who managed the family pharmacy in Missouri, was always calling and asking, "You're not getting a tattoo, are you? And keep those rings out of your nose." She didn't listen.

She really didn't care what he thought. After all, she was twenty-one. Can't a girl have a life?

"Architecture?"

The one-word question caught Meagan off guard. "What?"

Jesse had opened his eyes, and with them he gestured to her open backpack that sat on the counter. A copy of *Architectural Digest* leaned out.

"Call it a secret interest," she explained. "Who knows, someday . . ."

"Have any other secrets?"

Meagan sighed. Of all the come-ons. "None that you need to hear about." She shrugged.

Men never ceased to amaze her. Her mother's warning was right: no matter how nice they look, first the line, then the hook. For a couple of minutes neither spoke. Meagan liked it that way. She found safety in silence. Jesse, however, wasn't finished.

"Bishop asks a lot of you."

Meagan cocked her head. "Is that a question?"

"No, just the truth."

"He's all right." Meagan sidestepped the topic, intentionally avoiding Jesse's eyes as she dusted his forehead one last time.

Jesse's tone was solemn. "Meagan, don't let your heart get hard. You were not made to be this edgy, this crusty."

She dropped her hands to her side and looked at Jesse, at first offended, then curious.

"What do you know about me?"

"I know you are a better person than this. I also know it's not too late to make a change. This street you're traveling? The houses look nice, but the road goes nowhere."

She started to object, but his eyes caught hers. "I can help, Meagan. I really can."

"I don't need your help" were the words she started to say, but didn't. He smiled softly, reassuringly. More silence followed. Not awkward. Just silence. Meagan felt a smile forming in reply, but then . . .

"Five minutes!" shouted a studio voice. Meagan looked up to see Eric's face.

Meagan never watched the *Bentley Bishop Show.* The first couple of days she had tried but quickly grew weary of his piano-key smile and disc-jockey voice. So she lost interest. She tried chatting with other staff members, but they knew how she got and kept her job. Show veterans formed a tight club, and girls like Meagan needn't apply for membership. "You'd think I was a leper," she'd mumbled after her final attempt at conversation.

Meagan followed her daily ritual of cleaning her counter, pulling out her magazine, and sitting in the makeup chair. But on this day, as she lifted the remote to turn off the makeup-room monitor, she saw Jesse walk out on stage.

People offered polite applause. She watched Jesse greet the host, take his seat, and nod at the crowd. Bishop turned his attention to the index cards resting on the table, each bearing an Eric-prepared question. He gave them a shuffle and set things in motion.

"Tell us about yourself, Mr. Carpenter. I understand you teach at a community college."

"Night courses mainly."

"In Alabama?"

"Yessir. Sawgrass, Alabama."

"Do people in Sawgrass know the meaning of stress?"

Jesse nodded.

Bishop continued: "This is a tough, tough world, Jesse. Brutally competitive, highly demanding. Tell us, how do we handle the stress?"

The teacher sat up a bit straighter, made a tent with his hands, and began to speak. "Stress signals a deeper need, a longing. We long to fit in, to make a difference. Acceptance, significance—these matter to us. So we do what it takes; we go into debt to buy the house, we stretch the credit card to buy the clothes . . . and life on the treadmill begins."

"Treadmill?"

"Right, we spend a lot of energy going nowhere. At the end of the day, or the end of a life, we haven't moved one step. We're stuck."

"What do we do about it?"

"What we *typically* do doesn't work. We take vacations. We take pills. We take our chances in Vegas. We take advantage of younger women . . ." Jesse looked straight at Bishop as he spoke. But if Bishop connected the dots, he didn't show it.

Meagan did, and for the first time in a long time, she smiled.

"Doesn't work, Mr. Bishop. Back home we call it 'sipping out of the swamp.' There's stuff in that water we were never made to drink." This time Jesse turned toward the camera.

For a moment Meagan felt as if he were speaking to her, just to her. In self-defense, she muted the sound and watched him speak.

His minutes on the show totaled no more than seven. She later heard that Bishop and Eric were pleased, even interested in asking him to return.

She hoped they would.

Jesse spotted Meagan through the window of a café, squeezing lemon into her glass of water. For a couple of minutes he watched. The restaurant had a retro look, a throwback to diner days with soda counters and silver-rimmed tables. Two men in an adjacent booth said something to her; she ignored them. A server offered her a menu; she declined it. A car screeched to a stop and honked at a jay-walking pedestrian; she looked up. That's when Meagan saw him.

Jesse smiled. She didn't. But neither did she turn away. She watched him cross the narrow street, enter the café, and walk toward her booth. He asked if he could join her, and she nodded. As he signaled the server, Meagan noticed Jesse looked tired.

He said little as he waited on his coffee. She spoke even less, at first. But once she began, her whole story tumbled out. Dropped by a boyfriend in Missouri. Fed up with her family. Someone told her she could make fast money in commercials. Escaped to the West Coast. Audition after audition. Rejection after rejection. Finally cosmetics school. "I never even finished," she confessed. "I heard about the opening at Bentley Bishop's. Went for an interview and . . ."—she looked away—"after doing what he wanted, he hired me. And now"—a tear bubbled—"I'm here. I pay the rent and don't go hungry. Twenty-one years old and surviving L.A. Sounds like the chorus of a country-western song. But I'm okay. At least that's what I tell myself."

Jesse's sandwich arrived. He offered her half, but she declined. After a couple of bites, he wiped his mouth with a napkin.

"Meagan, I know you. I've watched you stain pillows with tears and walk streets because you couldn't sleep. I know you. And I know you hate who you are becoming."

"So"—Meagan touched the corner of her eye with the back of a knuckle—"if you're such a psychic, tell me: where's God in all this? I've been looking for him a long, long time." With a sudden increase in volume, she began listing misdeeds on her fingers. "I ran out on my folks. I sleep with my boss. I've spent more time on a barstool than a church pew. I'm tired, tired of it all." She bit her lip and looked away.

Jesse inclined the same direction and caught her attention. She looked up to see him beaming, energetic, as though he were an algebra professor and she was struggling with two plus two.

"Where is God in all this?" He repeated her question. "Nearer than you've ever dreamed." He took her glass and held it. "Meagan, everyone who drinks this water will get thirsty again. But I offer a different drink. Anyone who drinks the water I give will never thirst. Not ever."

Again, silence.

With a finger Meagan bounced the ice cubes in the glass. Finally she asked, "Never?"

"Not ever."

She looked away, then looked back, and, with every ounce of honesty she owned, asked, "Tell me, Jesse. Who in the world are you?"

Her new friend leaned forward in response and replied, "I thought you'd never ask."

One

The Dehydrated Heart

You're acquainted with physical thirst. Your body, according to some estimates, is 80 percent fluid. That means a man my size lugs around 160 pounds of water. Apart from brains, bones, and a few organs, we're walking water balloons.

We need to be. Stop drinking and see what happens. Coherent thoughts vanish, skin grows clammy, and vital organs wrinkle. Your eyes need fluid to cry; your mouth needs moisture to swallow; your glands need sweat to keep your body cool; your cells need blood to carry them; your joints need fluid to lubricate them. Your body needs water the same way a tire needs air.

In fact, your Maker wired you with thirst—a "low-fluid indicator." Let your fluid level grow low, and watch the signals flare. Dry mouth. Thick tongue. Achy head. Weak knees. Deprive your body of necessary fluid, and your body will tell you.

Deprive your soul of spiritual water, and your soul will tell you. Dehydrated hearts send desperate messages. Snarling tempers. Waves of worry. Growling mastodons of guilt and fear. You think

God wants you to live with these? Hopelessness. Sleeplessness. Loneliness. Resentment. Irritability. Insecurity. These are warnings. Symptoms of a dryness deep within.

Perhaps you've never seen them as such. You've thought they, like speed bumps, are a necessary part of the journey. Anxiety, you assume, runs in your genes like eye color. Some people have bad ankles; others, high cholesterol or receding hairlines. And you? You fret.

And moodiness? Everyone has gloomy days, sad Saturdays. Aren't such emotions inevitable? Absolutely. But unquenchable? No way. View the pains of your heart, not as struggles to endure, but as an inner thirst to slake—proof that something within you is starting to shrivel.

Treat your soul as you treat your thirst. Take a gulp. Imbibe moisture. Flood your heart with a good swallow of water.

Where do you find water for the soul? Jesus gave an answer one October day in Jerusalem. People had packed the streets for the annual reenactment of the rock-giving-water miracle of Moses. In honor of their nomadic ancestors, they slept in tents. In tribute to the desert stream, they poured out water. Each morning a priest filled a golden pitcher with water from the Gihon spring and carried it down a people-lined path to the temple. Announced by trumpets, the priest encircled the altar with a libation of liquid. He did this every day, once a day, for seven days. Then on the last day, the great day, the priest gave the altar a Jericho loop—seven circles—dousing it with seven vessels of water. It may have been at this very moment that the rustic rabbi from the northlands commanded the people's attention. "On the last day, that great day of the feast, Jesus stood and cried out, saying, 'If anyone thirsts, let him come to Me and drink. He who believes in Me, as the

Scripture has said, out of his heart will flow rivers of living water'" (John 7:37–38 NKJV).

Finely frocked priests turned. Surprised people looked. Wide-eyed children and toothless grandparents paused. They knew this man. Some had heard him preach in the Hebrew hills; others, in the city streets. Two and a half years had passed since he'd emerged from the Jordan waters. The crowd had seen this carpenter before.

But had they seen him this intense? He "stood and shouted" (NLT). The traditional rabbinic teaching posture was sitting and speaking. But Jesus stood up and shouted out. The blind man shouted, appealing for sight (Mark 10:46–47); the sinking Peter shouted, begging for help (Matt. 14:29–30); and the demon-possessed man shouted, pleading for mercy (Mark 5:2–7). John uses the same Greek verb to portray the volume of Jesus's voice. Forget a kind clearing of the throat. God was pounding his gavel on heaven's bench. Christ demanded attention.

He shouted because his time was short. The sand in the neck of his hourglass was down to measurable grains. In six months he'd be dragging a cross through these streets. And the people? The people thirsted. They needed water, not for their throats, but for their hearts. So Jesus invited: *Are your insides starting to shrivel? Drink me.*

What H_2O can do for your body, Jesus can do for your heart. Lubricate it. Aquify it. Soften what is crusty, flush what is rusty. How?

Like water, Jesus goes where we can't. Throw a person against a wall, his body thuds and drops. Splash water against a wall, and the liquid conforms and spreads. Its molecular makeup grants water great flexibility: one moment separating and seeping into a crack, another collecting and thundering over the Victoria Falls. Water goes where we cannot.

So does Jesus. He is a spirit and, although he forever has a body, he is not bound by a body. In fact, John parenthetically explains, "(When he said 'living water,' he was speaking of the Spirit, who would be given to everyone believing in him . . .)" (John 7:39). The Spirit of Jesus threads down the throat of your soul, flushing fears, dislodging regrets. He does for your soul what water does for your body. And, thankfully, we don't have to give him directions.

We give none to water, do we? Before swallowing, do you look at the liquid and say, "Ten drops of you go to my spleen. I need fifty on cardiovascular detail. The rest of you head north to my scalp. It's really itchy today." Water somehow knows where to go.

Jesus knows the same. Your directions are not needed, but your permission is. Like water, Jesus won't come in unless swallowed. That is, we must willingly surrender to his lordship. You can stand waist deep in the Colorado River and still die of thirst. Until you scoop and swallow, the water does your system no good. Until you gulp Christ, the same is true.

Don't you need a drink? Don't you long to flush out the fear, anxiety, and guilt? You can. Note the audience of his invitation. "If *anyone* thirsts, let him come to Me and drink" (v. 37 NKJV, emphasis mine). Are you *anyone?* If so, then step up to the well. You qualify for his water.

All ages are welcome. Both genders invited. No race excluded. Scoundrels. Scamps. Rascals and rubes. All welcome. You don't have to be rich to drink, religious to drink, successful to drink; you simply need to follow the instructions on what—or better, *who*—to drink. Him. In order for Jesus to do what water does, you must let him penetrate your heart. Deep, deep inside.

Internalize him. Ingest him. Welcome him into the inner workings of your life. Let Christ be the water of your soul.

How is this done? Begin by heeding your thirst. Don't dismiss your loneliness. Don't deny your anger. Your restless spirit, churning stomach, the sense of dread that turns your armpits into swamplands—these are signal flares exploding in the sky. *We could use a little moisture down here!* Don't let your heart shrink into a raisin. For the sake of those who need your love, hydrate your soul! Heed your thirst.

And drink good water. You don't gulp dirt or swallow rocks. Do you drink plastic or paper or pepper? Mercy no! When it comes to thirst of the body, we've learned how to reach for the right stuff. Do the same for your heart. Not everything you put to your lips will help your thirst. The arms of forbidden love may satisfy for a time, but only for a time. Eighty-hour workweeks grant a sense of fulfillment, but never remove the thirst.

Take special concern with the bottle labeled "religion." Jesus did. Note the setting in which he speaks. He isn't talking to prostitutes or troublemakers, penitentiary inmates or reform-school students. No, he addresses churchgoers at a religious convention. This day is an ecclesiastical highlight; like the Vatican on Easter Sunday. You half expect the pope to appear in the next verse. Religious symbols are laid out like a yard sale: the temple, the altar, trumpets, and robes. He could have pointed to any item as a source of drink. But he doesn't. These are mere symbols.

He points to himself, the one to whom the symbols point and in whom they are fulfilled. Religion pacifies, but never satisfies. Church activities might hide a thirst, but only Christ quenches it. Drink *him*.

And drink often. Jesus employs a verb that suggests repeated swallows. Literally, "Let him come to me and drink and keep drinking." One bottle won't satisfy your thirst. Regular sips satisfy thirsty throats. Ceaseless communion satisfies thirsty souls.

Toward this end, I give you this tool: a prayer for the thirsty heart. Carry it just as a cyclist carries a water bottle. The prayer outlines four essential fluids for soul hydration: God's work, God's energy, his lordship, and his love. You'll find the prayer easy to remember. Just think of the word *W-E-L-L*.

> Lord, I come thirsty. I come to drink, to receive. I receive your *work* on the cross and in your resurrection. My sins are pardoned, and my death is defeated. I receive your *energy*. Empowered by your Holy Spirit, I can do all things through Christ, who gives me strength. I receive your *lordship*. I belong to you. Nothing comes to me that hasn't passed through you. And I receive your *love*. Nothing can separate me from your love.

Don't you need regular sips from God's reservoir? I do. I've offered this prayer in countless situations: stressful meetings, dull days, long drives, demanding trips, character-testing decisions. Many times a day I step to the underground spring of God and receive anew his work for my sin and death, the energy of his Spirit, his lordship, and his love.

Drink with me from his bottomless well. You don't have to live with a dehydrated heart.

Receive Christ's *work* on the cross,
  the *energy* of his Spirit,
    his *lordship* over your life,
      his unending, unfailing *love*.

Drink deeply and often. And out of you will flow rivers of living water.

Part One

Accept His Work

TWO

Sin Vaccination

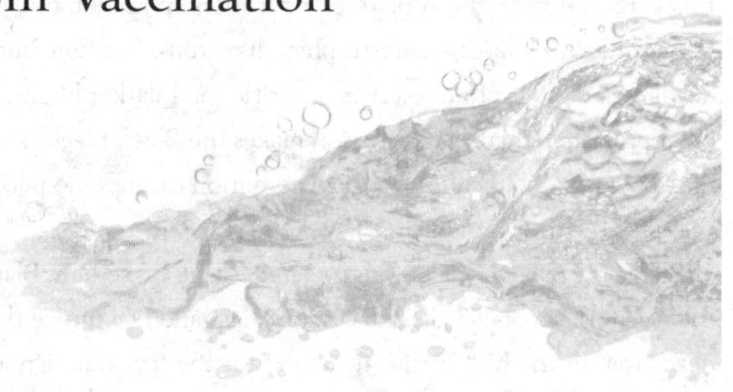

In October of 1347, a Genoese fleet returned from the Black Sea, carrying in its cargo the death sentence for Europe. By the time the ships landed in Messina, Italy, most of the sailors were dead. The few who survived wished they hadn't. Fever racked their bodies. Festering boils volcanoed on their skin. Authorities ordered the vessels out of the harbor, but it was too late. Flea-infested rats had already scampered down the ropes into the village, and the bubonic dictator had begun its ruthless march across the continent.

The disease followed trade routes northward through Italy into France and the northern nations. By spring it had breached the border of England. Within a short and brutal five years, twenty-five million people, one-third of Europe's population, had died. And that was just the beginning.

Three centuries later it still raged. As late as 1665 an epidemic left a hundred thousand Londoners dead, taking some seven thousand lives a week until a bitter, yet mercifully cold, winter killed the fleas.

No cure was known. No hope was offered. The healthy quarantined the infected. The infected counted their days.

When you make a list of history's harshest scourges, rank the Black Plague near the top. It earns a high spot. But not the highest. Call the disease catastrophic, disastrous. But humanity's deadliest? No. Scripture reserves that title for a darker blight, an older pandemic that by comparison makes the Black Plague seem like a cold sore. No culture avoids, no nation escapes, no person sidesteps the infection of sin.

Blame the bubonic plague on the *Yersinia pestis* bacterium. Blame the plague of sin on a godless decision. Adam and Eve turned their heads toward the hiss of the snake and for the first time ignored God. Eve did not ask, "God, what do you want?" Adam didn't suggest, "Let's consult the Creator." They acted as if they had no heavenly Father. His will was ignored, and sin, with death on its coattails, entered the world.

Sin sees the world with no God in it.

Where we might think of sin as slip-ups or missteps, God views sin as a godless attitude that leads to godless actions. "All of us have strayed away like sheep. We have left God's paths to follow our own" (Isa. 53:6). The sinful mind dismisses God. His counsel goes unconsulted. His opinion, unsolicited. His plan, unconsidered. The sin-infected grant God the same respect middle-schoolers give a substitute teacher—acknowledged, but not taken seriously.

The lack of God-centeredness leads to self-centeredness. Sin celebrates its middle letter—sIn. It proclaims, "It's your life, right? Pump your body with drugs, your mind with greed, your nights with pleasure." The godless lead a me-dominated, childish life, a life of "doing what we felt like doing, when we felt like doing it" (Eph. 2:3 MSG).

God says to love. I choose to hate.

God instructs, "Forgive." I opt to get even.

God calls for self-control. I promote self-indulgence.

Sin, for a season, quenches thirst. But so does salt water. Given time, the thirst returns, more demanding and demanding more than ever. "Having lost all sensitivity, they have given themselves over to sensuality so as to indulge in every kind of impurity, with a *continual lust for more*" (Eph. 4:19 NIV, emphasis mine).

We pay a high price for such self-obsession. "God isn't pleased at being ignored" (Rom. 8:8 MSG). Paul speaks of sinners when he describes those who

> knew God, but they wouldn't worship him as God or even give him thanks. And they began to think up foolish ideas of what God was like. The result was that their minds became dark and confused. . . .
>
> So God let them go ahead and do whatever shameful things their hearts desired. As a result, they did vile and degrading things with each other's bodies. (Rom. 1:21, 24)

You've seen the chaos. The husband ignoring his wife. The dictator murdering the millions. Grown men seducing the young. The young propositioning the old. When you do what you want, and I do what I want, and no one gives a lick as to what God wants, humanity implodes. The infection of the person leads to the corruption of the populace. As the Puritan clergyman Joseph Alleine wrote: "O miserable man, what a deformed monster has sin made you! God made you 'little lower than the angels'; sin has made you little better than the devils."[1] Extract God; expect earthly chaos and, many times worse, expect eternal misery.

God has made it clear. The plague of sin will not cross his shores. Infected souls never walk his streets. "Unjust people who don't care about God will not be joining in his kingdom. Those who use and abuse each other, use and abuse sex, use and abuse the earth and everything in it, don't qualify as citizens in God's kingdom" (1 Cor. 6:9–10 MSG). God refuses to compromise the spiritual purity of heaven.

Herein lies the awful fruit of sin. Lead a godless life, and expect a godless eternity. Spend a life telling God to leave you alone, and he will. He'll grant you an existence "without God and without hope" (Eph. 2:12). Jesus will "punish those who reject God and who do not obey the Good News about our Lord Jesus. They will suffer the punishment of eternal destruction, separated from the presence of the Lord and from his glorious might" (2 Thess. 1:8–9 TEV).

Christ keeps no secrets about hell. His description purposely chills the soul:

- A place of darkness (Matt. 8:12)
- A fiery furnace (Matt. 13:42)
- A place where "the worm does not die; the fire is never put out" (Mark 9:48 NCV)

Citizens of hell long to die, but cannot. Beg for water, but receive none. They pass into a dawnless night.

So what can we do? If all have been infected and the world is corrupted, to whom do we turn? Or, to re-ask the great question of Scripture: "What must I do to be saved?" (Acts 16:30). The answer offered then is the answer offered still: "Put your entire trust in the Master Jesus" (Acts 16:31 MSG).

Why Jesus? Why not Muhammad or Moses? Joseph Smith or Buddha? What uniquely qualifies Jesus to safeguard the sin-sick? In a sentence: *Christ, the sinless, became sin so that we, the sinners, could be counted sinless.* "God made him who had no sin to be sin for us, so that in him we might become the righteousness of God" (2 Cor. 5:21 NIV). Christ not only became the sin offering by receiving God's wrath for the sins of humanity, he overcame the punishment for sin (death) through his glorious resurrection from the dead.

Life's greatest calamity, from God's perspective, is that people die in sin. In one sentence Christ twice warned, "I told you that you would die in your sins; if you do not believe that I am the one I claim to be, you will indeed die in your sins" (John 8:24 NIV). Forget earthquakes or economic depressions. The ultimate disaster is carrying your sins to your casket. Heaven cannot fathom a worse tragedy. And heaven could not offer a greater gift than this one: "Christ . . . never sinned, but he died for sinners that he might bring us safely home to God" (1 Pet. 3:18).

What if a miracle worker had done something comparable with the Black Plague? Imagine a man born with bubonic resistance. The bacterium can't penetrate his system unless he allows it to do so. And, incredibly, he does. He pursues the infected and makes this offer: "Touch my hand. Give me your disease, and receive my health."

The boil-and-fever-ridden have nothing to lose. They look at his extended hand and reach to touch it. True to the man's word, bacteria pass from their system into his. But their relief spells his anguish. His skin erupts and his body heaves. And as the healed stand in awe, the disease bearer hobbles away.

Our history books tell no such story. But our Bible does.

> He took the punishment, and that made us whole.
> Through his bruises we get healed. . . .
> God has piled all our sins, everything we've done wrong
> on him, on him. . . .
> He took on his own shoulders the sin of the many,
> he took up the cause of all the black sheep.
> (Isa. 53:5–6, 12 MSG)

Christ responds to universal sin with a universal sacrifice, taking on the sins of the entire world. This is Christ's work *for* you. But God's salvation song has two verses. He not only took your place on the cross; he takes his place in your heart. This is the second stanza: Christ's work *in* you.

"It is no longer I who live," Paul explained, "but Christ lives in me" (Gal. 2:20 NKJV).

Or as he told one church: "Don't you realize that all of you together are the temple of God and that the Spirit of God lives in you?" (1 Cor. 3:16).

In salvation, God enters the hearts of his Adams and Eves. He permanently places himself within us. What powerful implications this brings. "When God lives and breathes in you (and he does, as surely as he did in Jesus), you are delivered from that dead life" (Rom. 8:11 MSG).

Let me show you how this works. It took three hundred years, but the Black Plague finally reached the quaint village of Eyam, England. George Viccars, a tailor, unpacked a parcel shipped from London. The cloth he'd ordered had arrived. But as he opened and shook it, he released plague-infected fleas. Within four days he was dead, and the village was doomed. The town unselfishly quarantined itself, seeking to protect the region.

Other villages deposited food in an open field and left the people of Eyam to die alone. But to everyone's amazement, many survived. A year later, when outsiders again visited the town, they found half the residents had resisted the disease. How so? They had touched it. Breathed it. One surviving mother had buried six children and her husband in one week. The gravedigger had handled hundreds of diseased corpses yet hadn't died. Why not? How did they survive?

Lineage. Through DNA studies of descendants, scientists found proof of a disease-blocking gene. The gene garrisoned the white blood cells, preventing the bacteria from gaining entrance. The plague, in other words, could touch people with this gene but not kill them. Hence a subpopulace swam in a sea of infection but emerged untouched. All because they had the right parents.[2] What's the secret for surviving the Black Plague? Pick the right ancestry.

Of course they couldn't. But by God you can. You can select your spiritual father. You can change your family tree from that of Adam to God. And when you do, he moves in. His resistance becomes your resistance. His Teflon coating becomes yours. Sin may entice you, but will never enslave you. Sin may, and will, touch you, discourage you, and distract you, but it cannot condemn you. Christ is in you, and you are in him, and "there is no condemnation for those who belong to Christ Jesus" (Rom. 8:1).

Can I urge you to trust this truth? Let your constant prayer be this: "Lord, I receive your work. My sins are pardoned." Trust the work of God *for* you. Then trust the presence of Christ *in* you. Take frequent, refreshing drinks from his well of grace. You need regular reminders that you are not fatally afflicted! Don't live as though you are.

A few years ago I noticed a tremor in my left thumb. Upon extension, it shook. I immediately imagined the worst. My father died from Lou Gehrig's disease; my turn was coming. By the time I consulted a doctor, I'd already prepared Denalyn for life as a young widow.

The medical report proved me wrong. No sickness was found. Trace the condition back to caffeine, stress, maybe a family tree, but the doctor informed, "You do not have ALS. You're in good health."

Upon hearing the news, I did what you might expect. I began to weep and asked, "How much time do I have left?"

The doctor cocked his head, puzzled.

"Any chance you could help me break the news to my wife?"

Still he didn't respond. Assuming he was too emotional, I gave him a hug and left.

Stopping at a hospital supply store, I ordered a wheelchair and hospital bed and inquired about home healthcare. I called Denalyn and told her I had some bad news.

Wait a second, you're thinking. *Did you not hear what the doctor told you?*

And I'm wondering, *Did you not hear what heaven told you?*

Christ indwells you! "The blood of Jesus . . . purifies us from all sin" (1 John 1:7 NIV). Then why the guilt on our faces? Why the regret? Why the shadow of shame? Shouldn't we live with a smile and a skip and a sparkle in the eye?

That response to the doctor about my trembling thumb? I made it up. Quite honestly, I gave my physician a handshake, smiled at the receptionist, and called Denalyn with the good news. And now, when I see that thumb shake, I chalk it up to an aging body and place my trust in the doctor's words.

Do the same. For just as my thumb will occasionally tremble, you will occasionally sin. And when you do, remember: sin may touch, but cannot claim you. Christ is in you! Trust his work *for* you. He took your place on the cross. And trust his work *in* you. Your heart is his home, and he is your master.

THREE

When Grace Goes Deep

The prodigal son trudges up the path. His pig stink makes passersby walk wide circles around him, but he doesn't notice. With eyes on the ground, he rehearses his speech: "Father"—his voice barely audible—"I have sinned against heaven and against you. I'm not worthy to be called your son." He rehashes the phrases, wondering if he should say more, less, or make a U-turn to the barnyard. After all, he cashed in the trust fund and trashed the family name. Over the last year, he'd awakened with more parched throats, headaches, women, and tattoos than a rock star. How could his father forgive him? *Maybe I could offer to pay off the credit cards*. He's so focused on penance planning that he fails to hear the sound of his father . . . running!

The dad embraces the mud-layered boy as if he were a returning war hero. He commands the servants to bring a robe, ring, and sandals, as if to say, "No boy of mine is going to look like a pigpen peasant. Fire up the grill. Bring on the drinks. It's time for a party!"

Big brother meanwhile stands on the porch and sulks. "No one ever gave me a party," he mumbles, arms crossed.

The father tries to explain, but the jealous son won't listen. He huffs and shrugs and grumbles something about cheap grace, saddles his high horse, and rides off. But you knew that. You've read the parable of the gracious father and the hostile brother (see Luke 15:11–32).

But have you heard what happened next? Have you read the second chapter? It's a page-turner. The older brother resolves to rain on the forgiveness parade. *If Dad won't exact justice on the boy, I will.*

"Nice robe there, little brother," he tells him one day. "Better keep it clean. One spot and Dad will send you to the cleaners with it."

The younger waves him away, but the next time he sees his father, he quickly checks his robe for stains.

A few days later big brother warns about the ring. "Quite a piece of jewelry Dad gave you. He prefers that you wear it on the thumb."

"The thumb? He didn't tell me that."

"Some things we're just supposed to know."

"But it won't fit my thumb."

"What's your goal—pleasing our father or your own personal comfort?" the spirituality monitor gibes, walking away.

Big brother isn't finished. With the pleasantness of a dyspeptic IRS auditor, he taunts, "If Dad sees you with loose laces, he'll take the sandals back."

"He will not. They were a gift. He wouldn't . . . would he?" The ex-prodigal then leans over to snug the strings. As he does, he spots a smudge on his robe. Trying to rub it off, he realizes the ring is on a finger, not his thumb. That's when he hears his father's voice. "Hello, Son."

There the boy sits, wearing a spotted robe, loose laces, and a misplaced ring. Overcome with fear, he reacts with a "Sorry, Dad" and turns and runs.

Too many tasks. Keeping the robe spotless, the ring positioned, the sandals snug—who could meet such standards? Gift preservation begins to wear on the young man. He avoids the father he feels he can't please. He quits wearing the gifts he can't maintain. And he even begins longing for the simpler days of the pigpen. "No one hounded me there."

That's the rest of the story. Wondering where I found it? On page 1,892 of my Bible, in the book of Galatians. Thanks to some legalistic big brothers, Paul's readers had gone from grace receiving to law keeping. Their Christian life had taken on the joy level of an upper G.I. endoscopy. Paul was puzzled.

> I am shocked that you are turning away so soon from God, who in his love and mercy called you to share the eternal life he gives through Christ. You are already following a different way that pretends to be the Good News but is not the Good News at all. You are being fooled by those who twist and change the truth concerning Christ. . . .
>
> And yet we Jewish Christians know that we become right with God, not by doing what the law commands, but by faith in Jesus Christ. So we have believed in Christ Jesus, that we might be accepted by God because of our faith in Christ—and not because we have obeyed the law. For no one will ever be saved by obeying the law. (Gal. 1:6–7; 2:16)

Joy snatchers infiltrated the Roman church as well. Paul had to remind them, "But people are declared righteous because of their faith, not because of their work" (Rom. 4:5).

Philippian Christians heard the same foolishness. Big brothers weren't telling them to wear a ring on their thumb, but they were insisting "you must be circumcised to be saved" (Phil. 3:2).

Even the Jerusalem church, the flagship congregation, heard the solemn monotones of the Quality Control Board. Non-Jewish believers were being told, "You cannot be saved if you are not circumcised as Moses taught us" (Acts 15:1 NCV).

The churches suffered from the same malady: grace blockage. The Father might let you in the gate, but you have to earn your place at the table. God makes the down payment on your redemption, but you pay the monthly installments. Heaven gives the boat, but you have to row it if you ever want to see the other shore.

Grace blockage. Taste, but don't drink. Wet your lips, but never slake your thirst. Can you imagine such instruction over a fountain? "No swallowing, please. Fill your mouth but not your belly."

Absurd. What good is water if you can't drink it? And what good is grace if you don't let it go deep?

Do you? What image best describes your heart? A water-drenched kid dancing in front of an open fire hydrant? Or a bristled desert tumbleweed? Here is how you know. One question. Does God's grace *define* you? Deeply flowing grace clarifies, once and for all, who we are.

> But God is so rich in mercy, and he loved us so very much, that even while we were dead because of our sins, he gave us life when he raised Christ from the dead. (It is only by God's special favor that you have been saved!) For he raised us from the dead

along with Christ, and we are seated with him in the heavenly realms—all because we are one with Christ Jesus. And so God can always point to us as examples of the incredible wealth of his favor and kindness toward us, as shown in all he has done for us through Christ Jesus.

God saved you by his special favor when you believed. And you can't take credit for this; it is a gift from God. Salvation is not a reward for the good things we have done, so none of us can boast about it. (Eph. 2:4–9)

Look how grace defines us. We are

- spiritually alive: "he gave us life" (v. 5);
- heavenly positioned: "seated with him in the heavenly realms" (v. 6);
- connected to God: "one with Christ Jesus" (v. 6);
- billboards of mercy: "examples of the incredible wealth of his favor and kindness toward us" (v. 7);
- honored children: "God saved you by his special favor" (v. 8).

Grace defines you. As grace sinks in, earthly labels fade. Society labels you like a can on an assembly line. Stupid. Unproductive. Slow learner. Fast talker. Quitter. Cheapskate. But as grace infiltrates, criticism disintegrates. You know you aren't who they say you are. You are who God says you are. Spiritually alive. Heavenly positioned. Connected to the Father. A billboard of mercy. An honored child.

Of course, not all labels are negative. Some people regard you as handsome, clever, successful, or efficient. But even a White House office doesn't compare with being "seated with him in the heavenly realms." Grace creates the Christian's résumé.

It certainly did so for Mephibosheth. Talk about a redefined life. After assuming the throne of Saul, "David began wondering if anyone in Saul's family was still alive, for he had promised Jonathan that he would show kindness to them" (2 Sam. 9:1).

The Philistines, you'll remember, defeated Saul in battle. After the smoke of conflict passed, David sought to display mercy to Saul's descendants. A servant named Ziba remembered: "Yes, one of Jonathan's sons is still alive, but he is crippled" (v. 3). No name offered. Just the pain. Labeled by misfortune. An earlier chapter reveals the mishap. When word of Saul's and Jonathan's deaths reached the capital, a nurse in Jonathan's house swept up his five-year-old boy and fled. But in her haste, she stumbled and dropped him, crippling the boy in both feet.

Where does such a child turn? Can't walk. Can't work. Father and grandfather dead. Where can the crippled grandson of a failed leader go?

How about Lo-debar? Sounds like a place charm forgot. Like No Trees, Texas, or Weed, Oregon, or French Lick, Indiana. Lo-debar, Israel. Appropriate place for Mephibosheth. Stuck with a name longer than his arm. Dropped like a cantaloupe from a torn paper sack. How low can you go? Low enough to end up living in the low-rent district of Lo-debar.

Acquainted with its streets? If you've been dropped, you are. Dropped from the list. Dropped by a guy. Dropped by the team. Dropped off at the orphanage. And now you walk with a limp. People don't remember your name, but they remember your pain. "He's the alcoholic." "Oh, I remember her. The widow." "You mean the divorced woman from Nowheresville?" "No. Lo-debarville." You live labeled.

But then something Cinderella-like happens. The king's men knock on your Lo-debar door. They load you in a wagon and carry you into the presence of the king. You assume the worst and begin praying for a nonsnoring prison cellmate. But the servants don't deposit you on the jailhouse steps; they set you at the king's table. Right above your plate sits a place card bearing your name. "And from that time on, Mephibosheth ate regularly with David, as though he were one of his own sons" (2 Sam. 9:11).

Charles Swindoll has penned a galaxy of fine paragraphs. But my favorite is this imagined scene from David's palace.

> Gold and bronze fixtures gleam from the walls. Lofty, wooden ceilings crown each spacious room. . . . David and his children gather for an evening meal. Absalom, tanned and handsome, is there, as is David's beautiful daughter Tamar. The call to dinner is given, and the king scans the room to see if all are present. One figure, though, is absent.
>
> *Clump, scraaape, clump, scraaape*. The sound coming down the hall echoes into the chamber. *Clump, scraaape, clump, scraaape*. Finally, the person appears at the door and slowly shuffles to his seat. It is the lame Mephibosheth seated in grace at David's table. And the tablecloth covers his feet. Now the feast can begin.[1]

From Lo-debar to the palace, from obscurity to royalty, from no future to the king's table. Quite a move for Mephibosheth. Quite a reminder for us. He models our journey. God lifted us from the dead-end street of Lo-debarville and sat us at his table. "We are seated with him in the heavenly realms" (Eph. 2:6).

Marinate your soul in that verse. Next time the arid desert winds blow, defining you by yesterday's struggles, reach for God's goblet of grace and drink. Grace defines who you are. The parent you can't please is as mistaken as the doting uncle you can't disappoint. People hold no clout. Only God does. According to him, you are his. Period. "For we are God's masterpiece. He has created us anew in Christ Jesus, so that we can do the good things he planned for us long ago" (Eph. 2:10).

Suppose Mephibosheth had seen this verse. Imagine someone back in the Lo-debar days telling him, "Don't be discouraged, friend. I know you can't dance or run. Others kick the soccer ball, and you're stuck here staring out the window. But listen, God wrote your story. He cast you in his drama. Three thousand years from now your story will stir an image of grace for some readers in the twenty-first century."

Would he have believed it? I don't know. But I pray that you will. You hang as God's work of art, a testimony in his gallery of grace.

Over a hundred years ago, a group of fishermen were relaxing in the dining room of a Scottish seaside inn, trading fish stories. One of the men gestured widely, depicting the size of a fish that got away. His arm struck the serving maid's tea tray, sending the teapot flying into the whitewashed wall, where its contents left an irregular brown splotch.

The innkeeper surveyed the damage and sighed, "The whole wall will have to be repainted."

"Perhaps not," offered a stranger. "Let me work with it."

Having nothing to lose, the proprietor consented. The man pulled pencils, brushes, some jars of linseed oil, and pigment out of an art box. He sketched lines around the stains and dabbed shades and colors throughout the splashes of tea. In time, an image began to emerge: a stag with a great rack of antlers. The man inscribed his signature at the bottom, paid for his meal, and left. His name: Sir Edwin Landseer, famous painter of wildlife.

In his hands, a mistake became a masterpiece.[2]

God's hands do the same, over and over. He draws together the disjointed blotches in our life and renders them an expression of his love. We become pictures: "examples of the incredible wealth of his favor and kindness toward us" (Eph. 2:7).

Who determines your identity? What defines you? The day you were dropped? Or the day you were carried to the King's table?

Receive God's work. Drink deeply from his well of grace. As grace sinks deep into your soul, Lo-debar will become a dot in the rearview mirror. Dark days will define you no more. You're in the palace now.

And now you know what to say to the big brothers of this world. No need for frantic robe cleaning or rules for ring wearing. Your deeds don't save you. And your deeds don't keep you saved. Grace does. The next time big brother starts dispensing more snarls than twin Dobermans, loosen your sandals, set your ring on your finger, and quote the apostle of grace who said, "By the grace of God I am what I am" (1 Cor. 15:10 NKJV).

FOUR

When Death Becomes Birth

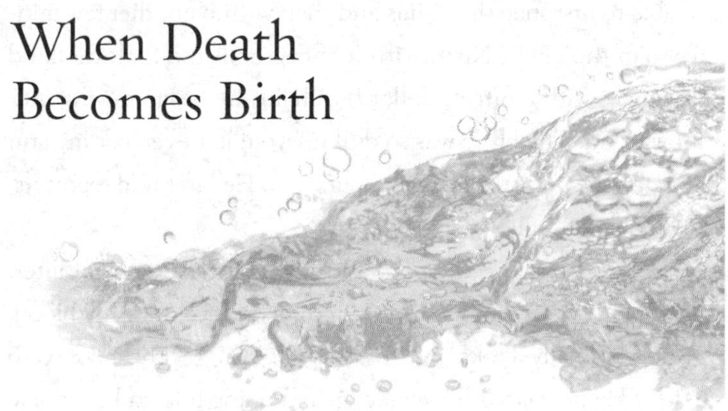

What would you do to sidestep death? Upon hearing the footsteps of the Grim Reaper at your door, what price would you pay for an extension? Would you give your right hand?

Aron Ralston did. The twenty-seven-year-old adventurer makes holiday treks out of climbing Rocky Mountain peaks. He's summited forty-five of them, alone, all in winter, most after midnight. Life on the edge isn't new to him. But life beneath an eight-hundred-pound boulder? He was climbing off one when it shifted, trapping his right hand against the wall of a narrow crevice in a remote Utah canyon.

He shoved the rock with his shoulder and tried to chisel it with his knife; he even attempted to hoist the thing with his climbing rope and pulley. The boulder didn't budge. After five days, with food and water gone and having drifted back and forth between depression and visions of friends and margaritas, he made a decision, the thought of which makes mere mortals gulp. He resolved to sever his right hand.

"It occurred to me that if I could break my bones up at the wrist, where they were trapped, I could be freed," he later said. "I was able to first snap the radius and then within another few minutes snap the ulna." Next, with a cheap multiuse tool, the kind that comes with a fifteen-dollar flashlight, he began sawing into his own skin. The blade was so dull it "wouldn't even cut my arm hairs," but he persisted in the amputation. He later told reporters, "It took about an hour."[1]

Don't even imagine the pops and snaps of those sixty minutes. I grow faint when the nurse takes ten seconds to draw my blood.

Ralston finally broke free of the boulder. (Sorry. Poor verb choice.) He now faced the challenge of finding human beings. He crawled through a 150-foot ravine, rappelled (one-handed, remember) down a 60-foot wall, and then hiked six miles. Only then did he run into some Dutch tourists who, no doubt, got more for their money than their travel agent ever promised. Downplaying his courage, Ralston explained the escape as a "matter of pragmatics."[2]

Pragmatic indeed. On one hand, death. Without the other hand, life. When faced with the choice, he chose life. Would we do the same?

We do everything short of it. Death is Public Enemy Number One. Buckle up. Sleep more. Run regularly. Eat less fat. More protein. Less caffeine. More vegetables. Ducking the shadow of death dominates our days.

But no one ducks it forever. Regarding death, Scripture offers some grim facts.

> Some people die in the prime of life,
>   with everything going for them—
>   fat and sassy.

Others die bitter and bereft,
  never getting a taste of happiness.
They're laid out side by side in the cemetery,
  where the worms can't tell one from the other.
  (Job 21:23–26 MSG)

Ecclesiastes 8:8 is equally uplifting. "None of us can hold back our spirit from departing. None of us has the power to prevent the day of our death. There is no escaping that obligation, that dark battle."

This troubles us. We'd appreciate some say-so regarding our death. Couldn't God let us sign up for a departure date? Most would request the one-hundred-year package of good health followed by a long nap from which we wake up in heaven.

God, however, didn't delegate death's datebook. For reasons undisclosed, he runs it without our advice. But while the date of your death isn't revealed, its inevitability is. "It is destined that each person dies only once and after that comes judgment" (Heb. 9:27).

The Utah mountain climber isn't the only one caught between a rock and a hard place. "What man can live and not see death?" (Ps. 89:48 NKJV). You won't find one in your mirror. You, as all God's children, live one final breath from your own funeral.

Which, from God's perspective, is nothing to grieve. He responds to these grave facts with this great news: "The day you die is better than the day you are born" (Eccles. 7:1). Now there is a twist. Heaven enjoys a maternity-ward reaction to funerals. Angels watch body burials the same way grandparents monitor delivery-room doors. "He'll be coming through any minute!" They can't wait to see the new arrival. While we're driving hearses and wearing black, they're hanging pink and blue streamers and passing out cigars. We don't grieve when babies enter the world. The hosts of heaven don't weep when we leave it.

Oh, but many of us weep at the thought of death. Do you? Do you dread your death? And is your dread of death robbing your joy of life? It can. It did for a young woman named Florence. At the age of thirty-seven she told her friends that her life hung by a thread that might snap at any moment. So she went to bed. And stayed there. For fifty-three years! Her death declaration proved true. She did die . . . at the age of ninety.

Doctors could find nothing wrong. Examiners left her bedside shaking their heads. Most diagnosed her as a hopeless hypochondriac—dreading death, ever obsessed by its imminence. Except for three years, Florence cowered before the giant of death. But during those three years on the Crimean battlefront, she made a name for herself, not as one who suffered, but as a friend of those who did. History's most famous nurse, Florence Nightingale, lived as a slave of death.[3]

What about you? Is your fear of dying robbing your joy of living? Then drink up! After all, Jesus came to "deliver those who have lived all their lives as slaves to the fear of dying" (Heb. 2:15).

Death sits well within his jurisdiction. Morticians answer to him. "Christ died and rose again for this very purpose, so that he might be Lord of those who are alive and of those who have died" (Rom. 14:9). Your death may surprise you and sadden others, but heaven knows no untimely death: "You saw me before I was born. Every day of my life was recorded in your book. Every moment was laid out before a single day had passed" (Ps. 139:16).

God dispenses days the way a store clerk dispenses change. For all who doubt his power, Jesus has three words: "Lazarus, come out!" (John 11:43).

If Scripture boasted a list of the famous dead, Lazarus would be near the top. He lived in Bethany, a sleepy hamlet that sat a short walk from Jerusalem. Jesus spent a lot of time there. Maybe he liked the kitchen of Martha or the devotion of Mary. One thing is for sure: he considered Lazarus a friend. News of Lazarus's death prompts Jesus to say, "Our friend Lazarus has fallen asleep, but now I will go and wake him up" (John 11:11).

And now, four days after the funeral, Jesus has come calling. Literally calling, "Lazarus, come out!" Can we try to picture Lazarus as he hears those words? Heaven-sent Lazarus. Heaven-happy Lazarus. Four days into his measureless days. By now he's forming fast friendships with other saints. King David shows him the harps. Moses invites him over for tea and manna. Elijah and Elisha take him for a spin in the fiery chariot. Daniel has promised him a lion of a Bible story. He's on his way to hear it when a voice booms through the celestial city.

"Lazarus, come out!"

Everybody knows that voice. No one wonders, *Who was that?* Angels stop. Hosts of holy-city dwellers turn toward the boy from Bethany, and someone says, "Looks like you're going back for another tour of duty."

Lazarus doesn't question the call. Perfect understanding comes with a heavenly passport. He doesn't object. But had he done so, who could have faulted him? His heavenly body knows no fever. His future no fear. He indwells a city that is void of padlocks, prisons, and Prozac. With sin and death nonexistent, preachers, doctors, and lawyers are free to worship. Would anyone blame Lazarus for saying, "Do I have to go back?"

But he doesn't second-guess the command. Nor does anyone else. Return trips have been frequent of late. The daughter of the synagogue ruler. The boy from Nain. Now Lazarus from Bethany. Lazarus turns toward the rarely used exit door. The very one, I suppose, Jesus used some thirty earth years earlier. With a wave and within a wink, he's reunited with his body and waking up on a cold slab in a wall-hewn grave. The rock to the entrance has been moved, and Lazarus attempts to do the same. Mummy-wrapped, he stiffly sits up and walks out of the tomb with the grace of Frankenstein's monster.

People stare and wonder.

We read and may ask, "Why did Jesus let him die only to call him back?"

To show who runs the show. To trump the cemetery card. To display the unsquashable strength of the One who danced the Watusi on the neck of the devil, who stood face to clammy face with death and declared, "You call that a dead end? I call it an escalator."

"Lazarus, come out!"

Those words, incidentally, were only a warmup for the big day. He's preparing a worldwide grave evacuation. "Joe, come out!" "Maria, come out!" "Giuseppe, come out!" "Jacob, come out!" Grave after grave will empty. What happened to Lazarus will happen to us. Only our spirit-body reunion will occur in heaven, not Bethany Memorial Cemetery.

> When this happens—when our perishable earthly bodies have been transformed into heavenly bodies that will never die—then at last the Scriptures will come true:
>
> "Death is swallowed up in victory.
> O death, where is your victory?
> O death, where is your sting?"
> (1 Cor. 15:54–55)

Till then, where does that leave us? It leaves us checking our list of friends. Because Lazarus called Jesus his friend, Jesus called Lazarus from the grave. Regarding death, you need a friend in the highest place. Without one, you're in big trouble. "When the wicked die, their hopes all perish, for they rely on their own feeble strength" (Prov. 11:7). Make sure Jesus refers to you with the same term of endearment he used with Lazarus. Prepare for death by making friends with Christ. "When they arrive at the gates of death, GOD welcomes those who love him" (Ps. 116:15 MSG).

Dread of death ends when you know heaven is your true home. In all my air travels I've never seen one passenger weep when the plane landed. Never. No one clings to the armrests and begs, "Don't make me leave. Don't make me leave. Let me stay and eat more peanuts." We're willing to exit because the plane has no permanent mailing address. Nor does this world. "But we are citizens of heaven, where the Lord Jesus Christ lives. And we are eagerly waiting for him to return as our Savior" (Phil. 3:20).

John Knox could relate. Born in 1505 in Scotland, his preaching regenerated a society. He inspired the masses and defied the excesses of the throne. Some loved him, others despised him, but Scotland has never forgotten him. To this day you can visit his home in Edinburgh and stand in the room where some believe he took his final breath.

Here is what happened. His coworker Richard Bannatyne stood near his bedside. Knox's breath became labored and slow. Bannatyne leaned over his friend's form. "The time to end your battle has come. Have you hope?" he whispered to his friend.

The answer from the old reformer came in the form of a finger. He lifted his finger and pointed it upward and died, inspiring a poet to write:

> . . . the death angel left him, what time earth's bonds were riven,
> the cold, stark, stiffening finger still pointing up to heaven.[4]

May your death find you pointing in the same direction. Why don't you do this: give God your death. Imagine your last breath, envision your final minutes, and offer them to him. Deliberately. Regularly. "Lord, I receive your work on the cross and in your resurrection. I entrust you with my departure from earth." With Christ as your friend and heaven as your home, the day of death becomes sweeter than the day of birth.

FIVE

With Heart Headed Home

Search the faces of the Cap Haitian orphanage for Carinette. Study the fifty-seven dark-skinned, bright-eyed, curly-haired, Creole-speaking, fun-loving children for a unique seven-year-old girl. She appears no different from the others. Eats the same rice and beans. Plays on the same grassless playground. Sleeps beneath a tin roof as do the other girls, hearing the nearly nightly pounding of the Haitian rain. But though she appears the same, don't be fooled. She lives in a different world—a world called home-to-be.

See the slender girl wearing the pink shirt? The girl with the long nose and bushy hair and a handful of photos. Ask to see them; Carinette will let you. Fail to ask; she'll show you anyway. The photos bear the images of her future family. She's been adopted.

Her adoptive parents are friends of mine. They brought her pictures, a teddy bear, granola bars, and cookies. Carinette shared the goodies and asked the director to guard her bear, but she keeps the pictures. They remind her of her home-to-be. Within a month, two at the most, she'll be there. She knows the day is coming. Every opening of the gate jumps her heart. Any day now her father will appear. He promised he'd be back. He came once to claim her. He'll come again to carry her home.

Till then she lives with a heart headed home.

Shouldn't we all? Carinette's situation mirrors ours. Our Father paid us a visit too. Have we not been claimed? Adopted? "So you should not be like cowering, fearful slaves. You should behave instead like God's very own children, adopted into his family—calling him 'Father, dear Father'" (Rom. 8:15).

God searched you out. Before you knew you needed adopting, he'd already filed the papers and selected the wallpaper for your room. "For God knew his people in advance, and he chose them to become like his Son, so that his Son would be the firstborn, with many brothers and sisters" (Rom. 8:29).

Abandon you to a fatherless world? No way. Those privy to God's family Bible can read your name. He wrote it there. What's more, he covered the adoption fees. Neither you nor Carinette can pay your way out of the orphanage, so "God sent [Christ] to buy freedom for us who were slaves to the law, so that he could adopt us as his very own children" (Gal. 4:5).

We don't finance our adoption, but we do accept it. Carinette could tell the prospective parents to get lost. But she hasn't. In the same way, you could tell God to get lost. But you wouldn't dare, would you? The moment we accept his offer we go from orphans to heirs.

"Heirs of God and joint heirs with Christ" (Rom. 8:17 NKJV). Heirs! Heaven knows no stepchildren or grandchildren. You and Christ share the same will. What he inherits, you inherit. You are headed home.

Oh, but we forget. Don't we grow accustomed to hard bunks

and tin plates? Seldom do we peer over the fence into the world to come. And how long has it been since you showed someone your pictures? Is Peter speaking to you when he urges, "Friends, this world is not your home, so don't make yourselves cozy in it" (1 Pet. 2:11 MSG)?

Adopted, but not transported. We have a new family, but not our heavenly house. We know our Father's name, but we haven't seen his face. He has claimed us, but has yet to come for us.

So here we are. Caught between what is and what will be. No longer orphans, but not yet home. What do we do in the meantime? Indeed, it can be just that—a *mean* time. Time made mean with chemotherapy, drivers driving with more beer than brains in their bodies, and backstabbers who make life on earth feel like a time-share in Afghanistan. How do we live in the *mean*time? How do we keep our hearts headed home? Paul weighs in with some suggestions.

> And even we Christians, although we have the Holy Spirit within us as a foretaste of future glory, also groan to be released from pain and suffering. We, too, wait anxiously for that day when God will give us our full rights as his children, including the new bodies he has promised us. Now that we are saved, we eagerly look forward to this freedom. For if you already have something, you don't need to hope for it. But if we look forward to something we don't have yet, we must wait patiently and confidently. (Rom. 8:23–25)

Paul calls the Holy Spirit a foretaste. "We have the Holy Spirit . . . as a foretaste of future glory" (v. 23). No person with a healthy appetite needs a definition for that word. Even as I draft this chapter, my mind drifts toward a few foretastes. Within an hour

I'll be in Denalyn's kitchen sniffing the dinner trimmings like a Labrador sniffing for wild game. When she's not looking, I'll snatch a foretaste. Just a bite of turkey, a spoon of chili, a corner of bread . . . predinner snacks stir appetites for the table.

Samplings from heaven's kitchen do likewise. There are moments, perhaps far too few, when time evaporates and joy modulates and heaven hands you an hors d'oeuvre.

- Your newborn has passed from restlessness to rest. Beneath the amber light of a midnight moon, you trace a soft finger across tiny, sleeping eyes and wonder, *God gave you to me?* A prelibation from heaven's winery.
- You're lost in the work you love to do, were made to do. As you step back from the moist canvas or hoed garden or rebuilt V-eight engine, satisfaction flows within like a gulp of cool water, and the angel asks, "Another apéritif?"
- The lyrics to the hymn say what you couldn't but wanted to, and for a moment, a splendid moment, there are no wars, wounds, or tax returns. Just you, God, and a silent assurance that everything is right with the world.

Rather than dismiss or disregard such moments as good luck, relish them. They can attune you to heaven. So can tough ones. "Although we have the Holy Spirit within us as a foretaste of future glory, [we] also groan to be released from pain and suffering. We, too, wait anxiously for that day when God will give us our full rights as his children, including the new bodies he has promised us" (v. 23).

Do you think Carinette groans? Orphans tend to. They live

lonely lives. Upon seeing a child with a mother and father, they groan. They see a house and think of their bunk; they groan. When they wonder what happened to their biological parents, wouldn't they groan? Of course.

But Carinette's groans are numbered. Every cafeteria meal brings her closer to home cooking, and each dormitory night carries her closer to a room of her own. And every time she longs to call someone mama, she remembers that she soon will.

Her struggles stir longings for home. Let your bursitis-plagued body remind you of your eternal one; let acid-inducing days prompt thoughts of unending peace. Are you falsely accused? Acquainted with abuse? Mudslinging is a part of this life, but not the next. Rather than begrudge life's troubles, listen to them.

Certain moments are so hideous, nothing else will do. A few years ago a *Time* magazine essay escorted readers into the ugly world of abused children. We met Antwan, age ten, puppet-stringed to neighborhood bullies and drug peddlers. They demanded his presence. He feared their punishment. When police appeared, the troublemakers stashed their drugs in his socks, thinking the boy wouldn't be searched. Antwan knew the police better than he knew his schoolteachers. What hope does a boy like Antwan have? The writer took us to his sparse apartment. His mother owned one light bulb. When she left the kitchen, she carried the lone bulb to the living room. As she screwed it into the lamp, the dim glow illuminated a poster on a far wall of a young black boy crying. The caption at the bottom read, "He will wipe away all tears from their eyes, and there shall be no more death, nor sorrow, nor crying, nor pain. All of that has gone forever" (Rev. 21:4 TLB).[1]

Write checks of hope on this promise. Do not bemoan passing time; applaud it. The more you drink from God's well, the more you urge the clock to tick. Every bump of the second hand brings you closer to a completed adoption. As Paul writes, "We, too, wait anxiously for that day when God will give us our full rights as his children" (Rom. 8:23).

My daughters have long since stopped doing this, but there was a time when they celebrated my daily arrival. Jenna was five years old, Andrea three. Denalyn would alert them, and they would scamper to the window, pressing noses and hands against the tall pane that paralleled the front door. As I pulled into the drive, I would see them: Andrea and Jenna, a head taller than her sister, squeezed into the frame. Seeing me, they squealed. My, how they jumped and clapped. You'd think someone had switched their M&M's for coffee beans. No returning Caesar ever felt more welcomed. As I opened the door, they tackled my knees and flooded the entryway with tsunami-size joy.

Their father was home.

It's been too long since I searched for God that way. Too seldom do I hear thunder and think, *Is that God?* I've been known to let a day, even two, pass without a glance to the eastern sky. Let's do better. "Let heaven fill your thoughts. Do not think only about things down here on earth" (Col. 3:2). How about regular ladle dips into the well of God's return? Don't you know Carinette's home-to-be dominates her thoughts? The pictures, the teddy bear—can she see them and not think of it?

Blessings and burdens. Both can alarm-clock us out of slumber. Gifts stir homeward longings. So do struggles. Every homeless day carries us closer to the day our Father will come.

Part Two

Rely on His Energy

SIX

Hope for Tuckered Town

Turn north at Stress Village, drive a few miles east of Worryville, bear right at the fork leading through Worn-Out Valley, and you'll find yourself entering the weary streets of Tuckered Town.

Her residents live up to the name. They lumber like pack mules on a Pike's Peak climb. Eyes down. Faces long. Shoulders slumped. Ask them to explain their sluggish ways, and they point to the cars. "You'd be tired too if you had to push one of these."

To your amazement that's what they do! Shoulders pressing, feet digging, lungs puffing, they muscle automobiles up and down the street. Rather than sit behind the wheel, they lean into the trunk.

The sight puzzles you. The sound stuns you. Do you hear what you think you hear? Running engines. Citizens of Tuckered Town turn the key, start the car, slip it into neutral, and shove!

You have to ask someone why. A young mother rolls her minivan into the grocery store parking lot. "Ever thought of pressing the gas?" you question.

"I do," she replies, brushing sweat away. "I press the gas to start the car; then I take over."

A bizarre answer. But no more bizarre than that of the out-of-breath fellow leaning against his eighteen-wheeler, wheezing like an overweight marathoner. "Did you push this truck?" you ask.

"I did," he gasps, covering his mouth with an oxygen mask.

"Why not use your accelerator?"

He cocks an eyebrow. "Because I'm a Tucker trucker, and we're strong enough to do our own work."

He doesn't look strong to you. But you say nothing. Just walk away wondering, *What kind of people are these? A pedal push away from power, yet they ignore it. Who would live in such a way?*

Paul asked the Galatian church an identical question. "You began your life in Christ by the Spirit. Now are you trying to make it complete by your own power? That is foolish" (Gal. 3:3 NCV). Is God nothing more than a jumper cable? Start-up strength and nothing more?

Corinthian Christians pushed a few cars too. "You are still not spiritual," the apostle accused (1 Cor. 3:3 NCV). What are you saying, Paul? Are they saved? Yes. He addresses them as "brothers and sisters" (1 Cor. 3:1 NCV). He considers them to be God's children. Heaven bound. Saved, but not spiritual. Plugged in, but not flipped on. "Brothers and sisters . . . I had to talk to you as I would to people without the Spirit—babies in Christ. . . . You are still not spiritual, because there is jealousy and quarreling among you, and this shows that you are not spiritual. You are acting like people of the world" (1 Cor. 3:1–3 NCV).

I used to think there were two kinds of people: the saved and unsaved. Paul corrects me by describing a third: the *saved, but unspiritual*. The spiritual person is Spirit dependent, Spirit directed,

Spirit dominated. He seeks to "walk in the Spirit" (Gal. 5:16 NKJV). Conversely, the unspiritual person cranks the car and hunkers behind it. Tragically, these people act "like people of the world" (1 Cor. 3:3 NCV). In language, lifestyle, priorities, and personality, they blend in with nonbelievers. They let God save them, but not change them.

Such carnal Christianity frustrates Paul. "You began your life in Christ by the Spirit. Now are you trying to make it complete by your own power? That is foolish" (Gal. 3:3 NCV).

Foolish and miserable. You don't want to carpool with unspiritual Christians. They have no kind words to share. "There is jealousy and strife" among them (1 Cor. 3:3 NASB). The only joy they know graduated from high school last year. And gratitude? Gratitude for what? The two-ton Hummer that daily has to be pushed uphill? The saved but unspiritual see salvation the way a farmer sees a hundred acres of untilled soil—lots of work. *Church attendance, sin resistance—have I done enough?* No wonder they're tired. No wonder they argue. "You are jealous of one another and quarrel with each other. Doesn't that prove you are controlled by your own desires?" (1 Cor. 3:3).

Harsh words
Joyless days
Contentious relationships
Thirsty hearts

You'll find more excitement at an Amish prom. Who wants to live in Tuckered Town? Moreover, who wants to move there? Nothing repels non-Christians more than gloomy Christians. No one wants a free truck if you have to push it. Your neighbor doesn't.

You don't. And God doesn't want it for any of us. He never intended for you to perambulate your life.

His word for tuckered-out Christians? "As you received Christ Jesus the Lord, so continue to live in him" (Col. 2:6 NCV).

How does one receive Christ? By coming thirsty and drinking deeply. How, then, does one live in Christ? By coming thirsty and drinking deeply.

When you do, saving power becomes staying power. "God, who began the good work within you, will continue his work until it is finally finished on that day when Christ Jesus comes back again" (Phil. 1:6).

Christ did not give you a car and tell you to push it. He didn't even give you a car and tell you to drive it. You know what he did? He threw open the passenger door, invited you to take a seat, and told you to buckle up for the adventure of your life.

When Christ enters the Tuckered Towns of the world, he stands at the intersection of Dead-Tired Avenue and Done-In Street and compels, "'If you are thirsty, come to me! If you believe in me, come and drink! For the Scriptures declare that rivers of living water will flow out from within.' (When he said 'living water,' he was speaking of the Spirit, who would be given to everyone believing in him)" (John 7:37–39).

"Come to me!" Not "come to my church" or "come to my system," but "come to me!"

Come to me and drink. No sipping. No tasting. It's time to chug-a-lug. Thirsty throats gulp water. Thirsty souls gulp Christ. The margin notes of the New American Standard Bible state: "Keep coming to Me and . . . keep drinking." Annual fill-ups or monthly ingestions won't do. You aren't sampling wine at a California vineyard. You're hiking through Death Valley, and that mirage you see is not a mirage but really is the river you need. Dive in and drink.

And as you do, look what happens: "rivers of living water will flow out from within" (John 7:38). The word for *rivers* can be translated *floods* (see Matt. 7:25, 27; Rev. 12:15–16). We've seen torrents torrential enough to carry homes. Newscasts run and rerun images of a house floating downstream. What is this force that can float a house?

One smaller than the power who floods you. "He was speaking of the Spirit, who would be given to everyone believing in him" (John 7:39). God's Spirit. God's powerful, unseen, undeniable presence pulsating through heart canals. A "spring of water gushing up inside that person, giving eternal life" (John 4:14 NCV).

God's Spirit rages within you. Whether you feel him or not is unimportant. Whether you understand him is insignificant. Jesus said, "Living water will flow out from within" (7:38). Not "may flow," "could flow," or "has been known to flow." But "will flow."

If such is the case, Max, then explain my weariness and irritability. If God's Spirit lives within me, why do I have the compassion of Hermann Goering? I can't tolerate my mother or control my temper or forgive myself. I'm so tired.

God through Paul answers that question with five rich words: "Be filled with the Spirit" (Eph. 5:18 NCV). The verb tense caused original readers to see capital letters: BE FILLED. With the same imperative gusto that he instructs, "Forgive," "Pray," and "Speak truth," God commands, "BE FILLED."

Not only does Paul give a command; he gives a continuous, collective command. Continuous in the sense that the filling is a daily privilege. Collective because the invitation is offered to all people. "You *all* be filled with the Spirit." Young, old, servants, businessmen, seasoned saints, and new converts. The Spirit will fill all. No SAT (Spiritual Aptitude Test) required. You don't need to persuade him to enter; he already has. Better set another plate for dinner. You've got company. "Your body is a temple for the Holy Spirit who is in you" (1 Cor. 6:19 NCV). As a Christian, you have all the power you need for all the problems you face.

The real question is not, how do I get more of the Spirit? but rather, how can you, Spirit, have more of me? We'd expect a Mother Teresa–size answer to that question. Build an orphanage. Memorize Leviticus. Bathe lepers. Stay awake through a dozen Lucado books. *Do this and be filled,* we think.

"Do this on your own and be tired," God corrects. Do you desire God's Spirit? Here is what you do. Ask. "Everyone who asks will receive. . . . You know how to give good things to your children. How much more your heavenly Father will give the Holy Spirit to those who ask him!" (Luke 11:10, 13 NCV).

The Spirit fills as prayers flow. Desire to be filled with strength? Of course you do. Then pray, "Lord, I receive your energy. Empowered by your Holy Spirit, I can do all things through Christ, who gives me strength." Welcome the Spirit into every room of your heart.

I did something similar with the air of my air conditioner. As I study in my dining room, cool air surrounds me. Outside the sidewalk sizzles in brick-oven heat. But inside I'm as cool as the other side of the pillow. Why? Two reasons. A compressor sits next to the house. I did not build nor install it. It came with the mortgage. Credit the cool house on a good compressor.

But equally credit the open vents. I did not install the "air makers," but I did open the "air blockers." Cool air fills the house because vents are open. I went from room to room, lowering the levers and releasing the air. The Holy Spirit will fill your life as you do the same: as you, room by room, invite him to flow in.

Try this: before you climb out of bed, mentally escort the Spirit into every room of your house. Before your feet touch the floor, open each vent. Got anger in a bedroom? Unpayable bills on a desk? Conflicts in an office? Need some air in the cellar or a change of atmosphere in the hallways? Invite him to fill each corridor of your life. Then, having welcomed him into your whole heart, go to your garage, climb into the passenger seat, buckle up, and thank your Driver that you don't live in Tuckered Town anymore.

SEVEN

Waiting for Power

Buried like a grass burr in Matthew's rose bed is this disclosure: "Then the eleven disciples left for Galilee, going to the mountain where Jesus had told them to go. When they saw him, they worshiped him—but *some of them still doubted!*" (Matt. 28:16–17, emphasis mine). Three years of miracles weren't enough. Nor were forty days at the Resurrection Retreat Center. They've seen him vacate tombs and dictate weather patterns, but still they doubt.

You have to be kidding. Who knows him better than they? Ask them a Christ question. Go ahead. Anything. Did he hum as he walked? Pray before he ate? Did he talk to storms in his sleep? And, if he did, did storms listen? They know. They know the person of Christ.

And, my, how they could speak on the passion of Christ. John winced as the hammer clanged. Mary wept as her son groaned. Close enough to be splattered by his blood, they knew his passion. When it came time to prepare the body for burial, they did.

And when it came time to see the empty tomb, they did that,

too. Peter ran a finger down the stone slab. Thomas studied Christ's pierced hands like a palm reader. And for forty days Jesus taught them. Forty days! Can you imagine a six-week seminar with the mind behind the microbes? "Tell us again, Jesus. Tell us how you got the hell out of hell."

Hand trained by Christ. Witnesses to the hinge moments of history. These folks are ready, aren't they? Apparently not. "Some of them still doubted."

Questions keep buzzing like a summer fly. Even after a thousand campfire conversations and a scrapbook full of jaw-dropping moments, some disciples resist. *I'm still not sure*.

What will Jesus do with them? We'd like to know, wouldn't we? We'd really like to know. *Still* stalks our sentences too.

"I still worry."

"I still gossip."

"Permafrost still chills my marriage."

"I'm still torn between the AA meeting and the corner bar."

"I still clench my teeth every time I get a call from that speck-of-dandruff ex-boyfriend of mine."

We find odd comfort in the lingering doubts of the disciples. For we still have our own. And so we wonder, *Does Christ have a word for those who linger near the dis-*still*-ery of doubt?*

His "yes" resounds. And his instruction will surprise you. What he told them, he tells us. "Don't leave Jerusalem yet. Wait here for the Father to give you the Holy Spirit, just as I told you he has promised to do" (Acts 1:4 CEV).

Jesus's word to the doubting disciples? "Wait." Before you go out, stand still. Prior to stepping forth, sit down. "Stay here in the city until the Holy Spirit comes and fills you with power from heaven" (Luke 24:49).

So they do. "They went to the upstairs room of the house where they were staying. . . . They all met together continually for prayer, along with Mary the mother of Jesus, several other women, and the brothers of Jesus" (Acts 1:13–14).

They have reasons to leave. Someone has a business to run or field to farm. Besides, the same soldiers who killed Christ still walk Jerusalem's streets. The disciples have ample reason to leave . . . but they don't. They stay. And they stay together.

"They all met together continually." As many as 120 souls huddle in the same house. How many potential conflicts exist in this group? Talk about a powder keg. Nathanael might glare at Peter for denying Christ at the fire. Then again, at least Peter stood near the fire. He could resent the others for running. So could the women. Faithful females who stood near the cross share the room with cowardly men who fled the cross. The room is ripe for conflict. Mary could demand special treatment. Jesus's blood brothers are in the room. They once tried to lock up Christ. Who's to say they won't lock up his followers? And the women. Isn't this a men's meeting? Who let the ladies in? Bitterness, arrogance, distrust, chauvinism—the room is a kindling box for all four. But no one strikes a match. They stay together, and most of all, they pray together.

"They all met together continually for prayer." Mark uses the same Greek word here translated "continually" to describe a boat floating in the water, waiting on Jesus. The Master, speaking on the beach of Galilee, told the disciples to have a boat ready and waiting (Mark 3:9). The boat was "continually" in the presence of Christ. So are the Upper Room disciples. One day passes. Then two. Then a week. For all they know a hundred more will come and go. But they aren't leaving. They persist in the presence of Christ.

Then, ten days later, hang on to your turban:

> On the day of Pentecost, seven weeks after Jesus' resurrection, the believers were meeting together in one place. Suddenly, there was a sound from heaven like the roaring of a mighty windstorm in the skies above them, and it filled the house where they were meeting. Then, what looked like flames or tongues of fire appeared and settled on each of them. And everyone present was filled with the Holy Spirit. (Acts 2:1–4a)

Doubters became prophets. Peter preached, and people came, and God opened the floodgates on the greatest movement in history. It began because the followers were willing to do one thing: wait in the right place for power.

We're so reluctant to do what they did. Who has time to wait? We groan at such a thought. But waiting doesn't mean inactivity—rather inHIMactivity. Waiting means watching for him. If you are waiting on a bus, you are watching for the bus. If you are waiting on God, you are watching for God, searching for God, hoping in God. Great promises come to those who do. "But those who wait on the LORD will find new strength. They will fly high on wings like eagles. They will run and not grow weary. They will walk and not faint" (Isa. 40:31).

To those who still struggle, God says, "Wait on me." And wait in the right place. Jesus doesn't tell us to stay in Jerusalem, but he does tell us to stay honest, stay faithful, stay true. "If you rebel against the LORD's commands and refuse to listen to him, then his hand will be as heavy upon you as it was upon your ancestors" (1 Sam. 12:15). Are you illegally padding your pocket? Are you giving your body to someone who doesn't share your name and wear your ring? Is your mouth a Mississippi River of gossip? If you intentionally hang out at the bus stop of disobedience, you need to know something—God's bus doesn't stop there. Go to the place of obedience. "The Holy Spirit . . . is God's gift to those who obey him" (Acts 5:32 TEV).

While you're waiting in the right place, get along with people. Would the Holy Spirit have anointed contentious disciples? According to Peter, disharmony hinders prayers. He tells husbands, "Live with your wives in an understanding way. . . . Do this so that nothing will stop your prayers" (1 Pet. 3:7 NCV). Waiting on God means working through conflicts, forgiving offenses, resolving disputes. "Always keep yourselves united in the Holy Spirit, and bind yourselves together with peace" (Eph. 4:3).

Some years ago our family had a backyard trampoline. One Saturday afternoon I noticed all three of our girls bouncing on it. My daughters, like all siblings, don't always get along. But for some reason, that afternoon they were one another's biggest fans. When one jumped, the other two applauded. If one fell, the other two helped her stand. My chest swelled with pride. After a few moments, you know what I did? I joined them. I couldn't resist. Their alliance pleased me. Our alliance pleases Christ. Jesus promised, "When two or three of you are together because of me, you can be sure that I'll be there" (Matt. 18:20 MSG).

Desire power for your life? It will come as you "do your part to live in peace with everyone, as much as possible" (Rom. 12:18).

It will also come as you pray. For ten days the disciples prayed. Ten days of prayer plus a few minutes of preaching led to three thousand saved souls. Perhaps we invert the numbers. We're prone to pray for a few minutes and preach for ten days. Not the apostles. Like the boat waiting for Christ, they lingered in his presence. They never left the place of prayer.

Biblical writers spoke often of this place. Early Christians were urged to

- "pray without ceasing" (1 Thess. 5:17 NASB);
- "always be prayerful" (Rom. 12:12);
- "pray at all times and on every occasion" (Eph. 6:18).

Remember the adverb *continually* that described the Upper Room prayer of the apostles? It's used to describe our prayers as well: "Continue earnestly in prayer, being vigilant in it with thanksgiving" (Col. 4:2 NKJV).

Sound burdensome? Are you wondering, *My business needs attention, my children need dinner, my bills need paying. How can I stay in a place of prayer?* Unceasing prayer may sound complicated, but it needn't be that way.

Do this. Change your definition of prayer. Think of prayers less as an activity for God and more as an awareness of God. Seek to live in uninterrupted awareness. Acknowledge his presence everywhere you go. As you stand in line to register your car, think, *Thank you, Lord, for being here*. In the grocery as you shop, *Your presence, my King, I welcome*. As you wash the dishes, worship your Maker. Brother Lawrence did. This well-known saint called himself the "lord of pots and pans." In his book *The Practice of the Presence of God*, he wrote:

> The time of business does not with me differ from the time of prayer; and in the noise and clatter of my kitchen, while several persons are at the same time calling for different things, I possess God in as great tranquility as if I were upon my knees at the blessed sacrament.[1]

Though a rookie in the League of Unceasing Prayer, I sure enjoy the pursuit. I've discovered the strength of carrying on two conversations: one with a person, another with the Person. One can, at once, listen and petition. As a person unfolds his problem, I'm often silently saying, *God, a little help here, please.* He always provides it. I've also discovered the delight of regular drinks from his water cooler. Throughout the day, my thoughts are marked with phrases: *Guide me, dear Father. Forgive that idea, please. Protect my daughters today.*

A final thought. The Upper Room was occupied by 120 disciples. Since there were about 4,000,000 people in Palestine at the time, this means that fewer than 1 in 30,000 was a Christian.[2] Yet look at the fruit of their work. Better said, look at the fruit of God's Spirit in them. We can only wonder what would happen today if we, who *still* struggle, did what they did: wait on the Lord in the right place.

EIGHT
God's Body Glove

You are so proud of the new gloves you just bought. Your old set was worn and threadbare, defenseless against winter's bite. So you shopped until you found just the right pair. How many did you examine? Dozens. And how many did you try on? Nearly the same number. After all, what good are gloves if you don't like them or they don't fit?

Ah, but then you found these. The clerk did you a favor. She reached under the counter and produced a set still wrapped in plastic. You paid the price and walked out the door, unsealing the bag. And now, walking down the avenue on a chilly morning, you prepare to wear your brand-new gloves.

You step to the side of the foot traffic, tear open the plastic cover, and plunge your hand into the woolen warmth, only to be stopped. You can't get your fingers into the fingers! The five entryways are stitched together. Mistake of the factory? Oversight of the store? Who knows? One thing is certain: your fingers won't fill the glove. A closed fist will, but an extended hand won't.

No problem, you say to yourself. *I'll make do*. You fist your way into the palm and park there, your fingers folded, the glove fingers flopping. Not exactly what you had in mind, but, hey, when it comes to warmth, you can't complain. Folded fingers stay nice and toasty. Frostbite is no concern.

Function, however, is. Ever tried to pick up a newspaper with your fingers folded inside a glove? Not easy. Neither is tying your shoes. Your hands feel like horse hoofs. Wave at someone, and he thinks you are shaking your fist. And forget grabbing a pencil or dialing a cell phone. Floppy wool has no grip.

You want extended fingers, stretched and strong. Why? You have leaves to rake. A steering wheel to grip. A neighbor's hand to shake. Simply put, you have things to do.

So does God. Babies need hugs. Children need good-night tucks. AIDS orphans need homes. Stressed-out executives need hope. God has work to do. And he uses our hands to do it.

What the hand is to the glove, the Spirit is to the Christian. "Behold, I stand at the door and knock; if anyone hears My voice and opens the door, I will *come in* to him" (Rev. 3:20 NASB, emphasis mine). God gets into us. At times, imperceptibly. Other times, disruptively. God gets his fingers into our lives, inch by inch reclaiming the territory that is rightfully his.

Your tongue. He claims it for his message.

Your feet. He requisitions them for his purpose.

Your mind? He made it and intends to use it for his glory.

Your eyes, face, and hands? Through them he will weep, smile, and touch.

As a glove responds to the strength of the hand, so you will respond to the leading of Christ to the point where you say, "I myself no longer live, but Christ lives in me" (Gal. 2:20). Oh, but the process can come so slowly. Why do some walk with such confidence and others stumble with such regularity?

Receiving the unseen is not easy. Most Christians find the cross of Christ easier to accept than the Spirit of Christ. Good Friday makes more sense than Pentecost. Christ, our substitute. Jesus taking our place. The Savior paying for our sins. These are astounding, yet embraceable, concepts. They fall in the arena of transaction and substitution, familiar territory for us. But Holy Spirit discussions lead us into the realm of the supernatural and unseen. We grow quickly quiet and cautious, fearing what we can't see or explain.

It helps to consider the Spirit's work from this angle. What Jesus did in Galilee is what the Holy Spirit does in us. Jesus *dwelt among* the people, teaching, comforting, and convicting. The Holy Spirit *dwells within* us, teaching, comforting, and convicting. The preferred New Testament word for this promise is *oikeo*, which means "live or dwell." *Oikeo* descends from the Greek noun *oikos*, which means "house." The Holy Spirit indwells the believer in the same way a homeowner indwells a house.

> Those who trust God's action in them find that God's Spirit is in them—living and breathing God! . . .
>
> But if God himself has taken up residence in your life, you can hardly be thinking more of yourself than of him. Anyone, of course, who has not welcomed this invisible but clearly present God, the Spirit of Christ, won't know what we're talking about. But for you who welcome him, in whom he dwells—even though you still experience all the limitations of sin—you yourself experience life on God's terms. (Rom. 8:5, 9–10 MSG)

Did you see the phrases of permanence? *God's Spirit is in them. . . . God himself has taken up residence in your life . . . in whom he dwells*. To Timothy, Paul urges, "You have been trusted with a wonderful treasure. Guard it with the help of the Holy Spirit, who lives within you" (2 Tim. 1:14 CEV). Could the apostle's words have been clearer than "Don't you realize that all of you together are the temple of God and that the Spirit of God lives in you?" (1 Cor. 3:16)?

All believers have God in their heart. But not all believers have given their whole heart to God. Remember, the question is not, how can I have more of the Spirit? but rather, how can the Spirit have more of me? A palm and a few fingers will not suffice. C. S. Lewis put it well:

> Christ says, "Give me All. I don't want so much of your time and so much of your money and so much of your work: I want You. I have not come to torment your natural self, but to kill it. No half-measures are any good. I don't want to cut off a branch here and a branch there, I want to have the whole tree down. . . . Hand over the whole natural self, all the desires which you think innocent as well as the desires you think wicked—the whole outfit. I will give you a new self instead. In fact, I will give you Myself: my own will shall become yours."[1]

Take inventory. As you look around your life, do you see any resistant pockets? Any stitched-up fingers? Go down the list.

Your tongue. Do you tend to stretch the truth? Puff up the facts? Your language? Is your language a sewer of profanities and foul talk? And grudges? Do you keep resentments parked in your "garudge"? Are you unproductive and lazy? Do you live off the system, assuming that the church or the country should take care of you?

If you find these questions too personal, blame Paul. He crafted the list.

> So put away all falsehood and "tell your neighbor the truth" because we belong to each other. And "don't sin by letting anger gain control over you." Don't let the sun go down while you are still angry, for anger gives a mighty foothold to the Devil.
>
> If you are a thief, stop stealing. Begin using your hands for honest work, and then give generously to others in need. Don't use foul or abusive language. Let everything you say be good and helpful, so that your words will be an encouragement to those who hear them.
>
> And *do not bring sorrow to God's Holy Spirit by the way you live*. Remember, he is the one who has identified you as his own, guaranteeing that you will be saved on the day of redemption.
>
> Get rid of all bitterness, rage, anger, harsh words, and slander, as well as all types of malicious behavior. (Eph. 4:25–31, emphasis mine)

Do your actions interrupt the flow of the Spirit in your life?

Our life was interrupted recently by an uninvited guest. I had turned on the television to watch the baseball play-offs. The reception was erratic. The game appeared and disappeared. I did all the professional stuff, like jiggling the connection and pounding on the set . . . Nothing helped.

The cable company checked the system and determined that the originating signal was strong and that the problem was on my end. A couple of days later a serviceman discovered what was wrong. Denalyn couldn't resist calling me with the news. "Remember the ring-tailed cat we heard scampering in the attic?" she asked.

A week earlier we'd awakened to the pitter-patter of furred feet over our bedroom ceiling. The pest-control guy had found clues of a ring-tailed cat—a little round-faced feline with a bushy tail. He set out a cage, and, sure enough, the sound stopped. To be honest, I thought he'd retrieved the critter. He hadn't. For a day or so, the caged cat sat in the attic.

I knew nothing about caged, ring-tailed cats, but this much I learned. They don't like major-league baseball games. While poor reception was yanking me in and out of Yankee Stadium, he was upstairs chewing on the cable. The wire cage had an opening just large enough for his nose and just close enough to the wire to keep me from seeing Boston beat New York.

Acknowledging pests isn't enough; you have to do something to get them out of the house.

You're likely aware of a few critters of your own: jealousy, bigotry, greed, anxiety. You can hear them scamper. You don't like the sound of them, and you may have even set out a few traps. "I'm working on my temper." "This bad habit needs attention." Good start, but don't stop there. Trapping varmints isn't enough. Call the heavenly pest control. Ask God to help you get rid of them.

Remember Paul's instruction? "Get rid of all bitterness, rage, anger, harsh words, and slander, as well as all types of malicious behavior" (Eph. 4:31). Harbored sin interferes with Spirit circulation. Confessed sin, however, splices the cable and restores the power.

This could take time. Don't give up on it. Don't let stumbles stop you. Come and keep coming. Drink and keep drinking. Ask and keep asking. "Your heavenly Father [will] give the Holy Spirit to those who ask and continue to ask Him!" (Luke 11:13 AMP).

Don't make the mistake of the fly I encountered in the airplane. That's right, on a recent flight a fly buzzed about in the cabin. How odd. A fly flying inside a flying plane. Why would a fly fly during a flight? Was he helping the plane? Doing his part to keep the craft airborne? Why did the fly in the plane fly in the plane?

I asked him. Catching his attention, I inquired, "Mr. Fly, why do you fly? Why don't you sit down and enjoy the journey?"

His reply smacked of smugness. "And let the plane crash? Why, this craft needs me. My wings are essential to our safety." And with a puff of the chest he flew toward the front of the plane. As he returned some moments later, he didn't look so confident. Fear flickered in his tiny eyes. "I don't think I can keep it up!"

"Keep what up?"

"The plane! I don't think I can keep the plane up. I'm flying as furiously as I can. But my wings are weary. I don't know how long I can do this."

I opted for frankness. "Don't you know it's not up to you? You are surrounded by strength, held aloft by power that is not yours. Stop flying! It's not up to you to get this plane home."

He looked at me as if I were crazy and told me to buzz off.

I so hope you won't. Some of you need to sit down. You fly furiously back and forth, ever busy, always thinking the success of this journey is up to you. Do you fear letting up?

Look out the windows. God's wings sustain you. God's engines empower you. You can flap like a fly and not accelerate this flight. It's your job to sit and trust: to receive.

Accept his power. You be the glove and let him get his hand deep into your life.

Surrender to his plan. Get rid of those cable-nibbling varmints.

And *keep* at it. Unceasingly seek God's Spirit.

Accept. Surrender. Keep at it. A-S-K. "Your Heavenly Father will give the Holy Spirit to those who ask him!" (Luke 11:13 PHILLIPS).

NINE

It's Not Up to You

Why anyone would pester Hannah Lake is beyond me. If the sweet face of this ten-year-old doesn't de-starch your shirt, her cherubic voice will. But, according to her dad, a grade school bully tried to stir some trouble. Intimidation tactics, pressure—the pest tried it all. But Hannah didn't fold. And in the end, it was not her dimples or tender voice but her faith that pulled her through.

The older student warned Hannah to prepare for battle. "Any day now I'm coming after you." Hannah didn't flinch or cry. She simply informed the perpetrator about the facts. "Do whatever you need to do," she explained. "But just know this: God is on my side."

Last word has it that no more threats have been made.

Elementary school bullies don't await you, but funeral homes do. Job transfers and fair-weather friends do. Challenges pockmark the pathway of your life. Where do you find energy to face them? God never promises an absence of distress. But he does promise the assuring presence of his Holy Spirit.

At first blush, a person might assume that the Holy Spirit is all about the spectacular and stupendous. We've seen the television images of sweating preachers, fainting and falling audiences, unintelligible tongue speaking, and questionable miracle working. While no one would deny the pupil-popping nature of the Holy Spirit's work (tongues of fire over the apostles' heads), a focus on the phenomenal might lead you to miss his quieter stabilizing work.

The Holy Spirit invisibly, yet indispensably, serves as a rudder for the ship of your soul, keeping you afloat and on track. This is no solo journey. Next time you feel as though it is, review some of the gifts the Spirit gives. For example, "you were sealed in Him with the Holy Spirit of promise, who is given as a pledge of our inheritance" (Eph. 1:13–14 NASB).

The Spirit seals you. The verb *sealed* stirs a variety of images. To protect a letter, you seal the envelope. To keep air out of a jar, you seal its mouth with a rubber-ringed lid. To keep oxygen from the wine, you seal the opening with cork and wax. To seal a deal, you might sign a contract or notarize a signature. Sealing declares ownership and secures contents.

The most famous New Testament "sealing" occurred with the tomb of Jesus. Roman soldiers rolled a rock over the entrance and "set a seal on the stone" (Matt. 27:66 NASB). Archaeologists envision two ribbons stretched in front of the entrance, glued together with hardened wax that bore the imprimatur of the Roman government—SPQR *(Senatus Populusque Romanus)*—as if to say, "Stay away! The contents of this tomb belong to Rome." Their seal, of course, proved futile.

The seal of the Spirit, however, proves forceful. When you accepted Christ, God sealed you with the Spirit. "Having believed, you were marked in him with a seal, the promised Holy Spirit" (Eph. 1:13 NIV). When hell's interlopers come seeking to snatch you from God, the seal turns them away. He bought you, owns you, and protects you. God paid too high a price to leave you unguarded. As Paul writes later, "Remember, he is the one who has identified you as his own, guaranteeing that you will be saved on the day of redemption" (Eph. 4:30).

In his delightful book *The Dance of Hope,* my friend Bill Frey tells of a blind student named John, whom he tutored at the University of Colorado in 1951. One day Bill asked John how he had become blind. The sightless student described an accident that had happened in his teenage years. The tragedy took not just the boy's sight but also his hope. He told Bill, "I was bitter and angry with God for letting it happen, and I took my anger out on everyone around me. I felt that since I had no future, I wouldn't lift a finger on my own behalf. Let others wait on me. I shut my bedroom door and refused to come out except for meals."

His admission surprised Bill. The student he assisted displayed no bitterness or anger. He asked John to explain the change. John credited his father. Weary of the pity party and ready for his son to get on with life, he reminded the boy of the impending winter and told him to mount the storm windows. "Do the work before I get home or else," the dad insisted, slamming the door on the way out.

John reacted with anger. Muttering and cursing and groping all the way to the garage, he found the windows, stepladder, and tools and went to work. "They'll be sorry when I fall off my ladder and break my neck." But he didn't fall. Little by little he inched around the house and finished the chore.

The assignment achieved the dad's goal. John reluctantly realized he could still work and began to reconstruct his life. Years later he learned something else about that day. When he shared this detail with Bill, his blind eyes misted. "I later discovered that at no time during the day had my father ever been more than four or five feet from my side."[1]

The father had no intention of letting the boy fall.

Your Father has no intention of letting you fall, either. You can't see him, but he is present. You are "shielded by God's power" (1 Pet. 1:5 NIV). He is "able to keep you from falling and to present you before his glorious presence without fault and with great joy" (Jude 24 NIV).

Drink deeply from this truth. God is able to keep you from falling! Does he want you living in fear? No! Just the opposite. "The Spirit we received does not make us slaves again to fear; it makes us children of God. With that Spirit we cry out, 'Father.' And the Spirit himself joins with our spirits to say we are God's children" (Rom. 8:15–16 NCV).

What an intriguing statement. Deep within you, God's Spirit confirms with your spirit that you belong to him. Beneath the vitals of the heart, God's Spirit whispers, "You are mine. I bought you and sealed you, and no one can take you." The Spirit offers an inward, comforting witness.

He is like a father who walks hand in hand with his little child. The child knows he belongs to his daddy, his small hand happily lost in the large one. He feels no uncertainty about his papa's love. But suddenly the father, moved by some impulse, swings his boy up into the air and into his arms and says, "I love you, Son." He puts a big kiss on the bubbly cheek, lowers the boy to the ground, and the two go on walking together.

Has the relationship between the two changed? On one level, no. The father is no more the father than he was before the expression of love. But on a deeper level, yes. The dad drenched, showered, and saturated the boy in love. God's Spirit does the same with us. "The love of God has been poured out in our hearts by the Holy Spirit who was given to us" (Rom. 5:5 NKJV). Note the preposition *of*. The Holy Spirit pours the love *of* God in our hearts, not love *for* God. God hands a bucket of love to the Spirit and instructs, "Douse their hearts."

There are moments when the Spirit enchants us with sweet rhapsody. *You belong to the Father. Signed, sealed, and soon-to-be delivered.* Been a while since you heard him whisper words of assurance? Then tell him. He's listening to you. And—get this!—he's speaking for you.

> The Spirit comes to the aid of our weakness. We do not even know how we ought to pray, but through our inarticulate groans the Spirit himself is pleading for us, and God who searches our inmost being knows what the Spirit means, because he pleads for God's own people in God's own way. (Rom. 8:26–27 NEB)

The Spirit comes to the aid of our weakness. What a sentence worthy of a highlighter. Who does not need this reminder? Weak bodies. Weak wills. Weakened resolves. We've known them all. The word *weakness* can refer to physical infirmities, as with the invalid who had been unable to walk for thirty-eight years (John 5:5), or spiritual impotence, as with the spiritually "helpless" of Romans 5:6.

Whether we are feeble of soul or body or both, how good to know it's not up to us. "The Spirit himself is pleading for us."

I witnessed a picture of the strong speaking for the weak during a White House briefing on the AIDS crisis. While most of the attendees represented relief organizations, a few ministers were invited. The agenda of the day included a Q and A with a White House staffer charged with partial oversight of several billion dollars earmarked for AIDS prevention and treatment. There were many questions. How does one qualify? How much can an organization hope to receive? What are the requirements, if any, for using the moneys? Most of the questions came from organizations. Most of us ministers were silent.

But not Bob Coy. Bob serves a large congregation in Fort Lauderdale, Florida. From earlier conversations, I knew of his heart for AIDS victims. When he raised his hand, I expected a policy question. Wrong. He had a personal question. "One of my friends in Miami is dying from AIDS. He spends two thousand dollars a month on medication. With insurance balking at coverage, I'm wondering if I might find him some assistance."

The White House policy staffer was surprised, but polite. "Uh, sure. After the meeting I'll put you in touch with the right person."

The minister, determined to bring the problem to the top of the food chain, remained standing. He held up a few sheets of stapled paper. "I brought his documents with me. If more is needed, I can run them down."

The government official remained polite. "Absolutely. After the meeting."

He had fielded another question or two when he noticed the minister from Florida had raised his hand again. This time the preacher went to the bottom line. "I'm still thinking of my friend," he explained. "Who signs the checks?"

"Excuse me?"

"Who signs the checks? I just want to talk to the person who makes the decisions. So I want to know, who signs the checks?"

My initial response was, *What audacity!* The minister seizing a White House moment to help a friend. Then I thought, *What loyalty! Does the bedridden friend in Florida have any idea that his cause is being presented a few hundred feet from the Oval Office?*

Do you have any idea that your needs are being described in heaven? The Holy Spirit "prays for us with groanings that cannot be expressed in words. And the Father who knows all hearts knows what the Spirit is saying, for the Spirit pleads for us believers in harmony with God's own will" (Rom. 8:26–27).

The AIDS-infected man has no voice, no clout, and no influence. But he has a friend. And his friend speaks on his behalf. The impoverished orphan of Russia, the distraught widow of the battle-field, the aging saint in the convalescent home—they may think they have no voice, no clout, no influence. But they have a friend—a counselor, a comforter—the blessed Spirit of God, who speaks the language of heaven in heaven. "He does our praying in and for us, making prayer out of our wordless sighs, our aching groans. He . . . keeps us present before God" (vv. 26–27 MSG).

It's not up to you to pray your prayers. None of us pray as much as we should, but all of us pray more than we think, because the Holy Spirit turns our sighs into petitions and tears into entreaties. He speaks for you and protects you. He makes sure you get heard. He makes sure you get home.

Now, suppose a person never hears this, never learns about the sealing and intercession of the Spirit. This individual thinks that salvation security resides in self, not God, that prayer power depends on the person, not the Spirit. What kind of life will this person lead?

A parched and prayerless one. Fighting to stay spiritually afloat drains him. Thinking he stands alone before God discourages him. So he lives parched and prayerless.

But what about the one who believes in the work of the Spirit? Really believes. Suppose a person drinks from this fountain? Better still, suppose you do. Suppose you let the Spirit saturate you with assurance. After all, "we can't round up enough containers to hold everything God generously pours into our lives through the Holy Spirit!" (Rom. 5:5 MSG).

Will you be different as a result? You bet your sweet Sunday you will. Your shoulders will lift as you lower the buckling weight of self-salvation. Your knees will bend as you discover the buoyant power of the praying Spirit. Higher walk. Deeper prayers. And, most of all, a quiet confidence that comes from knowing it's not up to you. And you, like Hannah, can tell the pests of the world, "Do whatever you need to do. But just know this: God is on my side."

Part Three

Trust His Lordship

TEN

In God We (Nearly) Trust

A few days before our wedding, Denalyn and I enjoyed and endured a sailing voyage. Milt, a Miami church friend, had invited Denalyn, her mom, and me to join him and a few others on a leisurely cruise along the Florida coast.

Initially it was just that. Leisure. We stretched out on cushions, hung feet over the side, caught some zzz's and rays. Nice.

But then came the storm. The sky darkened, the rain started, and the flat ocean humped like a dragon's neck. Sudden waves of water tilted the vessel up until we saw nothing but sky and then downward until we saw nothing but blue. I learned this about sailing: there is nothing swell about a swell. Tanning stopped. Napping ceased. Eyes turned first to the thunderclouds, then to the captain. We looked to Milt.

He was deliberate and decisive. He told some people where to sit, others what to do, and all of us to hang on. And we did what he said. Why? We knew he knew best. No one else knew the difference between starboard and stern. Only Milt did. We trusted him. We knew he knew.

And we knew we didn't. Prior to the winds, we might have boasted about Boy Scout merit badges in sailing or bass-boat excursions. But once the storm hit, we shut up. (Except for Denalyn, who threw up.) We had no choice but to trust Milt. He knew what we didn't—and he cared. The vessel was captained, not by a hireling or a stranger, but by a pal. Our safety mattered to him. So we trusted him.

Oh, that the choice were equally easy in life. Need I remind you about your westerly winds? With the speed of lightning and the force of a thunderclap, williwaws anger tranquil waters. Victims of sudden storms populate unemployment lines and ICU wards. You know the winds. You've felt the waves. Good-bye, smooth sailing. Hello, rough waters.

Such typhoons test our trust in the Captain. Does God know what he is doing? Can he get us out? Why did he allow the storm? The conditions worsen, and his instructions perplex: he calls on you to endure disaster, tolerate criticism, forgive an enemy . . . How do you respond?

Can you say about God what I said about Milt?

I know God knows what's best.

I know I don't.

I know he cares.

Such words come easily when the water is calm. But when you're looking at a wrecked car or a suspicious-looking mole, when war breaks out or thieves break in, do you trust him?

If yes, then you're scoring high marks in the classroom of sovereignty. This important biblical phrase defines itself. Zero in on the middle portion of the term. See the word within the word?

Sove-*reign*-ty. To confess the sovereignty of God is to acknowledge the reign of God, his regal authority and veto power over everything that happens. To embrace God's sovereignty is to drink from the well of his lordship and make a sailboat-in-the-storm decision. Not in regard to Milt and the sea, but in regard to God and life. You look toward the Captain and resolve: he knows what's best.

After all, doesn't he quarterback the activities of the universe?

> For our God is in the heavens,
> and he does as he wishes.
> (Ps. 115:3)

> From eternity to eternity I am God. No one can oppose what I do. No one can reverse my actions. (Isa. 43:13)

> Only I can tell you what is going to happen even before it happens. Everything I plan will come to pass, for I do whatever I wish. (Isa. 46:10)

> He chose us from the beginning, and all things happen just as he decided long ago. (Eph. 1:11)

Divine decrees direct the cosmos. Jesus informed Pilate, "You would have no power over me if it were not given to you from above" (John 19:11 NIV). The Jewish leaders thought they were the ones who sent Christ to the cross. Peter corrected them. Jesus was "delivered over by the predetermined plan and foreknowledge of God" (Acts 2:23 NASB).

Jeremiah rhetorically inquired, "Can anything happen without the Lord's permission?" (Lam. 3:37).

The book of Daniel declares no! "[God] has the power to do as he pleases among the angels of heaven and with those who live on earth. No one can stop him or challenge him, saying, 'What do you mean by doing these things?'" (Dan. 4:35).

Scripture, from Old Testament to New, from prophets to poets to preachers, renders one unanimous chorus: God directs the affairs of humanity. As Paul wrote, "God . . . is the *blessed controller* of all things, the king over all kings and the master of all masters" (1 Tim. 6:15 PHILLIPS, emphasis mine).

No leaf falls without God's knowledge. No dolphin gives birth without his permission. No wave crashes on the shore apart from his calculation. God has never been surprised. Not once. "The Son is . . . sustaining all things by his powerful word" (Heb. 1:3 NIV). "He himself gives life and breath to everything, and he satisfies every need there is" (Acts 17:25). King David proclaimed, "In Your book were written all the days that were ordained for me, when as yet there was not one of them" (Ps. 139:16 NASB).

Denying the sovereignty of God requires busy scissors and results in a hole-y Bible, for many holes are made as the verses are cut out. Amazingly, some people opt to extract such passages. Unable to reconcile human suffering with absolute sovereignty, they dilute God's Word. Rabbi Kushner did.

His book *When Bad Things Happen to Good People* reached a disturbing conclusion: God can't run the world. Kushner suggested that Job, the most famous sufferer, was "forced to choose between a good God who is not totally powerful, or a powerful God who is not totally good."[1]

The rabbi speaks for many. *God is strong. Or God is good. But God is not both.* Else, how do you explain birth defects, coast-crashing hurricanes, AIDS, or the genocide of the Tutsi in the 1990s? If God cares, he isn't strong; if he is strong, he doesn't care. He can't be both.

But according to the Bible, he is exactly that. Furthermore, according to the Bible, the problem is not the strength or kindness of God. The problem is the agenda of the human race. We pursue the wrong priority. We want good health, a good income, a good night's rest, and a good retirement. Our priority is *We*.

God's priority, however, is God. Why do the heavens exist? To flaunt God. "The heavens declare the glory of God" (Ps. 19:1 NIV).

Why do people struggle? To display his strength. "I have tested you in the furnace of affliction. For My own sake, for My own sake, I will act" (Isa. 48:10–11 NASB). The prophet proclaimed, "You lead Your people, to make Yourself a glorious name" (Isa. 63:14 NKJV).

God unfurls his own flag. He flexes his own muscles. Heaven does not ask, "How can I make Max happy?" Heaven asks, "How can I use Max to reveal my excellencies?" He may use blessings. Then again, he may use buffetings. Both belong to him.

> I am the one who creates the light and makes the darkness. I am the one who sends good times and bad times. I, the LORD, am the one who does these things. (Isa. 45:7)

> Enjoy prosperity while you can. But when hard times strike, realize that both come from God. (Eccles. 7:14)

> Is it not from the mouth of the Most High
> That woe and well-being proceed?
> (Lam. 3:38 NKJV)

Sometime ago I went to the Indianapolis airport to catch a return flight to San Antonio. Upon reaching the terminal, I realized I had lost my itinerary. But that was okay, because I knew which airline would carry me home. Continental. Having flown from San Antonio on Continental, I would return on Continental. Right? But the Continental counter was closed. The lights were off. No ticket agent was in sight. With the clock ticking toward my 7:40 p.m. departure, I called for help. "Hello? Anyone back there? I'm here for the 7:40 flight."

From within the catacombs emerged a Continental baggage handler. He looked at me and said, "We don't have a 7:40 flight."

I replied, "Yes, you do. I flew Continental here, and I need to fly it home."

He shrugged. "We don't have another flight tonight."

I turned to the automated ticket machine, entered my information, and requested a boarding pass for the 7:40 flight. It informed me that there was no such thing. Wouldn't you know? Even the machine was wrong!

The employee, much to his credit, bore with me. Scratching his bald head, he offered a solution. "You know, Northwest Airlines has a 7:40 flight. Maybe you should check with them."

Sure enough, they did. And I had to admit that the airline's schedule ranked higher than my opinion. Their authority checkmated mine. I could have stood in front of the Continental counter all night, stamping my feet and demanding my way. But what good would it have done? Eventually I had to submit to the truth of the itinerary.

Every so often in life, we find ourselves standing before God's counter, thinking we know the itinerary. Good health, a job promotion, a pregnancy. Many times God checks the itinerary he created and says yes. But there are times when he says, "No. That isn't the journey I have planned for you. I have you routed through the city of Struggle."

We can stamp our feet and shake our fists. Or we can make a sailor-in-the-storm decision. *I know God knows what is best.*

Some find the thought impossible to accept. One dear woman did. After I shared these ideas in a public setting, she asked to speak with me. Husband at her side, she related the story of her horrible childhood. First abused, then abandoned by her father. Unimaginable and undeserved hurts scar her early memories. Through tear-filled eyes she asked, "Do you mean to tell me God was watching the whole time?"

The question vibrated in the room. I shifted in my chair and answered, "Yes, he was. I don't know why he allowed your abuse, but I do know this. He loves you and hurts with you." She didn't like the answer. But dare we say anything else? Dare we suggest that God dozed off? Abandoned his post? That heaven sees but can't act? That our Father is kind but not strong, or strong but doesn't care?

I wish she could have spoken to Joseph. His brothers abused him, selling him into slavery. Was God watching? Yes. And our sovereign God used their rebellious hearts to save a nation from famine and the family of the Messiah from extinction. As Joseph told them, "God turned into good what you meant for evil" (Gen. 50:20).

I wish she could have spoken to Lazarus. He grew deathly ill. When Jesus heard the news, he did nothing. Jesus waited until Lazarus was four-days dead in the grave. Why? "For the glory of God, so that the Son of God may be glorified by it" (John 11:4 NASB).

Best of all would have been a conversation with Jesus himself. He begged God for a different itinerary: a crossless death. From Gethsemane's garden Christ pleaded for a plan B. Redemption with no nails. " 'Father, if you are willing, please take this cup of suffering away from me. Yet I want your will, not mine.' Then an angel from heaven appeared and strengthened him" (Luke 22:42–43).

Did God hear the prayer of his Son? Enough to send an angel. Did God spare his Son from death? No. The glory of God outranked the comfort of Christ. So Christ suffered, and God's grace was displayed and deployed.

Are you called to endure a Gethsemane season? Have you "been granted for Christ's sake, not only to believe in Him, but also to suffer for His sake" (Phil. 1:29 NASB)?

If so, then come thirsty and drink deeply from his lordship. He authors all itineraries. He knows what is best. No struggle will come your way apart from his purpose, presence, and permission. What encouragement this brings! You are never the victim of nature or the prey of fate. Chance is eliminated. You are more than a weather vane whipped about by the winds of fortune. Would God truly abandon you to the whims of drug-crazed thieves, greedy corporate raiders, or evil leaders? Perish the thought!

> When you pass through the waters, I will be with you;
> And through the rivers, they will not overflow you.
> When you walk through the fire, you will not be scorched,
> Nor will the flame burn you.
> For I am the LORD your God.
> (Isa. 43:2–3 NASB)

We live beneath the protective palm of a sovereign King who superintends every circumstance of our lives and delights in doing us good.

Nothing comes your way that has not first passed through the filter of his love. Margaret Clarkson, in her wonderfully titled book *Grace Grows Best in Winter*, wrote:

> The sovereignty of God is the one impregnable rock to which the suffering human heart must cling. The circumstances surrounding our lives are no accident: they may be the work of evil, but that evil is held firmly within the mighty hand of our sovereign God. . . . All evil is subject to Him, and evil cannot touch His children unless He permits it. God is the Lord of human history and the personal history of every member of his redeemed family.[2]

Learn well the song of sovereignty: *I know God knows what's best.* Pray humbly the prayer of trust: "I trust your lordship. I belong to you. Nothing comes to me that hasn't passed through you."

A word of caution: the doctrine of sovereignty challenges us. Study it gradually. Don't share it capriciously. When someone you love faces adversity, don't insensitively declare, "God is in control." A cavalier tone can eclipse the right truth. Be careful.

And be encouraged. God's ways are always right. They may not make sense to us. They may be mysterious, inexplicable, difficult, and even painful. But they are right. "And we know that God causes everything to work together for the good of those who love God and are called according to his purpose for them" (Rom. 8:28).

As John Oxenham wrote in 1913:

God's Handwriting

He writes in characters too grand
For our short sight to understand;
We catch but broken strokes, and try
To fathom all the mystery
Of withered hopes, of death, of life,
The endless war, the useless strife,—
But there, with larger, clearer sight,
We shall see this—His way was right.[3]

ELEVEN

Worry? You Don't Have To

The idea captured the fancy of futuristic scientists: an eight-story, glass-and-steel dome in which eight scientists could lead a self-sustained life. The outside elements of the Sonora Desert would not touch them. Let the sun blaze. Let the winds blow. Let the sand fly. Safe within the dome the researchers would be untouched.

So, with the hope of developing a space-colony prototype, the biospherians entered the two-hundred-million-dollar, three-acre terrarium in 1991.[1] They planted their seeds and grew their food; scientists watched with fascination, and not too few of us felt a tinge of envy.

Who hasn't longed for a rotunda of relief? Not from an Arizona desert, but from the harsh winds and hot sun of life. The bank demands the mortgage each month. Hospital bills pack a knockout punch. Semester finals lurk around the corner.

And look around you. You have reason to worry. The sun blasts cancer-causing rays. Air vents blow lung-clotting molds. Potato chips have too many carbs. Vegetables, too many toxins. And do they have to call an airport a terminal? Why does the pilot tell passengers, "We are about to make our *final* approach"? Even on the ground, the flight attendant urges us to stay seated until we have reached a "complete stop." Is there any other kind? Do some airlines have "sort of stops," "partial stops," or "little bits of stops"?

Some of us have postgraduate degrees from the University of Anxiety. We go to sleep worried that we won't wake up; we wake up worried that we didn't sleep. We worry that someone will discover that lettuce was fattening all along. The mother of one teenager bemoaned, "My daughter doesn't tell me anything. I'm a nervous wreck." Another mother replied, "My daughter tells me everything. I'm a nervous wreck." Wouldn't you love to stop worrying? Could you use a strong shelter from life's harsh elements?

God offers you just that: the possibility of a worry-free life. Not just less worry, but no worry. He created a dome for your heart. "His peace will guard your hearts and minds as you live in Christ Jesus" (Phil. 4:7).

Interested? Then take a good look at the rest of the passage.

> Don't worry about anything; instead, pray about everything. Tell God what you need, and thank him for all he has done. If you do this, you will experience God's peace, which is far more wonderful than the human mind can understand. His peace will guard your hearts and minds as you live in Christ Jesus. (vv. 6–7)

The Christians in Philippi needed a biosphere. Attacks were coming at them from all angles. Preachers served for selfish gain (1:15–17). Squabbling church members threatened the unity of the church (4:2). False teachers preached a crossless gospel (3:2–3, 18–19). Some believers struggled to find food and shelter (4:19). Persecutions outside. Problems inside.

Enough hornets' nests to make you worry. Folks in Philippi had them. Folks today have them. To them and us God gives the staggering proposal: "Don't worry about anything."

Yeah, right. And while I'm at it, I'll leapfrog the moon. Are you kidding?

Jesus isn't. Two words summarize his opinion of worry: *irrelevant* and *irreverent*.

"Can all your worries add a single moment to your life? Of course not" (Matt. 6:27). Worry is irrelevant. It alters nothing. When was the last time you solved a problem by worrying about it? Imagine someone saying, "I got behind in my bills, so I resolved to worry my way out of debt. And, you know, it worked! A few sleepless nights, a day of puking and hand wringing. I yelled at my kids and took some pills, and—glory to worry—money appeared on my desk."

It doesn't happen! Worry changes nothing. You don't add one day to your life or one bit of life to your day by worrying. Your anxiety earns you heartburn, nothing more. Regarding the things about which we fret:

- 40 percent never happen
- 30 percent regard unchangeable deeds of the past
- 12 percent focus on the opinions of others that cannot be controlled
- 10 percent center on personal health, which only worsens as we worry about it
- 8 percent concern real problems that we can influence[2]

Ninety-two percent of our worries are needless! Not only is worry irrelevant, doing nothing; worry is irreverent, distrusting God.

> And why worry about your clothes? Look at the lilies and how they grow. They don't work or make their clothing, yet Solomon in all his glory was not dressed as beautifully as they are. And if God cares so wonderfully for flowers that are here today and gone tomorrow, won't he more surely care for you? *You have so little faith!* (Matt. 6:28–30, emphasis mine)

Worry betrays a fragile faith, an "unconscious blasphemy."[3] We don't intentionally doubt God, but don't we, when we worry, essentially doubt God? We assume the attitude of a kid asking Michelangelo, "You sure you know what to do with that rock?" No wonder the apostle urges us to "be anxious for nothing" (Phil. 4:6 NASB). Paul is not promoting an irresponsible, careless life. We are not to be like the procrastinating minister. *I won't worry*, he told himself. *The Holy Spirit will give me my message*. All week long he avoided his work, saying, *The Holy Spirit will give me my message*. Finally, on Sunday, he stood before the church and prayed aloud, "All right, Lord. Give me a message." Much to the surprise of the church, a heavenly voice filled the sanctuary. "Tell the people you didn't study."

Manage your problems? Of course. But let your problems manage you? The worrisome heart does.

And the worrisome heart pays a high price for doing so. *Worry* comes from the Greek word that means "to divide the mind." Anxiety splits us right down the middle, creating a double-minded thinker. Rather than take away tomorrow's trouble, worry voids today's strength. Perception is divided, distorting your vision.

Strength is divided, wasting your energy. Who can afford to lose power?

But how can we stop doing so? Paul offers a two-pronged answer: God's part and our part. Our part includes prayer and gratitude. "Don't worry about anything; instead, *pray* about everything. Tell God what you need, and *thank him* for all he has done" (Phil. 4:6, emphasis mine).

Want to worry less? Then pray more. Rather than look forward in fear, look upward in faith. This command surprises no one. Regarding prayer, the Bible never blushes. Jesus taught people that "it was necessary for them to pray consistently and never quit" (Luke 18:1 MSG). Paul told believers, "Devote yourselves to prayer with an alert mind and a thankful heart" (Col. 4:2). James declared, "Are any among you suffering? They should keep on praying about it" (James 5:13).

Rather than worry about anything, "pray about everything." Everything? Diaper changes and dates? Business meetings and broken bathtubs? Procrastinations and prognostications? Pray about everything. "In everything . . . let your requests be made known to God" (Phil. 4:6 NKJV).

When we lived in Rio de Janeiro, Brazil, I used to take my daughters on bus rides. For a few pennies, we could board a bus and ride all over the city. May sound dull to us, but if you are two years old, such a day generates World Cup excitement. The girls did nothing on the trip. I bought the token, carried the backpack, and selected the route. My only request of them was this: "Stay close to me." Why? I knew the kind of characters who might board a bus. And God forbid that my daughters and I got separated.

Our Father makes the same request. "Stay close to me. Talk to me. Pray to me. Breathe me in and exhale your worry." Worry diminishes as we look upward. God knows what can happen on this journey, and he wants to bring us home.

Pray about everything.

And don't skip Paul's ingredient of gratitude. "Tell God what you need, and thank him for all he has done."

Do what the shepherd boy David did when he faced Goliath. David didn't cower before the giant's strength. He focused on God's success. When Saul refused to let him go head to knee with Goliath, David produced God's track record.

> "I have been taking care of my father's sheep," he said. "When a lion or a bear comes to steal a lamb from the flock, I go after it with a club and take the lamb from its mouth. If the animal turns on me, I catch it by the jaw and club it to death. I have done this to both lions and bears, and I'll do it to this pagan Philistine, too, for he has defied the armies of the living God! The LORD who saved me from the claws of the lion and the bear will save me from this Philistine!"
>
> Saul finally consented. "All right, go ahead," he said. "And may the LORD be with you!" (1 Sam. 17:34–37)

Are you afraid of a giant? Then recall the lion and the bear. Don't look forward in fear; look backward in appreciation. God's proof is God's past. Forgetfulness sires fearfulness, but a good memory makes for a good heart.

It works like this. Let's say a stress stirrer comes your way. The doctor decides you need an operation. She detects a lump and thinks it best that you have it removed. So there you are, walking out of her office. You've just been handed this cup of anxiety. What are you going to do with it? You can place it in one of two pots.

You can dump your bad news in the vat of worry and pull out the spoon. Turn on the fire. Stew on it. Stir it. Mope for a while. Brood for a time. Won't be long before you'll have a delightful pot of pessimism. Some of you have been sipping from this vat for a long time. Your friends and family have asked me to tell you that the stuff you're drinking is getting to you.

How about a different idea? The pot of prayer. Before the door of the doctor's office closes, give the problem to God. "I receive your lordship. Nothing comes to me that hasn't passed through you." In addition, stir in a healthy helping of gratitude. You don't think about a lion and bear, but you do remember the tax refund, the timely counsel, or the suddenly open seat on the overbooked flight. A glimpse into the past generates strength for the future.

Your part is prayer and gratitude.

God's part? Peace and protection. "If you do this, you will experience God's peace, which is far more wonderful than the human mind can understand. His peace will guard your hearts and minds as you live in Christ Jesus" (Phil. 4:7).

Believing prayer ushers in God's peace. Not a random, nebulous, earthly peace, but his peace. Imported from heaven. The same tranquillity that marks the throne room, God offers to you.

Do you think he battles anxiety? You suppose he ever wrings his hands or asks the angels for antacids? Of course not. A problem is no more a challenge to God than a twig is to an elephant. God enjoys perfect peace because God enjoys perfect power.

And he offers his peace to you. A peace that will "guard your hearts and minds as you live in Christ Jesus." Paul employs a military metaphor here. The Philippians, living in a garrison town, were accustomed to the Roman sentries maintaining their watch. Before any enemy could get inside, he had to pass through the guards. God gives you the same offer. His supernatural peace overshadows you like a protective dome, guarding your heart.

After twenty-four months, the biosphere in Arizona proved to be a total flop. Biological balance between the plants got out of whack. Oxygen dipped dangerously low. Researchers squabbled among themselves. The ants ran amuck and conquered most of the other bugs. The experiment failed, and the dome was abandoned.

But the dome of God still stands. We need only stay beneath it. Are you tied up in knots? "Cast all your anxiety on him because he cares for you" (1 Pet. 5:7 NIV). Strong verb there. *Cast*. Not *place*, *lay*, or *occasionally offer*. Peter enlisted the same verb Gospel writers used to describe the way Jesus treated demons. He cast them out. An authoritative hand on the collar, another on the belt, and a "Don't come back." Do the same with your fears. Get serious with them. Immediately cast them upon God.

Worry is an option, not an assignment. God can lead you into a worry-free world. Be quick to pray. Focus less on the problems ahead and more on the victories behind. Do your part, and God will do his. He will guard your heart with his peace . . . a peace that passes understanding.

TWELVE

Angels Watching over You

When seventeen-year-old Jake Porter ran onto the football field, both teams cheered. Odd that they would. In three years on the Northwest High squad, he'd barely dirtied a game jersey. The McDermott, Ohio, fans had never seen Jake carry the ball or make a tackle. Nor had they seen him read a book or write much more than a sentence. Kids with chromosomal fragile X syndrome, a common cause of mental retardation, seldom do.

But Jake loved sports. Each day after his special-ed classes, he dashed off to some practice: track, baseball, basketball. Never missed. Never played, either.

Until the Waverly game.

Jake's coach made his decision before the kickoff. If a lopsided score rendered the final seconds superfluous, Jake would come in. The lopsided part proved true. With five ticks remaining on the clock, his team was down 42–0. So the coach called a time-out.

He motioned to speak with the opposing coach. As his Waverly counterpart heard the plan, he began shaking his head and waving his hands. He disagreed with something. A referee intervened, and play resumed.

The quarterback took the ball and handed it to Jake. Jake knew what do: take a knee and let the clock expire. They'd practiced this play all week. But, to his surprise, the players wouldn't let him. His teammates told him to run. So he did. In the wrong direction. So the back judge stopped and turned him around.

That's when the Waverly defense did their part. The visiting coach, as it turns out, wasn't objecting to the play. He was happy for Porter to carry the ball but not for him just to run out the clock. He wanted Jake to score. Waverly players parted like the Red Sea for Moses and shouted for Jake to run. Run he did. Grinning and dancing and jumping all the way to the end zone.

Both sidelines celebrated. Moms cried, cheerleaders whooped, and Jake smiled as if he'd won the lottery without buying a ticket.[1]

How often do such things happen? According to the Bible, more often than you might think. In fact, what Jake's team did for him, the Lord of the universe does for you every day of your life. And you ought to see the team he coaches.

> The angels keep their ancient places—
> Turn but a stone and start a wing!
> 'Tis ye, 'tis your estrangéd faces,
> That miss the many-splendored thing.[2]

Has your face missed the angels? With over three hundred scriptural references, these celestial servants occupy an unquestioned role in the Bible. If you believe in God's Word, you have to believe in angels. At the same time, you have to be puzzled by them. Angel study is biblical whale watching. Angels surface just long enough to grant a glimpse and raise a question but then disappear before we have a full view.

One thing is certain: biblical and contemporary portrayals of angels don't match up. Grocery store tabloids present angels as Thumbelina fairies with see-through wings. They exist to do us favors—heaven's version of bottled genies who find parking places, lost keys, and missing cats. Snap your finger and "poof," they appear. Snap again and they vanish.

Not quite a biblical image. Two adjectives capture the greater truth about angels: *many* and *mighty*.

Multitudes of angels populate the world. Hebrews 12:22 speaks of "thousands of angels in joyful assembly." Jude declared, "The Lord is coming with thousands and thousands of holy angels to judge everyone" (vv. 14–15 CEV). An inspired King David wrote, "The chariots of God are twenty thousand, even thousands of angels: the Lord is among them, as in Sinai, in the holy place" (Ps. 68:17 KJV). When referring to Mt. Sinai, David was thinking of the time ten thousand angels descended on the mountain as God gave the law to Moses. "GOD came down from Sinai . . . coming with ten thousand holy angels" (Deut. 33:2 MSG).

Thousands of angels awaited the call of Christ on the day of the cross. "Do you think that I cannot appeal to My Father, and He will at once put at My disposal more than twelve legions of angels?" (Matt. 26:53 NASB). One legion equated to six thousand soldiers. Quick math reveals that seventy-two thousand hosts of heaven (enough to fill Los Angeles's Angel Stadium more than one and a half times) stood poised to rescue their Master. The book of Revelation, brimming as it is with glimpses into the soon-to-be world, refers to angels around the heavenly throne, "and the number of them was ten thousand times ten thousand, and thousands of thousands" (Rev. 5:11 NKJV).

And don't forget the vision given to Elisha's servant. When an army threatened to take the lives of them both, Elisha asked God to open the eyes of the boy. "Then the LORD opened the eyes of the young man, and he saw. And behold, the mountain was full of horses and chariots of fire all around Elisha" (2 Kings 6:17 NKJV).

If God opened our eyes, what would we see? Moms and dads, you'd see angels escorting your child to school. Travelers, you'd see angels encircling the aircraft. Patients, you'd see angels monitoring the moves of the surgeon. Teenagers, you'd see angels overseeing your sleep. Many, many angels. Hundreds of years ago John Milton wrote, "Millions of spiritual creatures walk the Earth unseen, both when we wake, and when we sleep."[3]

The poet was right: "Turn but a stone and start a wing."

You need an adjective to describe angels? Start with *many*.

Continue with *mighty*. Chiffon wings and meringue sweetness? Perhaps for angels in the gift books and specialty shops, but God's angels are marked by indescribable strength. Paul says Christ "will come with his mighty angels" (2 Thess. 1:7). From the word translated *mighty*, we have the English word *dynamic*. Angels pack dynamic force. It took only one angel to slay the firstborn of Egypt and only one angel to close the mouths of the lions to protect Daniel. David called angels "mighty creatures who carry out his plans, listening for each of his commands" (Ps. 103:20).

No need for you to talk to angels; they won't listen. Their ears incline only to God's voice. They are "spirits who serve God" (Heb. 1:14 NCV), responding to his command and following only his directions. Jesus said they "always see the face of my Father in heaven" (Matt. 18:10 NIV). Only one sound matters to angels—

God's voice. Only one sight enthralls angels—God's face. They know that he is Lord of all.

And as a result, they worship him. Whether in the temple with Isaiah or the pasture with the Bethlehem shepherds, angels worship. "When he presented his honored Son to the world, God said, 'Let all the angels of God worship him'" (Heb. 1:6). They did and they do.

Remember the earlier reference to the ten thousand times ten thousand angels encircling the throne of heaven? Guess what they are doing? "All the angels stood around the throne . . . saying: 'Amen! Blessing and glory and wisdom, thanksgiving and honor and power and might, be to our God forever and ever. Amen'" (Rev. 7:11–12 NKJV).

Doesn't their worship proclaim volumes about God's beauty? Angels could gaze at the Grand Tetons and Grand Canyon, Picasso paintings and the Sistine Chapel, but they choose, instead, to fix their eyes on the glory of God. They can't see enough of him, and they can't be silent about what they see.

At the very moment you read these words, God's sinless servants offer unceasing worship to their Maker. He is, remember, their creator. At one time no angels existed. And then, by God's decree, they did. "He made the things we can see and the things we can't see—kings, kingdoms, rulers, and authorities. Everything has been created through him and for him" (Col. 1:16). Angels fill God's invisible creation.

They worship him, and—here is a drink for thirsty hearts—they protect us. "All the angels are spirits who serve God and are sent to *help those who will receive salvation*" (Heb. 1:14 NCV, emphasis mine).

One of my friends recently took a heart-stopping mission trip to Vietnam. He and two companions set out to smuggle Bibles and money to Christians there. Upon landing, however, he was separated from the other two. He spoke no Vietnamese and had never traveled in Hanoi. Imagine his thoughts, then, as he stood in front of the airport, holding a bag of Bibles, wearing a belt of cash, and knowing nothing more than the name of his hotel.

Taxi driver after taxi driver offered his services, but he waited and prayed. Finally, knowing he needed to do something, he climbed into a taxi and spoke the name of the hotel. After an hour and a thousand turns, he found himself deposited at the designated place. He paid his drivers, and they went on their way.

That's right, "they" drove off. The front seat of his taxi had been occupied by two men. Only later did the uniqueness of this fact strike him. He saw hundreds of taxis during his days in Vietnam, but not another one of them had two drivers.

Meaningless detail? Quite possibly.

Affirming clue? Equally possible. Perhaps he was safely delivered, not by Vietnamese motorists, but by a tandem of heavenly couriers. His associates arrived but only after they'd been scammed by another taxi driver. Did God command a dynamic duo to protect my friend?

He certainly sent a powerful protector to Shadrach, Meshach, and Abednego. King Nebuchadnezzar commanded that the furnace fire be cranked up seven times its normal heat and that they be thrown into it. The king looked in, expecting to see a trio of misery; instead, the men were in fine company. A visitor stood next to them amid the flames. "'Look!' Nebuchadnezzar shouted. 'I see four men, unbound, walking around in the fire. They aren't even hurt by the flames! And the fourth looks like a divine being!'" (Dan. 3:25). An angel ministered to God's people.

And look at Peter, sleeping on a pallet in a Jerusalem prison's death row. One word from Herod and his head would roll. All earthly efforts to save him had expired. Heavenly efforts had not, however. An angel not only woke Peter up but also walked him out! The fisherman enjoyed a Jake Porter escort. "Suddenly, there was a bright light in the cell, and an angel of the Lord stood before Peter. The angel tapped him on the side to awaken him and said, 'Quick! Get up!' And the chains fell off his wrists" (Acts 12:7).

Angels minister to God's people. "[God] has put his angels in charge of you to watch over you wherever you go" (Ps. 91:11 NCV).

Billy Graham reminds us, "If you are a believer, expect powerful angels to accompany you in your life experience."[4] But what if you are not a believer? Do angels offer equal surveillance to God's enemies? No, they don't. The promise of angelic protection is limited to those who trust God. "All the angels are spirits who serve God and are sent to *help those who will receive salvation*." David speaks of this restricted coverage: "For the angel of the LORD guards *all who fear him*, and he rescues them" (Ps. 34:7, emphasis mine). Refuse God at the risk of an unguarded back. But receive his lordship, and be assured that many mighty angels will guard you in all your ways.

"The angel of the LORD encamps all around those who fear Him, and delivers them" (v. 7 NKJV). He doesn't wave as he flies past; he encamps, he lingers, he keeps vigilance over you. You traffic beneath the care of celestial beings. Let that truth lower your anxiety level! The wealthiest of the world don't have the protection God's servants give you.

And angels love to give it! Angels not only serve you, they are stunned by you. "Do you realize how fortunate you are? Angels would have given anything to be in on this" (1 Pet. 1:12 MSG). Amazed angels behold the gifts God has given you. Does the Holy

Spirit indwell angels? No. But he dwells in you. Do angels thank God for salvation? No, they've never been lost. But you have. Did Christ become an angel? No. But he became a human. And angels stood in awe when he did. Worshiping angels attended his birth. Awaiting angels witnessed his death. Excited angels announced his resurrection. Attentive angels watch the work of the church. "Through Christians like yourselves gathered in churches, this extraordinary plan of God is becoming known and talked about even among the angels!" (Eph. 3:10 MSG).

God's work in you leaves angels wide-eyed and applauding. Jesus said, "There is joy in the presence of God's angels when even one sinner repents" (Luke 15:10). When angels gather in the break room for angel food cake, they discuss the church.

"Have you seen what is happening in Nigeria?"

"The Australians are taking great strides."

"Hey, I just returned from New York. Let me tell you about the Bronx believers."

The Hebrew writer describes a "great cloud of witnesses" (Heb. 12:1 NIV). Certainly angels are numbered among them.

God sends his best troops to oversee your life. Imagine the president assigning his Secret Service to protect you, telling his agents to motorcade your car through traffic and safeguard you through crowds. How would you sleep if you knew D.C.'s finest guarded your door? How *will* you sleep knowing heaven's finest are doing just that? You are not alone. Receive God's lordship over your life. Heaven's many, mighty angels watch over you.

And when you cross the goal line, they'll be the first to applaud.

THIRTEEN

With God as Your Guardian

Did I just read what I think I read? I drove around the block for a second glance. The announcement, taped to a stop-sign pole, had a home computer look to it: yellow paper and thick letters. Our neighbors, like yours, print and post all types of fliers. The presence of the announcement didn't surprise me, but the words did.

Found: Potbellied Pig

Two phone numbers followed: one to call during the day and another to call at night. I'd never seen such an announcement. Similar ones, sure.

Found: Black Retriever
Found: Psychedelic Skateboard
Found: Gold Brooch

But "Found: Potbellied Pig"? Who loses a pig? Who *owns* a pig? I know many pet owners, but pet-pig owners? Can you imagine providing daily care for a pig? (Denalyn says she can.) Do pig owners invite dinner guests to pet the pig? Do they hang a sign on the outside gate: "Potbelly on Patrol"? Pig owners must be a special breed.

Even more so, those who rescue them. The sign presupposes a curious moment. Someone spotted the pig lumbering down the sidewalk. "Poor thing. Climb in little piggy, piggy, piggy. The street is no place for a lonely sow. I'll take you home."

Suppose one appeared on your porch. Upon hearing a snort at your front door, would you open it? Not me. Golden retriever? You bet. German shepherd? Will do. St. Bernard? Count on me for a few nights and a few neighborhood signs. But a potbellied pig? Sorry. I'd leave him on Jericho Road.

I wouldn't claim one. But God would. God did. God did when he claimed us.

We assume God cares for the purebreds of the world. The clean-nosed, tidy-living, convent-created souls of society. When God sees French poodles and Great Danes wandering the streets, he swings his door open. But what about the rest of us? We're prone to wander too. We find ourselves far from home. Do we warrant his oversight?

Psalm 91 offers a rousing yes! If you need to know the nature and size of God's lordship, nestle under the broad branches of David's poetry.

> Those who live in the shelter of the Most High
>   will find rest in the shadow of the Almighty.
> This I declare of the LORD:

He alone is my refuge, my place of safety;
he is my God, and I am trusting him.
For he will rescue you from every trap
and protect you from the fatal plague.
He will shield you with his wings.
He will shelter you with his feathers.
His faithful promises are your armor and protection.
Do not be afraid of the terrors of the night,
nor fear the dangers of the day,
nor dread the plague that stalks in darkness,
nor the disaster that strikes at midday.
Though a thousand fall at your side,
though ten thousand are dying around you,
these evils will not touch you.
But you will see it with your eyes;
you will see how the wicked are punished.

If you make the LORD your refuge,
if you make the Most High your shelter,
no evil will conquer you;
no plague will come near your dwelling.
For he orders his angels
to protect you wherever you go.
They will hold you with their hands
to keep you from striking your foot on a stone.
You will trample down lions and poisonous snakes;
you will crush fierce lions and serpents under your feet!

The LORD says, "I will rescue those who love me.
I will protect those who trust in my name.

When they call on me, I will answer;
    I will be with them in trouble.
    I will rescue them and honor them.
I will satisfy them with a long life
    and give them my salvation."
    (Ps. 91:1–16)

Sixteen verses collaborate to envision one image: God as your guardian. See if you can spot the most common word of the psalm:

"Those who live in the shelter of the Most High *will* find rest."
"He *will* rescue you."
"He *will* shield you."
"He *will* shelter you."
"Evils *will* not touch you."
"They [angels] *will* hold you."
"The LORD says, 'I *will* rescue.'"
"I *will* protect."
"I *will* answer."
"I *will* be with them."
"I *will* rescue."
"I *will* satisfy."

Okay, I gave you a good hint, but I don't want you to miss this point: God offers more than the possibility of protection or the likelihood of protection. Will God guard you? Is the pope Catholic? Your serenity matters to heaven. God's presence encapsulates your life. Separating you from evil is God, your guardian.

During the Clinton-Lewinsky scandal, special prosecutor Kenneth Starr spoke at our church. Because of the combustible days, a couple of tougher-than-two-dollar-steak U.S. marshals monitored his every move. One walked ahead, the other behind. Between services they silently sized up all well-wishers. While Judge Starr sat in the break room, they stood at the door, the American version of Great Britain's Foot Guards. When I asked if he minded their presence, Judge Starr shrugged. "You know, their protection comforts."

So much more does God's. He sizes up every person who comes your way. As you walk, he leads. As you sleep, he patrols. "He will shield you with his wings. He will shelter you with his feathers" (v. 4).

The image of living beneath *Shaddai*'s shadow reminds me of a rained-out picnic. My college friends and I barely escaped a West Texas storm before it pummeled the park where we were spending a Saturday afternoon. As we were leaving, my buddy brought the car to a sudden stop and gestured to a tender sight on the ground. A mother bird sat exposed to the rain, her wing extended over her baby who had fallen out of the nest. The fierce storm prohibited her from returning to the tree, so she covered her child until the wind passed.

From how many winds is God protecting you? His wing, at this moment, shields you. A slanderous critic heading toward your desk is interrupted by a phone call. A burglar en route to your house has a flat tire. A drunk driver runs out of gas before your car passes his. God, your guardian, protects you from

"every trap" (v. 3);
"the fatal plague" (v. 3);
"the plague that stalks in darkness" (v. 6);
"the terrors of the night . . . the dangers of the day" (v. 5).

One translation boldly promises: "Nothing bad will happen to you" (v. 10 NCV).

"Then why does it?" someone erupts. "Explain my job transfer. Or the bum who called himself my dad. Or the death of our child." Here is where potbellied-pig thoughts surface. God protects Alaskan malamutes and English setters, but little runts like me? Perhaps your Rubik's Cube has a square that won't turn. If God is our guardian, why do bad things happen to us?

Have they? Have bad things *really* happened to you? You and God may have different definitions for the word *bad*. Parents and children do. Look up the word *bad* in a middle-schooler's dictionary, and you'll read definitions such as "pimple on nose," "Friday night all alone," or "pop quiz in geometry." "Dad, this is really bad!" the youngster says. Dad, having been around the block a time or two, thinks differently. Pimples pass. And it won't be long before you'll treasure a quiet evening at home. Inconvenience? Yes. Misfortune? Sure. But *bad?* Save that adjective for emergency rooms and cemeteries.

What's bad to a child isn't always bad to a dad.

What you and I might rate as an absolute disaster, God may rate as a pimple-level problem that will pass. He views your life the way you view a movie after you've read the book. When something bad happens, you feel the air sucked out of the theater. Everyone else gasps at the crisis on the screen. Not you. Why? You've read the book. You know how the good guy gets out of the tight spot. God views your life with the same confidence. He's not only read your story . . . he wrote it. His perspective is different, and his purpose is clear.

God uses struggles to toughen our spiritual skin.

> Consider it a sheer gift, friends, when tests and challenges come at you from all sides. You know that under pressure, your faith-life is forced into the open and shows its true colors. So don't try to get out of anything prematurely. Let it do its work so you become mature and well-developed, not deficient in any way. (James 1:2–4 MSG)

One of God's cures for weak faith? A good, healthy struggle. Several years ago our family visited Colonial Williamsburg, a re-creation of eighteenth-century America in Williamsburg, Virginia. If you ever visit there, pay special attention to the work of the silversmith. The craftsman places an ingot of silver on an anvil and pounds it with a sledgehammer. Once the metal is flat enough for shaping, into the furnace it goes. The worker alternately heats and pounds the metal until it takes the shape of a tool he can use.

Heating, pounding.

Heating, pounding.

Deadlines, traffic.

Arguments, disrespect.

Loud sirens, silent phones.

Heating, pounding.

Heating, pounding.

Did you know that the *smith* in *silversmith* comes from the old English word *smite*? Silversmiths are accomplished smiters. So is God. Once the worker is satisfied with the form of his tool, he begins to planish and pumice it. Using smaller hammers and abrasive pads, he taps, rubs, and decorates. And no one stops him. No one yanks the hammer out of his hand and says, "Go easy on that silver. You've pounded enough!" No, the craftsman buffets the metal until he is finished with it. Some silversmiths, I'm told, keep polishing until they can see their face in the tool. When will God stop with you? When he sees his reflection in you. "The LORD will *perfect* that which concerns me" (Ps. 138:8 NKJV, emphasis mine). Jesus said, "My Father never stops working" (John 5:17).

God guards those who turn to him. The pounding you feel does not suggest his distance, but proves his nearness. Trust his sovereignty. Hasn't he earned your trust?

Has he ever spoken a word that proved to be false? Given a promise that proved to be a lie? Decades of following God led Joshua to conclude: "Not a word failed of any good thing which the LORD had spoken" (Josh. 21:45 NKJV). Look up *reliability* in heaven's dictionary and read its one-word definition: God. "If we are faithless he always remains faithful. He cannot deny his own nature" (2 Tim. 2:13 PHILLIPS).

Make a list of his mistakes. Pretty short, eh? Now make a list of the times he has forgiven you for yours. Who on earth has such a record? "The One who called you is completely dependable. If he said it, he'll do it!" (1 Thess. 5:24 MSG).

You can depend on him. He is "the same yesterday and today and forever" (Heb. 13:8 ESV). And because he is the Lord, "He will be the stability of your times" (Isa. 33:6 NASB).

Trust him. "But when I am afraid, I put my trust in you" (Ps. 56:3). Join with Isaiah, who resolved, "I will trust in him and not be afraid" (Isa. 12:2).

God is directing your steps and delighting in every detail of your life (Ps. 37:23–24). Doesn't matter who you are. Potbellied pig or prized purebred? God sees no difference. But he does see you. In fact, that's his car pulling over to the side of the road. That's God opening the door. And that's you climbing into the passenger seat.

There now, don't you feel safer knowing he is in control?

Part Four

Receive His Love

FOURTEEN

Going Deep

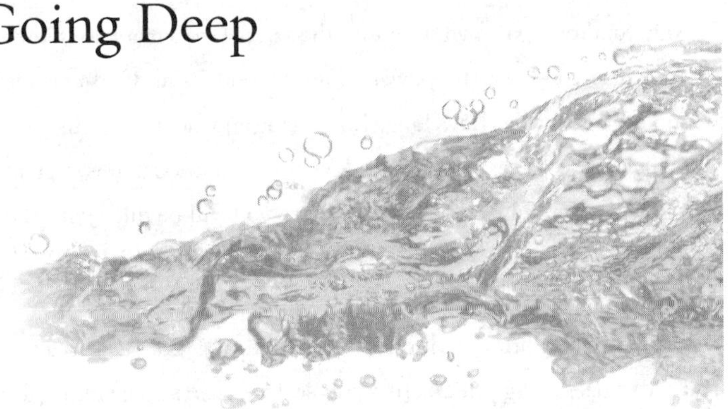

Pipín Ferreras wants to go deep, deeper than any person has ever gone. You and I are content with 10 or 20 feet of water. Certain risktakers descend 40, maybe 50. Not Pipín. This legendary Cuban diver has descended into 531 feet of ocean water, armed with nothing but flippers, a wet suit, deep resolve, and one breath of air.

His round trip lasted three minutes and twelve seconds. To prepare for such a dive, he loads his lungs with 8.2 liters of air—nearly twice the capacity of a normal human being—inhaling and exhaling for several minutes, his windpipe sounding like a bicycle pump. He then wraps his knees around the crossbar of an aluminum sled that lowers him to the sea bottom.[1]

No free diver has gone farther. Still, he wants more. Though he's acquainted with water pressure that tested World War II submarines, it's not enough. The mystery of the deep calls him. He wants to go deeper.

Could I interest you in a similar ear-popping descent? Not into the waters of the ocean, but into the limitless love of God.

> May your roots go down deep into the soil of God's marvelous love. And may you have the power to understand, as all God's people should, how wide, how long, how high, and how deep his love really is. May you experience the love of Christ, though it is so great you will never fully understand it. Then you will be filled with the fullness of life and power that comes from God. (Eph. 3:17–19)

When Paul wants to describe the love of God, he can't avoid the word *deep*. Dig "deep into the soil of God's marvelous love" (v. 17). Discover "how deep his love really is" (v. 18).

Envision Ferreras deep beneath the ocean surface. Having plunged the equivalent of five stories, where can he turn and not see water? To the right, to the left, beneath him, above him—the common consistency of his world is water. Water defines his dives, dictates his direction, liberates him, limits him. His world is water.

Can a person go equally deep into God's love? Sink so deep that he or she sees nothing but? David Brainerd, the eighteenth-century missionary to American Indians, would say so. He journaled:

> I withdrew to my usual place of retirement, in great tranquility. I knew only to breathe out my desire for a perfect conformity to Him in all things. God was so precious that the world with all its enjoyments seemed infinitely vile. I had no more desire for the favor of men than for pebbles.
>
> At noon I had the most ardent longings after God which I ever felt in my life.

In my secret retirement, I could do nothing but tell my dear Lord in a sweet calmness that He knew I desired nothing but Him, nothing but holiness, that He had given me these desires and He only could give the thing desired.

I never seemed to be so unhinged from myself, and to be so wholly devoted to God.

My heart was swallowed up in God most of the day.[2]

For any desiring a descent into such love, Scripture offers an anchor. Grab hold of this verse and let it lower you down: "God is love" (1 John 4:16).

One word into the passage reveals the supreme surprise of God's love—it has nothing to do with you. Others love you because of you, because your dimples dip when you smile or your rhetoric charms when you flirt. Some people love you because of you. Not God. He loves you because he is he. He loves you because he decides to. Self-generated, uncaused, and spontaneous, his constant-level love depends on his choice to give it. "The LORD did not set his affection on you and choose you because you were more numerous than other peoples, for you were the fewest of all peoples. But it was because the LORD loved you" (Deut. 7:7–8 NIV).

You don't influence God's love. You can't impact the treeness of a tree, the skyness of the sky, or the rockness of a rock. Nor can you affect the love of God. If you could, John would have used more ink: "God is *occasional* love" or "*sporadic* love" or "*fair-weather* love." If your actions altered his devotion, then God would not be love; indeed, he would be human, for this is human love.

And you've had enough of human love. Haven't you? Enough guys wooing you with Elvis-impersonator sincerity. Enough tabloids telling you that true love is just a diet away. Enough helium-filled expectations of bosses and parents and pastors. Enough mornings smelling like the mistakes you made while searching for love the night before.

Don't you need a fountain of love that won't run dry? You'll find one on a stone-cropped hill outside Jerusalem's walls where Jesus hangs, cross-nailed and thorn-crowned. When you feel unloved, ascend this mount. Meditate long and hard on heaven's love for you. Both eyes beaten shut, shoulders as raw as ground beef, lips bloody and split. Fists of hair yanked from his beard. Gasps of air escaping his lungs. As you peer into the crimsoned face of heaven's only Son, remember this: "God showed his great love for us by sending Christ to die for us while we were still sinners" (Rom. 5:8).

Don't trust other yardsticks. We often do. The sight of the healthy or successful prompts us to conclude, *God must really love him. He's so blessed with health, money, good looks, and skill.*

Or we gravitate to the other extreme. Lonely and frail in the hospital bed, we deduce, *God does not love me. How could he? Look at me.*

Rebuff such thoughts! Success signals God's love no more than struggles indicate the lack of it. The definitive, God-sanctioned gauge is not a good day or a bad break but the dying hours of his Son. Consider them often. Let the gap between trips to the cross diminish daily. Discover what Brainerd meant when he said, "My heart was swallowed up in God most of the day." Accept this invitation of Jesus: "Abide in My love" (John 15:9 NASB).

When you abide somewhere, you live there. You grow familiar with the surroundings. You don't pull in the driveway and ask, "Where is the garage?" You don't consult the blueprint to find the kitchen. To abide is to be at home.

To abide in Christ's love is to make his love your home. Not a roadside park or hotel room you occasionally visit, but your preferred dwelling. You rest in him. Eat in him. When thunder claps, you step beneath his roof. His walls secure you from the winds. His fireplace warms you from the winters of life. As John urged, "We take up permanent residence in a life of love" (1 John 4:16 MSG). You abandon the old house of false love and move into his home of real love.

Adapting to this new home takes time. First few nights in a new home you can wake up and walk into a wall. I did. Not in a new home, but in a motel. Climbed out of bed to get a glass of water, turned left, and flattened my nose. The dimensions to the room were different.

The dimensions of God's love are different too. You've lived a life in a house of imperfect love. You think God is going to cut you as the coach did, or abandon you as your father did, or judge you as false religion did, or curse you as your friend did. He won't, but it takes time to be convinced.

For that reason, abide in him. Hang on to Christ the same way a branch clutches the vine. According to Jesus, the branch models his definition of *abiding*. "As the branch cannot bear fruit of itself unless it abides in the vine, so neither can you unless you abide in Me" (John 15:4 NASB).

Does a branch ever release the vine? Only at the risk of death. Does the branch ever stop eating? Nope. It receives nutrients twenty-four hours a day. Would you say the branch is vine-dependent? I would. If branches had seminars, the topic would be "Get a Grip: Secrets of Vine Grabbing." But branches don't have seminars because attendance requires releasing the vine, something they refuse to do.

How well do you pass the vine test? Do you ever release yourself from Christ's love? Go unnourished? Do you ever stop drinking from his reservoir? Do so at the certain risk of a parched heart. Do so and expect a roundworm existence.

By sealing itself off against the world, the roundworm can endure extended seasons of drought. It essentially shuts down all systems. Releasing water until it's as dry as a cotton ball, the roundworm enters a state known as anhydrobiosis, meaning "life without water." A quarter of its body weight is converted to a material that encircles and protects its inner organs. It then shrinks to about 7 percent of its normal size and waits out the dry spell.[3]

Scientists assure us that humans can't do this. I'm not so sure.

- My friend's wife left him. "Now that the kids are grown," she announced, "it's my time to have fun."
- Recent headlines told of a man who murdered his estranged wife and kids. His justification? If he can't have them, no one will.
- Yesterday's e-mail came from a good man with a persistent porn problem. He's not convinced that God can forgive him.

Anhydrobiosis of the heart. In-drawn emotions. Callous souls. Coiled and re-coiled against the love drought of life. Hard shelled to survive the harsh desert. We were not made to live this way. What can we do?

From the file entitled "It Ain't Gonna Happen," I pull and pose this suggestion. Let's make Christ's command a federal law.

Everyone has to make God's love his or her home. Let it herewith be stated and hereby declared:

> *No person may walk out into the world to begin the day until he or she has stood beneath the cross to receive God's love.*

Cabbies. Presidents. Preachers. Tooth pullers and truck drivers. All required to linger at the fountain of his favor until all thirst is gone. I mean a can't-drink-another-drop satisfaction. All hearts hydrous. Then, and only then, are they permitted to enter the interstates, biology labs, classrooms, and boardrooms of the world.

Don't you ache for the change we'd see? Less honking and locking horns, more hugging and helping kids. We'd pass fewer judgments and more compliments. Forgiveness would skyrocket. How could you refuse to give a second chance when God has made your life one big mulligan? Doctors would replace sedative prescriptions with Scripture meditation: "Six times an hour reflect on God's promise: '*I have loved you with an everlasting love*' " (Jer. 31:3 NASB, emphasis mine). And can't you hear the newscast? "Since the implementation of the love law, divorce rates have dropped, cases of runaway children have plummeted, and Republicans and Democrats have disbanded their parties and decided to work together."

Wild idea? I agree. God's love can't be legislated, but it can be chosen. Choose it, won't you? For the sake of your heart. For the sake of your home. For Christ's sake, and yours, choose it. The prayer is as powerful as it is simple: "Lord, I receive your love. Nothing can separate me from your love."

My friend Keith took his wife, Sarah, to Cozumel, Mexico, to celebrate their anniversary. Sarah loves to snorkel. Give her fins, a mask, and a breathing tube, and watch her go deep. Down she swims, searching for the mysteries below.

Keith's idea of snorkeling includes fins, a mask, and a breathing tube, but it also includes a bellyboard. The surface satisfies him.

Sarah, however, convinced him to take the plunge. Forty feet offshore, she shouted for him to paddle out. He did. The two plunged into the water where she showed him a twenty-foot-tall submerged cross. "If I'd had another breath," he confessed, "the sight would have taken it away."

Jesus waves for you to descend and see the same. Forget surface glances. No more sunburned back. Go deep. Take a breath and descend so deeply into his love that you see nothing else.

Join the psalmist in saying:

> Whom have I in heaven but you?
> And earth has nothing I desire besides you.
> My flesh and my heart may fail,
> but God is the strength of my heart
> and my portion forever. . . .
> My heart has heard you say, "Come and talk
> with me, O my people." And my heart responds,
> "Lord, I am coming."
> (Ps. 73:25–26 NIV; 27:8 TLB)

FIFTEEN

Have You Heard the Clanging Door?

Nine-year-old Al trudges through the London streets, his hand squeezing a note, his heart pounding with fear. He has not read the letter; his father forbade him to do so. He doesn't know the message, but he knows its destination. The police station.

Young boys might covet a trip to the police station. Not Al. At least not today. Punishment, not pleasure, spawned this visit. Al failed to meet the family curfew. The fun of the day made him forget the time of day, so he came home late and in trouble.

His father, a stern disciplinarian, met Al at the front door and, with no greeting, gave him the note and the instruction, "Take it to the jailhouse." Al has no idea what to expect, but he fears the worst.

The fears prove justifiable. The officer, a friend of his father, opens the note, reads it, and nods. "Follow me." He leads the wide-eyed youngster to a jail cell, opens the door, and tells him to enter. The officer clangs the door shut. "This is what we do to naughty boys," he explains and walks away.

Al's face pales as he draws the only possible conclusion. He has crossed his father's line. Exhausted his supply of grace. Outspent the cache of mercy. So his dad has locked him away. Young Al has no reason to think he'll ever see his family again.

He was wrong. The jail sentence lasted only five minutes. But those five minutes felt like five months. Al never forgot that day. The sound of the clanging door, he often told people, stayed with him the rest of his life.[1]

Easy to understand why. Can you imagine a more ominous noise? Its echo wordlessly announced, "Your father rejects you. Search all you want; he isn't near. Plead all you want; he won't hear. You are separated from your father's love."

The slamming of the cell door. Many fear they have heard it. Al forgot the curfew. You forgot your virtue. Little Al came home late. Maybe you came home drunk. Or didn't come home at all. Al lost track of time. You lost your sense of direction and ended up in the wrong place doing the wrong thing, and heaven knows, heaven has no place for the likes of . . . Cheaters. Aborters. Adulterers. Secret sinners. Public scoundrels. Impostors. Church hypocrites. Locked away, not by an earthly father, but by your heavenly one. Incarcerated, not in a British jail, but in personal guilt, shame. No need to request mercy; the account is empty. Make no appeal for grace; the check will bounce. You've gone too far.

The fear of losing a father's love exacts a high toll. Al spent the rest of his life hearing the clanging door. That early taste of terror contributed to his lifelong devotion to creating the same in others. For Al—Alfred Hitchcock—made a career out of scaring people.

You may be scaring some folks yourself. You don't mean to. But you cannot produce what you do not possess. If you aren't convinced of God's love, how can you love others?

Do you fear you have heard the clanging door? If so, be assured. You have not. Your imagination says you did; logic says you did; some parent or pulpiteer says you did. But according to the Bible, according to Paul, you did not.

> And I am convinced that nothing can ever separate us from his love. Death can't, and life can't. The angels can't, and the demons can't. Our fears for today, our worries about tomorrow, and even the powers of hell can't keep God's love away. Whether we are high above the sky or in the deepest ocean, nothing in all creation will ever be able to separate us from the love of God that is revealed in Christ Jesus our Lord. (Rom. 8:38–39)

The words are the "Eureka!" at the end of Paul's love hunt. He initiates his search with five life-changing questions.

Question one: "If God is for us, who can ever be against us?" (v. 31). The presence of God tilts the scales of security forever in our direction. Who could hurt us?

Question two: "Since God did not spare even his own Son but gave him up for us all, won't God, who gave us Christ, also give us everything else?" (v. 32). Would God save our soul and then leave us to fend for ourselves? Will he address eternal needs and ignore earthly? Of course not.

Question three poses: "Who dares accuse us whom God has chosen for his own? Will God? No! He is the one who has given us right standing with himself" (v. 33). Once God accepts you, what other opinion matters? Every voice that accuses you, including your own, sounds wimpy in the tribunal of heaven. God's acceptance trumps earthly rejection.

Question four continues: "Who then will condemn us? Will Christ Jesus? No, for he is the one who died for us and was raised to life for us and is sitting at the place of highest honor next to God, pleading for us" (v. 34). Adjacent to God, within whispering distance of your Maker, sits the One who died for you. He occupies the place of high authority. So let your accusers or your conscience speak against you. Your divine defense attorney mutes their voices. Why? Because he loves you.

Question five asks the question of this chapter, even the question of life: "Can anything ever separate us from Christ's love?" (v. 35). This question crests the top step of a great staircase. As we stand with Paul at the top, he bids us to look around for anything that can separate us from God's love. Can you name one element of life that signals the end of God's devotion?

Or as the apostle asks, "Does it mean he no longer loves us if we have trouble or calamity, or are persecuted, or are hungry or cold or in danger or threatened with death?" (v. 35). Assembling adversaries like a jailhouse lineup, Paul waves them off one by one: "not trouble, not hard times, not hatred, not hunger, not homelessness, not bullying threats, not backstabbing, not even the worst sins listed in Scripture" (v. 35 MSG). No one can drive a wedge between you and God's love. "No, despite all these things, overwhelming victory is ours through Christ, who loved us" (v. 37). Earthly affliction does not equate to heavenly rejection.

Paul is convinced of this! He turns to the musician who holds the cymbals and gives him the nod. "And I am convinced that nothing can ever separate us from his love" (v. 38). He uses the perfect tense, implying, "I have become and I remain convinced." This is no passing idea or fluffy thought but rather a deeply rooted conviction. Paul is convinced. What do you suppose convinced him?

Maybe the disciples did. Paul gives no clue, so I'm just speculating, but maybe he asked the followers of Jesus to describe the length of God's love. In quick response they talked of the Passover party. It promised to be a great night. Good food. Good friends. Uninterrupted time with Christ. But in the middle of the meal, Jesus had dropped a bombshell: "Tonight all of you will desert me" (Matt. 26:31).

The disciples scoffed at the idea. "Peter declared, 'Even if everyone else deserts you, I never will.' . . . And all the other disciples vowed the same" (vv. 33, 35). "Abandon Jesus? Impossible. He's the flypaper; we're the flies." "In his corner, in his pocket. You can count on us, right?"

Wrong. Before the dark became dawn "all his disciples deserted him and ran away" (Mark 14:50). John. Andrew. They ran. Bartholomew. James. Thaddaeus. They scooted. When the Romans appeared, the followers disappeared in a blur of knees and elbows. Those mighty men who are today stained-glassed in a thousand cathedrals spent the night crawling beneath donkeys and hiding in haystacks. They abandoned him and ran away. When the kitchen got hot, they got out. Amazing.

But even more amazing is this. When Christ rose from the dead, he never brought it up. Never. Not even one "I told you so." Entering the Upper Room of vow violators, he could have quoted to them their own words, reminded them of their betrayal. "Boy, Andrew, some friend you are. And, John, to think I was going to let you write one of the Gospels."

He could have left them hearing the sound of a closing door. But he didn't. "That evening, on the first day of the week, the disciples were meeting behind locked doors because they were afraid of the Jewish leaders. Suddenly, Jesus was standing there among them! 'Peace be with you,' he said" (John 20:19).

They outran the guards. But they couldn't outrun the love of Christ.

Did Paul hear this story? If so, it would have been enough to convince him. Desert Jesus, and he'll still love you.

Peter might strengthen the verb. He might upgrade *desert* to *deny. Deny Jesus, and he'll still love you.* For while Christ faced a trial, Peter faced his own. As he warmed near a fire, "a servant girl came over and said to him, 'You were one of those with Jesus the Galilean.' But Peter denied it in front of everyone. 'I don't know what you are talking about,' he said" (Matt. 26:69–70).

Oh, the bouncing faith of Peter. It soared so high, Christ nicknamed him the Rock (Matt. 16:16–19); plummeted so low, Jesus called him Satan (Matt. 16:21–23). Who promised loyalty more insistently? Who fell more inexcusably?

Others we might understand, but this is Peter denying Jesus. His feet walked on water. His hands distributed the miracle food to the five thousand. His eyes saw Moses and Elijah standing next to Jesus on Transfiguration Hill. His lips swore allegiance. Remember what Jesus told him? "'Before the rooster crows, you will deny me three times.' 'No!' Peter insisted. 'Not even if I have to die with you! I will never deny you!'" (Matt. 26:34–35).

But he did. Thrice. Salting the air with vulgarity, he cursed the name of his dearest friend. Then the rooster crowed. Don't you know the crowing of the bird had the effect of a cell-door clang? "At that moment the Lord turned and looked at Peter. Then Peter remembered that the Lord had said, 'Before the rooster crows tomorrow morning, you will deny me three times.' And Peter left the courtyard, crying bitterly" (Luke 22:61–62).

Jesus will never look at me again, Peter must have thought.

He was wrong. Days after the resurrection Peter and some other disciples decided to go back to Galilee and fish. Why? Why would a witness of the resurrection go fishing? He may have been hungry. Or he may have been unconvinced. Christ can defeat death, but can he love a two-timer? Maybe Peter had his doubts.

If so, the doubts began to fade when he heard the voice. Jesus called to his friends, urging them to cast their net on the right side of the boat. The fact that they didn't recognize Jesus didn't keep them from trying. After they pulled in a large haul of fish, John recognized the Master. "It is the Lord!" (John 21:7 NKJV). Peter barely got his britches on before he bailed out of the boat and swam toward Christ. Before long, the two were standing, of all places, next to a fire. Peter had denied Christ at the first fire, but he couldn't deny the love of Christ at this one.

Maybe Peter told this story to Paul. Maybe by the time he finished, Paul was brushing away a tear and saying, "I'm convinced. Nothing can separate us from God's love."

"Deny Jesus," Peter testified, "and he'll still love you."

"Doubt Jesus," Thomas could add, "and the same is true."

Thomas had his doubts. Didn't matter to him that ten sets of eyes had seen the resurrected Jesus. Or that the women who had watched him being placed in the tomb watched him walk into the room. Let them shout and clap; Thomas was going to sit and wait. He wasn't in the room when Jesus came in. Maybe he was out for bagels, or maybe he took the death of Jesus harder than the others. In one of the four times he is quoted in Scripture, Thomas pledges, "Let's go, too—and die with Jesus" (John 11:16).

Thomas would die for Christ. Surely he'd die for the chance to see the risen Christ. But he wasn't about to be fooled. He'd buried his hopes once, thank you. Not about to bury them again. No matter what the others said, he needed to see for himself. So for seven days he sat. Others rejoiced; he resisted. They celebrated; he was silent. Thomas needed firsthand evidence. So Jesus gave it. First one hand, then the other, then the pierced side. "Put your finger here and see my hands. Put your hand into the wound in my side. Don't be faithless any longer. Believe!" (John 20:27).

And Thomas did. "My Lord and my God!" (v. 28).

Only a God could come back from the dead. And only a God of love would come back for a doubter.

Desert God—he'll still love you.

Deny God—he'll still love you.

Doubt God—he'll still love you.

Paul was convinced. Are you? Are you convinced that you have never lived a loveless day? Not one. Never unloved. Those times you deserted Christ? He loved you. You hid from him; he came looking for you.

And those occasions you denied Christ? Though you belonged to him, you hung with them, and when his name surfaced, you cursed like a drunken sailor. God let you hear the crowing of conscience and feel the heat of tears. But he never let you go. Your denials cannot diminish his love.

Nor can your doubts. You've had them. You may have them even now. While there is much we cannot know, may never know, can't we be sure of this? Doubts don't separate doubters from God's love.

The jail door has never closed. God's love supply is never

empty. "For his unfailing love toward those who fear him is as great as the height of the heavens above the earth" (Ps. 103:11).

The big news of the Bible is not that you love God but that God loves you; not that you can know God but that God already knows you! He tattooed your name on the palm of his hand. His thoughts of you outnumber the sand on the shore. You never leave his mind, escape his sight, flee his thoughts. He sees the worst of you and loves you still. Your sins of tomorrow and failings of the future will not surprise him; he sees them now. Every day and deed of your life has passed before his eyes and been calculated in his decision. He knows you better than you know you and has reached his verdict: he loves you still. No discovery will disillusion him; no rebellion will dissuade him. He loves you with an everlasting love.

I wrote parts of this chapter while staying at a Florida hotel. Early one morning I spent some time seated near an Olympic-size swimming pool. After reading the verses you just read, I lifted my gaze to see a bird swoop down out of the sky and park on the edge of the water. He dipped his beak in the pool, took a drink, and flew away. "Is that an image of your love?" I asked God. The gulp of the bird didn't diminish the water volume of the pool. Your sins and mine don't lower the love level of God.

The greatest discovery in the universe is the greatest love in the universe—God's love. "Nothing can ever separate us from his love" (Rom. 8:38). Think what those words mean. You may be separated from your spouse, from your folks, from your kids, from your hair, but you are not separated from the love of God. And you never will be. Ever.

Step to the well of his love and drink up. It may take some time to feel the difference. Occasional drinks won't bedew the evaporated heart. Ceaseless swallows will. Once filled up by his love, you'll never be the same.

Peter wasn't. He traded his boat for a pulpit and never looked back. The disciples weren't. The same men who fled the garden in fear traveled the world in faith. Thomas was never the same. If the legends be true, he carried the story of God's love for doubters and deserters all the way to India, where he, like his friends and Savior, died because of love.

The fear of love lost haunted young Al. But the joy of a love found changed the disciples. May you be changed. The next time you fear you hear a clanging door, remember, "Nothing can ever separate us from his love" (Rom. 8:38).

SIXTEEN

Fearlessly Facing Eternity

Dry mouth. Moist palms. Pulse pounding like a marching-band bass drum. Eyes darting over your shoulder. Heart vaulting into your throat. You know the feeling. You know the moment. You know exactly what it's like to see the flashing lights of the highway patrol in your rearview mirror.

Response #1? Prayer life spikes. "Oh, Lord." "God help me." "Jesus, have mercy on me a sinner." Policemen have stirred more prayers than a thousand pulpits.

Our requests are unanimous, predictable, and selfish. "Let there be a wreck down the highway." "See the kid driving the red truck, God? Send the officer after him." But he doesn't. Your back window fills with red and white strobes, floodlights, and flashing headlights, and as you pull to the side of the road, response #2 kicks in. Upward prayers become backward thoughts. *What did I do? How fast was I going? Whose dog did I hit?*

The highway patrol's version of Arnold Schwarzenegger fills your side mirror. Don't dare open your door. The second you do, his hand will Marshal Dillon its way to his holster, and he'll tell you to "stay in the car, please." Your best option is to return to prayer. Only God can help you now.

We dread such moments. Remember when the teacher took you outside the classroom? When your dad heard you climbing in the bedroom window past midnight? When my oldest daughter was small, I caught her in a misdemeanor. Anticipating my reaction, she told me, "My bottom tickles." We have a word for such moments. Judgment.

Payback. The evidence is in. The truth is out. And the policeman is standing at your door. No one likes the thought of judgment.

The Ephesian Christians didn't. They feared the judgment, not of the highway patrol, but of God. Knowing he sees all sin, knowing he hates all sin, knowing he must hate what he sees—not a comforting thought—they were afraid.

So John comforted them. He dipped the quill of his pen into the inkwell of God's love and wrote:

> As we live in God, our love grows more perfect. So we will not be afraid on the day of judgment, but we can face him with confidence because we are like Christ here in this world.
>
> Such love has no fear because *perfect love expels all fear*. If we are afraid, it is for fear of judgment, and this shows that his love has not been perfected in us. (1 John 4:17–18, emphasis mine)

"Perfect love expels all fear." Couldn't you use some fear expulsion? We can relate to the story of Louis Armstrong. The famous trumpeter grew up in rural Louisiana in the early 1900s. When he was a young boy, his Aunt Haddie often sent him to the creek for water. On one occasion, as he leaned over to fill his bucket, an alligator so scared the youngster that he dropped the pail and ran. His aunt told him to go back and get the water. "That alligator," she assured, "is just as scared of you as you are of it."

"If that's the case," he answered, "then that creek water ain't fit to drink."[1]

Alligators lurk in our creeks too. And when we see them, we react. We fear rejection, so we follow the crowd. We fear not fitting in, so we take the drugs. For fear of standing out, we wear what everyone else wears. For fear of blending in, we wear what no one else wears. For fear of sleeping alone, we sleep with anyone. For fear of not being loved, we search for love in all the wrong places.

But God flushes those fears. Those saturated in God's love don't sell out to win the love of others. They don't even sell out to win the love of God.

Do you think you need to? Do you think, *If I cuss less, pray more, drink less, study more . . . if I try harder, God will love me more*? Sniff and smell Satan's stench behind those words. We all need improvement, but we don't need to woo God's love. We change because we already have God's love. God's *perfect* love.

Perfect love is just that—perfect, a perfect knowledge of the past and a perfect vision of the future. You cannot shock God with your actions. There will never be a day that you cause him to gasp, "Whoa, did you see what she just did?" Never will he turn to his angels and bemoan, "Had I known Max was going to go Spam-brained on me, I wouldn't have saved his soul." God knows your entire story, from first word to final breath, and with clear assessment declares, "You are mine."

My publisher made a similar decision with this book. Before agreeing to publish it, they read it—every single word. Multiple sets of editorial eyes scoured the manuscript, moaning at my bad jokes, grading my word crafting, suggesting a tune-up here and a tone-down there. We volleyed pages back and forth, writer to editor to writer, until finally we all agreed—this is it. It's time to publish or pass. The publisher could pass, mind you. Sometimes they do. But in this case, obviously they didn't. With perfect knowledge of this imperfect product, they signed on. What you read may surprise you, but not them.

What you do may stun you, but not God. With perfect knowledge of your imperfect life, God signed on.

Years ago I met a woman who has tasted a form of such love. Brain surgery has left her without the use of a facial nerve. As a result, she faces the world with a crooked smile. After the operation she met the love of her life. Here's how she describes him: "He sees nothing strange or ugly about me and has never, even in anger, made a joke about my appearance. He has never seen me any other way. When I look in the mirror, I see deformity, but my husband sees beauty."

See what perfect love does? It drives out the fear of judgment. In fact, it purges the fear of the day of judgment. As John wrote, "So we will not be afraid on the day of judgment, but we can face him with confidence because we are like Christ here in this world" (v. 17).

On this topic, John makes no apology and pulls no punches. The day of judgment is not a phrase in a fiction novel but a day circled on heaven's calendar. Of the twenty-seven New Testament books, only the postcard-size epistles of Philemon and Third John fail to reference our divine court appearance.[2] While the details of the day are unrevealed to us and debated by us, we know this: The day is coming. On that day, earthly wealth will not matter. Physical beauty won't be factored. Fame will be forgotten. You might be positioned next to Napoleon or Julius Caesar, but you won't ask questions about Waterloo or Brutus. All eyes will be on Christ.

Those who ignored him have high cause for fear. "Then He will also say to those on His left, 'Depart from Me, accursed ones, into the eternal fire which has been prepared for the devil and his angels'" (Matt. 25:41 NASB).

But those who accepted him have none whatsoever. "We can face him with confidence because we are like Christ here in this world" (1 John 4:17). Think about that statement. God views Christians the way he views Christ: sinless and perfect. Hence, Christians can view judgment the way Christ does: with confidence and hope. Does Jesus fear the judgment? No. A sinless soul needn't. Does Jesus fear death? No. The giver of life wouldn't. Should the Christian fear judgment or death? Not at all. "Our standing in the world is identical with Christ's" (v. 17 MSG). The Son of God stands next to you doing what the son of Joe Allbright did for me.

Joe Allbright is a fair and fearless West Texas rancher, a square-jawed, rawboned man with a neck by Rawlings. In Andrews County, where I was raised, everyone knew him.

One of Joe's sons, James, and I were best friends in high school. We played football together. (More honest, he played while I guarded the team bench.) One Friday night after an out-of-town game, James invited me to stay at his house. By the time we reached his property, the hour was way past midnight, and he hadn't told his father he was bringing anyone home.

Mr. Allbright didn't know me or my vehicle, so when I stepped out of the car in front of his house, he popped on a floodlight and aimed it right at my face. Through the glare I saw this block of a man (I think he was in his underwear), and I heard his deep voice. "Who are you?" I gulped. My mind moved at the speed of cold honey. I started to say my name but didn't. Mr. *Allbright doesn't know me*. My only hope was that James would speak up. A glacier could have melted before he did so. Finally he interceded. "It's okay, Dad. That's my friend Max. He's with me." The light went off, and Mr. Allbright threw open the door. "Come on in, boys. Food is in the kitchen."

What changed? What made Mr. Allbright flip off the light? One fact. I had aligned myself with his son. My sudden safety had nothing to do with my accomplishments or offerings. I knew his son. Period.

For the same reason, you need never fear God's judgment. Not today. Not on Judgment Day. Jesus, in the light of God's glory, is speaking on your behalf. "That's my friend," he says. And when he does, the door of heaven opens.

Trust God's love. His perfect love. Don't fear he will discover your past. He already has. Don't fear disappointing him in the future. He can show you the chapter in which you will. With perfect knowledge of the past and perfect vision of the future, he loves you perfectly in spite of both.

Perfect love can handle your fear of judgment.

(And slower driving can handle your fear of policemen.)

SEVENTEEN

If God Wrote You a Letter

Christmas comes to El Sunza, El Salvador, via the shoebox. In a village where the wealthiest make fifty dollars a month and nicer homes are distinguished by tin roofs instead of plywood, the shoebox shipment highlights the year. The delivery originates in San Antonio where the children of the church in which I serve "adopt" a Salvadoran child and prepare the boxes.

Couriers grow misty eyed describing the joy of delivery day: children squeezing their brightly wrapped box, not wanting to hurry the moment. When they finally remove the paper, eyes pop saucer-wide at the toys—a Slinky, yo-yo, doll, or truck. They find toothbrushes and toothpaste, perhaps a set of underwear or socks. But the gift they cherish most is the letter. Tucked somewhere between toys and books, occupying little space but bringing torrential excitement, is a handwritten note.

The envelope bears the child's name. José Castillo. Beatrice Gonzales. Lines form around the translators as, one by one, the children hear words intended for their ears.

"Dear Diego," one might read. "My name is Matthew. I am in the fourth grade. Do you go to school? I play soccer. Do you? We call my dog Scratch because he itches all the time . . ."

Or,

"Dear Maria, this is Kara. I would like to meet you someday. Mom says El Salvador is 'forever' from here. What do you like to do? I love to sing and read and listen to Max Lucado preach sermons." (Some of these children show such taste.)

Many of the Salvadoran kids sleep with their notes, amazed that someone in far-off Texas is thinking about them. Astounding what a letter from afar can do for children.

But you know that. Like the gifts of the children, your gifts come from a distant land. Unlike the village children, you have Christmas every day. Your shoebox bears, not toys and books, but God himself!

His work: on the cross and in the resurrection. As a result, your sin brings no guilt, and the grave brings no fear.

His energy: it's not up to you. You can do all things through Christ, who gives you strength.

His lordship: he is in charge of you and looks out for you.

His love: what can separate you from it?

Who could imagine such gifts? Who could imagine not opening them? Curiously, some of the Salvadoran children have to be told to open theirs. Bless their hearts, they think the box is the gift. It outpaces any prior possession. Some see the bright ribbon and colorful wrapping and think, *This is it. This is the present.* Were no one to tell them, they would carry the box to their dirt-floored home, place it in a prime location, and admire it, display it, but never open it.

Don't we do the same with Christ? Aren't we prone to keep

him at arm's length? We place him on the mantel of our heart: respect him, revere his name, but never open his gifts. Never dig into the box. Never unpack his presence on the dirt floor of our worry and work, sin and sorrows.

He is so willing to enter your world. The hospital room? He goes there. Late-night deadlines? He'll stay up with you. Are you watching the slow death of someone you love? He'll sit by your side every single minute. Just invite him. "Look! Here I stand at the door and knock. If you hear me calling and open the door, I will come in, and we will share a meal as friends" (Rev. 3:20).

Don't make the mistake that the associates of Lawrence of Arabia made. He took them to Paris after World War I. They had never seen such sights. The Arc de Triomphe, Napoleon's tomb, the Champs Élysées. But nothing impressed these men from the Arabian Desert more than the faucet in the bathtub of their hotel room. They turned it on and off, on and off, amazed that with a twist of the wrist they could have all the water they wanted.

When the time came to leave Paris and return to the east, Lawrence found them in the bathroom with wrenches, trying to disconnect the spout. "We need faucets," they explained. "If we have them, we will have all the water we want."[1]

They didn't understand the role of the faucet. Spouts carry water, not produce it. Spigots are the tool, not the source. The valve might direct fluid, but generate it? No. We know this . . .

Or do we? Through what faucets has God poured his love into your life? A faithful church? A prayerful spouse? Time-tested traditions? A girlfriend in college or a grandma from childhood? God's water passes through many faucets. His gift comes in many packages. The treasure, however, is not the plumbing or the box, not the container of the gift. No, the treasure is the Giver himself.

On my list of things I wish I had learned earlier, this truth hovers near the top. Grace came my way packaged in a church. Congregations and their leaders changed me. But then the churches struggled, even divided. Mature men acted less than that. The box ripped, the faucet clogged, and my heart, for a time, sank.

Not a moment too soon, I heard the invitation of the still-running fountain. "If anyone is thirsty, let him come to me [not to my prophets or people] and drink" (John 7:37 NIV).

God describes himself as "the fountain of living water" (Jer. 2:13). Thank him for the faucets, but don't trust them to nourish you. Thank him for the boxes in which his gifts come. But don't fail to open them. And most of all, don't fail to read the letter. For buried amid the gifts of daily mercy and unquenchable commitment rests a letter, a personal letter. It might read something like this:

> Dear child of mine,
>
> Are you thirsty? Come and drink. ✣ I am one who comforts you. ✣ I bought you ✣ and complete you. ✣ I delight in you and claim you as my own, rejoicing over you as a bridegroom rejoices over his bride. ✣ I will never fail you or forsake you.[2]

Accept My Work

> I know your manifold transgressions and your mighty sins, ✣ yet my grace is sufficient for you. ✣ I have cast all your sins behind my back, ✣ trampled them under my feet, and thrown them into the depths of the ocean! ✣ Your sins have been washed away, ✣ swept away like the morning mists, scattered like the clouds. Oh, return to me, for I have paid the price to set you free.[3]

Your death is swallowed up in victory. ◈ I disarmed the evil rulers and authorities ◈ and broke the power of the devil, who had the power of death. ◈ Blessed are those who die in the Lord. ◈ Your citizenship is in heaven. ◈ Come, inherit the kingdom prepared for you ◈ where I will remove all of your sorrows, and there will be no more death or sadness or crying or pain.[4]

Rely on My Energy

You are worried and troubled about many things; ◈ trust me with all your heart. ◈ I know how to rescue godly people from their trials. ◈ My Spirit helps you in your distress. ◈ Let me strengthen you with my glorious power. ◈ I did not spare my Son but gave him up for you. Won't I give you everything else? ◈ March on, dear soul, with courage! ◈ Never give up. ◈ I will help you. I will uphold you.[5]

Trust My Lordship

Trust in me always. I am the eternal Rock, ◈ your Shepherd, the Guardian of your soul. ◈ When you go through deep waters and great trouble, I will be with you. When you go through rivers of difficulty, you will not drown! When you walk through the fire of oppression, you will not be burned up; the flames will not consume you.[6]

So, don't worry. ◈ I never tire or sleep. I stand beside you. ◈ The angel of the LORD encamps around you. ◈ I hide you in the shelter of my presence. ◈ I will go ahead of you, ◈ directing your steps and delighting in every detail of your life. If you stumble, you will not fall, for I hold you by the hand. ◈ I will guide you along the best pathway for your life.[7]

Wars will break out near and far, but don't panic. ✦ I have overcome the world. ✦ Don't worry about anything; instead, pray about everything. ✦ I surround you with a shield of love.[8]

I will make you fruitful in the land of suffering, ✦ trading beauty for ashes, joy for mourning, praise for despair. ✦ I live with the low spirited and spirit crushed. I put new spirit in you and get you on your feet again. ✦ Weeping may go on all night, but joy comes with the morning. ✦ If I am for you, who can ever be against you?[9]

Receive My Love

I throw my arms around you, lavish attention on you, and guard you as the apple of my eye. ✦ I rejoice over you with great gladness. ✦ My thoughts of you cannot be counted; they outnumber the grains of sand! ✦ Nothing can ever separate you from my love. Death can't, and life can't. The angels can't, and the demons can't. Your fears for today, your worries about tomorrow, and even the powers of hell can't keep my love away.[10]

You sometimes say, "The Lord has deserted me; the Lord has forgotten me." But can a mother forget her nursing child? Can she feel no love for a child she has borne? Even if that were possible, I would not forget you! ✦ I paid for you with the precious lifeblood of Christ, my sinless, spotless Lamb. ✦ No one will snatch you away from me. ✦ See, I have written your name on my hand. ✦ I call you my friend. ✦ Why, the very hairs on your head are all numbered. So don't be afraid; you are valuable to me.[11]

Give me your burdens; I will take care of you. ✥ I know how weak you are, that you are made of dust. ✥ Give all your worries and cares to me, because I care about what happens to you.[12]

Remember, I am at hand. ✥ Come to me when you are weary and carry heavy burdens, and I will give you rest. ✥ I delight in you, ✥ and I can be trusted to keep my promises. ✥ Come and drink the water of life.[13]

Your Maker, your Father,
God

Reader's Guide

Come Thirsty

Prepared by Steve Halliday

Meagan

Come to the Well

1. I know you are a better person than this. I also know it's not too late to make a change. This street you're traveling? The houses look nice, but the road goes nowhere.

   A. Are you satisfied with the life you're leading? Explain.

   B. Do you ever feel that it's too late to make a change? If so, explain.

   C. What street are you currently traveling? Where does the road appear to lead?

2. Stress signals a deeper need, a longing. We long to fit in, to make a difference. Acceptance, significance—these matter to us. So we do what it takes; we go into debt to buy the house, we stretch the credit card to buy the clothes . . . and life on the treadmill begins.

   A. Describe your current stress level.

   B. What "deeper need" or "longing" can you identify in your own heart?

   C. When do you most feel as though you're living on a treadmill?

3. We spend a lot of energy going nowhere. At the end of the day, or the end of a life, we haven't moved one step. We're stuck.
   A. On what do you spend most of your energy? Is the outcome positive?
   B. Describe a time in your life that you felt stuck. What did you do to get unstuck?
   C. If you continue on your present course, where do you think you'll be in ten years? Fifteen? Twenty? Is that where you want to be? Explain.

4. "Where is God in all this?" He repeated her question. "Nearer than you've ever dreamed."
   A. What would you tell someone who asked you, "Where is God in all this?"
   B. Does God feel near to you right now? Explain.
   C. Does your present path keep you near God? What path change should you consider to keep God close?

Fill Your Cup

1. Read John 4:1–42.
   A. What parallels do you see between Meagan's story and the life circumstances of the woman described in John 4?
   B. Why do you think Jesus did not immediately identify himself when he met the Samaritan woman?
   C. Why do you think Jesus called attention to the woman's unsavory sexual past (vv. 16–18)?
   D. Describe Jesus's main goal in his interaction with this woman (vv. 21–24).

E. Why do you think the woman immediately became an evangelist (vv. 28–30, 39–41)?

Drink Deeply

Spend a few minutes thanking God for his amazing love for you, and ask him to open your eyes to new discoveries about him and his plans for you as you read *Come Thirsty*.

ONE

The Dehydrated Heart

Come to the Well

1. Deprive your soul of spiritual water, and your soul will tell you. Dehydrated hearts send desperate messages. Snarling tempers. Waves of worry. Growling mastodons of guilt and fear.

   A. How would you describe "spiritual water" to someone else? What is it?

   B. Describe a time when you felt deprived of spiritual water. What happened?

   C. What "desperate message" does your soul most often send you when you are deprived of spiritual water? How do you generally respond to this message?

2. What H_2O can do for your body, Jesus can do for your heart. Lubricate it. Aquify it. Soften what is crusty, flush what is rusty.

   A. In your life, have you needed Jesus to "lubricate" and "aquify" your heart? Explain.

   B. Describe a specific time when you allowed Jesus to soften what was crusty or flush what was rusty.

   C. Take stock of your heart at this very moment. Do you need Jesus to do anything for it? Explain.

3. In order for Jesus to do what water does, you must let him go where water goes. Deep, deep inside. Internalize him. Ingest him. Welcome him into the inner workings of your life. Let Christ be the water of your soul.
   A. How deeply do you normally allow Christ to penetrate your life? Explain.
   B. What areas of your life seem most resistant to Christ?
   C. How can you better welcome Christ into the inner workings of your life? What specific steps can you take?

4. Religion pacifies, but never satisfies. Church activities might hide a thirst, but only Christ quenches it. Drink *him.* And drink often. . . . Regular sips satisfy thirsty throats.
   A. In what way does religion pacify? Why can it never satisfy?
   B. How can church activities hide a spiritual thirst? Have they ever done so for you? If so, explain.
   C. How does one "drink" Christ? Describe the process as you know it.

Fill Your Cup

1. Read John 7:14–39.
   A. What do you think so amazed the religious professionals about Jesus's teaching (v. 15)?
   B. How did Jesus explain his extraordinary teaching (v. 16)?
   C. What key to effective Bible study does Jesus describe in verse 17?
   D. What miracle did Jesus perform that upset the religious professionals (v. 23)? Why did it upset them? Why did Jesus think it should not have upset them?

E. From where did Jesus claim to have come (vv. 16, 29)? Why did this upset some in the crowd?

F. What did Jesus say in verses 33–34 that confused his opponents? Why do you think Jesus spoke in such a cloaked fashion? What do you believe he really meant?

G. How do you "come" to Jesus and "drink" (v. 37)?

H. What connection does Jesus make between believing in him and living water (v. 38)?

I. What did Jesus mean by "living water" (v. 39)? Is this living water in you? Explain.

Drink Deeply

Even if it is not your regular habit, schedule at least half an hour to get alone with God. Use the time both to thank him for his desire to fill you with living water and to ask him to reveal those areas of your heart that are most "dehydrated." Ask him, "Where have I not allowed the living water of Jesus to penetrate my heart? In my relationships? In my work life? In my desire for some particular thing?" Once the Lord has clearly answered your prayer, ask for the strength and wisdom to give that area over to the healing waters of Jesus.

TWO

Sin Vaccination

Come to the Well

1. Sin, for a season, quenches thirst. But so does salt water. Given time, the thirst returns, more demanding and demanding more than ever.
   A. In what way does sin temporarily quench thirst? Why is it only temporary?
   B. Have you experienced the temporary thirst-quenching power of sin? Explain.
   C. In what way do the demands of sin get more demanding?
2. Lead a godless life, and expect a godless eternity. Spend a life telling God to leave you alone, and he will.
   A. How would you describe a "godless life"? What does it look like?
   B. How would you describe a "godless eternity"? What would it look like?
   C. In what ways do we tell God to leave us alone?
3. You can select your spiritual father. You can change your family tree from that of Adam to God. And when you do, he moves in. His resistance becomes your resistance.
   A. How can someone select his or her spiritual father? Describe the process.

B. Have you changed your family tree from that of Adam to God? How can you know for sure?

C. How can you tell when you're battling sin through God's resistance and not through your own?

4. Trust the work of God *for* you. Then trust the presence of Christ *in* you. Take frequent, refreshing drinks from his well of grace. You need regular reminders that you are not fatally afflicted! Don't live as though you are.

   A. What does it mean to trust the work of God *for* you?

   B. What does it mean to trust the presence of Christ *in* you?

   C. How do some believers live as though they are fatally afflicted with sin?

Fill Your Cup

1. Read Ephesians 2:1–10.

   A. How does Paul paint our lives before we placed our faith in Christ (vv. 1–3)?

   B. What changed our desperate situation (v. 4)?

   C. What did God do for us that we couldn't do ourselves (v. 5)?

   D. What is yet in store for every believer (vv. 6–7)?

   E. How did we receive these amazing blessings (vv. 8–9)?

   F. What is expected of us now (v. 10)?

2. Read Isaiah 53:4–6.

   A. Who is the "he" in verse 4?

   B. What did he do for us (vv. 4–5)?

   C. What have we done to make this necessary (v. 6)?

3. Read 1 John 1:5–9.
   A. How does verse 5 portray God?
   B. What hypocrisy is revealed in verse 6?
   C. What does Jesus do for us, according to verse 7? What condition do we have to meet?
   D. How do we sometimes deceive ourselves (v. 8)?
   E. What promise are we given in verse 9?

Drink Deeply

Go somewhere quiet, taking your Bible with you. First, invite God to meet with you in a special way. Then turn to Psalm 51 and silently read through it. Then pray through it, this time reading it out loud, pausing after each verse to ask God to apply David's prayer to your own heart. Continue in this way through the psalm, inviting God to cleanse your heart so you might serve him with joy.

THREE

When Grace Goes Deep

Come to the Well

1. Thanks to some legalistic big brothers, Paul's readers had gone from grace receiving to law keeping. Their Christian life had taken on the joy level of an upper G.I. endoscopy. Paul was puzzled.

   A. Describe the difference between "grace receiving" and "law keeping."

   B. Why does law keeping generally deflate joy?

   C. What most puzzled Paul about the choice his friends had made? Would he be puzzled if he witnessed your life? Explain.

2. The churches suffered from . . . grace blockage. The Father might let you in the gate, but you have to earn your place at the table. God makes the down payment on your redemption, but you pay the monthly installments. Heaven gives the boat, but you have to row it if you ever want to see the other shore.

   A. In your own terms, define "grace blockage."

   B. How do we sometimes try to earn our place at God's table?

   C. Why do you think we face the continual temptation to mix grace and good works?

3. Grace defines who you are. The parent you can't please is as mistaken as the doting uncle you can't disappoint. People hold no clout. Only God does. According to him, you are his. Period.
   - A. Does grace define who *you* are? Explain.
   - B. In what way does grace shape how you live? How did it shape the way you acted today?
   - C. Have you ever let people hold the clout that belongs only to God? If so, describe what happened.

4. God's hands . . . draw together the disjointed blotches in our life and render them an expression of his love.
   - A. What disjointed blotches in your life has God rendered an expression of his love?
   - B. How is God working in your life right now?
   - C. How do you see God's love active in the lives of your loved ones?

Fill Your Cup

1. Read Galatians 1:6–9; 2:16.
   - A. What event greatly surprised Paul (v. 6)? Why did it surprise him?
   - B. What caused this surprising event (v. 7)?
   - C. What strong statement does Paul make in verse 8? Why does he say this so strongly?
   - D. What is the significance of his repeating his strong statement in verse 9?
   - E. How does a person get right with God, according to 2:16?
   - F. Who gets right with God through perfect behavior (2:16)?

2. Read 2 Samuel 9:1–13.
   A. Why did David show such kindness to Mephibosheth (v. 1)?
   B. Why did David tell Mephibosheth not to fear (v. 7)? Why might the man have felt afraid?
   C. How did Mephibosheth see himself (v. 8)?
   D. What privilege did Mephibosheth receive (v. 11)?
   E. Why do you think the story is summarized in verse 13? What's the point?

Drink Deeply

Whenever genuine grace shows up, it makes a powerful difference in the lives of those it touches. For a slight change of pace, plan an evening to gather friends or loved ones and together watch *Les Misérables,* the film adaptation of Victor Hugo's classic work. Watch it specifically for any illustrations of grace in action. Then discuss what you saw, especially in terms of its portrayal of grace.

Also, if you'd like to learn more about the wonders of God's grace, especially regarding how it can change the way you live, consider reading a quality book on the topic, such as Philip Yancey's *What's So Amazing about Grace?* or Charles Swindoll's *The Grace Awakening.*

FOUR

When Death Becomes Birth

Come to the Well

1. Many of us weep at the thought of death. Do you? Do you dread your death? And is your dread of death robbing your joy of life?

   A. Answer each of Max's questions.

   B. Why is death hard for most of us to contemplate, let alone discuss?

   C. Why do we often describe the death of a loved one as "loss"?

2. Why did Jesus let Lazarus die only to call him back? To show who runs the show. To trump the cemetery card. To display the unsquashable strength of the One who danced the Watusi on the neck of the devil, who stood face to clammy face with death and declared, "You call that a dead end? I call it an escalator."

   A. Why do you think Jesus let Lazarus die?

   B. In what way has Jesus made death an escalator?

   C. How did Jesus "trump the cemetery card"? Do you think he will do this for you? Explain.

3. Dread of death ends when you know heaven is your true home.

A. How does knowing that heaven is your true home alter your thinking about death?

B. Why do many Christians still dread death?

C. Describe your true home.

4. Give God your death. Imagine your last breath, envision your final minutes, and offer them to him. Deliberately. Regularly.

A. What do you envision when you think of your final minutes?

B. What does it mean to "give God your death"? Have you done this? Explain.

C. Why is it wise to regularly think of your own death? How can you keep this from becoming morbid?

Fill Your Cup

1. Read Hebrews 9:27–28.

A. What is the destiny of every man and woman (v. 27)?

B. What happens after this event (v. 27)?

C. What did Christ do the first time he came to earth (v. 28)?

D. What will Christ do the second time he comes to earth (v. 28)?

2. Read Hebrews 2:14–16.

A. Why did Jesus have to become human (v. 14)?

B. What mission did Jesus accomplish by his death (vv. 14–15)?

C. What group did Jesus intend to help by his death (v. 16)?

3. Read 1 Corinthians 15:54–58.

A. When do the events described in this passage take place?

B. What specifically takes place (v. 54)?

C. How would you answer the questions in verse 55?

D. What cause and effect is described in verse 56? What provides the power?

E. What victory is described in verse 57? Who wins this victory? Who gets to enjoy this victory?

F. What conclusion does Paul draw from the truth he has just declared (v. 58)? How should these truths affect our lives?

Drink Deeply

To help you grapple with your own death, write out your own obituary. Make it as long or as short as you like, but make sure it reflects the reality of your life, not merely how you hope to be remembered. What do you think survivors would really say about you?

FIVE

With Heart Headed Home

Come to the Well

1. Heaven knows no stepchildren or grandchildren. You and Christ share the same will. What he inherits, you inherit. You are headed home.
   A. What does it mean that heaven knows no stepchildren or grandchildren?
   B. What must first happen for Christ and you to share the same will?
   C. When you consider heaven your true home, what difference does this make in the way you live right now?

2. Let your bursitis-plagued body remind you of your eternal one; let acid-inducing days prompt thoughts of unending peace. Are you falsely accused? Acquainted with abuse? Mudslinging is a part of this life, but not the next. Rather than begrudge life's troubles, listen to them.
   A. How can you allow your current troubles to remind you of your eternal home?
   B. What in life tends to trouble you the most? How can you use even this to prompt "thoughts of unending peace"?
   C. Do you tend to begrudge life's troubles or listen to them? Explain.

3. The more you drink from God's well, the more you urge the clock to tick. Every bump of the second hand brings you closer to a completed adoption.
   A. In what ways do you "drink from God's well"?
   B. List the things you won't miss about earthly life.
   C. What comforts you the most about your future "completed adoption"? Explain.

4. Blessings and burdens. Both can alarm-clock us out of slumber. Gifts stir homeward longings. So do struggles. Every homeless day carries us closer to the day our Father will come.
   A. Describe some blessings that have alarm-clocked you out of slumber.
   B. Describe some burdens that have alarm-clocked you out of slumber.
   C. What pictures come to mind when you think of the day your Father will come for you?

Fill Your Cup

1. Read Romans 8:15–25.
   A. What two things are contrasted in verse 15? What is important to remember about this contrast?
   B. What (or who) reminds us of our true identity (v. 16)?
   C. What promise is made in verse 17? What advisory is given?
   D. What two things are compared in verse 18? What is the point of this comparison?
   E. What future event is described in verses 19–21?
   F. What truth is proclaimed in verse 22?

G. What present truth and future reality are proclaimed in verse 23? Why is it important to keep both things in mind?

H. What are we told to do in verse 24?

I. How are we told to do this in verse 25?

2. Read Galatians 4:4–7.

A. What event is described in verse 4?

B. What two things did Christ accomplish for us, according to verse 5?

C. What cry goes out from our hearts, according to verse 6? Who prompts this cry?

D. What promise is made in verse 7?

Drink Deeply

To remind you of your inheritance in Christ, take steps to get your own will in order. As you consider your own estate and where you want it to go after your death, consciously bring to mind the amazing inheritance Christ has bestowed on you.

SIX

Hope for Tuckered Town

Come to the Well

1. I used to think there were two kinds of people: the saved and unsaved. Paul corrects me by describing a third: the *saved, but unspiritual.*

   A. Describe a saved person.

   B. Describe an unsaved person.

   C. Describe a saved, but unspiritual person.

   D. Which one of the three are you? Explain.

2. The unspiritual person cranks the car and hunkers behind it. Tragically, these people act "like people of the world" (1 Cor. 3:3 NCV). In language, lifestyle, priorities, and personality, they blend in with nonbelievers. They let God save them, but not change them.

   A. Describe a few expected differences between the actions of believers and "people of the world."

   B. How does your language compare with that of nonbelievers? How about your lifestyle? Priorities? Personality?

   C. What areas of your life do you think God most wants to change?

3. The saved but unspiritual see salvation the way a farmer sees a hundred acres of untilled soil—lots of work. *Church attendance, sin resistance—have I done enough?* No wonder they're tired.
   A. Do you see the Christian life as "lots of work"? Explain.
   B. What risk is there in this view of Christianity?
   C. Be honest. Do you feel tired in your walk with Christ? Explain.

4. Annual fill-ups or monthly ingestions won't do. You aren't sampling wine at a California vineyard. You're hiking through Death Valley, and that mirage you see is not a mirage but really is the river you need. Dive in and drink.
   A. What are the most personal ways you "fill up" with the Savior?
   B. What image or metaphor most clearly conveys this idea for you? Why?
   C. How do we so often "sample" Christ rather than "drink" him?

Fill Your Cup

1. Read Galatians 3:1–14.
   A. What question does Paul ask in verse 2? What answer is he expecting? Why is this crucial?
   B. What question does Paul ask in verse 3? What answer is he expecting?
   C. What question does Paul ask in verse 4? What answer is he expecting?
   D. What question does Paul ask in verse 5? What answer is he expecting?

E. What example does Paul give in verses 6–9? How does this example illustrate his point?

F. What general principle is given in verse 10?

G. What general principle is given in verse 11?

H. What did Christ do for us, according to verse 13?

I. Why did Christ do this for us, according to verse 14?

2. Read Ephesians 5:18.

A. What are believers instructed not to do in this verse?

B. What are believers instead instructed to do?

C. Describe someone you know who seems to be infused with the Spirit.

Drink Deeply

Sometimes the best cure for residents of Tuckered Town is simply to rest awhile in the presence of God—no other agenda, no other activity. Turn off your cell phone, go somewhere quiet, and spend at least an hour or two in God's presence—just you and him. "Be silent, and know that I am God!" (Ps. 46:10).

SEVEN

Waiting for Power

Come to the Well

1. Even after a thousand campfire conversations and a scrapbook full of jaw-dropping moments, some disciples resist. *I'm still not sure.*
   A. What do you think kept these disciples from feeling sure about Jesus?
   B. What do you think keeps us from feeling sure about Jesus?
   C. In what way(s) do you sometimes feel unsure about Jesus?
2. Doubters became prophets. Peter preached, and people came, and God opened the floodgates on the greatest movement in history. It began because the followers were willing to do one thing: wait in the right place for power.
   A. What turned doubters into prophets?
   B. Why do you think God waited to send the Spirit to the disciples? Why didn't God send him immediately after Christ ascended to heaven?
   C. Is God asking you to wait for something right now? If so, what do you think he wants to teach you?
3. Unceasing prayer may sound complicated, but it needn't be that way. . . . Think of prayers less as an activity for God and more as an awareness of God. Seek to live in uninterrupted awareness. Acknowledge his presence everywhere you go.

A. What needs to change for you to start thinking of prayer as "an awareness of God"?

B. In what new ways could you acknowledge God's presence?

C. What do you expect to happen when you acknowledge God's presence everywhere you go?

4. We can only wonder what would happen today if we, who *still* struggle, did what they did: wait on the Lord in the right place.

   A. In what ways do you still struggle to have faith?

   B. How is the Lord asking you to wait on him right now?

   C. What has happened in the past when you have waited on the Lord in the right "place"? Describe your experience.

Fill Your Cup

1. Read Matthew 28:16–17.

   A. What group is described in this passage? What were they doing? Why were they doing it?

   B. What two things happened when members of this group saw Jesus? What do you think accounts for the difference?

2. Read Luke 24:49; Acts 1:4–5.

   A. What promise was Jesus talking about in Luke 24:49? How did he instruct them to receive the benefits of this promise?

   B. What command did Jesus give his followers in Acts 1:4? What is the promise he mentions?

   C. What promise did Jesus make in verse 5? How does this expand on his earlier statement?

3. Read Acts 2:1–4.

   A. What group is described in verse 1? Why were they there?

   B. What sound did these individuals hear (v. 2)? What is significant about it?

   C. What sight did these individuals see (v. 3)? What is significant about it?

   D. What happened to these individuals (v. 4)? What accounted for this activity?

   E. What lesson(s) can we learn for our lives today from this passage?

Drink Deeply

Do a personal study of the power of the Spirit in the life of the early church. Over a number of days or weeks, sit down with your Bible and read through the book of Acts, noting in particular the passages where the Spirit's activity is specifically mentioned. You might be surprised at the vast number of ways in which the Spirit moves in power!

EIGHT

God's Body Glove

Come to the Well

1. What Jesus did in Galilee is what the Holy Spirit does in us. Jesus *dwelt among* the people, teaching, comforting, and convicting. The Holy Spirit *dwells within* us, teaching, comforting, and convicting.
   A. Does the Holy Spirit "dwell within" you? How do you know for sure?
   B. What is the Holy Spirit teaching you these days?
   C. How is the Holy Spirit comforting you these days?
   D. Of what is the Holy Spirit convicting you these days?

2. Do your actions interrupt the flow of the Spirit in your life?
   A. What does it mean to "interrupt the flow of the Spirit"?
   B. How do someone's actions interrupt the flow of the Spirit?
   C. How do you know when your actions have interrupted the flow of the Spirit in your life? What do you do about this?

3. Harbored sin interferes with Spirit circulation. Confessed sin, however, splices the cable and restores the power.
   A. Define "harbored sin." Is this ever a problem in your life? Explain.

B. What does it take for you to confess your sins to God?

C. Why is confession of sin so important in the life of a growing believer?

4. *Accept* his power. . . . *Surrender* to his plan. . . . And *keep* at it.

A. How can you accept God's power in your current circumstances?

B. What does it mean *today* for you to surrender to God's plan?

C. Why is it important to keep at this discipline?

Fill Your Cup

1. Read Galatians 2:19–20.

A. What does it mean to be "crucified with Christ"?

B. Can you say, as did Paul, that "I myself no longer live"?

C. What does it mean to say that "Christ lives in me"?

D. How does one live "by trusting in the Son of God"?

E. What two things does Paul remind us about Christ in his last phrase of verse 20?

2. Read Romans 8:5–11.

A. How can you tell if you're living in your own strength, according to verse 5? How can you tell if you're living in the power of God?

B. What two ways of life are described in verse 6? How do they differ in outcome?

C. How does Paul describe the mind-set of those who try to live by their own power (v. 7)?

D. What blanket statement does Paul make about those who don't rely on God's power (v. 8)?

E. What definition of a Christian does Paul give in verse 9?

F. What general principle for the Christian life does Paul give in verses 10–11?

3. Read Ephesians 4:25–32.

A. What things are we to avoid, according to this passage?

B. What things are we to pursue, according to this passage?

C. How do both of these things depend on being filled with the Holy Spirit?

Drink Deeply

What does it mean to be "filled with the Spirit"? Many believers make it too complicated. Really, it's just inviting the Spirit to work in you and through you. If you're not familiar with how this works, try an experiment for one week. Get a little notebook and carry it with you. Then, throughout the week, whenever you are faced with a temptation or a difficult decision or a problem or another challenge, pray that God's Holy Spirit will guide you or strengthen you or do whatever else you need him to do—and note your request in your notebook. After the week has passed, go back through your notebook to see how the Spirit really *has* filled you and done remarkable things in your life.

NINE

It's Not Up to You

Come to the Well

1. The Holy Spirit invisibly, yet indispensably, serves as a rudder for the ship of your soul, keeping you afloat and on track. This is no solo journey.
   - A. How does the Holy Spirit serve as the rudder for your ship?
   - B. When you feel as though you're in this battle alone, how can you remind yourself that the Spirit of God is within you and for you?
   - C. Describe a specific time when the Holy Spirit kept you "afloat and on track."
2. When hell's interlopers come seeking to snatch you from God, the seal turns them away. He bought you, owns you, and protects you. God paid too high a price to leave you unguarded.
   - A. In your own words, describe the "seal" of the Holy Spirit.
   - B. How does it make you feel to know that God guards you through the ministry of the Holy Spirit?
   - C. Describe a time when you know the Holy Spirit guarded you and kept you from serious injury.

3. The father had no intention of letting the boy fall. Your Father has no intention of letting you fall, either. You can't see him, but he is present.
   - A. In what situations do you feel most likely to fall?
   - B. How does your Father tend to keep you from falling?
   - C. Why do you think so much of God's work remains invisible to our eyes?
4. The impoverished orphan of Russia, the distraught widow of the battlefield, the aging saint in the convalescent home—they may think they have no voice, no clout, no influence. But they have a friend—a counselor, a comforter—the blessed Spirit of God, who speaks the language of heaven in heaven.
   - A. When are you most likely to think you have no voice, no clout, no influence in heaven? How do you combat this?
   - B. How does it make you feel to know that the Spirit of God prays for you?
   - C. What can you do to help others know they have a voice and clout in heaven?

Fill Your Cup

1. Read Ephesians 1:13–14; 4:30.
   - A. What happens to everyone who believes in Christ (v. 13)?
   - B. What is one important role of the Spirit within us (v. 14)?
   - C. To what future day does verse 14 look forward?
   - D. Why does Paul remind us of this day in 4:30? What are we warned against doing?

2. Read Romans 8:26–27.
   A. Why does the Spirit intercede for us in our prayers (v. 26)? How can this give us great hope?
   B. How can we be sure that these prayers will *always* be effective (v. 27)? How can this give us great hope?

Drink Deeply

Make a list of all the major challenges facing you at this moment. Whether these challenges occur in your home, at work, in church, in your neighborhood, or elsewhere, write them down. What strategies have you used to meet these challenges? Have your attempts worked? Commit each one of these concerns to the Lord, reminding yourself in every case that you are not alone in this battle. Keep a journal to record (1) the dates you prayed about the challenge; (2) any change you noticed in your attitude or anxiety level; (3) how God answered your prayers.

TEN

In God We (Nearly) Trust

Come to the Well

1. Typhoons test our trust in the Captain. Does God know what he is doing? Can he get us out? Why did he allow the storm?

   A. How do "typhoons" test your trust in the Captain?

   B. When was the last time you wondered, *God, do you know what you're doing?*

   C. Describe a typhoon experience that caused you to cry out to your Captain for rescue. What did this experience do for your faith?

2. No struggle will come your way apart from God's purpose, presence, and permission. What encouragement this brings! You are never the victim of nature or the prey of fate. Chance is eliminated. You are more than a weather vane whipped about by the winds of fortune.

   A. Does it comfort you to know that no struggle comes your way apart from God's purpose, presence, and permission? Explain.

   B. How is chance or fate eliminated in the life of the believer?

   C. When bad things happen to you, how do you look for God's purpose and his presence?

3. When someone you love faces adversity, don't insensitively declare, "God is in control." A cavalier tone can eclipse the right truth. Be careful.
   - A. Why is it a bad idea to declare, "God is in control," without taking into account the specifics of the situation?
   - B. Describe a time when you saw someone violate this guideline. What happened?
   - C. In what way can a "cavalier tone" tend to "eclipse the right truth"?
4. God's ways are always right. They may not make sense to us. They may be mysterious, inexplicable, difficult, and even painful. But they are right.
   - A. How do we know that God's ways are always right?
   - B. Describe a time when God's ways did not make sense to you. Has hindsight provided any insight? If so, explain.
   - C. Why is it important to remember that God's ways are always right?

Fill Your Cup

1. Read Daniel 4:1–37.
   - A. What did Nebuchadnezzar, the mightiest king of his era, learn about the sovereign rule of God (vv. 1–3)?
   - B. What dream did the king have (vv. 4–18)? Why did this dream frighten him so badly?
   - C. What interpretation of the dream did Daniel give the king (vv. 19–26)?
   - D. What advice did Daniel give the king (v. 27)?

E. What happened to the king when he ignored Daniel's advice (vv. 29–33)?

F. How did the king's experience change his outlook (v. 34)?

G. What conclusion did the king reach regarding the sovereign rule of God (vv. 35, 37)?

2. Read Luke 22:39–44.

A. What request did Jesus make of his Father in verse 42?

B. What answer did he receive?

C. What was more important to Jesus than getting a yes response to his request?

D. How did God show Jesus that he had heard his prayer, even though he would not grant the request (v. 43)?

E. How do we know this was a sincere request (v. 44)?

F. How does this episode reveal that Jesus told the truth in John 4:34; 6:38–39; and 8:29?

G. What would have been the consequences if Jesus had not trusted God?

Drink Deeply

When we speak of God's sovereignty, we sometimes express it as a cold doctrine that doesn't seem to connect much with real life. To remind yourself of how God's sovereignty often works, read the biblical book of Esther. Although God's name is not mentioned in the book, his sovereign hand is evident. In what instances do you see it? In what ways do God's actions in this book echo what he's doing in your own life?

For a very different picture of the way God's sovereignty at times expresses itself, read the fourth chapter of Daniel. How do the lessons of this book differ from those of Esther?

ELEVEN

Worry? You Don't Have To

Come to the Well

1. Worry changes nothing. You don't add one day to your life or one bit of life to your day by worrying. Your anxiety earns you heartburn, nothing more.
   A. What kind of things do you tend to worry about?
   B. In a given week, how often would you say you worry about something?
   C. Describe what worry has accomplished for you.
2. Worry betrays a fragile faith, an "unconscious blasphemy." We don't intentionally doubt God, but don't we, when we worry, essentially doubt God?
   A. How does worry betray a "fragile faith"? In what way is it an "unconscious blasphemy"?
   B. What's the problem with doubting God?
   C. Select one of the worries you identified in 1.A. If you aren't trusting God to take care of it, whom or what are you trusting to take care of it? What steps can you take to turn it over to God?
3. Worry diminishes as we look upward. God knows what can happen on this journey, and he wants to bring us home.

   A. Why does worry diminish as we look upward?

   B. How does knowing that God wants to bring us home help diminish worry?

   C. How do you personally battle worry?

4. God's proof is God's past. Forgetfulness sires fearfulness, but a good memory makes for a good heart.

   A. How does thinking about what God has done in the past help you in the present?

   B. What good things has God done for you in the past week? The past month? The past year?

   C. What most makes you afraid? How can "God's past" help you to overcome this fear?

Fill Your Cup

1. Read Philippians 4:6–8.

   A. What are we told *not* to do in verse 6?

   B. What are we told to do instead?

   C. Concerning what particular things are we to do this?

   D. In what particular way are we to do this?

   E. What is the promised result of doing this (v. 7)?

2. Read Matthew 6:24–32.

   A. According to verse 24, who is to be our "master"?

   B. How does compliance with verse 24 make possible our obedience to the command of verse 25?

   C. How is the illustration in verse 26 supposed to bolster our faith?

D. How would you answer the question of verse 27?

E. How would you answer the question of verse 28?

F. How is the illustration in verses 28–29 supposed to bolster our faith?

G. How would you answer the question of verse 30?

H. How is the comment in verse 32 supposed to motivate us?

3. Read 1 Peter 5:7.

A. What does this verse command?

B. To whom is this command directed?

C. What reason for the command is given?

Drink Deeply

If you struggle to control your worry and anxiety, it might help to get assistance from others who have dealt with the same problem. Seek out the counsel of someone whose wisdom you respect.

Then remind yourself of a saying attributed to A. J. Cronin: "Worry never robs tomorrow of its sorrow; it only saps today of its strength." It has been said that more than 90 percent of what we worry about never happens. Test this statement in your own life. Keep a "worry journal" for three months. Divide each page into two columns: "What I Worry About" and "The Date This Worry Actually Took Shape." How many of the things you worried about in those three months actually occurred?

TWELVE

Angels Watching over You

Come to the Well

1. If you believe in God's Word, you have to believe in angels. At the same time, you have to be puzzled by them.
   A. What do you believe about angels?
   B. Why does the Bible's description of angels tend to puzzle us?
   C. What is the biggest misconception about angels, in your opinion?
2. Two adjectives capture the greater truth about angels: *many* and *mighty*.
   A. What difference does it make to you that there are *many* angels?
   B. Why do you think the Bible makes a point to tell us that angels are *mighty*?
   C. Describe your favorite angel story in the Bible. Why is it your favorite?
3. Only one sound matters to angels—God's voice. Only one sight enthralls angels—God's face. They know that he is Lord of all.
   A. Do you consider it a good thing that angels respond only to God's command? Explain.
   B. What does it mean to you that God is Lord of all?

4. Refuse God at the risk of an unguarded back. But receive his lordship, and be assured that many mighty angels will guard you in all your ways.
   A. In what ways do we "refuse God"?
   B. What does it mean to "receive" God's lordship?
   C. Do you believe that angels are guarding you right now? Explain.

Fill Your Cup

1. Read Hebrews 1:6–7, 14; 2:2, 7, 9; 12:22; 13:2.
   A. What did God command the angels to do when Christ was born (1:6; see also Luke 2:8–15)?
   B. Name one primary angelic function (1:7).
   C. Whom are angels charged to serve (1:14)?
   D. Where do angels rank among God's creatures (2:7, 9)?
   E. Name another angelic function (12:22).
   F. Do we always know when an angel has visited us (13:2)?
2. Read Psalms 34:7; 35:1–6; 78:49; 103:20.
   A. What promise is given in Psalm 34:7?
   B. What angelic function is described in Psalm 35:5–6?
   C. What angelic function is described in Psalm 78:49?
   D. What angelic functions are described in Psalm 103:20?

Drink Deeply

If you'd like to get a fuller biblical picture of the nature and activity of angels, get a good concordance and look up the words *angel* and *angels.* Then make a study of all the references you find. But be prepared for a lot of work, since Scripture uses these terms alone more than three hundred times! You might also benefit from reading what others have written about God's angelic servants: Billy Graham's *Angels* and Herbert Lockyer's *All the Angels in the Bible* are both considered classics.

THIRTEEN

With God as Your Guardian

Come to the Well

1. God sizes up every person who comes your way. As you walk, he leads. As you sleep, he patrols.
   - A. Do you see God as your Guardian? Explain.
   - B. In what ways has God led you?
   - C. Describe a time that God "patrolled" as you slept.
2. What's bad to a child isn't always bad to a dad. What you and I might rate as an absolute disaster, God may rate as a pimple-level problem that will pass.
   - A. Name some things that seem bad to a child, but not to a dad.
   - B. Describe a time in your life when you experienced an "absolute disaster." Did you see God's hand in this situation? Explain.
   - C. How has God personally shown you his faithfulness?
3. God uses struggles to toughen our spiritual skin.
   - A. How can struggles toughen our spiritual skin?
   - B. How has God used struggles to toughen your spiritual skin?
   - C. In what ways does it help to remember that God uses struggles to toughen our spiritual skin?

4. God guards those who turn to him. The pounding you feel does not suggest his distance, but proves his nearness. Trust his sovereignty. Hasn't he earned your trust?
   - A. What does it mean to turn to God? Is this a one-time event? Explain.
   - B. What "pounding" do you feel right now? How can this suggest God's nearness rather than his distance?
   - C. What does it mean to trust God's sovereignty? How can you learn to do this more and more?

Fill Your Cup

1. Read Psalm 91:1–16.
   - A. How does the psalmist picture God in verses 1–2? What images does he use?
   - B. What additional images are used in verses 3–8? How is each image calculated to increase our trust in God?
   - C. What promise is made in verses 11–12? How did the devil misuse this promise (see Matt. 4:5–7)? What can we learn from this encounter between Jesus and Satan about claiming promises?
   - D. What reason does the Lord give for his actions in verse 14?
   - E. What promises does God give in verses 15–16? How does an eternal perspective on life help us understand God's promises?

2. Read James 1:2–4.
   - A. What does James tell us to do when troubles come our way (v. 2)?
   - B. What reason does James give for his instruction (v. 3)?

C. What is the outcome of complying with James's instruction (v. 4)?

Drink Deeply

Take a look at your life, especially the past ten years, and ask yourself, "What things that I once considered bad do I now consider good? How has God used the 'bad' events of my life for my good?" After you complete your personal historical survey, make sure you thank God for his good care of you—even when you don't feel it's quite what you'd have it to be.

FOURTEEN

Going Deep

Come to the Well

1. Some people love you because of you. Not God. He loves you because he is he. He loves you because he decides to. Self-generated, uncaused, and spontaneous, his constant-level love depends on his choice to give it.
   - A. Who in your life loves you because of you?
   - B. What does it mean that God loves you because he is he? How can this truth give you great confidence?
   - C. Discuss each element of God's love just mentioned: self-generated, uncaused, spontaneous, constant-level. How does each of these terms expand your concept of God's love?
2. Success signals God's love no more than struggles indicate the lack of it. The definitive, God-sanctioned gauge is not a good day or a bad break but the dying hours of his Son. Consider them often.
   - A. Why does success not necessarily signal God's love? Why do struggles not indicate the lack of God's love?
   - B. How do the dying hours of Jesus best show us God's love?
   - C. How can you train yourself to think often of Christ's sacrifice? Name some practical steps you could take, starting today.

3. To abide in Christ's love is to make his love your home. Not a roadside park or hotel room you occasionally visit, but your preferred dwelling.
   A. What does it mean to you to "abide in Christ's love"?
   B. How can you make Christ's love your "preferred dwelling"?
   C. What tends to keep you from abiding in Christ's love? How can you overcome this obstacle?
4. God's love can't be legislated, but it can be chosen. Choose it, won't you? For the sake of your heart. For the sake of your home. For Christ's sake, and yours, choose it.
   A. Have you chosen God's love? Why or why not?
   B. How can choosing God's love improve your heart? How can it improve your home?
   C. How does it benefit Christ ("for Christ's sake") for you to choose God's love?

Fill Your Cup

1. Read Ephesians 3:16–19.
   A. For what did Paul pray in verse 16?
   B. What was the purpose of his prayer (v. 17)?
   C. For what else did Paul pray in verse 17?
   D. How does the apostle describe God's love in verses 18–19?
   E. What was the ultimate prayer of Paul in verse 19?
2. Read John 15:1–8.
   A. To what did Jesus compare himself in verse 1? To what did he compare his Father? What is significant about both images?

B. What divine activity does Jesus describe in verse 2?

C. What general principle of the Christian life is laid out in verse 4?

D. What promise is given in verse 5?

E. What warning is given in verse 6?

F. What additional promise is given in verse 7? On what does the promise depend?

G. What gives God glory, according to verse 8? How does this provide evidence of relationship to Christ?

Drink Deeply

Perhaps one of the best ways to celebrate God's amazing love and grace is to share some of that love and grace with others. Who in your life—family member, coworker, neighbor, fellow church member—most needs encouragement right now? Think of some special, maybe even unusual way to show that person God's love. And remember this: *you* are not the center of attention! Maybe you could do something anonymously and leave the person wondering who could have been so thoughtful. Sometimes, secret displays of grace are the most fun!

FIFTEEN

Have You Heard the Clanging Door?

Come to the Well

1. "Deny Jesus," Peter testified, "and he'll still love you." "Doubt Jesus," Thomas could add, "and the same is true."
   A. How could Jesus still love Peter after Peter had denied him?
   B. How could Jesus still love Thomas after Thomas had doubted him?
   C. If Jesus will still love us regardless of what we do, does it matter how we live? Explain.
2. Are you convinced that you have never lived a loveless day? Not one. Never unloved. Those times you deserted Christ? He loved you. You hid from him; he came looking for you.
   A. Answer the previous question.
   B. In what ways have you "deserted" Christ? What happened?
   C. How did Jesus come looking for you?
3. The jail door has never closed. God's love supply is never empty.
   A. How do we know that God's love supply is never empty?
   B. How have you most recently experienced God's love?
   C. How can you, today, show God's love to others?

4. The big news of the Bible is not that you love God but that God loves you; not that you can know God but that God already knows you! He tattooed your name on the palm of his hand. His thoughts of you outnumber the sand on the shore. You never leave his mind, escape his sight, flee his thoughts. He sees the worst of you and loves you still.
   A. How does it make you feel to realize that God knows you completely and still loves you utterly?
   B. How does it make you feel to know that God has tattooed your name on the palm of his hand?
   C. What do you imagine God is thinking about you at this moment?

Fill Your Cup

1. Read Romans 8:31–39.
   A. What question is asked in verse 31? What is the expected answer?
   B. What question is asked in verse 32? What is the expected answer?
   C. What questions are asked in verse 33? What are the expected answers?
   D. What questions are asked in verse 34? What is the apostle's response?
   E. What questions are asked in verse 35? What is the expected answer?
   F. What is the purpose of the Bible quotation in verse 36?
   G. How did the apostle see the troubles of life when viewed from his close connection to God (v. 37)?

H. What final conclusion does the apostle reach in verses 38–39?

2. Read 1 John 4:7–12.

   A. What instruction is given in verse 7? What reason is given for the instruction? What general truth is expressed?

   B. What bold statement is made in verse 8? What reason is given for this statement?

   C. What major proof of the love of God is cited in verse 9?

   D. What is true love, according to verse 10?

   E. What instruction is given in verse 11? On what basis is this instruction given?

   F. How can others see the invisible God and his love (v. 12)?

Drink Deeply

To help remind you that, as Paul says, "If we are faithless, he will remain faithful, for he cannot disown himself" (2 Tim. 2:13 NIV), do a little exercise that might feel a bit uncomfortable. Sit down and make a catalog of the specific ways you believe you may have failed your Lord in the last year (let's not make this too depressing!). After you have finished your list, burn it—and remind yourself of the goodness of the Lord. Then give him joyful thanks and full-bodied praise for being who he is and acting as he does!

SIXTEEN

Fearlessly Facing Eternity

Come to the Well

1. Payback. The evidence is in. The truth is out. And the policeman is standing at your door. No one likes the thought of judgment.
   - A. What thoughts and feelings does judgment stir in you?
   - B. If you were being paid back today, what kind of payment would you expect?
   - C. Why do you think the Bible talks so much about judgment?
2. You will not be helped or hindered by the deeds of your family, church, or nation. You will be personally judged according to one question: "What did you do with Jesus?"
   - A. Why will the deeds of your family, church, or nation not help you in the judgment to come?
   - B. What have you done with Jesus?
   - C. Why does everything hinge on your answer to this last question?
3. God views Christians the way he views Christ: sinless and perfect. Hence, Christians can view judgment the way Christ does: with confidence and hope.

A. How can God view Christians in the same way he views Christ?

B. Do you view judgment the same way Christ does? Explain.

C. What gives you the right to feel confidence and hope as you contemplate God's judgment? What have you done to deserve that right?

4. You need never fear God's judgment. Not today. Not on Judgment Day. Jesus, in the light of God's glory, is speaking on your behalf. "That's my friend," he says. And when he does, the door of heaven opens.

A. Do you think Jesus considers you his friend? Explain.

B. Do you expect the door of heaven to be opened for you on the day of judgment? Explain.

Fill Your Cup

1. Read 1 John 4:16–18.

A. What does it mean to "know" the love of God (v. 16)? How is it different to trust it or rely on it?

B. How is love made complete, or perfect, in us (v. 17)? What effect does this love have on us in the day of judgment? In what specific way does John expect followers of Jesus to be "like" him?

C. How do fear and love interact (v. 18)? If one fears divine judgment, what conclusion can be made?

2. Read Romans 2:5–11; 14:10–12; 2 Corinthians 5:9–10.

A. What "day" is in view in Romans 2:5?

B. What general principle of divine judgment is described in verse 6?

C. What group is described in verse 7? What can they expect to receive at the judgment (v. 10)?

D. What group is described in verses 8–9?

E. Why is it important to recognize the truth of verse 11?

F. What further details are given about this event in Romans 14:10–12?

G. What personal goal will serve us well when the day of judgment comes (2 Cor. 5:9)?

H. What additional details are given in 2 Corinthians 5:10?

Drink Deeply

The Gospel of Matthew presents some of the most extended biblical teaching on the final judgment to be found anywhere in Scripture. In your quiet time some day, read Matthew 24:36–25:46. Put yourself into each of the varied scenes that Jesus describes. Where do you think you fit?

When you're ready for another study, take a close look at the little book of 1 Thessalonians. Each chapter of this book ends with a reference to the second coming of Christ. List the various things you learn about the return of Christ, take a whole day to meditate on each of these things, and then take a personal inventory to see how your study *has been* and *is* changing the way you live.

SEVENTEEN

If God Wrote You a Letter

Come to the Well

1. Were no one to tell them, they would carry the box to their dirt-floored home, place it in a prime location, and admire it, display it, but never open it. Don't we do the same with Christ? Aren't we prone to keep him at arm's length?

   A. How do we tend to keep Christ at arm's length?

   B. Why do you think we tend to keep Christ at arm's length?

   C. What can you do today to personally experience the gift of Christ?

2. Through what faucets has God poured his love into your life? A faithful church? A prayerful spouse? Time-tested traditions? A girlfriend in college or a grandma from childhood?

   A. Answer the previous question.

   B. Why do you think God uses so many "faucets" to pour out his love?

   C. How can you be a "faucet" to pour out God's love on others?

3. The treasure is the Giver himself. On my list of things I wish I had learned earlier, this truth hovers near the top.

   A. Why is it so easy for our hearts to be captured by the gifts of God rather than by God himself?

   B. What about God do you value the most? Why?

   C. How can you train yourself to want the Giver more than his gifts?

4. Max lists four things that can help us drink from the bottomless well of Christ (these are also the four main divisions of the book): accept his work; rely on his energy; trust his lordship; receive his love.

   A. In what ways have you accepted the work of God on your behalf? In what ways do you struggle to accept his work?

   B. How have you learned to rely on God's energy? How do you still tend to rely on your own strength?

   C. In what areas of life do you find it easiest to trust God's lordship? In what areas of life is this still a struggle?

   D. How have you learned to receive God's love? When do you sometimes have a problem receiving God's love?

Fill Your Cup

1. Read Jeremiah 2:12–13.

   A. How do you know that the statement about to be made in Jeremiah 2:13 is of enormous significance?

   B. What two sins had the people of Jeremiah's time committed? What exchange had they made? What was so foolish about this exchange? How do we often make the same exchange? Why do you think we make it?

2. Read Isaiah 55:1–3.

   A. Who is addressed in verse 1? What invitation is given?

   B. What question is asked in verse 2? What answer could be given? What promise is made?

C. What ultimate benefit is offered in verse 3? Have you accepted this benefit? Explain.

3. Read John 7:37–39.

A. What claim about himself is Jesus making in verse 37?

B. What benefit does he promise to his listeners (v. 39)?

C. What do his listeners have to do to enjoy this benefit (v. 38)?

Drink Deeply

If you could write a letter to God that could be delivered this very day, what would you say in that letter? Take some time to write that letter—of thanks, of praise, of petition, or whatever you would like to say in such a special note—and then offer it to God. Keep the letter in a safe and special place and revisit it later, especially on dark and difficult days, so you can say along with the psalmist, "I am still confident of this: I will see the goodness of the LORD in the land of the living" (Ps. 27:13 NIV).

Notes

Chapter 2: Sin Vaccination

1. I. D. E. Thomas, comp., *The Golden Treasury of Puritan Quotations* (Chicago: Moody Press, 1975), 266, quoted in Bruce A. Demarest, *The Cross and Salvation: The Doctrine of Salvation* (Wheaton, IL: Crossway Books, 1997), 29.
2. "Secrets of the Dead: Mystery of the Black Death," Public Broadcasting Service, http://www.pbs.org/wnet/secrets/case_plague/index.html and http://www.pbs.org/wnet/secrets/case_plague/clues.html.

Chapter 3: When Grace Goes Deep

1. Charles Swindoll, *The Tale of the Tardy Oxcart and 1,501 Other Stories* (Nashville: Word Publishing, 1998), 250.
2. Ron Lee Davis with James D. Denny, *Mistreated* (Portland, OR: Multnomah Press, 1989), 147–48.

Chapter 4: When Death Becomes Birth

1. Rick Reilly, "Extreme Measures," *Sports Illustrated*, http://sportsillustrated.cnn.com./inside_game /rick_reilly/news/2003/05/20/life_of_reilly0519/3; Shane Burrows, "Cheating Death in Bluejohn Canyon," http://www.climb-utah.com/Roost/bluejohn2.htm; "Climber Describes Amputation Ordeal," CBS News, http://www.cbsnews.com/stories/2003/05/02/national/main551979.shtml; "A Rational Choice," ABC News, http://abcnews.go.com/sections/GMA/US/GMA030506Climber_amputate.html.
2. "Climber Recounts Canyon Ordeal," http://www.msnbc.com/news/908232.asp.
3. Paul Aurandt, *Destiny and 102 Other Real Life Mysteries* (New York: Bantam Books, 1983), 28.
4. F. W. Boreham, *Life Verses: The Bible's Impact on Famous Lives* (Grand Rapids: Kregel Publications, 1994), 1:118.

Chapter 5: With Heart Headed Home

1. "Corridors of Agony," *Time*, 27 January 1992, quoted in Maxie Dunnam, *This Is Christianity* (Nashville: Abingdon Press, 1994), 133–34.

Chapter 7: Waiting for Power

1. Brother Lawrence, *The Practice of the Presence of God* (Old Tappan, NJ: Revell, 1958), 9.
2. William Barclay, *The Acts of the Apostles* (Philadelphia: Westminster Press, 1976), 15.

Chapter 8: God's Body Glove

1. C. S. Lewis, *Mere Christianity* (New York: Macmillan Publishing Co., 1952), 167.

Chapter 9: It's Not Up to you

1. William C. Frey, *The Dance of Hope: Finding Ourselves in the Rhythm of God's Great Story* (Colorado Springs, CO: WaterBrook Press, 2003), 174.

Chapter 10: In God We (Nearly) Trust

1. Harold S. Kushner, *When Bad Things Happen to Good People* (New York: Avon Books, 1983), 42–43.
2. Margaret Clarkson, *Grace Grows Best in Winter: Help for Those Who Must Suffer* (Grand Rapids: W. B. Eerdmans, 1984), 40–41.
3. John Oxenham, *Bees in Amber: A Little Book of Thoughtful Verse*, The Project Gutenberg, http://www.gutenberg.net/etext06/8bees10.txt.

Chapter 11: Worry? You Don't Have To

1. "Biosphere 2 Today, A New Dynamic for Ecosystem Study and Education," http://www.accessexcellence.org/LC/ST/st4bg.html.
2. Bob Russell with Rusty Russell, *Jesus, Lord of Your Personality: Four Powerful Principles for Change* (West Monroe: LA: Howard Publishing, 2002), 41.
3. R. G. V. Tasker, ed., *Tyndale New Testament Commentaries: The Epistle of Paul to the Philippians* (Grand Rapids: W. B. Eerdmans, 1976), 169.

Chapter 12: Angels Watching over You

1. Rick Reilly, "The Play of the Year," *Sports Illustrated*, 18 November 2002.
2. Francis Thompson, *The Kingdom of God*, quoted in Herbert Lockyer Jr., *All the Angels in the Bible* (Peabody, MA: Hendrickson Publishers, 1995), xv.
3. John Milton, *Paradise Lost*, bk. 4, lines 678–79.

4. Billy Graham, *Angels: God's Secret Agents* (Garden City, NY: Doubleday, 1975), 24.

Chapter 14: Going Deep

1. Gary Smith, "The Rapture of the Deep," *Sports Illustrated*, 16 June 2003, 62–78.
2. David Brainerd, quoted in Cynthia Heald, "Becoming a Friend of God," *Discipleship Journal*, no. 54 (1989): 22.
3. Craig Childs, *The Secret Knowledge of Water: Discovering the Essence of the American Desert* (Boston: Little, Brown and Company, 2000), 61–62.

Chapter 15: Have You Heard the Clanging Door?

1. Patrick McGilligan, *Alfred Hitchcock: A Life in Darkness and Light* (New York: HarperCollins, 2003), 7–8. There are many variations to this story, and some believe it may be apocryphal.

Chapter 16: Fearlessly Facing Eternity

1. "Fear," sample illustrations, http://www.preachingplus.com.
2. H. A. Guy, *The New Testament Doctrine of the Last Things* (New York: Oxford University Press, 1948), 173, quoted in Frank Stagg, *New Testament Theology* (Nashville: Broadman Press, 1962), 305.

Chapter 17: If God Wrote You a Letter

1. Spiros Zodhiates et al., *A Treasury of Bible Illustrations* (Chattanooga, TN: AMG Publishers, 1995), 135.
2. Isa. 55:1; Isa. 51:12; 1 Cor. 6:20; Col. 2:10; Isa. 62:4–5; Heb. 13:5.
3. Amos 5:12; 2 Cor. 12:9; Isa. 38:17; Mic. 7:19; 1 Cor. 6:11; Isa. 44:22.
4. 1 Cor. 15:54; Col. 2:15; Heb. 2:14; Rev. 14:13; Phil. 3:20; Matt. 25:34; Rev. 21:4.
5. Luke 10:41; Prov. 3:5; 2 Pet. 2:9; Rom. 8:26; Col. 1:11; Rom. 8:32; Judg. 5:21; 2 Cor. 4:1; Isa. 41:10.
6. Isa. 26:4; 1 Pet. 2:25; Isa. 43:2.
7. Matt. 6:34; Ps. 121:4–5; Ps. 34:7; Ps. 31:20; Deut. 31:6; Ps. 37:23–24; Ps. 32:8.
8. Matt. 24:6; John 16:33; Phil. 4:6; Ps. 5:12.
9. Gen. 41:52; Isa. 61:3; Isa. 57:15; Ps. 30:5; Rom. 8:31.
10. Deut. 32:10 MSG; Zeph. 3:17; Ps. 139:17–18; Rom. 8:38.
11. Isa. 49:14–15; 1 Pet. 1:19; John 10:28; Isa. 49:16; John 15:15; Matt. 10:30–31.
12. Ps. 55:22; Ps. 103:13–14; 1 Pet. 5:7.
13. Phil. 4:5; Matt. 11:28; Ps. 149:4; Heb. 10:23; Rev. 22:17.

TRAVELING LIGHT

Releasing the Burdens
You Were Never Intended to Bear

Max Lucado

Traveling Light

Published in Nashville, Tennessee, by Thomas Nelson. Thomas Nelson is a registered trademark of Thomas Nelson, Inc.

Thomas Nelson, Inc., titles may be purchased in bulk for educational, business, fund-raising, or sales promotional use. For information, please e-mail SpecialMarkets@ThomasNelson.com.

Library of Congress Cataloging-in-Publication Data

Lucado, Max.
Traveling light / by Max Lucado.
p. cm.
Includes bibliographical references.
ISBN-10: 0-8499-1345-4 (tp)
ISBN-13: 978-0-8499-1345-7 (tp)
ISBN-10: 0-8499-1297-0 (hc)
ISBN-13: 978-0-8499-1297-9 (hc)
1. Christian life—Meditations. I. Title.

BV4501.3 .L86 2001
242—dc21

2001026267

To my dear friend Joey Paul,
celebrating thirty years of words at Word,
sharing the Word

Acknowledgments

Here are well-deserved pats on some sturdy backs:

To Liz Heaney and Karen Hill—my editors and my assistant, midwives of the manuscript. Sorry I groaned so much.

To Steve and Cheryl Green—my representative and my friends. Because of you, contracts are read, and bills are paid, and this old boy sleeps well at night.

To Greg Pruett—Bible translator and Hebrew student. Thanks for the great insights.

To Eugene Peterson—Bible translator, author, and hero to many. Thanks for letting me use the title. And, much more, thanks for sharing your heart.

To Steve Halliday—study guide author par excellence.

To my friends at Thomas Nelson. Once again, you're the best.

To Laura Kendall and Carol Bartley—the great sleuths of the English language. Thanks for making me look smart.

To Jenna, Andrea, and Sara—my delightful daughters. I couldn't be prouder.

To Denalyn—my wife of two decades. Before you were born, where did poets go for inspiration?

To you—the reader. May the real Author speak to you.

And, most of all, to you, Jesus. The only reason we can release a burden is because you are there to take it. All the applause is yours.

1

The Luggage of Life

I've never been one to travel light.

I've tried. Believe me, I've tried. But ever since I stuck three fingers in the air and took the Boy Scout pledge to be prepared, I've been determined to be exactly that—prepared.

Prepared for a bar mitzvah, baby dedication, or costume party. Prepared to parachute behind enemy lines or enter a cricket tournament. And if, perchance, the Dalai Lama might be on my flight and invite me to dine in Tibet, I carry snowshoes. One has to be prepared.

I don't know how to travel light.

Fact is, there's a lot about travel I don't know. I don't know how to interpret the restrictions of a supersaver seat—*half price if you leave on Wednesdays during duck-hunting season and return when the moon is full in a nonelection year.* I don't know why they don't build the whole plane out of the same metal they use to build the little black box. I don't know how to escape the airplane toilet without sacrificing one of my extremities to the jaws of the folding door. And I don't know what to say to guys like the taxi driver in Rio who learned I was an American and asked me if I knew his cousin Eddie who lives in the U.S.

There's a lot about traveling I don't know.

I don't know why we men would rather floss a crocodile than ask for directions. I don't know why vacation slides aren't used to treat insomnia, and I don't know when I'll learn not to eat food whose names I can't pronounce.

But most of all, I don't know how to travel light.

I don't know how to travel without granola bars, sodas, and rain gear. I don't know how to travel without flashlights and a generator and a global tracking system. I don't know how to travel without an ice chest of wieners. What if I stumble upon a backyard barbecue? To bring nothing to the party would be rude.

Every travel-catalog company in the world has my credit-card number. I've got an iron that doubles as a paperweight, a hair dryer the size of a coach's whistle, a Swiss Army knife that expands into a pup tent, and a pair of pants that inflate upon impact. (On one flight my wife, Denalyn, gave me a swat on the leg, and I couldn't get out of my seat.)

I don't know how to travel light. But I need to learn. Denalyn refuses to give birth to any more children even though the airlines allow each passenger three checked bags and two carry-ons.

I need to learn to travel light.

You're wondering why I can't. *Loosen up!* you're thinking. *You can't enjoy a journey carrying so much stuff. Why don't you just drop all that luggage?*

Funny you should ask. I'd like to inquire the same of you. Haven't you been known to pick up a few bags?

Odds are, you did this morning. Somewhere between the first step on the floor and the last step out the door, you grabbed some luggage. You stepped over to the baggage carousel and loaded up. Don't remember doing so? That's because you did it without thinking. Don't remember seeing a baggage terminal? That's because the carousel is not the one in the airport; it's the one in the mind. And the bags we grab are not made of leather; they're made of burdens.

The suitcase of guilt. A sack of discontent. You drape a duffel bag of weariness on one shoulder and a hanging bag of grief on the other. Add on a backpack of doubt, an overnight bag of loneliness, and a trunk of fear. Pretty soon you're pulling more stuff than a skycap. No wonder you're so tired at the end of the day. Lugging luggage is exhausting.

What you were saying to me, God is saying to you, "Set that stuff down! You're carrying burdens you don't need to bear."

"Come to me," he invites, "all of you who are weary and carry heavy burdens, and I will give you rest" (Matt. 11:28 NLT).

If we let him, God will lighten our loads . . . but how do we let him? May I invite an old friend to show us? The Twenty-third Psalm.

> The LORD is my shepherd;
> I shall not want.
> He makes me to lie down in green pastures;
> He leads me beside the still waters.
> He restores my soul;
> He leads me in the paths of righteousness
> For His name's sake.
>
> Yea, though I walk through the valley of the shadow of death,
> I will fear no evil;
> For You are with me;
> Your rod and Your staff, they comfort me.
>
> You prepare a table before me in the presence of my enemies;
> You anoint my head with oil.
> My cup runs over.
> Surely goodness and mercy shall follow me
> All the days of my life;
> And I will dwell in the house of the LORD
> Forever. (NKJV)

Do more beloved words exist? Framed and hung in hospital halls, scratched on prison walls, quoted by the young, and whispered by the dying. In these lines sailors have found a harbor, the frightened have found a father, and strugglers have found a friend.

And because the passage is so deeply loved, it is widely known. Can you find ears on which these words have never fallen? Set to music in a hundred songs, translated into a thousand tongues, domiciled in a million hearts.

One of those hearts might be yours. What kinship do you feel with these words? Where do the verses transport you? To a fireside? Bedside? Graveside?

Hardly a week passes that I don't turn to them. This passage is to the minister what balm is to the physician. I recently applied them to the heart of a dear friend. Summoned to his house with the words "The doctors aren't giving him more than a few days," I looked at him and understood. Face pale. Lips stretched and parched. Skin draping between bones like old umbrella cloth between spokes. The cancer had taken so much: his appetite, his strength, his days. But the cancer hadn't touched his faith. Pulling a chair to his bed and squeezing his hand, I whispered, "Bill, 'The Lord is my shepherd; I shall not want.'" He rolled his head toward me as if to welcome the words.

"He makes me to lie down in green pastures; He leads me beside the still waters. He restores my soul; He leads me in the paths of righteousness for His name's sake."

Reaching the fourth verse, fearful that he might not hear, I leaned forward until I was a couple of inches from his ear and said, "Though I walk through the valley of the shadow of death, I will fear no evil; for You are with me; Your rod and Your staff, they comfort me."

He didn't open his eyes, but he arched his brows. He didn't speak, but his thin fingers curled around mine, and I wondered if the Lord was helping him set down some luggage, the fear of dying.

Do you have some luggage of your own? Do you think God might use David's psalm to lighten your load? *Traveling light means trusting God with the burdens you were never intended to bear.*

Why don't you try traveling light? Try it for the sake of those you love. Have you ever considered the impact that excess baggage has on relationships? We've made this point at our church by virtue of a drama. A wedding is reenacted in which we hear the thoughts of the bride and groom. The groom enters, laden with luggage. A bag dangles from every appendage. And each bag is labeled: guilt, anger, arrogance, insecurities. This fellow is loaded. As he stands at the altar, the audience hears him thinking, *Finally, a woman who will help me carry all my burdens. She's so strong, so stable, so . . .*

As his thoughts continue, hers begin. She enters, wearing a wedding gown but, like her fiancé, covered with luggage. Pulling a hanging bag, shouldering a carry-on, hauling a makeup kit, paper sack—everything you could imagine and everything labeled. She has her own bags: prejudice, loneliness, disappointments. And her expectations? Listen to what she is thinking: *Just a few more minutes and I've got me a man. No more counselors. No more group sessions. So long, discouragement and worry. I won't be seeing you anymore. He's going to fix me.*

Finally they stand at the altar, lost in a mountain of luggage. They smile their way through the ceremony, but when given the invitation to kiss each other, they can't. How do you embrace someone if your arms are full of bags?

For the sake of those you love, learn to set them down.

And, for the sake of the God you serve, do the same. He wants to use you, you know. But how can he if you are exhausted? This truth came home to me yesterday afternoon on a run. Preparing for a jog, I couldn't decide what to wear. The sun was out, but the wind was chilly. The sky was clear, but the forecast said rain. Jacket or sweatshirt? The Boy Scout within me prevailed. I wore both.

I grabbed my Walkman but couldn't decide which tape to bring. A sermon or music? You guessed it, I took both. Needing to stay in touch with my kids, I carried a cell phone. So no one would steal my car, I pocketed my keys. As a precaution against thirst, I brought along some drink money in a pouch. I looked more like a pack mule than a runner! Within half a mile I was peeling off the jacket and hiding it in a bush. That kind of weight will slow you down.

What's true in jogging is true in faith. God has a great race for you to run. Under his care you will go where you've never been and serve in ways you've never dreamed. But you have to drop some stuff. How can you share grace if you are full of guilt? How can you offer comfort if you are disheartened? How can you lift someone else's load if your arms are full with your own?

For the sake of those you love, travel light.

For the sake of the God you serve, travel light.

For the sake of your own joy, travel light.

There are certain weights in life you simply cannot carry. Your Lord is asking you to set them down and trust him. He is the father at the baggage claim. When a dad sees his five-year-old son trying to drag the family trunk off the carousel, what does he say? The father will say to his son what God is saying to you.

"Set it down, child. I'll carry that one."

What do you say we take God up on his offer? We just might find ourselves traveling a little lighter.

By the way, I may have overstated my packing problems. (I don't usually take snowshoes.) But I can't overstate God's promise: "Unload all your worries onto him, since he is looking after you" (1 Pet. 5:7 JB).

2

The Middle C of Life

The Burden of a Lesser God

The Lord . . .

Psalm 23:1

I'm only five feet from an eagle. His wings are spread, and his talons are lifted above the branch. White feathers cap his head, and black eyes peer at me from both sides of a golden beak. He is so close I could touch him. So near I could stroke him. With only a lean and a stretch of my right arm, I could cover the eagle's crown with my hand.

But I don't. I don't reach. Why not? Am I afraid of him?

Hardly. He hasn't budged in two years. When I first opened the box, he impressed me. When I first set him on the shelf, I admired him. Man-made eagles are nice for a while, but you quickly get used to them.

David is concerned that you and I don't make the same mistake with God. His pen has scarcely touched papyrus, and he's urging us to avoid gods of our own making. With his very first words in this psalm, David sets out to deliver us from the burden of a lesser deity.

One might argue that he seeks to do nothing else. For though he will speak of green pastures, his thesis is not rest. He will describe death's somber valley, but this poem is not an ode to dying. He will tell of the Lord's forever house, but his theme is not heaven. Why did David write the Twenty-third Psalm? To build our trust in God . . . to remind us of who he is.

In this psalm David devotes one hundred and fifteen words to explaining the first two:[1] "The Lord." In the arena of unnecessary luggage, the psalmist begins with the weightiest: the refashioned god. One who looks nice but does little. God as . . .

A genie in a bottle. Convenient. Congenial. Need a parking place, date, field goal made or missed? All you do is rub the bottle and *poof*—it's yours. And, what's even better, this god goes back into the bottle after he's done.

A sweet grandpa. So soft hearted. So wise. So kind. But very, very, very old. Grandpas are great when they are awake, but they tend to doze off when you need them.

A busy dad. Leaves on Mondays, returns on Saturdays. Lots of road trips and business meetings. He'll show up on Sunday, however, so clean up and look spiritual. On Monday, be yourself again. He'll never know.

Ever held these views of God? If so, you know the problems they cause. A busy dad doesn't have time for your questions. A kind grandpa is too weak to carry your load. And if your god is a genie in a bottle, then you are greater than he is. He comes and goes at your command.

A god who looks nice but does little.

Reminds me of a briefcase I own. Though I'd like to fault the salesman, I can't. The purchase was my decision. But he certainly made it easy. I didn't need a new satchel. The one I had was fine. Scarred and scratched but fine. The paint was worn off the zippers, and the edges were scuffed, but the bag was fine.

Oh, but this new one, to use the words of the college-age boy in the leather store, was "really fine." Loaded with features: copper covers on the corners, smooth leather from Spain, and, most of all, an Italian name near the handle. The salesman gave his line and handed me the bag, and I bought them both.

I left the store with a briefcase that I have used maybe twice. What was I thinking? It carries so little. My old bag had no copper-covered corners, but it had a belly like a beluga. This new one reminds me of a high-fashion model: slim, stiff, and tight-lipped. A book and a newspaper, and this Italian satchel is *"fullisimo."*

The bag looks nice but does nothing.

Is that the kind of God you want? Is that the kind of God we have?

David's answer is a resounding no. "You want to know who God really is?" he asks. "Then read this." And he writes the name *Yahweh.* "Yahweh is my shepherd."

Though foreign to us, the name was rich to David. So rich, in fact, that David chose *Yahweh* over *El Shaddai* (God Almighty), *El Elyon* (God Most High), and *El Olam* (God the Everlasting). These and many other titles for God were at David's disposal. But when he considered all the options, David chose *Yahweh.*

Why *Yahweh?* Because *Yahweh* is God's name. You can call me preacher or writer or half-baked golfer—these are accurate descriptions, but these aren't my names. I might call you dad, mom, doctor, or student, and those terms may describe you, but they aren't your name. If you want to call me by my name, say *Max.* If I call you by your name, I say it. And if you want to call God by his name, say *Yahweh.*

God has told us his name. (How he must long to be close to us.)

Moses was the first to learn it. Seven centuries prior to David, the eighty-year-old shepherd was tending sheep when the bush began to blaze and his life began to change. Moses was told to return to Egypt and rescue the enslaved Hebrews. He raised more excuses than a kid at bedtime, but God trumped each one. Finally Moses asked,

> "When I go to the Israelites, I will say to them, 'The God of your fathers sent me to you.' What if the people say, 'What is his name?' What should I tell them?"
>
> Then God said to Moses, "I AM WHO I AM. When you go to the people of Israel, tell them, 'I AM sent me to you.'" (Exod. 3:13–14)

God would later remind Moses: "I am Yahweh. To Abraham and Isaac and Jacob I appeared as El Shaddai; I did not make myself known to them by my name Yahweh" (Exod. 6:2–3 JB).

The Israelites considered the name too holy to be spoken by human lips. Whenever they needed to say *Yahweh,* they substituted the word *Adonai,* which means "Lord." If the name needed to be written, the scribes would take a bath before they wrote it and destroy the pen afterward.[2]

God never gives a definition of the word *Yahweh,* and Moses never requests one. Many scholars wish he had, for the study of the name has raised some healthy discussions.

The name I AM sounds strikingly close to the Hebrew verb *to be—havah.* It's quite possibly a combination of the present tense form (I am) and the causative tense (I cause to be). *Yahweh,* then, seems to mean "I AM" and "I cause." God is the "One who is" and the "One who causes."

Why is that important? Because we need a big God. And if God is the "One who is," then he is an unchanging God.

Think about it. Do you know anyone who goes around saying, "I am"? Neither do I. When we say "I am," we always add another word. "I am *happy.*" "I am *sad.*" "I am *strong.*" "I am *Max.*" God, however, starkly states, "I AM" and adds nothing else.

"You are what?" we want to ask. "I AM," he replies. God needs no descriptive word because he never changes. God is what he is. He is what he has always been. His immutability motivated the psalmist to declare, "But thou art the same" (Ps. 102:27 KJV). The writer is saying, "You are the One who is. You never change."[3] Yahweh is an unchanging God.

He is also an uncaused God.

Though he creates, God was never created. Though he makes, he was never made. Though he causes, he was never caused. Hence the psalmist's proclamation: "Before the mountains were born or you brought forth the earth and the world, from everlasting to everlasting you are God" (Ps. 90:2 NIV).

God is Yahweh—an unchanging God, an uncaused God, and an ungoverned God.

You and I are governed. The weather determines what we wear. The terrain tells us how to travel. Gravity dictates our speed, and health determines our strength. We may challenge these forces and alter them slightly, but we never remove them.

God—our Shepherd—doesn't check the weather; he makes it. He doesn't defy gravity; he created it. He isn't affected by health; he has no body. Jesus said, "God is spirit" (John 4:24). Since he has no body, he has no limitations—equally active in Cambodia as he is in Connecticut. "Where can I go to get away from your Spirit?" asked David. "Where can I run from you? If I go up to the heavens, you are there. If I lie down in the grave, you are there" (Ps. 139:7–8).

Unchanging. Uncaused. Ungoverned. These are only a fraction of God's qualities, but aren't they enough to give you a glimpse of your Father? Don't we need this kind of shepherd? Don't we need an unchanging shepherd?

When Lloyd Douglas, author of *The Robe* and other novels, attended college, he lived in a boardinghouse. A retired, wheelchair-bound music professor resided on the first floor. Each morning Douglas would stick his head in the door of the teacher's apartment and ask the same question, "Well, what's the good news?" The old man would pick up his tuning fork, tap it on the side of the wheelchair, and say, "That's middle C! It was middle C yesterday; it will be middle C tomorrow; it will be middle C a thousand years from now. The tenor upstairs sings flat. The piano across the hall is out of tune, but, my friend, that is middle C."[4]

You and I need a middle C. Haven't you had enough change in your life? Relationships change. Health changes. The weather changes. But the Yahweh who ruled the earth last night is the same Yahweh who rules it today. Same convictions. Same plan. Same mood. Same love. He never changes. You can no more alter God than a pebble can alter the rhythm of the Pacific. Yahweh is our middle C. A still point in a turning world. Don't we need a still point? Don't we need an unchanging shepherd?

We equally need an uncaused shepherd. No one breathed life into Yahweh. No one sired him. No one gave birth to him. No one caused him. No act brought him forth.

And since no act brought him forth, no act can take him out. Does he fear an earthquake? Does he tremble at a tornado? Hardly. Yahweh sleeps through storms and calms the winds with a word. Cancer does not trouble him, and cemeteries do not disturb him. He was here before they came. He'll be here after they are gone. He is uncaused.

And he is ungoverned. Counselors can comfort you *in* the storm, but you need a God who can *still* the storm. Friends can hold your hand at your deathbed, but you need a Yahweh who has defeated the grave. Philosophers can debate the meaning of life, but you need a Lord who can declare the meaning of life.

You need a Yahweh.

You don't need what Dorothy found. Remember her discovery in *The Wonderful Wizard of Oz*? She and her trio followed the yellow-brick road only to discover that the wizard was a wimp! Nothing but smoke and mirrors and tin-drum thunder. Is that the kind of god you need?

You don't need to carry the burden of a lesser god . . . a god on a shelf, a god in a box, or a god in a bottle. No, you need a God who can place 100 billion stars in our galaxy and 100 billion galaxies in the universe. You need a God who can shape two fists of flesh into 75 to 100 billion nerve cells, each with as many as 10,000 connections to other nerve cells, place it in a skull, and call it a brain.[5]

And you need a God who, while so mind-numbingly mighty, can come in the soft of night and touch you with the tenderness of an April snow.

You need a Yahweh.

And, according to David, you have one. He is your shepherd.

3

I'll Do It My Way

The Burden of Self-Reliance

The Lord *is my shepherd.*

Psalm 23:1 NKJV

ou say you can swing a club like Tiger Woods? That's saying a lot.

You hope to score touchdowns like Joe Montana? You'll have to work hard.

And you, young lady? You aspire to be the next Mia Hamm? Good for you.

And me? Well, actually there is one fellow who's caught my attention. He reminds me of me. You've probably never heard of him. Did you see the British Open in '99? Yeah, the one in Carnoustie, Scotland? Remember the player who had a seven-stroke lead with one hole to go?

That's right, the Frenchman. Jean Van de Velde. He was six strokes and 480 yards away from a major championship, a wad of cash, and a place in history. All he needed to do was score a six on a par four.

I could shoot a six on a par four. My mother could make a six on a par four. This guy could shoot a six with a waffle iron and a banana. Tell the trophy engraver to warm up the pen and practice his *V*s. He'll need two to write "Jean Van de Velde."

Granted the hole was not easy. Bisected three times by a "wee burn," the Scottish term for a marshy creek. No sweat. Hit three short shots . . . putt three times if you have to. Just take a six, win the hole, and smile for the cameras. Besides it's windy, and the "wee burn" is wee deep. Don't flirt with it.

Oh, but the French love to flirt. Van de Velde pulls out his driver, and somewhere in Des Moines an armchair duffer who'd been lured to sleep by the seven-stroke lead opens one eye. *He's holding a driver?*

Van de Velde's caddie was a thirty-year-old Parisian named Christopher with untidy English and a paintbrush on his chin and bleached hair under his hat. "I think he and I—we want too much show," he later confessed.

Van de Velde pushes his drive halfway to the Eiffel Tower. Now he has 240 yards to the green with nothing but deep grass and heartache in between. Surely he will hit a short shot back in the fairway.

Logic says, "Don't go for the green."

Golf 101 says, "Don't go for the green."

Every Scot in the gallery says, "Aye, laddie. Don't go for the green."

Van de Velde says, "I'm going for the green."

He pulls out a two iron, and the armchair golfer in Des Moines opens the other eye. *A two iron!? Maybe if you're teed up on the beach, trying to hit into the Caribbean!* The spectators are silent. Most out of respect. A few in prayer. Van de Velde's two iron becomes a FORE! iron. *Whack. Clang. Plop.* The ball caroms off the bleachers and disappears into marsh tall enough to hide a lawn gnome.

His lie would've made Pinocchio's nose grow. The next shot lands in the water and the next in the sand. Tally the damage, and you've got four strokes plus a penalty. He's lying five and not on the green. So much for winning the hole. By now he's praying for a seven and a tie. To the great relief of the civilized world, Van de Velde makes the seven. You've got to wonder if he ever recovered from the "wee burn." He lost the play-off.

Golf, like nylon running shorts, reveals a lot about a person. What the eighteenth hole revealed about Van de Velde reminds me of me.

I've done the same thing. The same blasted thing. All he needed was a five iron, but he had to go and pull out the driver. Or, in my case:

All I needed to do was apologize, but I had to argue.

All I needed to do was listen, but I had to open my big mouth.

All I needed to do was be patient, but I had to take control.

All I had to do was give it to God, but I tried to fix it myself.

Why don't I leave the driver in the bag? I know how Christopher the caddie would answer: "I think he and I and Max—we want too much show."

Too much stubbornness. Too much independence. Too much self-reliance.

I don't need advice—*Whack.*

I can handle this myself—*Clang.*

I don't need a shepherd, thank you—*Plop.*

Can you relate? Are Jean and I the only ones to make an anthem out of Sinatra's song "I Did It My Way"? Are we the only two dragging around the cast-iron chest of self-reliance? I don't think so.

We humans want to do things our way. Forget the easy way. Forget the common way. Forget the best way. Forget God's way. We want to do things *our* way.

And, according to the Bible, that's precisely our problem. "We all have wandered away like sheep; each of us has gone his own way" (Isa. 53:6).

You wouldn't think sheep would be obstinate. Of all God's animals, the sheep is the least able to take care of himself.

Sheep are dumb! Have you ever met a sheep trainer? Ever seen sheep tricks? Know anyone who has taught his sheep to roll over? Ever witnessed a circus sideshow featuring "Mazadon and his jumping sheep"? No. Sheep are just too dumb.

And defenseless. They have no fangs or claws. They can't bite you or outrun you. That's why you never see sheep as team mascots. We've heard of the St. Louis Rams and the Chicago Bulls and the Seattle

Seahawks, but the New York Lambs? Who wants to be a lamb? You couldn't even stir up a decent yell for the cheerleaders.

> We are the sheep.
> We don't make a peep.
> Victory is yours to keep.
> But count us if you want to sleep.

What's more, sheep are dirty. A cat can clean itself. So can a dog. We see a bird in a birdbath or a bear in a river. But sheep? They get dirty and stay that way.

Couldn't David have thought of a better metaphor? Surely he could have. After all, he outran Saul and outgunned Goliath. Why didn't he choose something other than sheep?

How about:

"The Lord is my commander in chief, and I am his warrior." There. We like that better. A warrior gets a uniform and a weapon, maybe even a medal.

Or, "The Lord is my inspiration, and I am his singer." We are in God's choir; what a flattering assignment.

Or, "The Lord is my king, and I am his ambassador." Who wouldn't like to be a spokesperson for God?

Everyone stops when the ambassador speaks. Everyone listens when God's minstrel sings. Everyone applauds when God's warrior passes.

But who notices when God's sheep show up? Who notices when the sheep sing or speak or act? Only one person notices. The shepherd. And that is precisely David's point.

When David, who was a warrior, minstrel, and ambassador for God, searched for an illustration of God, he remembered his days as a shepherd. He remembered how he lavished attention on the sheep day and night. How he slept with them and watched over them.

And the way he cared for the sheep reminded him of the way God cares for us. David rejoiced to say, "The LORD is my shepherd," and in so doing he proudly implied, "I am his sheep."

Still uncomfortable with being considered a sheep? Will you humor me and take a simple quiz? See if you succeed in self-reliance. Raise your hand if any of the following describe you.

You can control your moods. You're never grumpy or sullen. You can't relate to Jekyll and Hyde. You're always upbeat and upright. Does that describe you? No? Well, let's try another.

You are at peace with everyone. Every relationship as sweet as fudge. Even your old flames speak highly of you. Love all and are loved by all. Is that you? If not, how about this description?

You have no fears. Call you the Teflon toughie. Wall Street plummets—no problem. Heart condition discovered—yawn. World War III starts—what's for dinner? Does this describe you?

You need no forgiveness. Never made a mistake. As square as a game of checkers. As clean as grandma's kitchen. Never cheated, never lied, never lied about cheating. Is that you? No?

Let's evaluate this. You can't control your moods. A few of your relationships are shaky. You have fears and faults. Hmmm. Do you really want to hang on to your chest of self-reliance? Sounds to me as if you could use a shepherd. Otherwise, you might end up with a Twenty-third Psalm like this:

> I am my own shepherd. I am always in need.
> I stumble from mall to mall and shrink to shrink, seeking relief but never finding it.
> I creep through the valley of the shadow of death and fall apart.

I fear everything from pesticides to power lines, and I'm starting to act like my mother.

I go down to the weekly staff meeting and am surrounded by enemies. I go home, and even my goldfish scowls at me.

I anoint my headache with extra-strength Tylenol.

My Jack Daniel's runneth over.

Surely misery and misfortune will follow me, and I will live in self-doubt for the rest of my lonely life.

Why is it that the ones who most need a shepherd resist him so?

Ah, now there is a question for the Van de Veldes of life. Scripture says, "Do it God's way." Experience says, "Do it God's way." Every Scot in heaven begs, "Aye, laddie, do it God's way."

And, every so often, we do. And when we do, when we follow the lead of *Notre Dieu* and keep the driver in the bag, somehow the ball stays in the fairway.

Yes, Van de Velde reminds me of me.

After losing the play-off hole, he kept his composure for the crowds. But once he sat in the scorer's tent, he buried his face in his hands. "Next time I'll hit zee wedge," he sobbed. "You'll say I'm a coward, but next time I'll hit zee wedge."

You and me both, Jean.[1]

4

The Prison of Want

The Burden of Discontent

The Lord *is my shepherd; I shall not want.*

Psalm 23:1 NKJV

Come with me to the most populated prison in the world. The facility has more inmates than bunks. More prisoners than plates. More residents than resources.

Come with me to the world's most oppressive prison. Just ask the inmates; they will tell you. They are overworked and underfed. Their walls are bare and bunks are hard.

No prison is so populated, no prison so oppressive, and, what's more, no prison is so permanent. Most inmates never leave. They never escape. They never get released. They serve a life sentence in this overcrowded, underprovisioned facility.

The name of the prison? You'll see it over the entrance. Rainbowed over the gate are four cast-iron letters that spell out its name:

W-A-N-T

The prison of want. You've seen her prisoners. They are "in want." They want something. They want something bigger. Nicer. Faster. Thinner. They want.

They don't want much, mind you. They want just one thing. One new job. One new car. One new house. One new spouse. They don't want much. They want just one.

And when they have "one," they will be happy. And they are right—

they will be happy. When they have "one," they will leave the prison. But then it happens. The new-car smell passes. The new job gets old. The neighbors buy a larger television set. The new spouse has bad habits. The sizzle fizzles, and before you know it, another ex-con breaks parole and returns to jail.

Are you in prison? You are if you feel better when you have more and worse when you have less. You are if joy is one delivery away, one transfer away, one award away, or one makeover away. If your happiness comes from something you deposit, drive, drink, or digest, then face it—you are in prison, the prison of want.

That's the bad news. The good news is, you have a visitor. And your visitor has a message that can get you paroled. Make your way to the receiving room. Take your seat in the chair, and look across the table at the psalmist David. He motions for you to lean forward. "I have a secret to tell you," he whispers, "the secret of satisfaction. 'The LORD is my shepherd; I shall not want'" (Ps. 23:1 NKJV).

David has found the pasture where discontent goes to die. It's as if he is saying, "What I have in God is greater than what I don't have in life."

You think you and I could learn to say the same?

Think for just a moment about the things you own. Think about the house you have, the car you drive, the money you've saved. Think about the jewelry you've inherited and the stocks you've traded and the clothes you've purchased. Envision all your stuff, and let me remind you of two biblical truths.

Your stuff isn't yours. Ask any coroner. Ask any embalmer. Ask any funeral-home director. No one takes anything with him. When one of the wealthiest men in history, John D. Rockefeller, died, his accountant was asked, "How much did John D. leave?" The accountant's reply? "All of it."[1]

"Naked a man comes from his mother's womb, and as he comes, so he departs. He takes nothing from his labor that he can carry in his hand" (Eccles. 5:15 NIV).

All that stuff—it's not yours. And you know what else about all that stuff? *It's not you.* Who you are has nothing to do with the clothes you wear or the car you drive. Jesus said, "Life is not defined by what you have, even when you have a lot" (Luke 12:15 MSG). Heaven does not know you as the fellow with the nice suit or the woman with the big house or the kid with the new bike. Heaven knows your heart. "The LORD does not look at the things man looks at. Man looks at the outward appearance, but the LORD looks at the heart" (1 Sam. 16:7 NIV). When God thinks of you, he may see your compassion, your devotion, your tenderness or quick mind, but he doesn't think of your things.

And when you think of you, you shouldn't either. Define yourself by your stuff, and you'll feel good when you have a lot and bad when you don't. Contentment comes when we can honestly say with Paul: "I have learned to be satisfied with the things I have. . . . I know how to live when I am poor, and I know how to live when I have plenty" (Phil. 4:11–12).

Doug McKnight could say those words. At the age of thirty-two he was diagnosed with multiple sclerosis. Over the next sixteen years it would cost him his career, his mobility, and eventually his life. Because of MS, he couldn't feed himself or walk; he battled depression and fear. But through it all, Doug never lost his sense of gratitude. Evidence of this was seen in his prayer list. Friends in his congregation asked him to compile a list of requests so they could intercede for him. His response included eighteen blessings for which to be grateful and six concerns for which to be prayerful. His blessings outweighed his needs by three times. Doug McKnight had learned to be content.[2]

So had the leper on the island of Tobago. A short-term missionary met her on a mission trip. On the final day, he was leading worship in a leper colony. He asked if anyone had a favorite song. When he did, a woman turned around, and he saw the most disfigured face he'd ever seen. She had no ears and no nose. Her lips were gone. But she raised a fingerless hand and asked, "Could we sing 'Count Your Many Blessings'?"

The missionary started the song but couldn't finish. Someone later commented, "I suppose you'll never be able to sing the song again." He answered, "No, I'll sing it again. Just never in the same way."[3]

Are you hoping that a change in circumstances will bring a change in your attitude? If so, you are in prison, and you need to learn a secret of traveling light. *What you have in your Shepherd is greater than what you don't have in life.*

May I meddle for a moment? What is the one thing separating you from joy? How do you fill in this blank: "I will be happy when ____________________"? When I am healed. When I am promoted. When I am married. When I am single. When I am rich. How would you finish that statement?

Now, with your answer firmly in mind, answer this. If your ship never comes in, if your dream never comes true, if the situation never changes, could you be happy? If not, then you are sleeping in the cold cell of discontent. You are in prison. And you need to know what you have in your Shepherd.

You have a God who hears you, the power of love behind you, the Holy Spirit within you, and all of heaven ahead of you. If you have the Shepherd, you have grace for every sin, direction for every turn, a candle for every corner, and an anchor for every storm. You have everything you need.

And who can take it from you? Can leukemia infect your salvation? Can bankruptcy impoverish your prayers? A tornado might take your earthly house, but will it touch your heavenly home?

And look at your position. Why clamor for prestige and power? Are you not already privileged to be part of the greatest work in history?

According to Russ Blowers, we are. He is a minister in Indianapolis. Knowing he would be asked about his profession at a Rotary Club meeting, he resolved to say more than "I'm a preacher."

Instead he explained, "Hi, I'm Russ Blowers. I'm with a global enterprise. We have branches in every country in the world. We have representatives in nearly every parliament and boardroom on earth. We're into motivation and behavior alteration. We run hospitals, feeding stations, crisis-pregnancy centers, universities, publishing houses, and nursing homes. We care for our clients from birth to death. We are into life insurance and fire insurance. We perform spiritual heart transplants. Our original Organizer owns all the real estate on earth plus an assortment of galaxies and constellations. He knows everything and lives everywhere. Our product is free for the asking. (There's not enough money to buy it.) Our CEO was born in a hick town, worked as a carpenter, didn't own a home, was misunderstood by his family and hated by his enemies, walked on water, was condemned to death without a trial, and arose from the dead. I talk with him every day."[4]

If you can say the same, don't you have reason to be content?

A man once went to a minister for counseling. He was in the midst of a financial collapse. "I've lost everything," he bemoaned.

"Oh, I'm so sorry to hear that you've lost your faith."

"No," the man corrected him, "I haven't lost my faith."

"Well, then I'm sad to hear that you've lost your character."

"I didn't say that," he corrected. "I still have my character."

"I'm so sorry to hear that you've lost your salvation."

"That's not what I said," the man objected. "I haven't lost my salvation."

"You have your faith, your character, your salvation. Seems to me," the minister observed, "that you've lost none of the things that really matter."

We haven't either. You and I could pray like the Puritan. He sat down to a meal of bread and water. He bowed his head and declared, "All this and Jesus too?"

Can't we be equally content? Paul says that "godliness with contentment is great gain" (1 Tim. 6:6 NIV). When we surrender to God the cumbersome sack of discontent, we don't just give up something; we gain something. God replaces it with a lightweight, tailor-made, sorrow-resistant attaché of gratitude.

What will you gain with contentment? You may gain your marriage. You may gain precious hours with your children. You may gain your self-respect. You may gain joy. You may gain the faith to say, "The LORD is my shepherd; I shall not want."

Try saying it slowly. "The LORD is my shepherd; I shall not want."

Again, "The LORD is my shepherd; I shall not want."

Again, "The LORD is my shepherd; I shall not want."

Shhhhhhh. Did you hear something? I think I did. I'm not sure . . . but I think I heard the opening of a jail door.

5

I Will Give You Rest

The Burden of Weariness

He makes me to lie down in green pastures.

PSALM 23:2 NKJV

I'll give you the consequences of the burden; you guess the cause.

- It afflicts 70 million Americans and is faulted for 38,000 deaths each year.
- The condition annually costs the U.S. $70 billion worth of productivity.
- Teenagers suffer from it. Studies show that 64 percent of teens blame it for poor school performance.
- Middle agers face it. Researchers say the most severe cases occur between ages thirty and forty.
- Senior citizens are afflicted by it. One study suggests that the condition impacts 50 percent of the over-sixty-five population.
- Treatments involve everything from mouth guards to herbal teas to medication.[1]

Any idea what's being described?

Chemical abuse? Divorce? Long sermons? None of those answers are correct, though the last one was a good hunch. The answer may surprise you. Insomnia. America can't get to sleep.

For most of my life I secretly snickered at the thought of sleep difficulties. My problem was not in going to sleep. My problem was staying awake. But a few years ago I went to bed one night, closed my eyes, and nothing happened. I didn't fall asleep. Rather than slow to a halt, my mind kicked into high gear. A thousand and one obligations rushed at me. Midnight passed, and I was still awake. I drank some milk, returned to bed. I was still awake. I woke up Denalyn, using the blue ribbon of dumb questions, "Are you awake?" She told me to quit thinking about things. So I did. I quit thinking about things and started thinking about people. But as I thought of people, I thought of what those people were doing. They were sleeping. That made me mad and kept me awake. Finally, somewhere in the early hours of the morning, having been initiated into the fraternity of 70 million sleepless Americans, I dozed off.

I don't snicker at the thought of sleep difficulties anymore. Nor do I question the inclusion of the verse about rest in the Twenty-third Psalm.

People with too much work and too little sleep step over to the baggage claim of life and grab the duffel bag of weariness. You don't carry this one. You don't hoist it onto your shoulder and stride down the street. You drag it as you would a stubborn St. Bernard. Weariness wearies.

Why are we so tired? Have you read a newspaper lately? We long to have the life of Huck and Tom on the Mississippi, but look at us riding the white waters of the Rio Grande. Forks in the river. Rocks in the water. Heart attacks, betrayal, credit-card debt, and custody battles. Huck and Tom didn't have to face these kinds of things. We do, however, and they keep us awake. And since we can't sleep, we have a second problem.

Our bodies are tired. Think about it. If 70 million Americans aren't sleeping enough, what does that mean? That means one-third of our country is dozing off at work, napping through class, or sleeping at the wheel. (Fifteen hundred road deaths per year are blamed on heavy-eyed truckdrivers.) Some even snooze while reading Lucado books.

(Hard to fathom, I know.) Thirty tons of aspirins, sleeping pills, and tranquilizers are consumed every day![2] The energy gauge on the dashboard of our forehead says empty.

Were we to invite an alien to solve our problem, he'd suggest a simple solution—everybody go to sleep. We'd laugh at him. He doesn't understand the way we work. Literally. He doesn't understand *the way* we work. We work hard. There is money to be made. Degrees to be earned. Ladders to be climbed. In our book, busyness is next to godliness. We idolize Thomas Edison, who claimed he could live on fifteen-minute naps. Somehow we forget to mention Albert Einstein, who averaged eleven hours of sleep a night.[3] In 1910 Americans slept nine hours a night; today we sleep seven and are proud of it. And we are tired because of it. Our minds are tired. Our bodies are tired. But much more important, our souls are tired.

We are eternal creatures, and we ask eternal questions: Where did I come from? Where am I going? What is the meaning of life? What is right? What is wrong? Is there life after death? These are the primal questions of the soul. And left unanswered, such questions will steal our rest.

Only one other living creature has as much trouble resting as we do. Not dogs. They doze. Not bears. They hibernate. Cats invented the catnap, and the sloths slumber twenty hours a day. (So that's what I was rooming with my sophomore year in college.) Most animals know how to rest. There is one exception. These creatures are woolly, simpleminded, and slow. No, not husbands on Saturday—sheep! Sheep can't sleep.

For sheep to sleep, everything must be just right. No predators. No tension in the flock. No bugs in the air. No hunger in the belly.[4] Everything has to be just so.

Unfortunately, sheep cannot find safe pasture, nor can they spray insecticide, deal with the frictions, or find food. They need help. They need a shepherd to "lead them" and help them "lie down in green pastures." Without a shepherd, they can't rest.

Without a shepherd, neither can we.

In the second verse of the Twenty-third Psalm, David the poet becomes David the artist. His quill becomes a brush, his parchment a canvas, and his words paint a picture. A flock of sheep on folded legs, encircling a shepherd. Bellies nestled deep in the long shoots of grass. A still pond on one side, the watching shepherd on the other. "He makes me to lie down in green pastures; He leads me beside the still waters" (Ps. 23:2 NKJV).

Note the two pronouns preceding the two verbs. *He* makes me . . . *He* leads me . . .

Who is the active one? Who is in charge? The shepherd. The shepherd selects the trail and prepares the pasture. The sheep's job—our job—is to watch the shepherd. With our eyes on our Shepherd, we'll be able to get some sleep. "You will keep him in perfect peace, whose mind is stayed on You" (Isa. 26:3 NKJV).

May I show you something? Flip to the back of this book, and look at an empty page. When you look at it, what do you see? What you see is a white piece of paper. Now place a dot in the center of the sheet. Look at it again. Now what do you see? You see the dot, don't you? And isn't that our problem? We let the dark marks eclipse the white space.

We see the waves of the water rather than the Savior walking through them. We focus on our paltry provisions rather than on the One who can feed five thousand hungry people. We concentrate on the dark Fridays of crucifixion and miss the bright Sundays of resurrection.

Change your focus and relax.

And while you are at it, change your schedule and rest!

The other day my wife met a friend at a restaurant for coffee. The two entered the parking lot at the same time. When Denalyn stepped out of her car, she saw her friend waving her over. Denalyn thought she was saying something, but she couldn't hear a word. A jack-hammer was pounding pavement only a few feet away. She walked toward her friend, who, as it turned out, was just saying hello, and the two entered the restaurant.

When it came time to leave, my wife couldn't find her keys. She looked in her purse, on the floor, in her friend's car. Finally when she went to her car, there they were. Not only were the keys in the ignition, the car was running. It had been running the entire time she and her friend were in the café.

Denalyn blames the oversight on the noise. "Everything was so loud, I forgot to turn it off."

The world gets that way. Life can get so loud we forget to shut it down. Maybe that's why God made such a big deal about rest in the Ten Commandments.

Since you did so well on the dot exercise, let me give you another. Of the ten declarations carved in the tablets, which one occupies the most space? Murder? Adultery? Stealing? You'd think so. Certainly each is worthy of ample coverage. But curiously, these commands are tributes to brevity. God needed only five English words to condemn adultery and four to denounce thievery and murder.

But when he came to the topic of rest, one sentence would not suffice.

> Remember the Sabbath day, to keep it holy. Six days you shall labor and do all your work, but the seventh day is the Sabbath of the LORD your God. In it you shall do no work: you, nor your son, nor your daughter, nor your manservant, nor your maidservant, nor your cattle, nor your stranger who is within your gates. For in six days the LORD made the heavens and the earth, the sea, and all that is in them, and rested the

> seventh day. Therefore the LORD blessed the Sabbath day and hallowed it. (Exod. 20:8–11 NKJV)

God knows us so well. He can see the store owner reading this verse and thinking, "Somebody needs to work that day. If I can't, my son will." So God says, *Nor your son.* "Then my daughter will." *Nor your daughter.* "Then maybe an employee." *Nor them.* "I guess I'll have to send my cow to run the store, or maybe I'll find some stranger to help me." *No,* God says. *One day of the week you will say no to work and yes to worship. You will slow and sit down and lie down and rest.*

Still we object. "But . . . but . . . but . . . who is going to run the store?" "What about my grades?" "I've got my sales quota." We offer up one reason after another, but God silences them all with a poignant reminder: "In six days the LORD made the heavens and the earth, the sea, and all that is in them, and rested the seventh day." God's message is plain: "If creation didn't crash when I rested, it won't crash when you do."

Repeat these words after me: It is not my job to run the world.

A century ago Charles Spurgeon gave this advice to his preaching students:

> Even beasts of burden must be turned out to grass occasionally; the very sea pauses at ebb and flood; earth keeps the Sabbath of the wintry months; and man, even when exalted to God's ambassador, must rest or faint, must trim his lamp or let it burn low; must recruit his vigor or grow prematurely old. . . . In the long run we shall do more by sometimes doing less.[5]

The bow cannot always be bent without fear of breaking. For a field to bear fruit, it must occasionally lie fallow. And for you to be healthy, you must rest. Slow down, and God will heal you. He will bring rest to your mind, to your body, and most of all to your soul. He will lead you to green pastures.

Green pastures were not the natural terrain of Judea. The hills around Bethlehem where David kept his flock were not lush and green. Even today they are white and parched. Any green pasture in Judea is the work of some shepherd. He has cleared the rough, rocky land. Stumps have been torn out, and brush has been burned. Irrigation. Cultivation. Such are the work of a shepherd.

Hence, when David says, "He makes me to lie down in green pastures," he is saying, "My shepherd makes me lie down in his finished work." With his own pierced hands, Jesus created a pasture for the soul. He tore out the thorny underbrush of condemnation. He pried loose the huge boulders of sin. In their place he planted seeds of grace and dug ponds of mercy.

And he invites us to rest there. Can you imagine the satisfaction in the heart of the shepherd when, with work completed, he sees his sheep rest in the tender grass?

Can you imagine the satisfaction in the heart of God when we do the same? His pasture is his gift to us. This is not a pasture that you have made. Nor is it a pasture that you deserve. It is a gift of God. "For it is by grace you have been saved, through faith—and this not from yourselves, it is the gift of God" (Eph. 2:8 NIV).

In a world rocky with human failure, there is a land lush with divine mercy. Your Shepherd invites you there. He wants you to lie down. Nestle deeply until you are hidden, buried, in the tall shoots of his love, and there you will find rest.

6

Whaddifs and Howells

The Burden of Worry

He leads me beside the still waters.

PSALM 23:2 NKJV

Your ten-year-old is worried. So anxious he can't eat. So worried he can't sleep. "What's wrong?" you inquire. He shakes his head and moans, "I don't even have a pension plan."

Or your four-year-old is crying in bed. "What's wrong, sweetheart?" She whimpers, "I'll never pass college chemistry."

Your eight-year-old's face is stress-struck. "I'll be a rotten parent. What if I set a poor example for my kids?"

How would you respond to such statements? Besides calling a child psychologist, your response would be emphatic: "You're too young to worry about those things. When the time comes, you'll know what to do."

Fortunately, most kids don't have such thoughts.

Unfortunately, we adults have more than our share. Worry is the burlap bag of burdens. It's overflowing with "whaddifs" and "howells." "Whaddif it rains at my wedding?" "Howell I know when to discipline my kids?" "Whaddif I marry a guy who snores?" "Howell we pay our baby's tuition?" "Whaddif, after all my dieting, they learn that lettuce is fattening and chocolate isn't?"

The burlap bag of worry. Cumbersome. Chunky. Unattractive. Scratchy. Hard to get a handle on. Irritating to carry and impossible to give away. No one wants your worries.

The truth be told, you don't want them either. No one has to remind you of the high cost of anxiety. (But I will anyway.) Worry divides the mind. The biblical word for *worry (merimnao)* is a compound of two Greek words, *merizo* ("to divide") and *nous* ("the mind"). Anxiety splits our energy between today's priorities and tomorrow's problems. Part of our mind is on the now; the rest is on the not yet. The result is half-minded living.

That's not the only result. Worrying is not a disease, but it causes diseases. It has been connected to high blood pressure, heart trouble, blindness, migraine headaches, thyroid malfunctions, and a host of stomach disorders.

Anxiety is an expensive habit. Of course, it might be worth the cost if it worked. But it doesn't. Our frets are futile. Jesus said, "You cannot add any time to your life by worrying about it" (Matt. 6:27). Worry has never brightened a day, solved a problem, or cured a disease.

How can a person deal with anxiety? You might try what one fellow did. He worried so much that he decided to hire someone to do his worrying for him. He found a man who agreed to be his hired worrier for a salary of $200,000 per year. After the man accepted the job, his first question to his boss was, "Where are you going to get $200,000 per year?" To which the man responded, "That's your worry."

Sadly, worrying is one job you can't farm out, but you can overcome it. There is no better place to begin than in verse two of the shepherd's psalm.

"He leads me beside the still waters," David declares. And, in case we missed the point, he repeats the phrase in the next verse: "He leads me in the paths of righteousness."

"He leads me." God isn't behind me, yelling, "Go!" He is ahead of me, bidding, "Come!" He is in front, clearing the path, cutting the brush, showing the way. Just before the curve, he says, "Turn here."

Prior to the rise, he motions, "Step up here." Standing next to the rocks, he warns, "Watch your step here."

He leads us. He tells us what we need to know when we need to know it. As a New Testament writer would affirm: "We will find grace to help us *when we need it*" (Heb. 4:16 NLT, emphasis mine).

Listen to a different translation: "Let us therefore boldly approach the throne of our gracious God, where we may receive mercy and in his grace find *timely help*" (Heb. 4:16 NEB, emphasis mine).

God's help is timely. He helps us the same way a father gives plane tickets to his family. When I travel with my kids, I carry all our tickets in my satchel. When the moment comes to board the plane, I stand between the attendant and the child. As each daughter passes, I place a ticket in her hand. She, in turn, gives the ticket to the attendant. Each one receives the ticket in the nick of time.

What I do for my daughters God does for you. He places himself between you and the need. And at the right time, he gives you the ticket. Wasn't this the promise he gave his disciples? "When you are arrested and judged, don't worry ahead of time about what you should say. Say whatever *is given you to say at that time,* because it will not really be you speaking; it will be the Holy Spirit" (Mark 13:11, emphasis mine).

Isn't this the message God gave the children of Israel? He promised to supply them with manna each day. But he told them to collect only one day's supply at a time. Those who disobeyed and collected enough for two days found themselves with rotten manna. The only exception to the rule was the day prior to the Sabbath. On Friday they could gather twice as much. Otherwise, God would give them what they needed, in their time of need.

God leads us. God will do the right thing at the right time. And what a difference that makes.

Since I know his provision is timely, I can enjoy the present.

"Give your entire attention to what God is doing right now, and don't get worked up about what may or may not happen tomorrow. God will help you deal with whatever hard things come up when the time comes" (Matt. 6:34 MSG).

That last phrase is worthy of your highlighter: "when the time comes."

"I don't know what I'll do if my husband dies." You will, *when the time comes.*

"When my children leave the house, I don't think I can take it." It won't be easy, but strength will arrive *when the time comes.*

"I could never lead a church. There is too much I don't know." You may be right. Or you may be wanting to know everything too soon. Could it be that God will reveal answers to you *when the time comes?*

The key is this: Meet today's problems with today's strength. Don't start tackling tomorrow's problems until tomorrow. You do not have tomorrow's strength yet. You simply have enough for today.

More than eighty years ago a great Canadian man of medicine, Sir William Osler, delivered a speech to the students of Yale University entitled "A Way of Life." In the message he related an event that occurred while he was aboard an ocean liner.

One day while he was visiting with the ship's captain, a loud, piercing alarm sounded, followed by strange grinding and crashing sounds below the deck. "Those are our watertight compartments closing," the captain explained. "It's an important part of our safety drill. In case of real trouble, water leaking into one compartment would not affect the rest of the ship. Even if we should collide with an iceberg, as did the *Titanic,* water rushing in will fill only that particular ruptured compartment. The ship, however, will still remain afloat."

When he spoke to the students at Yale, Osler remembered the captain's description of the boat:

> Each one of you is certainly a much more marvelous organization than that great liner and bound on a far longer voyage. What I urge is that you learn to master your life by living each day in a day-tight compartment and this will certainly ensure your safety throughout your entire journey of life. Touch a button and hear, at every level of your life, the iron doors shutting out the Past—the dead yesterdays. Touch another and shut off, with a metal curtain, the Future—the unborn tomorrows. Then you are safe—safe for today.
>
> Think not of the amount to be accomplished, the difficulties to be overcome, but set earnestly at the little task near your elbow, letting that be sufficient for the day; for surely our plain duty is not to see what lies dimly at a distance but to do what lies clearly at hand.[1]

Jesus made the same point in fewer words: "So don't worry about tomorrow, because tomorrow will have its own worries. Each day has enough trouble of its own" (Matt. 6:34).

Easy to say. Not always easy to do, right? We are so prone to worry. Just last night I was worrying in my sleep. I dreamed that I was diagnosed with ALS, a degenerative muscle disease, which took the life of my father. I awakened from the dream and, right there in the middle of the night, began to worry. Then Jesus' words came to my mind, "Don't worry about tomorrow." And for once, I decided not to. I dropped the burlap sack. After all, why let tomorrow's imaginary problem rob tonight's rest? Can I prevent the disease by staying awake? Will I postpone the affliction by thinking about it? Of course not. So I did the most spiritual thing I could have done. I went back to sleep.

Why don't you do the same? God is leading you. Leave tomorrow's problems until tomorrow.

Arthur Hays Sulzberger was the publisher of the *New York Times* during the Second World War. Because of the world conflict, he found it almost impossible to sleep. He was never able to banish worries from his mind until he adopted as his motto these five words—"one step enough for me"—taken from the hymn "Lead Kindly Light."[2]

> Lead, kindly Light . . .
> Keep Thou my feet; I do not ask to see
> The distant scene; one step enough for me.

God isn't going to let you see the distant scene either. So you might as well quit looking for it. He promises a lamp unto our feet, not a crystal ball into the future.[3] We do not need to know what will happen tomorrow. We only need to know he leads us and "we will find grace to help us when we need it" (Heb. 4:16 NLT).

7

It's a Jungle Out There

The Burden of Hopelessness

He restores my soul.

Psalm 23:3 NKJV

I wonder if you could imagine yourself in a jungle. A dense jungle. A dark jungle. Your friends convinced you it was time for a once-in-a-lifetime trip, and here you are. You paid the fare. You crossed the ocean. You hired the guide and joined the group. And you ventured where you had never ventured before—into the thick, strange world of the jungle.

Sound interesting? Let's take it a step farther. Imagine that you are in the jungle, lost and alone. You paused to lace your boot, and when you looked up, no one was near. You took a chance and went to the right; now you're wondering if the others went to the left. (Or did you go left and they go right?)

Whatever, you are alone. And you have been alone for, well, you don't know how long it has been. Your watch was attached to your pack, and your pack is on the shoulder of the nice guy from New Jersey who volunteered to hold it while you tied your boots. You didn't intend for him to walk off with it. But he did. And here you are, stuck in the middle of nowhere.

You have a problem. First, you were not made for this place. Drop you in the center of avenues and buildings, and you could sniff your way home. But here in sky-blocking foliage? Here in trail-hiding thickets? You are out of your element. You weren't made for this jungle.

What's worse, you aren't equipped. You have no machete. No knife.

No matches. No flares. No food. You aren't equipped, but now you are trapped—and you haven't a clue how to get out.

Sound like fun to you? Me either. Before moving on, let's pause and ask how you would feel. Given such circumstances, what emotions would surface? With what thoughts would you wrestle?

Fear? Of course you would.

Anxiety? To say the least.

Anger? I could understand that. (You'd like to get your hands on those folks who convinced you to take this trip.)

But most of all, what about hopelessness? No idea where to turn. No hunch what to do. Who could blame you for sitting on a log (better check for snakes first), burying your face in your hands, and thinking, *I'll never get out of here.* You have no direction, no equipment, no hope.

Can you freeze frame that emotion for a moment? Can you sense, for just a second, how it feels to be out of your element? Out of solutions? Out of ideas and energy? Can you imagine, just for a moment, how it feels to be out of hope?

If you can, you can relate to many people in this world.

For many people, life is—well, life is a jungle. Not a jungle of trees and beasts. Would that it were so simple. Would that our jungles could be cut with a machete or our adversaries trapped in a cage. But our jungles are comprised of the thicker thickets of failing health, broken hearts, and empty wallets. Our forests are framed with hospital walls and divorce courts. We don't hear the screeching of birds or the roaring of lions, but we do hear the complaints of neighbors and the demands of bosses. Our predators are our creditors, and the brush that surrounds us is the rush that exhausts us.

It's a jungle out there.

And for some, even for many, hope is in short supply. Hopelessness is an odd bag. Unlike the others, it isn't full. It is empty, and its emptiness creates the burden. Unzip the top and examine all the pockets. Turn it upside down and shake it hard. The bag of hopelessness is painfully empty.

Not a very pretty picture, is it? Let's see if we can brighten it up. We've imagined the emotions of being lost; you think we can do the same with being rescued? What would it take to restore your hope? What would you need to reenergize your journey?

Though the answers are abundant, three come quickly to mind.

The first would be a person. Not just any person. You don't need someone equally confused. You need someone who knows the way out.

And from him you need some vision. You need someone to lift your spirits. You need someone to look you in the face and say, "This isn't the end. Don't give up. There is a better place than this. And I'll lead you there."

And, perhaps most important, you need direction. If you have only a person but no renewed vision, all you have is company. If he has a vision but no direction, you have a dreamer for company. But if you have a person with direction—who can take you from this place to the right place—ah, then you have one who can restore your hope.

Or, to use David's words, "He restores my soul."

Our Shepherd majors in restoring hope to the soul. Whether you are a lamb lost on a craggy ledge or a city slicker alone in a deep jungle, everything changes when your rescuer appears.

Your loneliness diminishes, because you have fellowship.

Your despair decreases, because you have vision.

Your confusion begins to lift, because you have direction.

Please note: You haven't left the jungle. The trees still eclipse the sky, and the thorns still cut the skin. Animals lurk and rodents scurry. The jungle is still a jungle. It hasn't changed, but you have. You have changed because you have hope. And you have hope because you have met someone who can lead you out.

Your Shepherd knows that you were not made for this place. He knows you are not equipped for this place. So he has come to guide you out.

He has come to restore your soul. He is the perfect one to do so.

He has the right vision. He reminds you that "you are like foreigners and strangers in this world" (1 Pet. 2:11). And he urges you to lift your eyes from the jungle around you to the heaven above you. "Don't shuffle along, eyes to the ground, absorbed with the things right in front of you. Look up, and be alert to what is going on around Christ. . . . See things from his perspective" (Col. 3:2 MSG).

David said it this way, "I lift up my eyes to the hills—where does my help come from? My help comes from the LORD, the Maker of heaven and earth. He will not let your foot slip—he who watches over you will not slumber. . . . The LORD watches over you . . . the sun will not harm you by day, nor the moon by night. The LORD will keep you from all harm—he will watch over your life" (Ps. 121:1–7 NIV).

God, your rescuer, has the right vision. He also has the right direction. He made the boldest claim in the history of man when he declared, "I am the way" (John 14:6). People wondered if the claim was accurate. He answered their questions by cutting a path through the underbrush of sin and death . . . and escaping alive. He's the only One who ever did. And he is the only One who can help you and me do the same.

He has the right vision: He has seen the homeland. He has the right directions: He has cut the path. But most of all, he is the right person, for he is our God. Who knows the jungle better than the One who made it? And who knows the pitfalls of the path better than the One who has walked it?

The story is told of a man on an African safari deep in the jungle. The guide before him had a machete and was whacking away the tall weeds and thick underbrush. The traveler, wearied and hot, asked in frustration, "Where are we? Do you know where you are taking me? Where is the path?!" The seasoned guide stopped and looked back at the man and replied, "I am the path."

We ask the same questions, don't we? We ask God, "Where are you taking me? Where is the path?" And he, like the guide, doesn't tell us. Oh, he may give us a hint or two, but that's all. If he did, would we understand? Would we comprehend our location? No, like the traveler, we are unacquainted with this jungle. So rather than give us an answer, Jesus gives us a far greater gift. He gives us himself.

Does he remove the jungle? No, the vegetation is still thick.

Does he purge the predators? No, danger still lurks.

Jesus doesn't give hope by changing the jungle; he restores our hope by giving us himself. And he has promised to stay until the very end. "I am with you always, to the very end of the age" (Matt. 28:20 NIV).

We need that reminder. We all need that reminder. For all of us need hope.

Some of you don't need it right now. Your jungle has become a meadow and your journey a delight. If such is the case, congratulations. But remember—we do not know what tomorrow holds. We do not know where this road will lead. You may be one turn from a cemetery, from a hospital bed, from an empty house. You may be a bend in the road from a jungle.

And though you don't need your hope restored today, you may tomorrow. And you need to know to whom to turn.

Or perhaps you do need hope today. You know you were not made for this place. You know you are not equipped. You want someone to lead you out.

If so, call out for your Shepherd. He knows your voice. And he's just waiting for your request.

8

A Heavenly Exchange

The Burden of Guilt

He leads me in the paths of righteousness for His name's sake.

PSALM 23:3 NKJV

A friend organized a Christmas cookie swap for our church office staff. The plan was simple. Price of admission was a tray of cookies. Your tray entitled you to pick cookies from the other trays. You could leave with as many cookies as you brought.

Sounds simple, if you know how to cook. But what if you can't? What if you can't tell a pan from a pot? What if, like me, you are culinarily challenged? What if you're as comfortable in an apron as a bodybuilder in a tutu? If such is the case, you've got a problem.

Such was the case, and I had a problem. I had no cookies to bring; hence I would have no place at the party. I would be left out, turned away, shunned, eschewed, and dismissed. (Are you feeling sorry for me yet?)

This was my plight.

And, forgive me for bringing it up, but your plight's even worse.

God is planning a party . . . a party to end all parties. Not a cookie party, but a feast. Not giggles and chitchat in the conference room, but wide-eyed wonder in the throne room of God.

Yes, the guestlist is impressive. Your question to Jonah about undergoing a gut check in a fish gut? You'll be able to ask him. But more impressive than the names of the guests is the nature of the guests. No egos, no power plays. Guilt, shame, and sorrow will be checked at the gate. Disease, death, and depression will be the Black Plagues of a distant past. What we now see daily, there we will never see.

And what we now see vaguely, there we will see clearly. We will see God. Not by faith. Not through the eyes of Moses or Abraham or David. Not via Scripture or sunsets or summer rains. We will see not God's work or words, but we will see him! For he is not the host of the party; he is the party. His goodness is the banquet. His voice is the music. His radiance is the light, and his love is the endless topic of discussion.

There is only one hitch. The price of admission is somewhat steep. In order to come to the party, you need to be righteous. Not good. Not decent. Not a taxpayer or churchgoer.

Citizens of heaven are righteous. R-i-g-h-t.

All of us *occasionally* do what is right. A few *predominantly* do what is right. But do any of us *always* do what is right? According to Paul we don't. "There is none righteous, no, not one" (Rom. 3:10 NKJV).

Paul is adamant about this. He goes on to say, "No one anywhere has kept on doing what is right; not one" (Rom. 3:12 TLB).

Some may beg to differ. "I'm not perfect, Max, but I'm better than most folks. I've led a good life. I don't break the rules. I don't break hearts. I help people. I like people. Compared to others, I think I could say I'm a righteous person."

I used to try that one on my mother. She'd tell me my room wasn't clean, and I'd ask her to go with me to my brother's room. His was always messier than mine. "See, my room is clean; just look at his."

Never worked. She'd walk me down the hall to her room. When it came to tidy rooms, my mom was righteous. Her closet was just right. Her bed was just right. Her bathroom was just right. Compared to hers, my room was, well, just wrong. She would show me her room and say, "This is what I mean by clean."

God does the same. He points to himself and says, "This is what I mean by righteousness."

Righteousness is who God is.

"Our God and Savior Jesus Christ does what is right" (2 Pet. 1:1).

"God is a righteous judge" (Ps. 7:11 NIV).

"The LORD is righteous, he loves justice" (Ps. 11:7 NIV).

God's righteousness "endures forever" (Ps. 112:3 NIV) and "reaches to the skies" (Ps. 71:19 NIV).

Isaiah described God as "a righteous God and a Savior" (Isa. 45:21 NIV).

On the eve of his death, Jesus began his prayer with the words "Righteous Father" (John 17:25 NIV).

Get the point? God is righteous. His decrees are righteous (Rom. 1:32). His judgment is righteous (Rom. 2:5). His requirements are righteous (Rom. 8:4). His acts are righteous (Dan. 9:16). Daniel declared, "Our God is right in everything he does" (Dan. 9:14).

God is never wrong. He has never rendered a wrong decision, experienced the wrong attitude, taken the wrong path, said the wrong thing, or acted the wrong way. He is never too late or too early, too loud or too soft, too fast or too slow. He has always been and always will be right. He is righteous.

When it comes to righteousness, God runs the table without so much as a bank shot. And when it comes to righteousness, we don't know which end of the cue stick to hold. Hence, our plight.

Will God, who is righteous, spend eternity with those who are not? Would Harvard admit a third-grade dropout? If it did, the act might be benevolent, but it wouldn't be right. If God accepted the unrighteous, the invitation would be even nicer, but would he be right? Would he be right to overlook our sins? Lower his standards? No. He wouldn't be right. And if God is anything, he is right.

He told Isaiah that righteousness would be his plumb line, the standard by which his house is measured (Isa. 28:17). If we are unrighteous, then, we are left in the hallway with no cookies. Or to use Paul's analogy, "we're sinners, every one of us, in the same sinking boat with everybody else" (Rom. 3:19 MSG). Then what are we to do?

Carry a load of guilt? Many do. So many do.

What if our spiritual baggage were visible? Suppose the luggage in our hearts was literal luggage on the street. You know what you'd see most of all? Suitcases of guilt. Bags bulging with binges, blowups, and compromises. Look around you. The fellow in the gray-flannel suit? He's dragging a decade of regrets. The kid with the baggy jeans and nose ring? He'd give anything to retract the words he said to his mother. But he can't. So he tows them along. The woman in the business suit? Looks as if she could run for senator? She'd rather run for help, but she can't run at all. Not hauling that carpetbag of cagmag everywhere she goes.

Listen. The weight of weariness pulls you down. Self-reliance misleads you. Disappointments discourage you. Anxiety plagues you. But guilt? Guilt consumes you.

So what do we do? Our Lord is right, and we are wrong. His party is for the guiltless, and we are anything but. What do we do?

I can tell you what I did. I confessed my need. Remember my cookie dilemma? This is the e-mail I sent to the whole staff. "I can't cook, so I can't be at the party."

Did any of the assistants have mercy on me? No.

Did any of the staff have mercy on me? No.

Did any of the Supreme Court justices have mercy upon me? No.

But a saintly sister in the church did have mercy on me. How she heard of my problem, I do not know. Perhaps my name found its way on an emergency prayer list. But I do know this. Only moments before the celebration, I was given a gift, a plate of cookies, twelve circles of kindness.

And by virtue of that gift, I was privileged a place at the party.

Did I go? You bet your cookies I did. Like a prince carrying a crown on a pillow, I carried my gift into the room, set it on the table, and stood tall. And because some good soul heard my plea, I was given a place at the table.

And because God hears your plea, you'll be given the same. Only, he did more—oh, so much more—than bake cookies for you.

It was, at once, history's most beautiful and most horrible moment. Jesus stood in the tribunal of heaven. Sweeping a hand over all creation, he pleaded, "Punish me for their mistakes. See the murderer? Give me his penalty. The adulteress? I'll take her shame. The bigot, the liar, the thief? Do to me what you would do to them. Treat me as you would a sinner."

And God did. "For Christ died for sins once for all, the righteous for the unrighteous, to bring you to God" (1 Pet. 3:18 NIV).

Yes, righteousness is what God is, and, yes, righteousness is what we are not, and, yes, righteousness is what God requires. But "God has a way to make people right with him" (Rom. 3:21).

David said it like this: "He leads me in the paths of righteousness" (Ps. 23:3 NKJV).

The path of righteousness is a narrow, winding trail up a steep hill. At the top of the hill is a cross. At the base of the cross are bags. Countless bags full of innumerable sins. Calvary is the compost pile for guilt. Would you like to leave yours there as well?

One final thought about the Christmas cookie party. Did everyone know I didn't cook the cookies? If they didn't, I told them. I told them I was present by virtue of someone else's work. My only contribution was my own confession.

We'll be saying the same for eternity.

9

Get Over Yourself

The Burden of Arrogance

For His name's sake . . .

PSALM 23:3 NKJV

Humility is such an elusive virtue. Once you think you have it, you don't, or you wouldn't think you did. You've heard the story of the boy who received the "Most Humble" badge and had it taken away because he wore it?

Something similar happened to me just the other morning. I had retreated to a nearby town to work on this book. The village is a perfect hideaway; it is quaint, quiet, and has great food.

I'd gone to a café for breakfast when I noticed that people were staring at me. As I parked, two fellows turned and looked in my direction. A woman did a double take as I entered, and several patrons looked up as I passed. When I took my seat, the waitress gave me a menu but not before she'd given me a good study.

Why the attention? Couldn't be my fly; I was wearing sweats. After some thought I took the mature posture and assumed they recognized me from my book jackets. *Why, this must be a town of readers. And,* I shrugged to myself, *they know a good author when they see one.* My appreciation for the village only increased.

Giving a smile to the folks at the other tables, I set about to enjoy my meal. When I walked to the cash register, the heads turned again. *I'm sure Steinbeck had the same problem.* The woman who took my money started to say something but then paused. Overwhelmed, I guessed.

It was only when I stopped in the rest room that I saw the real reason for the attention—a ribbon of dried blood on my chin. My patch job on the shaving nick hadn't worked, and I was left with my own turkey wattle.

So much for feeling famous. They probably thought I was an escapee from a Texas prison.

Oh, the things God does to keep us humble. He does it for our own good, you know. Would you set a saddle on the back of your five-year-old? Would God let you be saddled with arrogance? No way.

This is one piece of luggage God hates. He doesn't dislike arrogance. He doesn't disapprove of arrogance. He's not unfavorably disposed toward arrogance. God hates arrogance. What a meal of maggots does for our stomach, human pride does for God's.

"I hate pride and arrogance" (Prov. 8:13 NIV).

"The LORD despises pride" (Prov. 16:5 NLT).

God says, "Do nothing out of . . . vain conceit" (Phil. 2:3 NIV). And, "Do not let arrogance come out of your mouth" (1 Sam. 2:3 NASB). And, in the same way that he gives grace to the humble, "God opposes the proud" (1 Pet. 5:5 NIV). As humility goes before honor, "pride goes . . . before a fall" (Prov. 16:18 NIV).

Ever wonder why churches are powerful in one generation but empty the next? Perhaps the answer is found in Proverbs 15:25: "The LORD will tear down the house of the proud" (NASB).

God hates arrogance. He hates arrogance because we haven't done anything to be arrogant about. Do art critics give awards to the canvas? Is there a Pulitzer for ink? Can you imagine a scalpel growing smug after a successful heart transplant? Of course not. They are only tools, so they get no credit for the accomplishments.

And the message of the Twenty-third Psalm is that we have nothing to be proud about either. We have rest, salvation, blessings, and a home in heaven—and we did nothing to earn any of it. Who did? Who did the work? The answer threads through the psalm like a silk thread through pearls.

"He makes me . . ."

"He leads me . . ."

"He restores my soul . . ."

"You are with me . . ."

"Your rod and Your staff . . . comfort me . . ."

"You prepare a table . . ."

"You anoint my head . . ."

We may be the canvas, the paper, or the scalpel, but we are not the ones who deserve the applause. And just to make sure we get the point, right smack-dab in the middle of the poem, David declares who does. The shepherd leads his sheep, not for our names' sake, but "for His name's sake."

Why does God have anything to do with us? *For his name's sake.* No other name on the marquee. No other name up in lights. No other name on the front page. This is all done for God's glory.

Why? What's the big deal? Does God have an ego problem?

No, but we do. We are about as responsible with applause as I was with the cake I won in the first grade. In the grand finale of the musical chairs competition, guess who had a seat? And guess what the little red-headed, freckle-faced boy won? A tender, moist coconut cake. And guess what the boy wanted to do that night in one sitting? Eat the whole thing! Not half of it. Not a piece of it. All of it! After all, I'd won it.

But you know what my folks did? They rationed the cake. They gave me only what I could handle. Knowing that today's binge is tomorrow's bellyache, they made sure I didn't get sick on my success.

God does the same. He takes the cake. He takes the credit, not because he needs it, but because he knows we can't handle it. We aren't content with a bite of adulation; we tend to swallow it all. It messes with our systems. The praise swells our heads and shrinks our brains, and pretty soon we start thinking we had something to do with our survival. Pretty soon we forget we were made out of dirt and rescued from sin.

Pretty soon we start praying like the fellow at the religious caucus: "God, I thank you that the world has people like me. The man on the corner needs welfare—I don't. The prostitute on the street has AIDS—I don't. The drunk at the bar needs alcohol—I don't. The gay caucus needs morality—I don't. I thank you that the world has people like me."

Fortunately, there was a man in the same meeting who had deflected all the applause. Too contrite even to look to the skies, he bowed and prayed, "God, have mercy on me, a sinner. Like my brother on welfare, I'm dependent on your grace. Like my sister with AIDS, I'm infected with mistakes. Like my friend who drinks, I need something to ease my pain. And as you love and give direction to the gay, grant some to me as well. Have mercy on me, a sinner."

After telling a story like that, Jesus said, "I tell you, when this man went home, he was right with God, but the Pharisee was not. All who make themselves great will be made humble, but all who make themselves humble will be made great" (Luke 18:14).

With the same intensity that he hates arrogance, God loves humility. The Jesus who said, "I am gentle and humble in heart" (Matt. 11:29 NASB) loves those who are gentle and humble in heart. "Though the LORD is supreme, he takes care of those who are humble" (Ps. 138:6). God says, "I live with people who are . . . humble" (Isa. 57:15). He also says, "To this one I will look, to him who is humble and contrite" (Isa. 66:2 NASB). And to the humble, God gives great treasures:

He gives honor: "Humility goes before honor" (Prov. 15:33 NRSV).

He gives wisdom: "With the humble is wisdom" (Prov. 11:2 NASB).

He gives direction: "He teaches the humble His way" (Ps. 25:9 NASB).

And most significantly, he gives grace: "God . . . gives grace to the humble" (1 Pet. 5:5).

And this reassurance: "He crowns the humble with salvation" (Ps. 149:4 NIV).

The mightiest of the saints were known for their humility. Though Moses had served as prince of Egypt and emancipator of the slaves, the Bible says, "Moses was . . . more humble than anyone else" (Num. 12:3 NIV).

The apostle Paul was saved through a personal visit from Jesus. He was carried into the heavens and had the ability to raise the dead. But when he introduced himself, he mentioned none of these. He simply said, "I, Paul, am God's slave" (Titus 1:1 MSG).

John the Baptist was a blood relative of Jesus and the first evangelist in history, but he is remembered in Scripture as the one who resolved, "He must increase, but I must decrease" (John 3:30 NKJV).

God loves humility. Could that be the reason he offers so many tips on cultivating it? May I, ahem, humbly articulate a few?

1. *Assess yourself honestly.* Humility isn't the same as low self-esteem. Being humble doesn't mean you think you have nothing to offer; it means you know exactly what you have to offer and no more. "Don't cherish exaggerated ideas of yourself or your importance, but try to have a sane estimate of your capabilities by the light of the faith that God has given to you" (Rom. 12:3 PHILLIPS).

2. *Don't take success too seriously.* Scripture gives this warning: "When your . . . silver and gold increase, . . . your heart will become proud" (Deut. 8:13–14). Counteract this pride with reminders of the brevity of life and the frailty of wealth.

Ponder your success and count your money in a cemetery, and remember that neither of the two is buried with you. "People come into this world with nothing, and when they die they leave with nothing" (Eccles. 5:15). I saw a reminder of this in a cemetery. Parked next to the entrance was a nice recreational boat with a For Sale sign. You had to wonder if the fisherman realized he couldn't take it with him.

3. Celebrate the significance of others. "In humility consider others better than yourselves" (Phil. 2:3 NIV). Columnist Rick Reilly gave this advice to rookie professional athletes: "Stop thumping your chest. The line blocked, the quarterback threw you a perfect spiral while getting his head knocked off, and the *good* receiver blew the double coverage. Get over yourself."[1]

The truth is, every touchdown in life is a team effort. Applaud your teammates. An elementary-age boy came home from the tryouts for the school play. "Mommy, Mommy," he announced, "I got a part. I've been chosen to sit in the audience and clap and cheer." When you have a chance to clap and cheer, do you take it? If you do, your head is starting to fit your hat size.

4. Don't demand your own parking place. This was the instruction of Jesus to his followers: "Go sit in a seat that is not important. When the host comes to you, he may say, 'Friend, move up here to a more important place.' Then all the other guests will respect you" (Luke 14:10).

Demanding respect is like chasing a butterfly. Chase it, and you'll never catch it. Sit still, and it may light on your shoulder. The French philosopher Blaise Pascal asked, "Do you wish people to speak well of you? Then never speak well of yourself."[2] Maybe that's why the Bible says, "Don't praise yourself. Let someone else do it" (Prov. 27:2).

5. Never announce your success before it occurs. Or as one of the kings of Israel said, "One who puts on his armor should not boast like one who takes it off" (1 Kings 20:11 NIV). Charles Spurgeon trained many young ministers. On one occasion a student stepped up to preach with great confidence but failed miserably. He came down, humbled and meek. Spurgeon told him, "If you had gone up as you came down, you would have come down as you went up."[3] If humility precedes an event, then confidence may follow.

6. *Speak humbly.* "Let no arrogance come from your mouth" (1 Sam. 2:3 NKJV). Don't be cocky. People aren't impressed with your opinions. Take a tip from Benjamin Franklin.

> [I developed] the habit of expressing myself in terms of modest diffidence, never using when I advance any thing that may possibly be disputed, the words certainly, undoubtedly, or any others that give the air of positiveness to an opinion; but rather I say, I conceive or I apprehend a thing to be so or so. . . . This habit I believe has been a great advantage to me.[4]

It would be a great advantage to us as well.

One last thought to foster humility.

7. *Live at the foot of the cross.* Paul said, "The cross of our Lord Jesus Christ is my only reason for bragging" (Gal. 6:14). Do you feel a need for affirmation? Does your self-esteem need attention? You don't need to drop names or show off. You need only pause at the base of the cross and be reminded of this: The maker of the stars would rather die for you than live without you. And that is a fact. So if you need to brag, brag about that.

And check your chin occasionally.

10

I Will Lead You Home

The Burden of the Grave

Yea, though I walk through the valley of the shadow of death, I will fear no evil; for You are with me; Your rod and Your staff, they comfort me.

PSALM 23:4 NKJV

Summer in ancient Palestine. A woolly bunch of bobbing heads follow the shepherd out of the gate. The morning sun has scarcely crested the horizon, and he is already leading his flock. Like every other day, he guides them through the gate and out into the fields. But unlike most days, the shepherd will not return home tonight. He will not rest on his bed, and the sheep will not sleep in their fenced-in pasture. This is the day the shepherd takes the sheep to the high country. Today he leads his flock to the mountains.

He has no other choice. Springtime grazing has left his pasture bare, so he must seek new fields. With no companion other than his sheep and no desire other than their welfare, he leads them to the deep grass of the hillsides. The shepherd and his flock will be gone for weeks, perhaps months. They will stay well into the autumn, until the grass is gone and the chill is unbearable.

Not all shepherds make this journey. The trek is long. The path is dangerous. Poisonous plants can infect the flock. Wild animals can attack the flock. There are narrow trails and dark valleys. Some shepherds choose the security of the barren pasture below.

But the good shepherd doesn't. He knows the path. He has walked this trail many times. Besides, he is prepared. Staff in hand

and rod attached to his belt. With his staff he will nudge the flock; with his rod he will protect and lead the flock. He will lead them to the mountains.

David understood this annual pilgrimage. Before he led Israel, he led sheep. And could his time as a shepherd be the inspiration behind one of the greatest verses in the Bible? "Yea, though I walk through the valley of the shadow of death, I will fear no evil; for You are with me; Your rod and Your staff, they comfort me" (Ps. 23:4 NKJV).

For what the shepherd does with the flock, our Shepherd will do with us. He will lead us to the high country. When the pasture is bare down here, God will lead us up there. He will guide us through the gate, out of the flatlands, and up the path of the mountain.

As one shepherd writes:

> Every mountain has its valleys. Its sides are scarred by deep ravines and gulches and draws. And the best route to the top is always through these valleys.
>
> Any sheepman familiar with the high country knows this. He leads his flock gently, but persistently up the paths that wind through the dark valleys.[1]

Someday our Shepherd will do the same with us. He will take us to the mountain by way of the valley. He will guide us to his house through the valley of the shadow of death.

Many years ago when I lived in Miami, our church office received a call from a nearby funeral home. A man had identified the body of an indigent as his brother and wanted a memorial service. He didn't know any ministers in the area. Would we say a few words? The senior minister and I agreed. When we arrived, the brother of the deceased had selected a text from a Spanish Bible: "Yea, though I walk through the valley of the shadow of death, I will fear no evil; for You are with me; Your rod and Your staff, they comfort me" (Ps. 23:4 NKJV).

He needed assurance that, though his brother had lived alone, he did not die alone. And for that assurance, he turned to this verse. You've likely done the same.

If you've attended a memorial service, you've heard the words. If you've walked through a cemetery, you've read them. They're quoted at the gravesides of paupers, carved on the headstones of kings. Those who know nothing of the Bible know this part of the Bible. Those who quote no scripture can remember this scripture, the one about the valley and the shadow and the shepherd.

Why? Why are these words so treasured? Why is this verse so beloved? I can think of a couple of reasons. By virtue of this psalm, David grants us two important reminders that can help us surrender our fear of the grave.

We all have to face it. In a life marked by doctor appointments, dentist appointments, and school appointments, there is one appointment that none of us will miss, the appointment with death. "Everyone must die once, and after that be judged by God" (Heb. 9:27 TEV). Oh, how we'd like to change that verse. Just a word or two would suffice. "*Nearly* everyone must die . . ." or "*Everyone but me* must die . . ." or "*Everyone who forgets to eat right and take vitamins* must die . . ." But those are not God's words. In his plan everyone must die, even those who eat right and take their vitamins.

I could have gone all day without reminding you of that. We do our best to avoid the topic. One wise man, however, urges us to face it squarely: "We all must die, and everyone living should think about this" (Eccles. 7:2). Solomon isn't promoting a morbid obsession with death. He is reminding us to be honest about the inevitable.

Moses gave the same exhortation. In the only psalm attributed to his pen, he prayed, "Teach us how short our lives really are so that we may be wise" (Ps. 90:12).

The wise remember the brevity of life. Exercise may buy us a few more heartbeats. Medicine may grant us a few more breaths. But in the end, there is an end. And the best way to face life is to be honest about death.

David was. He may have slain Goliath, but he had no illusions about sidestepping the giant of death. And though his first reminder sobers us, his second reminder encourages us: *We don't have to face death alone.*

Don't miss the shift in David's vocabulary. Up to this point, you and I have been the audience and God has been the topic. "The LORD is my shepherd." "He makes me to lie down." "He leads me beside the still waters." "He restores my soul." "He leads me in the paths of righteousness." For the first three verses, David speaks to us and God listens.

But suddenly in verse four, David speaks to God and we listen. It's as if David's face, which was on us, now lifts toward God. His poem becomes a prayer. Rather than speak to us, he speaks to the Good Shepherd. "You are with me; Your rod and Your staff, they comfort me."

David's implied message is subtle but crucial. Don't face death without facing God. Don't even speak of death without speaking to God. He and he alone can guide you through the valley. Others may speculate or aspire, but only God knows the way to get you home. And only God is committed to getting you there safely.

Years after David wrote these words, another Bethlehem Shepherd would say: "There are many rooms in my Father's house; I would not tell you this if it were not true. I am going there to prepare a place for you. After I go and prepare a place for you, I will come back and take you to be with me so that you may be where I am" (John 14:2–3).

Note the promise of Jesus. "I will come back and take you to be with me." He pledges to take us home. He does not delegate this task. He may send missionaries to teach you, angels to protect you, teachers to guide you, singers to inspire you, and physicians to heal you, but he sends no one to take you. He reserves this job for himself. "I will come back and take you home." He is your personal Shepherd. And he is personally responsible to lead you home. And because he is present when any of his sheep dies, you can say what David said, "I will fear no evil."

When my daughters were younger, we enjoyed many fun afternoons in the swimming pool. Just like all of us, they had to overcome their fears in order to swim. One of the final fears they had to face was the fear of the deep. It's one thing to swim on the surface; it's another to plunge down to the bottom. I mean, who knows what kind of dragons and serpents dwell in the depths of an eight-foot pool? You and I know there is no evil to fear, but a six-year-old doesn't. A child feels the same way about the deep that you and I feel about death. We aren't sure what awaits us down there.

I didn't want my daughters to be afraid of the deep end, so with each I played Shamu the whale. My daughter would be the trainer. I would be Shamu. She would pinch her nose and put her arm around my neck, then down we would go. Deep, deep, deep until we could touch the bottom of the pool. Then up we would explode, breaking the surface. After several plunges they realized they had nothing to fear. They feared no evil. Why? Because I was with them.

And when God calls us into the deep valley of death, he will be with us. Dare we think that he would abandon us in the moment of death? Would a father force his child to swim the deep alone? Would the shepherd require his sheep to journey to the highlands alone? Of course not. Would God require his child to journey to eternity alone? Absolutely not! He is with you!

What God said to Moses, he says to you: "My Presence will go with you, and I will give you rest" (Exod. 33:14 NIV).

What God said to Jacob, he says to you: "I am with you and will watch over you wherever you go" (Gen. 28:15 NIV).

What God said to Joshua, he says to you: "As I was with Moses, so I will be with you; I will never leave you nor forsake you" (Josh. 1:5 NIV).

What God said to the nation of Israel, he says to you: "When you pass through the waters, I will be with you" (Isa. 43:2 NIV).

The Good Shepherd is with you. And because he is with you, you can say what David said: "I will fear no evil; for You are with me; Your rod and Your staff, they comfort me."

Years ago a chaplain in the French army used the Twenty-third Psalm to encourage soldiers before battle. He would urge them to repeat the opening clause of the psalm, ticking it off, one finger at a time. The little finger represented the word *the;* the ring finger represented the word *LORD;* the middle finger, *is;* the index finger, *my;* and the thumb, *shepherd*. Then he asked every soldier to write the words on the palm of his hand and to repeat the verse whenever he needed strength.

The chaplain placed special emphasis on the message of the index finger—*my*. He reminded the soldiers that God is a personal shepherd with a personal mission—to get them home safely.

Did the chaplain's words find their mark? In the life of one man they did. After a battle one of the young soldiers was found dead, his right hand clutching the index finger of the left. "The LORD is my shepherd . . ."[2]

I pray that your final hours will find you clutching the same hope.

11

When Mourning Comes

The Burden of Grief

Though I walk through the valley of the shadow of death . . .

Psalm 23:4 NKJV

Carlos Andres Baisdon-Niño lay down with his favorite Bible storybook. He began with the first chapter and turned every page until the end. When he finished, he blew his good-night kisses to Mami and Papi, to his three *"niñas,"* and then, as always, he blew one to Papa Dios. He closed his eyes, drifted off to sleep, and awoke in heaven.

Carlos was three years old.

When Tim and Betsa, his parents, and I met to plan the funeral, they wanted me to watch a video of Carlos. "You've got to see him dancing," Tim told me. One look and I could see why. What little Carlos did to the rhythm of a Latin song can't be described with words. He shook from top to bottom. His feet moved, his hands bounced, his head swayed. You got the impression that his heart rate had switched over to his native Colombian beat.

We laughed, the three of us did. And in the laughter, for just a moment, Carlos was with us. For just a moment there was no leukemia, syringes, blankets, or chemotherapy. There was no stone to carve or grave to dig. There was just Carlos. And Carlos was just dancing.

But then the video stopped, and so did the laughter. And this mom and dad resumed their slow walk through the valley of the shadow of death.

Are you passing through the same shadow? Is this book being held by the same hands that touched the cold face of a friend? And the eyes that fall upon this page, have they also fallen upon the breathless figure of a husband, wife, or child? Are you passing through the valley? If not, this chapter may seem unnecessary. Feel free to move on—it will be here when you need it.

If so, however, you know that the black bag of sorrow is hard to bear.

It's hard to bear because not everyone understands your grief. They did at first. They did at the funeral. They did at the graveside. But they don't now; they don't understand. Grief lingers.

As silently as a cloud slides between you and the afternoon sun, memories drift between you and joy, leaving you in a chilly shadow. No warning. No notice. Just a whiff of the cologne he wore or a verse of the song she loved, and you are saying good-bye all over again.

Why won't the sorrow leave you alone?

Because you buried more than a person. You buried some of yourself. Wasn't it John Donne who said, "Any man's death diminishes me"? It's as if the human race resides on a huge trampoline. The movements of one can be felt by all. And the closer the relationship, the more profound the exit. When someone you love dies, it affects you.

It affects your dreams.

Some years ago my wife and I served with other missionaries in Rio de Janeiro, Brazil. Our team consisted of several young couples who, by virtue of being far away from home, became very close. We rejoiced greatly when two of our team members, Marty and Angela, announced that she was pregnant with their first child.

The pregnancy was difficult, however, and the joy became concern. Angela was told to stay in bed, and we were urged to stay in prayer. We did. And the Lord answered our prayers, though not as we desired. The baby died in the womb.

I've never forgotten Marty's comment. "More than a baby died, Max. A dream died."

Why does grief linger? Because you are dealing with more than memories—you are dealing with unlived tomorrows. You're not just battling sorrow—you're battling disappointment. You're also battling anger.

It may be on the surface. It may subterranean. It may be a flame. It may be a blowtorch. But anger lives in sorrow's house. Anger at self. Anger at life. Anger at the military or the hospital or the highway system. But most of all, anger at God. Anger that takes the form of the three-letter question—why? Why him? Why her? Why now? Why us?

You and I both know I can't answer that question. Only God knows the reasons behind his actions. But here is a key truth on which we can stand.

Our God is a good God.

"You are good, LORD. The LORD is good and right" (Ps. 25:7–8).

"Taste and see that the LORD is good" (Ps. 34:8 NIV).

God is a good God. We must begin here. Though we don't understand his actions, we can trust his heart.

God does only what is good. But how can death be good? Some mourners don't ask this question. When the quantity of years has outstripped the quality of years, we don't ask how death can be good.

But the father of the dead teenager does. The thirty-year-old widow does. The parents of Carlos did. My friends in Rio did. How could death be good?

Part of the answer may be found in Isaiah 57:1–2: "Good people are taken away, but no one understands. Those who do right are being taken away from evil and are given peace. Those who live as God wants find rest in death."

Death is God's way of taking people away from evil. From what kind of evil? An extended disease? An addiction? A dark season of rebellion? We don't know. But we know that no person lives one day more or less than God intends. "All the days planned for me were written in your book before I was one day old" (Ps. 139:16).

But her days here were so few . . .

His life was so brief . . .

To us it seems that way. We speak of a short life, but compared to eternity, who has a long one? A person's days on earth may appear as a drop in the ocean. Yours and mine may seem like a thimbleful. But compared to the Pacific of eternity, even the years of Methuselah filled no more than a glass. James was not speaking just to the young when he said, "Your life is like a mist. You can see it for a short time, but then it goes away" (James 4:14).

In God's plan every life is long enough and every death is timely. And though you and I might wish for a longer life, God knows better.

And—this is important—though you and I may wish a longer life for our loved ones, they don't. Ironically, the first to accept God's decision of death is the one who dies.

While we are shaking heads in disbelief, they are lifting hands in worship. While we are mourning at a grave, they are marveling at heaven. While we are questioning God, they are praising God.

But, Max, what of those who die with no faith? My husband never prayed. My grandpa never worshiped. My mother never opened a Bible, much less her heart. What about the one who never believed?

How do we know he didn't?

Who among us is privy to a person's final thoughts? Who among us knows what transpires in those final moments? Are you sure no prayer was offered? Eternity can bend the proudest knees. Could a person stare into the yawning canyon of death without whispering a plea for mercy? And could our God, who is partial to the humble, resist it?

He couldn't on Calvary. The confession of the thief on the cross was both a first and final one. But Christ heard it. Christ received it. Maybe you never heard your loved one confess Christ, but who's to say Christ didn't?

We don't know the final thoughts of a dying soul, but we know this. We know our God is a good God. He is "not willing that any should perish but that all should come to repentance" (2 Pet. 3:9 NKJV). He wants your loved one in heaven more than you do. And he usually gets what he wants.

You know what else God wants? He wants you to face your sorrow. Denial and dismissal are not a part of God's grief therapy.

David faced his. When he learned of the death of Saul and Jonathan, David and the entire army tore their clothing, wept aloud, and fasted until sunset. His lament was intense and public. "May there be no dew or rain on the mountains of Gilboa," he mourned, "and may their fields produce no grain. . . . We loved Saul and Jonathan and enjoyed them while they lived. They are together even in death. They were faster than eagles. They were stronger than lions" (2 Sam. 1:21–23).

David not only sang this dirge, he "ordered that the people of Judah be taught this song" (v. 18). Death was not soft-pedaled or passed over. Face it, fight it, question it, or condemn it, but don't deny it. As his son Solomon explained, "There is . . . a time to mourn" (Eccles. 3:1, 4 NIV). Don't heed, but do forgive, those who urge you not to.

God will lead you *through*, not around, the valley of the shadow of death. And, by the way, aren't you glad it's just a shadow?

Dr. Donald Grey Barnhouse told of the occasion of his first wife's death. He and his children were driving home from the burial, overcome with grief. He searched for a word of comfort to offer but could think of nothing. Just then, a large moving van drove by. As it passed, the shadow of the truck swept over the car. An inspiration came to Dr. Barnhouse. He turned to his family and asked, "Children, would you rather be run over by a truck or by its shadow?"

The children said, "Well, of course, Dad, we'd rather be run over by the shadow. That can't hurt us at all."

Dr. Barnhouse explained, "Did you know that two thousand years ago the truck of death ran over the Lord Jesus . . . in order that only its shadow might run over us?"[1]

We face death, but thanks to Jesus, we only face its shadow. And thanks to Jesus, we believe that our loved ones are happy and that the little Carloses of the world are dancing as never before.

12

From Panic to Peace

The Burden of Fear

I will fear no evil.

Psalm 23:4 NKJV

It's the expression of Jesus that puzzles us. We've never seen his face like this.

Jesus smiling, yes.

Jesus weeping, absolutely.

Jesus stern, even that.

But Jesus anguished? Cheeks streaked with tears? Face flooded in sweat? Rivulets of blood dripping from his chin? You remember the night.

> Jesus left the city and went to the Mount of Olives, as he often did, and his followers went with him. When he reached the place, he said to them, "Pray for strength against temptation."
>
> Then Jesus went about a stone's throw away from them. He kneeled down and prayed, "Father, if you are willing, take away this cup of suffering. But do what you want, not what I want." Then an angel from heaven appeared to him to strengthen him. Being full of pain, Jesus prayed even harder. His sweat was like drops of blood falling to the ground. (Luke 22:39–44)

The Bible I carried as a child contained a picture of Jesus in the Garden of Gethsemane. His face was soft, hands calmly folded as he knelt beside a rock and prayed. Jesus seemed peaceful. One reading of the Gospels disrupts that image. Mark says, "Jesus fell to the ground" (Mark 14:35). Matthew tells us Jesus was "very sad and troubled . . . to the point of death" (Matt. 26:37–38). According to Luke, Jesus was "full of pain" (Luke 22:44).

Equipped with those passages, how would you paint this scene? Jesus flat on the ground? Face in the dirt? Extended hands gripping grass? Body rising and falling with sobs? Face as twisted as the olive trees that surround him?

What do we do with this image of Jesus?

Simple. We turn to it when we look the same. We read it when we feel the same; we read it when we feel afraid. For isn't it likely that fear is one of the emotions Jesus felt? One might even argue that fear was the primary emotion. He saw something in the future so fierce, so foreboding that he begged for a change of plans. "Father, if you are willing, take away this cup of suffering" (Luke 22:42).

What causes you to pray the same prayer? Boarding an airplane? Facing a crowd? Public speaking? Taking a job? Taking a spouse? Driving on a highway? The source of your fear may seem small to others. But to you, it freezes your feet, makes your heart pound, and brings blood to your face. That's what happened to Jesus.

He was so afraid that he bled. Doctors describe this condition as hematidrosis. Severe anxiety causes the release of chemicals that break down the capillaries in the sweat glands. When this occurs, sweat comes out tinged with blood.

Jesus was more than anxious; he was afraid. Fear is worry's big brother. If worry is a burlap bag, fear is a trunk of concrete. It wouldn't budge.

How remarkable that Jesus felt such fear. But how kind that he told us about it. We tend to do the opposite. Gloss over our fears. Cover them up. Keep our sweaty palms in our pockets, our nausea and dry mouths a secret. Not so with Jesus. We see no mask of strength. But we do hear a request for strength.

"Father, if you are willing, take away this cup of suffering." The first one to hear his fear is his Father. He could have gone to his mother. He could have confided in his disciples. He could have assembled a prayer meeting. All would have been appropriate, but none were his priority. He went first to his Father.

Oh, how we tend to go everywhere else. First to the bar, to the counselor, to the self-help book or the friend next door. Not Jesus. The first one to hear his fear was his Father in heaven.

A millennium earlier David was urging the fear-filled to do the same. "I will fear no evil." How could David make such a claim? Because he knew where to look. "You are with me; Your rod and Your staff, they comfort me."

Rather than turn to the other sheep, David turned to the Shepherd. Rather than stare at the problems, he stared at the rod and staff. Because he knew where to look, David was able to say, "I will fear no evil."

I know a fellow who has a fear of crowds. When encircled by large groups, his breath grows short, panic surfaces, and he begins to sweat like a sumo wrestler in a sauna. He received some help, curiously, from a golfing buddy.

The two were at a movie theatre, waiting their turn to enter, when fear struck again. The crowd closed in like a forest. He wanted out and out fast. His buddy told him to take a few deep breaths. Then he helped manage the crisis by reminding him of the golf course.

"When you are hitting your ball out of the rough, and you are surrounded by trees, what do you do?"

"I look for an opening."

"You don't stare at the trees?"

"Of course not. I find an opening and focus on hitting the ball through it."

"Do the same in the crowd. When you feel the panic, don't focus on the people; focus on the opening."

Good counsel in golf. Good counsel in life. Rather than focus on the fear, focus on the solution.

That's what Jesus did.

That's what David did.

And that's what the writer of Hebrews urges us to do. "Let us run with endurance the race that is set before us, looking unto Jesus, the author and finisher of our faith" (Heb. 12:1–2 NKJV).

The writer of Hebrews was not a golfer, but he could have been a jogger, for he speaks of a runner and a forerunner. The forerunner is Jesus, the "author and finisher of our faith." He is the author—that is to say he wrote the book on salvation. And he is the finisher—he not only charted the map, he blazed the trail. He is the forerunner, and we are the runners. And we runners are urged to keep our eyes on Jesus.

I'm a runner. More mornings than not I drag myself out of bed and onto the street. I don't run fast. And compared to marathoners, I don't run far. But I run. I run because I don't like cardiologists. Nothing personal, mind you. It's just that I come from a family that keeps them in business. One told my dad he needed to retire. Another opened the chests of both my mom and brother. I'd like to be the one family member who doesn't keep a heart surgeon's number on speed dial.

Since heart disease runs in our family, I run in our neighborhood. As the sun is rising, I am running. And as I am running, my body is groaning. It doesn't want to cooperate. My knee hurts. My hip is stiff. My ankles complain. Sometimes a passerby laughs at my legs, and my ego hurts.

Things hurt. And as things hurt, I've learned that I have three options. Go home. (Denalyn would laugh at me.) Meditate on my hurts until I start imagining I'm having chest pains. (Pleasant thought.) Or I can keep running and watch the sun come up. My trail has just enough easterly bend to give me a front-row seat for God's morning miracle. If I watch God's world go from dark to golden, guess what? The same happens to my attitude. The pain passes and the joints loosen, and before I know it, the run is half over and life ain't half bad. Everything improves as I fix my eyes on the sun.

Wasn't that the counsel of the Hebrew epistle—"looking unto Jesus"? What was the focus of David? "You are with me; Your rod and Your staff, they comfort me."

How did Jesus endure the terror of the crucifixion? He went first to the Father with his fears. He modeled the words of Psalm 56:3: "When I am afraid, I put my trust in you" (NLT).

Do the same with yours. Don't avoid life's Gardens of Gethsemane. Enter them. Just don't enter them alone. And while there, be honest. Pounding the ground is permitted. Tears are allowed. And if you sweat blood, you won't be the first. Do what Jesus did; open your heart.

And be specific. Jesus was. "Take *this* cup," he prayed. Give God the number of the flight. Tell him the length of the speech. Share the details of the job transfer. He has plenty of time. He also has plenty of compassion.

He doesn't think your fears are foolish or silly. He won't tell you to "buck up" or "get tough." He's been where you are. He knows how you feel.

And he knows what you need. That's why we punctuate our prayers as Jesus did. "If you are willing . . ."

Was God willing? Yes and no. He didn't take away the cross, but he took the fear. God didn't still the storm, but he calmed the sailor.

Who's to say he won't do the same for you?

"Do not be anxious about anything, but in everything, by prayer and petition, with thanksgiving, present your requests to God" (Phil. 4:6 NIV).

Don't measure the size of the mountain; talk to the One who can move it. Instead of carrying the world on your shoulders, talk to the One who holds the universe on his. Hope is a look away.

Now, what were you looking at?

13

Silent Nights and Solitary Days

The Burden of Loneliness

You are with me.

PSALM 23:4 NKJV

A friend of mine worked at a pharmacy while attending the University of Texas. Steve's primary job was to deliver supplies to nursing homes in the Austin area. An additional task, however, involved a short trip next door.

Every four days he shouldered a large jug of water and carried it fifty or so feet to a building behind the pharmacy. The customer was an older woman, perhaps in her seventies, who lived alone in a dark, sparse, and tarnished apartment. A single light bulb hung from the ceiling. The wallpaper was stained and peeling. The shades were drawn, and the room was shadowy. Steve would deliver the jug, receive the payment, thank the woman, and leave.

Over the weeks he grew puzzled by her purchase. He learned that the woman had no other source of water. She would rely on his delivery for four days of washing, bathing, and drinking. Odd choice. Municipal water was cheaper. The city would have charged her twelve to fifteen dollars a month; her expense at the pharmacy added up to fifty dollars a month. Why didn't she choose the less expensive source?

The answer was in the delivery system. Yes, the city water cost less. But the city sent only the water; they didn't send a person. She preferred to pay more and see a human being than pay less and see no one.

Could anyone be that lonely?

It seems that David was. Some of his psalms have the feel of a lone oak on a winter prairie.

He wrote:

> Turn to me and be gracious to me,
> for I am lonely and afflicted. (Ps. 25:16 NIV)
>
> I'm tired of all this—so tired. My bed
> has been floating forty days and nights
> On the flood of my tears.
> My mattress is soaked, soggy with tears.
> The sockets of my eyes are black holes;
> Nearly blind, I squint and grope. (Ps. 6:6–7 MSG)

David knew what it feels like to be lonely . . . betrayed.

> When they were sick, I dressed in black;
> instead of eating, I prayed.
> My prayers were like lead in my gut,
> like I'd lost my best friend, my brother.
> I paced, distraught as a motherless child,
> hunched and heavyhearted.
>
> But when I was down
> they threw a party!
> All the nameless riffraff of the town came
> chanting insults about me.
> Like barbarians desecrating a shrine,
> they destroyed my reputation.

> YAHWEH, how long are you going
> to stand there doing nothing? (Ps. 35:13–17 MSG)

David knew the feeling of loneliness.

He knew it in his family. He was one of eight sons of Jesse. But when Samuel the prophet asked to see Jesse's boys, David was overlooked. The prophet counted and asked if there wasn't another child somewhere. Jesse snapped his fingers as if he'd forgotten his keys. "I still have the youngest son. He is out taking care of the sheep" (1 Sam. 16:11).

Jesse's term for "youngest son" was not complimentary. He literally said, "I still have the runt." Some of you were the runt in your family. The runt is the one the others have to put up with and keep an eye on. And on this day the runt was left out. How would you feel if a family meeting was called and your name wasn't?

Things didn't improve when he changed households.

His inclusion in the royal family was King Saul's idea. His exclusion was Saul's idea as well. Had David not ducked, he would have been pinned to the wall by the spear of the jealous king. But David did duck, and David did run. For ten years he ran. Into the wilderness he ran. Sleeping in caves, surviving on wild animals. He was hated and hunted like a jackal.

David was no stranger to loneliness.

You aren't either. By now you've learned that you don't have to be alone to feel lonely. Two thousand years ago 250 million people populated the earth. Now there are more than 5 billion. If loneliness could be cured by the presence of people, then surely there would be less loneliness today. But loneliness lingers.

Very early in my ministry I offered this Sunday morning prayer: "Thank you, Lord, for all our friends. We have so many we can't spend time with them all." After the service a successful businessman corrected me, "You may have more friends than you can see. Not me. I have none." A person can be surrounded by a church and still be lonely.

Loneliness is not the absence of faces. It is the absence of intimacy. Loneliness doesn't come from being alone; it comes from feeling alone. Feeling as if you are

facing death alone,

facing disease alone,

facing the future alone.

Whether it strikes you in your bed at night or on your drive to the hospital, in the silence of an empty house or the noise of a crowded bar, loneliness is when you think, *I feel so alone. Does anyone care?*

Bags of loneliness show up everywhere. They litter the floors of boardrooms and clubs. We drag them into parties and usually drag them back out. You'll spot them near the desk of the overworker, beside the table of the overeater, and on the nightstand of the one-night stand. We'll try anything to unload our loneliness. This is one bag we want to drop quickly.

But should we? Should we be so quick to drop it? Rather than turn from loneliness, what if we turned toward it? Could it be that loneliness is not a curse but a gift? A gift from God?

Wait a minute, Max. That can't be. Loneliness heavies my heart. Loneliness leaves me empty and depressed. Loneliness is anything but a gift.

You may be right, but work with me for a moment. I wonder if loneliness is God's way of getting our attention.

Here's what I mean. Suppose you borrow a friend's car. His radio doesn't work, but his CD player does. You rummage through his collection, looking for your style of music—let's say, country-western. But you find nothing. He has nothing but his style of music—let's say, classical.

It's a long trip. And you can talk to yourself for only so long. So eventually you reach for a CD. You'd prefer some steel guitar, but you're stuck with soaring tenors. Initially it's tolerable. At least it fills the air. But eventually it's enjoyable. Your heart picks up the pattern of the kettledrums, your head rolls with the cellos, and you even catch yourself attempting a little Italian aria. "Hey, this isn't so bad."

Now, let me ask you. Would you have made this discovery on your own? No. What led to it? What caused you to hear music you'd never heard before? Simple. You had no other choice, no other option. You had nowhere else to go. Finally, when the silence was too loud, you took a chance on a song you'd never heard.

Oh, how God wants you to hear his music.

He has a rhythm that will race your heart and lyrics that will stir your tears. You want to journey to the stars? He can take you there. You want to lie down in peace? His music can soothe your soul.

But first, he's got to get rid of that country-western stuff. (Forgive me, Nashville. Only an example.)

And so he begins tossing the CDs. A friend turns away. The job goes bad. Your spouse doesn't understand. The church is dull. One by one he removes the options until all you have left is God.

He would do that? Absolutely. "The Lord disciplines those he loves" (Heb. 12:6). If he must silence every voice, he will. He wants you to hear his music. He wants you to discover what David discovered and to be able to say what David said.

"You are with me."

Yes, you, Lord, are in heaven. Yes, you rule the universe. Yes, you sit upon the stars and make your home in the deep. But yes, yes, yes, you are with me.

The Lord is with me. The Creator is with me. Yahweh is with me.

Moses proclaimed it: "What great nation has a god as near to them as the LORD our God is near to us" (Deut. 4:7 NLT).

Paul announced it: "He is not far from each one of us" (Acts 17:27 NIV).

And David discovered it: "You are with me."

Somewhere in the pasture, wilderness, or palace, David discovered that God meant business when he said:

"I will not leave you" (Gen. 28:15).

"I will . . . not forsake My people" (1 Kings 6:13 NKJV).

"The LORD will not abandon His people" (Ps. 94:14 NASB).

"God . . . will never leave you nor forsake you" (Deut. 31:6 NIV).

The discovery of David is indeed the message of Scripture—*the Lord is with us.* And, since the Lord is near, everything is different. Everything!

You may be facing death, but you aren't facing death alone; the Lord is with you. You may be facing unemployment, but you aren't facing unemployment alone; the Lord is with you. You may be facing marital struggles, but you aren't facing them alone; the Lord is with you. You may be facing debt, but you aren't facing debt alone; the Lord is with you.

Underline these words: You are not alone.

Your family may turn against you, but God won't. Your friends may betray you, but God won't. You may feel alone in the wilderness, but you are not. He is with you. And because he is, everything is different. *You* are different.

God changes your *n* into a *v*. You go from *lonely* to *lovely.*

When you know God loves you, you won't be desperate for the love of others.

You'll no longer be a hungry shopper at the market. Have you ever gone to the grocery on an empty stomach? You're a sitting duck. You buy everything you don't need. Doesn't matter if it is good for you—you just want to fill your tummy. When you're lonely, you do the same in life, pulling stuff off the shelf, not because you need it, but because you are hungry for love.

Why do we do it? Because we fear facing life alone. For fear of not fitting in, we take the drugs. For fear of standing out, we wear the clothes. For fear of appearing small, we go into debt and buy the house. For fear of going unnoticed, we dress to seduce or to impress. For fear of sleeping alone, we sleep with anyone. For fear of not being loved, we search for love in all the wrong places.

But all that changes when we discover God's perfect love. And "perfect love casts out fear" (1 John 4:18 NKJV).

Loneliness. Could it be one of God's finest gifts? If a season of solitude is his way to teach you to hear his song, don't you think it's worth it?

So do I.

14

The Crowing Rooster and Me

The Burden of Shame

You prepare a table before me in the presence of my enemies.

PSALM 23:5 NKJV

See the fellow in the shadows? That's Peter. Peter the apostle. Peter the impetuous. Peter the passionate. He once walked on water. Stepped right out of the boat onto the lake. He'll soon preach to thousands. Fearless before friends and foes alike. But tonight the one who stepped on the water has hurried into hiding. The one who will speak with power is weeping in pain.

Not sniffling or whimpering, but weeping. Bawling. Bearded face buried in thick hands. His howl echoing in the Jerusalem night. What hurts more? The fact that he did it? Or the fact that he swore he never would?

"Lord, I am ready to go with you to prison and even to die with you!" he pledged only hours earlier. "But Jesus said, 'Peter, before the rooster crows this day, you will say three times that you don't know me'" (Luke 22:33–34).

Denying Christ on the night of his betrayal was bad enough, but did he have to boast that he wouldn't? And one denial was pitiful, but three? Three denials were horrific, but did he have to curse? "Peter began to place a curse on himself and swear, 'I don't know the man'" (Matt. 26:74).

And now, awash in a whirlpool of sorrow, Peter is hiding. Peter is weeping. And soon Peter will be fishing.

We wonder why he goes fishing. We know why he goes to Galilee.

He had been told that the risen Christ would meet the disciples there. The arranged meeting place is not the sea, however, but a mountain (Matt. 28:16). If the followers were to meet Jesus on a mountain, what are they doing in a boat? No one told them to fish, but that's what they did. "Simon Peter said, 'I am going out to fish.' The others said, 'We will go with you'" (John 21:3). Besides, didn't Peter quit fishing? Two years earlier, when Jesus called him to fish for men, didn't he drop his net and follow? We haven't seen him fish since. We never see him fish again. Why is he fishing now? Especially now! Jesus has risen from the dead. Peter has seen the empty tomb. Who could fish at a time like this?

Were they hungry? Perhaps that's the sum of it. Maybe the expedition was born out of growling stomachs.

Or then again, maybe it was born out of a broken heart.

You see, Peter could not deny his denial. The empty tomb did not erase the crowing rooster. Christ had returned, but Peter wondered, he must have wondered, "After what I did, would he return for someone like me?"

We've wondered the same. Is Peter the only person to do the very thing he swore he'd never do?

"Infidelity is behind me!"

"From now on, I'm going to bridle my tongue."

"No more shady deals. I've learned my lesson."

Oh, the volume of our boasting. And, oh, the heartbreak of our shame.

Rather than resist the flirting, we return it.

Rather than ignore the gossip, we share it.

Rather than stick to the truth, we shade it.

And the rooster crows, and conviction pierces, and Peter has a partner in the shadows. We weep as Peter wept, and we do what Peter did. We go fishing. We go back to our old lives. We return to our pre-Jesus practices. We do what comes naturally, rather than what comes spiritually. And we question whether Jesus has a place for folks like us.

Jesus answers that question. He answers it for you and me and all who tend to "Peter out" on Christ. His answer came on the shore of the sea in a gift to Peter. You know what Jesus did? Split the waters? Turn the boat to gold and the nets to silver? No, Jesus did something much more meaningful. He invited Peter to breakfast. Jesus prepared a meal.

Of course, the breakfast was one special moment among several that morning. There was the great catch of fish and the recognition of Jesus. The plunge of Peter and the paddling of the disciples. And there was the moment they reached the shore and found Jesus next to a fire of coals. The fish were sizzling, and the bread was waiting, and the defeater of hell and the ruler of heaven invited his friends to sit down and have a bite to eat.

No one could have been more grateful than Peter. The one Satan had sifted like wheat was eating bread at the hand of God. Peter was welcomed to the meal of Christ. Right there for the devil and his tempters to see, Jesus "prepared a table in the presence of his enemies."

OK, so maybe Peter didn't say it that way. But David did. "You prepare a table before me in the presence of my enemies" (Ps. 23:5 NKJV). What the shepherd did for the sheep sounds a lot like what Jesus did for Peter.

At this point in the psalm, David's mind seems to be lingering in the high country with the sheep. Having guided the flock through the valley to the alp lands for greener grass, he remembers the shepherd's added responsibility. He must prepare the pasture.

This is new land, so the shepherd must be careful. Ideally, the grazing area will be flat, a mesa or tableland. The shepherd searches for poisonous plants and ample water. He looks for signs of wolves, coyotes, and bears.

Of special concern to the shepherd is the adder, a small brown snake that lives underground. Adders are known to pop out of their holes and nip the sheep on the nose. The bite often infects and can even kill. As defense against the snake, the shepherd pours a circle of oil at the top of each adder's hole. He also applies the oil to the noses of the animals. The oil on the snake's hole lubricates the exit, preventing the snake from climbing out. The smell of the oil on the sheep's nose drives the serpent away. The shepherd, in a very real sense, has prepared the table.[1]

What if your Shepherd did for you what the shepherd did for his flock? Suppose he dealt with your enemy, the devil, and prepared for you a safe place of nourishment? What if Jesus did for you what he did for Peter? Suppose he, in the hour of your failure, invited you to a meal?

What would you say if I told you he has done exactly that?

On the night before his death, Jesus prepared a table for his followers.

> On the first day of the Festival of Unleavened Bread, the day the lambs for the Passover meal were killed, Jesus' disciples asked him, "Where do you want us to go and get the Passover meal ready for you?"
>
> Then Jesus sent two of them with these instructions: "Go into the city, and a man carrying a jar of water will meet you. Follow him to the house he enters, and say to the owner of the house: 'The Teacher says, Where is the room where my disciples and I will eat the Passover meal?' Then he will show you a large, upstairs room, fixed up and furnished, where you will get everything ready for us." (Mark 14:12–15 TEV)

Look who did the "preparing" here. Jesus reserved a large room and arranged for the guide to lead the disciples. Jesus made certain the room was furnished and the food set out. What did the disciples do? They faithfully complied and were fed.

The Shepherd prepared the table.

Not only that, he dealt with the snakes. You'll remember that only one of the disciples didn't complete the meal that night. "The devil had already persuaded Judas Iscariot, the son of Simon, to turn against Jesus" (John 13:2). Judas started to eat, but Jesus didn't let him finish. On the command of Jesus, Judas left the room. "'The thing that you will do—do it quickly.' . . . Judas took the bread Jesus gave him and immediately went out. It was night" (John 13:27, 30).

There is something dynamic in this dismissal. Jesus prepared a table in the presence of the enemy. Judas was allowed to see the supper, but he wasn't allowed to stay there.

You are not welcome here. This table is for my children. You may tempt them. You may trip them. But you will never sit with them. This is how much he loves us.

And if any doubt remains, lest there be any "Peters" who wonder if there is a place at the table for them, Jesus issues a tender reminder as he passes the cup. "Every one of you drink this. This is my blood which is the new agreement that God makes with his people. This blood is poured out for many to forgive their sins" (Matt. 26:27–28).

"*Every one* of you drink this." Those who feel unworthy, drink this. Those who feel ashamed, drink this. Those who feel embarrassed, drink this.

May I share a time when I felt all three?

By the age of eighteen I was well on my way to a drinking problem. My system had become so resistant to alcohol that a six-pack of beer had little or no impact on me. At the age of twenty, God not only saved me from hell after this life, he saved me from hell during it. Only he knows where I was headed, but I have a pretty good idea.

For that reason, part of my decision to follow Christ included no more beer. So I quit. But, curiously, the thirst for beer never left. It hasn't hounded me or consumed me, but two or three times a week the thought of a good beer sure entices me. Proof to me that I have to be careful is this—nonalcoholic beers have no appeal. It's not the flavor of the drink; it's the buzz. But for more than twenty years, drinking has never been a major issue.

A couple of years ago, however, it nearly became one. I lowered my guard a bit. *One beer with barbecue won't hurt.* Then another time with Mexican food. Then a time or two with no food at all. Over a period of two months I went from no beers to maybe one or two a week. Again, for most people, no problem, but for me it could become one.

You know when I began to smell trouble? One hot Friday afternoon I was on my way to speak at our annual men's retreat. Did I say the day was hot? Brutally hot. I was thirsty. Soda wouldn't do. So I began to plot. Where could I buy a beer and not be seen by anyone I knew?

With that thought, I crossed a line. What's done in secret is best not done at all. But I did it anyway. I drove to an out-of-the-way convenience store, parked, and waited until all patrons had left. I entered, bought my beer, held it close to my side, and hurried to the car.

That's when the rooster crowed.

It crowed because I was sneaking around. It crowed because I knew better. It crowed because, and this really hurt, the night before I'd scolded one of my daughters for keeping secrets from me. And now, what was I doing?

I threw the beer in the trash and asked God to forgive me. A few days later I shared my struggle with the elders and some members of the congregation and was happy to chalk up the matter to experience and move on.

But I couldn't. The shame plagued me. Of all the people to do such a thing. So many could be hurt by my stupidity. And of all the times to do such a thing. En route to minister at a retreat. What hypocrisy!

I felt like a bum. Forgiveness found its way into my head, but the elevator designed to lower it eighteen inches to my heart was out of order.

And, to make matters worse, Sunday rolled around. I found myself on the front row of the church, awaiting my turn to speak. Again, I had been honest with God, honest with the elders, honest with myself. But still, I struggled. Would God want a guy like me to preach?

The answer came in the Supper. The Lord's Supper. The same Jesus who'd prepared a meal for Peter had prepared one for me. The same Shepherd who had trumped the devil trumped him again. The same Savior who had built a fire on the shore stirred a few embers in my heart.

"*Every one* of you drink this." And so I did. It felt good to be back at the table.

15

Slippery Sheep and Healed Hurts

The Burden of Disappointment

You anoint my head with oil.

PSALM 23:5 NKJV

D*is* changes everything. With *dis*, "obey" becomes "*dis*obey." "Respect" is changed to "*dis*respect." "Regard" is suddenly "*dis*regard." What was an "ability" becomes a "*dis*ability." "Engage" is now "*dis*engage," and "grace" is transformed into "*dis*grace." All because of *dis*.

We'd be hard pressed to find a more potent trio of letters. And we'd be hard pressed to find a better example of their power than the word *appointment*.

Most of us like appointments. Even the organizationally inept like appointments. Appointments create a sense of predictability in an unpredictable world. Down deep we know we control the future as much as a caboose controls the train, yet our Day-Timers give us the illusion that we do.

A disappointment reminds us that we don't. A disappointment is a missed appointment. What we hoped would happen, didn't. We wanted health; we got disease. We wanted retirement; we got reassignment. Divorce instead of family. Dismissal instead of promotion. Now what? What do we do with our disappointments?

We could do what Miss Haversham did. Remember her in Charles Dickens's *Great Expectations*? Jilted by her fiancé just prior to the wedding, her appointment became a missed appointment and a disappointment. How did she respond? Not too well. She closed all the blinds in the house, stopped every clock, left the wedding cake on the table to gather cobwebs, and continued to wear her wedding dress until it hung in yellow decay around her shrunken form. Her wounded heart consumed her life.

We can follow the same course.

Or we can follow the example of the apostle Paul. His goal was to be a missionary in Spain. Rather than send Paul to Spain, however, God sent him to prison. Sitting in a Roman jail, Paul could have made the same choice as Miss Haversham, but he didn't. Instead he said, "As long as I'm here, I might as well write a few letters." Hence your Bible has the Epistles to Philemon, the Philippians, the Colossians, and the Ephesians.[1] No doubt Paul would have done a great work in Spain. But would it have compared with the work of those four letters?

You've sat where Paul sat. I know you have. You were hotter than a two-dollar pistol on the trail to Spain or college or marriage or independence . . . but then came the layoff or the pregnancy or the sick parent. And you ended up in prison. So long, Spain. Hello, Rome. So long, appointment. Hello, disappointment. Hello, pain.

How did you handle it? Better asked, how are you handling it? Could you use some help? I've got just what you need. Six words in the fifth verse of the Twenty-third Psalm: "You anoint my head with oil."

Don't see the connection? What does a verse on oil have to do with the hurts that come from the disappointments of life?

A little livestock lesson might help. In ancient Israel shepherds used oil for three purposes: to repel insects, to prevent conflicts, and to heal wounds.

Bugs bug people, but they can kill sheep. Flies, mosquitoes, and gnats can turn the summer into a time of torture for the livestock. Consider nose flies, for example. If they succeed in depositing their eggs into the soft membrane of the sheep's nose, the eggs become wormlike larvae, which drive the sheep insane. One shepherd explains: "For relief from this agonizing annoyance sheep will deliberately beat their heads against trees, rocks, posts, or brush. . . . In extreme cases of intense infestation a sheep may even kill itself in a frenzied endeavor to gain respite from the aggravation."[2]

When a swarm of nose flies appears, sheep panic. They run. They hide. They toss their heads up and down for hours. They forget to eat. They aren't able to sleep. Ewes stop milking, and lambs stop growing. The entire flock can be disrupted, even destroyed by the presence of a few flies.

For this reason, the shepherd anoints the sheep. He covers their heads with an oil-like repellent. The fragrance keeps the insects at bay and the flock at peace.

At peace, that is, until mating season. Most of the year, sheep are calm, passive animals. But during mating season, everything changes. The rams put the "ram" in *rambunctious*. They strut around the pasture and flex their necks, trying to win the attention of the new gal on the block. When a ram catches her eye, he tosses his head back and says, "I want ewe, baby." About that time her boyfriend shows up and tells her to go someplace safe. "Ewe better move, sweetie. This could get ugly." The two rams lower their heads and POW! An old-fashioned head butt breaks out.

To prevent injury, the shepherd anoints the rams. He smears a slippery, greasy substance over the nose and head. This lubricant causes them to glance off rather than crash into each other.

They still tend to get hurt, however. And these wounds are the third reason the shepherd anoints the sheep.

Most of the wounds the shepherd treats are simply the result of living in a pasture. Thorns prick or rocks cut or a sheep rubs its head too hard against a tree. Sheep get hurt. As a result, the shepherd regularly, often daily, inspects the sheep, searching for cuts and abrasions. He doesn't want the cut to worsen. He doesn't want today's wound to become tomorrow's infection.

Neither does God. Just like sheep, we have wounds, but ours are wounds of the heart that come from disappointment after disappointment. If we're not careful, these wounds lead to bitterness. And so just like sheep, we need to be treated. "He made us, and we belong to him; we are his people, the sheep he tends" (Ps. 100:3).

Sheep aren't the only ones who need preventive care, and sheep aren't the only ones who need a healing touch. We also get irritated with each other, butt heads, and then get wounded. Many of our disappointments in life begin as irritations. The large portion of our problems are not lion-sized attacks, but rather the day-to-day swarm of frustrations and mishaps and heartaches. You don't get invited to the dinner party. You don't make the team. You don't get the scholarship. Your boss doesn't notice your hard work. Your husband doesn't notice your new dress. Your neighbor doesn't notice the mess in his yard. You find yourself more irritable, more gloomy, more . . . well, more hurt.

Like the sheep, you don't sleep well, you don't eat well. You may even hit your head against a tree a few times.

Or you may hit your head against a person. It's amazing how hard-headed we can be with each other. Some of our deepest hurts come from butting heads with people.

Like the sheep, the rest of our wounds come just from living in the pasture. The pasture of the sheep, however, is much more appealing. The sheep have to face wounds from thorns and thistles. We have to face aging, loss, and illness. Some of us face betrayal and injustice. Live long enough in this world, and most of us will face deep, deep hurts of some kind or another.

So we, like the sheep, get wounded. And we, like the sheep, have a shepherd. Remember the words we read? "We belong to him; we are his people, the sheep he tends" (Ps. 100:3). He will do for you what the shepherd does for the sheep. He will tend to you.

If the Gospels teach us anything, they teach us that Jesus is a Good Shepherd. "I am the good shepherd," Jesus announces. "The good shepherd gives his life for the sheep" (John 10:11).

Didn't Jesus spread the oil of prevention on his disciples? He prayed for them. He equipped them before he sent them out. He revealed to them the secrets of the parables. He interrupted their arguments and calmed their fears. Because he was a good shepherd, he protected them against disappointments.

Not only did Jesus prevent wounds, he healed them. He touched the eyes of the blind man. He touched the disease of the leper. He touched the body of the dead girl. Jesus tends to his sheep. He touched the searching heart of Nicodemus. He touched the open heart of Zacchaeus. He touched the broken heart of Mary Magdalene. He touched the confused heart of Cleopas. And he touched the stubborn heart of Paul and the repentant heart of Peter. Jesus tends to his sheep. And he will tend to you.

If you will let him. How? How do you let him? The steps are so simple.

First, go to him. David would trust his wounds to no other person but God. He said, "*You* anoint my head with oil." Not, "your prophets," "your teachers," or "your counselors." Others may guide us to God. Others may help us understand God. But no one does the work of God, for only God can heal. God "heals the brokenhearted" (Ps. 147:3).

Have you taken your disappointments to God? You've shared them with your neighbor, your relatives, your friends. But have you taken them to God? James says, "Anyone who is having troubles should pray" (James 5:13).

Before you go anywhere else with your disappointments, go to God.

Maybe you don't want to trouble God with your hurts. *After all, he's got famines and pestilence and wars; he won't care about my little struggles,* you think. Why don't you let him decide that? He cared enough about a wedding to provide the wine. He cared enough about Peter's tax payment to give him a coin. He cared enough about the woman at the well to give her answers. "He cares about you" (1 Pet. 5:7).

Your first step is to go to the right person. Go to God. Your second step is to assume the right posture. Bow before God.

In order to be anointed, the sheep must stand still, lower their heads, and let the shepherd do his work. Peter urges us to "be humble under God's powerful hand so he will lift you up when the right time comes" (1 Pet. 5:6).

When we come to God, we make requests; we don't make demands. We come with high hopes and a humble heart. We state what we want, but we pray for what is right. And if God gives us the prison of Rome instead of the mission of Spain, we accept it because we know "God will always give what is right to his people who cry to him night and day, and he will not be slow to answer them" (Luke 18:7).

We go to him. We bow before him, and we *trust in him.*

The sheep doesn't understand why the oil repels the flies. The sheep doesn't understand how the oil heals the wounds. In fact, all the sheep knows is that something happens in the presence of the shepherd. And that's all we need to know as well. "LORD, I give myself to you; my God, I trust you" (Ps. 25:1–2).

Go.

Bow.

Trust.

Worth a try, don't you think?

16

Jam Session

The Burden of Envy

My cup overflows with blessings.

Psalm 23:5 NLT

A member of our church gave me a jar of homemade peach preserves a couple of weeks ago. Few delicacies in life compare with her peach preserves. Should I someday face a firing squad, I'll pass on the cigarette but be the first to perk up if Sarah's peach preserves are offered. Each spoonful is a celestial experience. The only problem with her gift was that it didn't last. I'm sad to report that the bottom of my jar is in sight. I'll soon be shaking out the last drop like a lost cowboy shakes his canteen.

To be quite honest, I'm dreading the moment. Its proximity has affected my behavior. Anyone who requests a taste of my peach preserves is met with a Clint Eastwood snarl, "Don't even think about it."

If I were Sarah's husband, Keith, I wouldn't have such a problem. He gets all the peach preserves he wants. Does the clinking of the spoon at the bottom of the jar trigger tears for Keith? Hardly, he has an unlimited supply. One might even say that he has more than he deserves. And one might wonder why he has so much and I have so little. Why should he have a pantryful and I just a jarful? Who gave him the key to the jam-and-jelly castle? Who made him the master of marmalades? Who crowned Keith the king of confitures? It's not fair. It's not right. In fact, the more I think about it . . .

Which is exactly what I shouldn't do. I shouldn't think about it. For resting at the end of this trail of thought is the deadly briefcase of envy.

If you haven't seen one in real life, you've seen one in the spy movies. The assassin carries it up the back stairs into the vacated room at the top of the building. When he is sure no one can see him, he opens the case. The disassembled rifle sits in cushioned slots. The scope, the barrel, the stock—all await the hand of the marksman. The marksman awaits the arrival of his victim.

Who is his victim? Anyone who has more than he has. More karats, more horsepower, more office space, more church members. Jealousy sets her cross hairs on the one who has more. "You want something you don't have, and you will do anything to get it. You will even kill!" (James 4:2 CEV).

Honestly, Max, I would never do that. I would never kill.

With a rifle, maybe not. But with your tongue? With your glare? Your gossip? "Jealousy," informs Proverbs 6:34, "enrages a man" (NASB). Are your sights set on someone? If so, be careful; "jealousy will rot your bones" (Prov. 14:30).

Need a deterrent for envy? An antidote for jealousy? The psalm we are studying offers one. Rather than bemoan the peach preserves you don't have, rejoice in the abundant cup you do. "My cup overflows with blessings" (Ps. 23:5 NLT).

Is an overflowing cup full? Absolutely. The wine reaches the rim and then tumbles over the edge. The goblet is not large enough to contain the quantity. According to David, our hearts are not large enough to contain the blessings that God wants to give. He pours and pours until they literally flow over the edge and down on the table. You'll like the paragraph penned a century ago by F. B. Meyer:

> Whatever the blessing is in our cup, it is sure to run over. With him the calf is always the fatted calf; the robe is always the best robe; the joy is unspeakable; the peace passeth understanding. . . . There is no

> grudging in God's benevolence; He does not measure out his goodness as an apothecary counts his drops and measures his drams, slowly and exactly, drop by drop. God's way is always characterized by multitudinous and overflowing bounty.[1]

The last thing we need to worry about is not having enough. Our cup overflows with blessings.

Let me ask a question—a crucial question. If focusing on our diminishing items leads to envy, what would happen if we focused on the unending items? If awareness of what we don't have creates jealousy, is it possible that an awareness of our abundance will lead to contentment? Let's give it a try and see what happens. Let's dedicate a few paragraphs to a couple of blessings that, according to the Bible, are overflowing in our lives.

Abounding grace. "The more we see our sinfulness, the more we see God's *abounding grace* forgiving us" (Rom. 5:20 TLB, emphasis mine). To abound is to have a surplus, an abundance, an extravagant portion. Should the fish in the Pacific worry that it will run out of ocean? No. Why? The ocean abounds with water. Need the lark be anxious about finding room in the sky to fly? No. The sky abounds with space.

Should the Christian worry that the cup of mercy will run empty? He may. For he may not be aware of God's abounding grace. Are you? Are you aware that the cup God gives you *overflows* with mercy? Or are you afraid your cup will run dry? Your warranty will expire? Are you afraid your mistakes are too great for God's grace?

We can't help but wonder if the apostle Paul had the same fear. Before he was Paul the apostle, he was Saul the murderer. Before he encouraged Christians, he murdered Christians. What would it be like to live with such a past? Did he ever meet children whom he had made orphans? Did their faces haunt his sleep? Did Paul ever ask, "Can God forgive a man like me?"

The answer to his and our questions is found in a letter he wrote to Timothy: "The grace of our Lord was poured out on me abundantly, along with the faith and love that are in Christ Jesus" (1 Tim. 1:14 NIV).

God is not a miser with his grace. Your cup may be low on cash or clout, but it is overflowing with mercy. You may not have the prime parking place, but you have sufficient pardon. "He will abundantly pardon" (Isa. 55:7 NKJV). Your cup overflows with grace.

Hope. And because it does, your cup overflows with hope. "God will help you overflow with hope in him through the Holy Spirit's power within you" (Rom. 15:13 TLB).

Heaven's hope does for your world what the sunlight did for my grandmother's cellar. I owe my love of peach preserves to her. She canned her own and stored them in an underground cellar near her West Texas house. It was a deep hole with wooden steps, plywood walls, and a musty smell. As a youngster I used to climb in, close the door, and see how long I could last in the darkness. Not even a slit of light entered that underground hole. I would sit silently, listening to my breath and heartbeats, until I couldn't take it anymore and then would race up the stairs and throw open the door. Light would avalanche into the cellar. What a change! Moments before I couldn't see anything—all of a sudden I could see everything.

Just as light poured into the cellar, God's hope pours into your world. Upon the sick, he shines the ray of healing. To the bereaved, he gives the promise of reunion. For the dying, he lit the flame of resurrection. To the confused, he offers the light of Scripture.

God gives hope. So what if someone was born thinner or stronger, lighter or darker than you? Why count diplomas or compare résumés?

What does it matter if they have a place at the head table? You have a place at God's table. And he is filling your cup to overflowing.

The overflowing cup was a powerful symbol in the days of David. Hosts in the ancient East used it to send a message to the guest. As long as the cup was kept full, the guest knew he was welcome. But when the cup sat empty, the host was hinting that the hour was late. On those occasions, however, when the host really enjoyed the company of the person, he filled the cup to overflowing. He didn't stop when the wine reached the rim; he kept pouring until the liquid ran over the edge of the cup and down on the table.[2]

Have you noticed how wet your table is? God wants you to stay. Your cup overflows with joy. Overflows with grace. Shouldn't your heart overflow with gratitude?

The heart of the boy did. Not at first, mind you. Initially he was full of envy. But, in time, he was full of gratitude.

According to the fable, he lived with his father in a valley at the base of a large dam. Every day the father would go to work on the mountain behind their house and return home with a wheelbarrow full of dirt. "Pour the dirt in the sacks, Son," the father would say. "And stack them in front of the house."

And though the boy would obey, he also complained. He was tired of dirt. He was weary of bags. Why didn't his father give him what other fathers gave their sons? They had toys and games; he had dirt. When he saw what the others had, he grew mad at them. "It's not fair," he said to himself.

And when he saw his father, he objected. "They have fun. I have dirt."

The father would smile and place his arm on the boy's shoulders and say, "Trust me, Son. I'm doing what is best."

But it was so hard for the boy to trust. Every day the father would bring the load. Every day the boy would fill bags. "Stack them as high as you can," the father would say as he went for more. And so the boy filled the bags and piled them high. So high he couldn't see over them.

"Work hard, Son," the father said one day. "We're running out of time." As the father spoke, he looked at the darkening sky. The boy stared at the clouds and turned to ask about them, but when he did, the thunder cracked and the sky opened. The rain poured so hard he could scarcely see his father through the water. "Keep stacking, Son!" And as he did, the boy heard a mighty crash.

The water of the river poured through the dam and toward the little village. In a moment the tide swept everything in its path, but the dike of dirt gave the boy and the father the time they needed. "Hurry, Son. Follow me."

They ran to the side of the mountain behind their house and into a tunnel. In a matter of moments they exited the other side and scampered up the hill and came upon a new cottage.

"We'll be safe here," the father said to the boy.

Only then did the son realize what the father had done. He had burrowed an exit. Rather than give him what he wanted, the father gave his boy what he needed. He gave him a safe passage and a safe place.

Hasn't our Father given us the same? A strong wall of grace to protect us? A sure exit to deliver us? Of whom can we be envious? Who has more than we do? Rather than want what others have, shouldn't we wonder if they have what we do? Instead of being jealous of them, how about zealous for them? For heaven's sake, drop the rifles and hold out the cup. There is enough to go around.

One thing is certain. When the final storm comes and you are safe in your Father's house, you won't regret what he didn't give. You'll be stunned at what he did.

17

God's Loving Pursuit

The Burden of Doubt

Surely goodness and mercy shall follow me
all the days of my life.

Psalm 23:6 NKJV

Eric Hill had everything you'd need for a bright future. He was twenty-eight years old and a recent college grad with an athletic frame and a soft smile. His family loved him, girls took notice of him, and companies had contacted him about working for them. Although Eric appeared composed without, he was tormented within. Tormented by voices he could not still. Bothered by images he could not avoid. So, hoping to get away from them all, he got away from it all. On a gray rainy day in February 1982, Eric Hill walked out the back door of his Florida home and never came back.

His sister Debbie remembers seeing him leave, his tall frame ambling down the interstate. She assumed he would return. He didn't. She hoped he would call. He didn't. She thought she could find him. She couldn't. Where Eric journeyed, only God and Eric know, and neither of them has chosen to tell. What we do know is Eric heard a voice. And in that voice was an "assignment." And that assignment was to pick up garbage along a roadside in San Antonio, Texas.

To the commuters on Interstate 10, his lanky form and bearded face became a familiar sight. He made a home out of a hole in a vacant lot. He made a wardrobe out of split trousers and a torn sweatshirt. An old hat deferred the summer sun. A plastic bag on his shoulders softened the winter chill. His weathered skin and stooped shoulders made him look twice his forty-four years. But then, sixteen years on the side of the road would do that to you.

That's how long it had been since Debbie had seen her brother. She might never have seen him again had it not been for two events. The first was the construction of a car dealership on Eric's vacant lot. The second was a severe pain in his abdomen. The dealership took his home. The pain nearly took his life.

EMS found him curled in a ball on the side of the road, clutching his stomach. The hospital ran some tests and found that Eric had cancer. Terminal cancer. Another few months and he would be dead. And with no known family or relatives, he would die alone.

His court-appointed attorney couldn't handle this thought. "Surely someone is looking for Eric," he reasoned. So the lawyer scoured the Internet for anyone in search of a brown-haired, adult male with the last name Hill. That's how he met Debbie.

His description seemed to match her memory, but she had to know for sure.

So Debbie came to Texas. She and her husband and two children rented a hotel room and set out to find Eric. By now he'd been released from the hospital, but the chaplain knew where he was. They found him sitting against a building not far from the interstate. As they approached, he stood. They offered fruit; he refused. They offered juice; he declined. He was polite but unimpressed with this family who claimed to be his own.

His interest perked, however, when Debbie offered him a pin to wear, an angel pin. He said yes. Her first time to touch her brother in sixteen years was the moment he allowed her to pin the angel on his shirt.

Debbie intended to spend a week. But a week passed, and she stayed. Her husband returned home, and she stayed. Spring became summer, and Eric improved, and still she stayed. Debbie rented an apartment and began homeschooling her kids and reaching out to her brother.

It wasn't easy. He didn't recognize her. He didn't know her. One day he cursed her. He didn't want to sleep in her apartment. He didn't want her food. He didn't want to talk. He wanted his vacant lot. He wanted his "job." Who was this woman anyway?

But Debbie didn't give up on Eric. She understood that he didn't understand. So she stayed.

I met her one Sunday when she visited our congregation. When she shared her story, I asked what you might want to ask. "How do you keep from giving up?"

"Simple," she said. "He's my brother."

I told her that her pursuit reminded me of another pursuit—that her heart reminded me of another heart. Another kind heart who left home in search of the confused. Another compassionate soul who couldn't bear the thought of a brother or sister in pain. So, like Debbie, he left home. Like Debbie, he found his sibling.

And when Jesus found us, we acted like Eric. Our limitations kept us from recognizing the One who came to save us. We even doubted his presence—and sometimes we still do.

How does he deal with our doubts? He follows us. As Debbie followed Eric, God follows us. He pursues us until we finally see him as our Father, even if it takes *all the days of our lives.*

"Surely goodness and mercy shall follow me all the days of my life; and I will dwell in the house of the LORD forever" (Ps. 23:6 NKJV).

This must be one of the sweetest phrases ever penned. Can we read it from a few other translations?

"Goodness and love unfailing, these will follow me all the days of my life, and I shall dwell in the house of the LORD my whole life long" (NEB).

"I know that your goodness and love will be with me all my life; and your house will be my home as long as I live" (TEV).

"Your beauty and love chase after me every day of my life. I'm back home in the house of YAHWEH for the rest of my life" (MSG).

To read the verse is to open a box of jewels. Each word sparkles and begs to be examined in the face of our doubts: *goodness, mercy, all the days, dwell in the house of the LORD, forever.* They sweep in on insecurities like a SWAT team on a terrorist.

Look at the first word: *surely*. David didn't say, "*Maybe* goodness and mercy shall follow me." Or "*Possibly* goodness and mercy shall follow me." Or "*I have a hunch* that goodness and mercy shall follow me." David could have used one of those phrases. But he didn't. He believed in a sure God, who makes sure promises and provides a sure foundation. David would have loved the words of one of his great-great-grandsons, the apostle James. He described God as the one "with whom there is never the slightest variation or shadow of inconsistency" (James 1:17 PHILLIPS).

Our moods may shift, but God's doesn't. Our minds may change, but God's doesn't. Our devotion may falter, but God's never does. Even if we are faithless, he is faithful, for he cannot betray himself (2 Tim. 2:13). He is a sure God. And because he is a sure God, we can state confidently, "Surely goodness and mercy shall follow me all the days of my life."

And what follows the word *surely?* "Goodness and mercy." If the Lord is the shepherd who leads the flock, goodness and mercy are the two sheepdogs that guard the rear of the flock. Goodness *and* mercy. Not goodness alone, for we are sinners in need of mercy. Not mercy alone, for we are fragile, in need of goodness. We need them both. As one man wrote, "Goodness to supply every want. Mercy to forgive every sin. Goodness to provide. Mercy to pardon."[1]

Goodness and mercy—the celestial escort of God's flock. If that duo doesn't reinforce your faith, try this phrase: "all the days of my life."

What a huge statement. Look at the size of it! Goodness and mercy follow the child of God each and every day! Think of the days that lie ahead. What do you see? Days at home with only toddlers? God will be at your side. Days in a dead-end job? He will walk you through. Days of loneliness? He will take your hand. Surely goodness and mercy shall follow me—not some, not most, not nearly all—but all the days of my life.

And what will he do during those days? (Here is my favorite word.) He will "follow" you.

What a surprising way to describe God! We're accustomed to a God who remains in one place. A God who sits enthroned in the heavens and rules and ordains. David, however, envisions a mobile and active God. Dare we do the same? Dare we envision a God who follows us? Who pursues us? Who chases us? Who tracks us down and wins us over? Who follows us with "goodness and mercy" all the days of our lives?

Isn't this the kind of God described in the Bible? A God who follows us? There are many in the Scriptures who would say so. You have to go no farther than the third chapter of the first book before you find God in the role of a seeker. Adam and Eve are hiding in the bushes, partly to cover their bodies, partly to cover their sin. But does God wait for them to come to him? No, the words ring in the garden: "Where are you?" (Gen. 3:9). With that question God began a quest for the heart of humanity that continues up to and through the moment you read these words.

Moses can tell you about it. He was forty years in the desert when he looked over his shoulder and saw a bush blazing. God had followed him into the wilderness.

Jonah can tell you about it. He was a fugitive on a boat when he looked over his shoulder and saw clouds brewing. God had followed him onto the ocean.

The disciples of Jesus knew the feeling of being followed by God. They were rain soaked and shivering when they looked over their shoulders and saw Jesus walking toward them. God had followed them into the storm.

An unnamed Samaritan woman knew the same. She was alone in life and alone at the well when she looked over her shoulder and heard a Messiah speaking. God had followed her through her pain.

John the Apostle was banished on Patmos when he looked over his shoulder and saw the skies begin to open. God had followed him into his exile.

Lazarus was three days dead in a sealed tomb when he heard a voice, lifted his head, and looked over his shoulder and saw Jesus standing. God had followed him into death.

Peter had denied his Lord and gone back to fishing when he heard his name and looked over his shoulder and saw Jesus cooking breakfast. God had followed him in spite of his failure.

God is the God who follows. I wonder . . . have you sensed him following you? We often miss him. Like Eric, we don't know our Helper when he is near. But he comes.

Through the kindness of a stranger. The majesty of a sunset. The mystery of romance. Through the question of a child or the commitment of a spouse. Through a word well spoken or a touch well timed, have you sensed his presence?

If so, then release your doubts. Set them down. Be encumbered by them no longer. You are no candidate for insecurity. You are no longer a client of timidity. You can trust God. He has given his love to you; why don't you give your doubts to him?

Not easy to trust, you say? Maybe not, but neither is it as difficult as you think. Try these ideas:

Trust your faith and not your feelings. You don't feel spiritual each day? Of course you don't. But your feelings have no impact on God's presence. On the days you don't feel close to God, trust your faith and not your feelings. Goodness and mercy shall follow you all the days of your life.

Measure your value through God's eyes, not your own. To everyone else, Eric Hill was a homeless drifter. But to Debbie, he was a brother. There are times in our lives when we are gangrels—homeless, disoriented, hard to help, and hard to love. In those seasons remember this simple fact: God loves you. He follows you. Why? Because you are family, and he will follow you all the days of your life.

See the big picture, not the small. Eric's home was taken. His health was taken. But through the tragedy, his family was returned to him. Perhaps your home and health have been threatened as well. The immediate result might be pain. But the long-term result might be finding a Father you never knew. A Father who will follow you all the days of your life.

By the way, the last chapter in Eric Hill's life is the best one. Days before he died he recognized Debbie as his sister. And, in doing so, he discovered his home.

We will as well. Like Eric, we have doubted our Helper. But like Debbie, God has followed us. Like Eric, we are quick to turn away. But like Debbie, God is slow to anger and determined to stay. Like Eric, we don't accept God's gifts. But like Debbie, God still gives them. He gives us his angels, not just pinned on a lapel, but placed on our path.

And most of all, God gives us himself. Even when we choose our hovel over his house and our trash over his grace, still he follows. Never forcing us. Never leaving us. Patiently persistent. Faithfully present. Using all of his power to convince us that he is who he is and that he can be trusted to lead us home.

His goodness and mercy will follow us all the days of our lives.

18

Almost Heaven

The Burden of Homesickness

I will dwell in the house of the L*ORD* *forever.*

PSALM 23:6 NKJV

For the last twenty years, I've wanted a dog. A big dog. But there were always problems. The apartment was too small. The budget was too tight. The girls were too young. But most of all, Denalyn was unenthusiastic. Her logic? She'd already married one slobbering, shedding beast, why put up with a second? So we compromised and got a small dog.

I like Salty, but small dogs aren't really dogs. They don't bark; they yelp. They don't eat; they nibble. They don't lick you; they sniff you. I like Salty, but I wanted a real dog. A man's-best-friend type of dog. A fat-pawed, big-eating, slurp-you-on-the-face type of dog you could saddle or wrestle or both.

I was alone in my passion until Sara was born. She loves dogs. And the two of us were able to sway the household vote. Denalyn gave in, and Sara and I began the search. We discovered a woman in South Carolina who breeds golden retrievers in a Christian environment. From birth the dogs are surrounded by inspirational music and prayers. (No, I don't know if they tithe with dog biscuits.) When the trainer told me that she had read my books, I got on board. A woman with such good taste is bound to be a good breeder, right?

So we ordered a pup. We mailed the check, selected the name Molly, and cleared a corner for her dog pillow. The dog hadn't even been born, and she was named, claimed, and given a place in the house.

Can't the same be said about you? Long before your first whimper, your Master claimed you, named you, and hung a reserved sign on your room. You and Molly have more in common than odor and eating habits. (Just teasing.)

You're both being groomed for a trip. We prefer the terms *maturation* and *sanctification* to *weaning* and *training,* but it's all the same. You're being prepared for your Master's house. You don't know the departure date or flight number, but you can bet your puppy chow that you'll be seeing your Owner someday. Isn't this the concluding promise of David?

"And I will dwell in the house of the LORD forever" (Ps. 23:6 NKJV).

Where will you live forever? In the house of the Lord. If his house is your "forever house," what does that make this earthly house? You got it! Short-term housing. This is not our home. "Our homeland is in heaven" (Phil. 3:20).

This explains the homesickness we feel.

Have you ever longed to be home? May I share a time when I did? I was spending the summer of my nineteenth year working in northern Georgia. The folks in that region are very nice, but no one is too nice to a door-to-door salesman. There were times that summer when I was so lonely for home I felt my bones would melt.

One of those occasions came on the side of a country road. The hour was late, and I was lost. I'd stopped to pull out a flashlight and a map. To my right was a farmhouse. In the farmhouse was a family. I knew it was a family because I could see them. Right through the big plate-glass window, I could see the mother and father and boy and girl. Norman Rockwell would have placed them on a canvas. The mom was spooning out food, and the dad was telling a story, and the kids were laughing, and it was all I could do to keep from ringing the doorbell and asking for a place at the table. I felt so far from home.

What I felt that night, some of you have felt ever since . . .

your husband died.

your child was buried.

you learned about the lump in your breast or the spot in your lung.

Some of you have felt far from home ever since your home fell apart.

The twists and turns of life have a way of reminding us—we aren't home here. This is not our homeland. We aren't fluent in the languages of disease and death. The culture confuses the heart, the noise disrupts our sleep, and we feel far from home.

And, you know what? That's OK.

Homesickness is one of the burdens God doesn't mind if we carry. We, like Molly, are being prepared for another house. And we, like the parakeet from Green Bay, know we aren't there yet.

Pootsie was her name. She escaped from her owner and came into the keeping of the humane society. When no one else claimed her, Sue Gleason did. They hit it off. They talked and bathed together, becoming fast friends. But one day the little bird did something incredible. It flew over to Mrs. Gleason, put her beak in her ear, and whispered, "Fifteen hundred South Oneida Street, Green Bay."

Gleason was dumbfounded. She researched and found that the address existed. She went to the house and found a seventy-nine-year-old man named John Stroobants.

"Do you have a parakeet?" she asked.

"I used to; I miss him terribly."

When he saw his Pootsie, he was thrilled. "You know, he even knows his phone number."[1]

The story isn't as crazy as you might think. You have an eternal address fixed in your mind as well. God has "set eternity in the hearts of men" (Eccles. 3:11 NIV). Down deep you know you are not home yet.

So be careful not to act like you are. Don't lower the duffel bag too soon. Would you hang pictures on the wall of a Greyhound bus? Do you set up a bedroom at the roadside rest stop? Do you load your king-size bed on a commercial flight?

Would you treat this world like home? It isn't. The greatest calamity is not to feel far from home when you are, but to feel right at home when you are not. Don't quench, but rather, stir this longing for heaven.

God's home is a *forever* home. "And I will dwell in the house of the LORD forever" (Ps. 23:6 NKJV).

My friends Jeff and Carol just adopted two small children. Christopher, the older, is only three, but he knows the difference between Jeff's house and the foster home from which he came. He tells all visitors, "This is my forever home."

Won't it be great when we say the same? Couldn't we use a forever home? This home we're in won't last forever. Birthdays remind us of that.

During the writing of this book I turned forty-six. I'm closer to ninety than I am to infancy. All those things they say about aging are coming true. I'm patting myself less on the back and more under the chin. I have everything I had twenty years ago, except now it's all lower. The other day I tried to straighten out the wrinkles in my socks and found out I wasn't wearing any. I can relate to Dave Barry's description of aging:

> . . . dental problems, intestinal malfunctions, muscle deterioration, emotional instability, memory lapses, hearing and vision loss, impotence, seizures, growths, prostate problems, greatly reduced limb function, massive coronary failure, death, and, of course, painful hemorrhoidal swelling.[2]

Aging. It's no fun. The way we try to avoid it, you'd think we could. We paint the body, preserve the body, protect the body. And well we should. These bodies are God's gifts. We should be responsible. But we should also be realistic. This body must die so the new body can live. "Flesh and blood cannot have a part in the kingdom of God. Something that will ruin cannot have a part in something that never ruins" (1 Cor. 15:50).

Aging is God's idea. It's one of the ways he keeps us headed homeward. We can't change the process, but we can change our attitude. Here is a thought. What if we looked at the aging body as we look at the growth of a tulip?

Do you ever see anyone mourning over the passing of the tulip bulb? Do gardeners weep as the bulb begins to weaken? Of course not. We don't purchase tulip girdles or petal wrinkle cream or consult plastic-leaf surgeons. We don't mourn the passing of the bulb; we celebrate it. Tulip lovers rejoice the minute the bulb weakens. "Watch that one," they say. "It's about to blossom."

Could it be heaven does the same? The angels point to our bodies. The more frail we become, the more excited they become. "Watch that lady in the hospital," they say. "She's about to blossom." "Keep an eye on the fellow with the bad heart. He'll be coming home soon."

"We are waiting for God to finish making us his own children, which means our bodies will be made free" (Rom. 8:23).

Are our bodies now free? No. Paul describes them as our "earthy bodies" (Phil. 3:21 MSG). Or as other translations state:

"our lowly body" (NKJV)

"the body of our humble state" (NASB)

"these weak mortal bodies" (NLT)

"our vile body" (KJV)

"our simple bodies" (NCV)

You could add your own adjective, couldn't you? Which word describes your body? My *cancerous* body? My *arthritic* body? My *deformed* body? My *crippled* body? My *addicted* body? My *ever-expanding* body? The word may be different, but the message is the same: These bodies are weak. They began decaying the minute we began breathing.

And, according to God, that's a part of the plan. Every wrinkle and every needle take us one step closer to the last step when Jesus will change our simple bodies into forever bodies. No pain. No depression. No sickness. No end.

This is not our forever house. It will serve for the time being. But there is nothing like the moment we enter his door.

Molly can tell you. After a month in our house she ran away. I came home one night to find the place unusually quiet. Molly was gone.

She'd slipped out unnoticed. The search began immediately. Within an hour we knew that she was far, far from home. Now, if you don't like pets, what I'm about to say is going to sound strange. If you do like pets, you will understand.

You'll understand why we walked up and down the street, calling her name. You'll understand why I drove around the neighborhood at 10:30 P.M. You'll understand why I put up a poster in the convenience store and convened the family for a prayer. (Honestly, I did.) You'll understand why I sent e-mails to the staff, asking for prayers, and to her breeder, asking for advice. And you'll understand why we were ready to toss the confetti and party when she showed up.

Here is what happened. The next morning Denalyn was on her way home from taking the girls to school when she saw the trash truck. She asked the workers to keep an eye out for Molly and then hurried home to host a moms' prayer group. Soon after the ladies arrived, the trash truck pulled into our driveway, a worker opened the door, and out bounded our dog. She had been found.

When Denalyn called to tell me the news, I could barely hear her voice. It was Mardi Gras in the kitchen. The ladies were celebrating the return of Molly.

This story pops with symbolism. The master leaving his house, searching for the lost. Victories in the midst of prayer. Great things coming out of trash. But most of all: the celebration at the coming home. That's something else you have in common with Molly—a party at your homecoming.

By that moment only one bag will remain. Not guilt. It was dropped at Calvary. Not the fear of death. It was left at the grave. The only lingering luggage will be this God-given longing for home. And when you see him, you'll set it down. Just as a returning soldier drops his duffel when he sees his wife, you'll drop your longing when you see your Father. Those you love will shout. Those you know will applaud. But all the noise will cease when he cups your chin and says, "Welcome home." And with scarred hand he'll wipe every tear from your eye. And you will dwell in the house of your Lord—forever.

Conclusion

I fell asleep in the Louvre.

The most famous museum in the world. The best-known building in Paris. Tourists are oohing and aahing, and that's me, nodding and snoring. Seated on a bench. Back to the wall. Chin to my chest. Conked out.

The crown jewels are down the hall. Rembrandt is on the wall. Van Gogh is one floor up. The *Venus de Milo* is one floor down. I should have been star struck and wide eyed.

Denalyn was. You'd have thought she was at Foley's Red Apple sale. If there was a tour, she took it. If there was a button to push, she pushed it. If there was a brochure to read, she read it. She didn't even want to stop to eat.

But me? I gave the *Mona Lisa* five minutes.

Shameful, I know.

I should have been more like the fellow next to me. When I dozed off, he was transfixed on a seventeenth-century Dutch artist's rendering of a flower. When I awoke, the guy was still staring. I closed my eyes again. When I opened them, he hadn't moved.

I leaned toward him and tried to sound reflective. "Awesome, eh?" No response. "The shades are masterful." Still no reply. "Do you think it's a number painting?" He sighed and said nothing, but I knew what he was thinking, *Uncultured klutz.*

He's right. I was. But it wasn't my fault. I like seventeenth-century art as much as the next guy . . . well, maybe not that much. But at least I can usually stay awake.

But not that day. Why did I fall asleep at the Louvre?

Blame it on the bags, baby; blame it on the bags. I was worn out from lugging the family luggage. We checked more suitcases than the road show of the *Phantom of the Opera.*

I can't fault my wife and daughters. They learned it from me. Remember, I'm the one who travels prepared for an underwater wedding and a bowling tournament. It's bad enough for one person to travel like that, but five? It'll wear you out.

You think I'll ever learn to travel light?

I tell you what. Let's make a pact. I'll reduce the leather bags, and we'll both reduce the emotional ones. After all, it's one thing to sleep through the Louvre but quite another to sleep through life.

We can, you know. Do we not dwell in the gallery of our God? Isn't the sky his canvas and humanity his magnum opus? Are we not encircled by artistry? Sunsets burning. Waves billowing.

And isn't the soul his studio? The birthing of love, the bequeathing of grace. All around us miracles pop like fireflies—souls are touched, hearts are changed, and . . .

Yawn. We miss it. We sleep through it. We can't help it. It's hard work carrying yesterday's guilt around. This burlap bag of worry has my neck in a knot. The dread of death is enough to break a back.

It's also enough to make you miss the magic of life. Many miss it every Sunday. Good, well-meaning folks sitting in church, fighting to keep the eyes—if not of their heads at least of their hearts—awake.

And what do we miss? We miss God parting the heavens to hear us sing. Shouldn't we be stretching heavenward, tiptoed on our pews?

What do we miss? God is meeting us in communion! Shouldn't we be distributing, along with the wafers and wine, ammonia sticks so we could awaken each other from our faints of awe?

What do we miss? God's Word. Should we not hold it like nitroglycerin? Shouldn't we be wide-awake? We should, but we dragged that trunk of dissatisfaction all over town last week. And, besides that, we couldn't sleep last night; we kept rolling over on our duffel bag of disappointments.

Then let's get rid of the bags! Once and for all, let's give our luggage to him. Let's take him at his word! "Come to me, all of you who are weary and carry heavy burdens, and I will give you rest" (Matt. 11:28 NLT).

Rest from the burden of a small god. Why? Because I have found **the Lord.**

Rest from doing things my way. Why? Because **the Lord is my Shepherd.**

Rest from endless wants. Why? Because **I shall not want.**

Rest from weariness. Why? Because **he makes me to lie down.**

Rest from worry. Why? Because **he leads me.**

Rest from hopelessness. Why? Because **he restores my soul.**

Rest from guilt. Why? Because **he leads me in the paths of righteousness.**

Rest from arrogance. Why? Because of **his name's sake.**

Rest from the valley of death. Why? Because **he walks me through it.**

Rest from the shadow of grief. Why? Because **he guides me.**

Rest from fear. Why? Because **his presence comforts me.**

Rest from loneliness. Why? Because **he is with me.**

Rest from shame. Why? Because **he has prepared a place for me in the presence of my enemies.**

Rest from my disappointments. Why? Because **he anoints me.**

Rest from envy. Why? Because **my cup overflows.**

Rest from doubt. Why? Because **he follows me.**

Rest from homesickness. Why? Because **I will dwell in the house of my Lord forever.**

And tomorrow, when out of habit you pick your luggage back up, set it down again. Set it down again and again until that sweet day when you find you aren't picking it back up.

And on that day, when you feel the load lifted, when you've taken a step toward traveling light, when you have the energy to ponder the mysteries of life, do me a favor. Walk down the hall and turn to the left. Wait your turn behind the scarlet ropes. Take a good, long look at the *Mona Lisa,* and tell me, what's the big deal about her anyway?

Notes

Chapter 2: The Middle C of Life

1. Or, in Hebrew, fifty-four words describe the first one.
2. Around A.D. 200 Christian scholars began writing the vowels for *Adonai* beneath the Tetragrammaton (YHWH), reminding the reader to say "Adonai." The word was still unpronounceable until German scholars in the middle of the nineteenth century inserted the vowels of *Adonai* between the *Yahweh* consonants creating the name *Jehovah*—a name that had never existed in any language.
3. Nathan Stone, *Names of God* (Chicago: Moody Press, 1944), 20.
4. Donald W. McCullough, *The Trivialization of God: The Dangerous Illusion of a Manageable Deity* (Colorado Springs: NavPress, 1995), 66.
5. Ibid., 54.

Chapter 3: I'll Do It My Way

1. With appreciation to Rick Reilly and his chapter on Jean Van de Velde, "*Mon Dieu!* Better Safe Than Sorry!" in *The Life of Reilly* (New York: Total Sports Illustrated, 2000), 175–77.

Chapter 4: The Prison of Want

1. Randy C. Alcorn, *Money, Possessions, and Eternity* (Wheaton, Ill.: Tyndale Publishers, 1989), 55.

2. Chris Seidman, *Little Buddy* (Orange, Calif.: New Leaf Books, 2001), 138. Used with permission.

3. Rick Atchley, "I Have Learned the Secret," audiotape 7 of the 1997 Pepperdine Lectures (Malibu, Calif., 1997). Used with permission.

4. Used with permission.

Chapter 5: I Will Give You Rest

1. Robert Sullivan, "Sleepless in America," *Life,* February 1998, 56–66 and *Prime Time Live,* 2 March 1998.

2. Sullivan, "Sleepless," 63.

3. Ibid.

4. Phillip Keller, *A Shepherd Looks at Psalm 23* (Grand Rapids, Mich.: Zondervan Publishing, 1970; reprint, in *Phillip Keller: The Inspirational Writings,* New York: Inspirational Press, 1993), 28–29 (page citations are to the reprint edition).

5. Helmut Thielicke, *Encounter with Spurgeon,* trans. John W. Doberstein (Philadelphia: Fortress Press, 1963; reprint, Grand Rapids, Mich.: Baker Book House, 1975), 220 (page citation is to the reprint edition).

Chapter 6: Whaddifs and Howells

1. Og Mandino, *The Spellbinder's Gift* (New York: Fawcett Columbine, 1995), 70–71.

2. From "Worrier and Warrior," a sermon by Ted Schroder, Christ Episcopal Church, San Antonio, Texas, on 10 April 1994.

3. See Psalm 119:105.

Chapter 9: Get Over Yourself

1. Rick Reilly, *The Life of Reilly* (New York: Total Sports Illustrated, 2000), 73.

2. Paul Lee Tan, *Encyclopedia of 7700 Illustrations* (Rockville, Md.: Assurance Publishers, 1979), 211.
3. Ibid., 1100.
4. William J. Bennett, ed., *The Spirit of America: Words of Advice from the Founders in Stories, Letters, Poem and Speeches* (New York: Touchstone, 1997), 161.

Chapter 10: I Will Lead You Home

1. Phillip Keller, *A Shepherd Looks at Psalm 23* (Grand Rapids, Mich.: Zondervan Publishing, 1970; reprint, in *Phillip Keller: The Inspirational Writings,* New York: Inspirational Press, 1993), 70 (page citation is to the reprint edition).
2. F. W. Boreham, *Life Verses: The Bible's Impact on Famous Lives,* vol. 2 (Grand Rapids, Mich.: Kregel Publications, 1994), 211.

Chapter 11: When Mourning Comes

1. Michael P. Green, ed., *Illustrations for Biblical Preaching* (Grand Rapids, Mich.: Baker Book House, 1989), 91.

Chapter 14: The Crowing Rooster and Me

1. Charles W. Slemming, *He Leadeth Me: The Shepherd's Life in Palestine* (Fort Washington, Pa.: Christian Literature Crusade, 1964), quoted in Charles R. Swindoll, *Living Beyond the Daily Grind, Book 1: Reflections on the Songs and Sayings in Scripture* (Nashville: W Publishing Group, 1988), 77–78.

Chapter 15: Slippery Sheep and Healed Hurts

1. "Paul was in prison several times: Philippi (Acts 16:23); Jerusalem (Acts 23:18); Caesarea (Acts 23:33; 24:27; 25:14); and Rome (Acts 28:16, 20, 30)." Robert B. Hughes and J. Carl Laney, *New Bible Companion* (Wheaton, Ill.: Tyndale House Publishers, 1990), 681.

2. Phillip Keller, *A Shepherd Looks at Psalm 23* (Grand Rapids, Mich.: Zondervan Publishing, 1970; reprint, in *Phillip Keller: The Inspirational Writings,* New York: Inspirational Press, 1993), 99 (page citation is to the reprint edition).

Chapter 16: Jam Session

1. F. B. Meyer, *The Shepherd Psalm* (Grand Rapids, Mich.: Kregel Publications, 1991), 115.
2. From a sermon entitled "God's Antidote to Your Hurt" by Rick Warren.

Chapter 17: God's Loving Pursuit

1. F. B. Meyer, *The Shepherd Psalm* (Grand Rapids, Mich.: Kregel Publications, 1991), 125.
2. Though originally written for this book, this story initially appeared in *The Gift for All People.* Thanks to Multnomah Publishing for allowing us to use it in *Traveling Light*.

Chapter 18: Almost Heaven

1. Calvin Miller, *Into the Depths of God: Where Eyes See the Invisible, Ears Hear the Inaudible, and Minds Conceive the Inconceivable* (Minneapolis: Bethany House, 2000), 217.
2. Dave Barry, *Dave Barry Turns 40* (New York: Crown, 1990), quoted in Helen Exley, *A Spread of Over 40s Jokes* (New York: Exley Giftbooks, 1992).

Study Guide

Traveling Light

Prepared by Steve Halliday

1

The Luggage of Life

Traveling Back

1. *The bags we grab are not made of leather; they're made of burdens. The suitcase of guilt. A sack of discontent. You drape a duffel bag of weariness on one shoulder and a hanging bag of grief on the other. Add on a backpack of doubt, an overnight bag of loneliness, and a trunk of fear. Pretty soon you're pulling more stuff than a skycap. No wonder you're so tired at the end of the day. Lugging luggage is exhausting.*

   A. Which of the "bags" listed here trouble you the most? Why?

   B. Have you left any luggage behind? How did it feel to do so?

2. *God is saying to you, "Set that stuff down! You're carrying burdens you don't need to bear."*

   A. Why do you think we carry burdens we don't need to bear?

   B. What keeps you from setting down burdens you needn't bear?

3. *Traveling light means trusting God with the burdens you were never intended to bear.*

   A. What does it mean to trust God with a burden? How does one do this?

   B. What have you learned from observing others with their "luggagc"?

Traveling Up

1. Read Psalm 23.

   A. What pictures leap to mind when you read this psalm?

   B. What memories does this psalm conjure up for you?

C. What part of this psalm means the most to you? Why?

D. How does this psalm teach us to give up personal burdens?

2. Read Matthew 11:28–30.

A. To whom are these words addressed? Does this include you?

B. What promise does Jesus give to those who respond to his invitation?

C. Are you taking advantage of Jesus' invitation? Why or why not?

3. Read 1 Peter 5:7.

A. What does this verse instruct us to do? (How are we to obey?)

B. What reason does Peter give for obeying this command?

C. What benefit can we expect to receive when we obey?

Traveling On

1. Set aside at least a half-hour for prayer, and ask the Lord to reveal any burdens you need to lay down. Pray with a piece of paper and a pen in hand, and write down any burdens the Lord brings to mind. Show your completed list to your closest friend, and ask him or her to pray with you that God will show you how to release these burdens.

2. What burdens are your loved ones needlessly bearing? What can you do to help them lay down those unnecessary burdens?

2

The Middle C of Life

The Burden of a Lesser God

Traveling Back

1. *With his very first words in [Psalm 23], David sets out to deliver us from the burden of a lesser deity.*

   A. What lesser deities hold an attraction for your acquaintances?

   B. Why would anyone settle for a lesser deity?

2. Max says that many people settle for one of three lesser deities: God as a genie in a bottle, as a sweet grandpa, or as a busy dad.

   A. Describe in your own words each of these lesser deities. What seems attractive about them?

   B. Have any of these three lesser deities appealed to you? Why or why not?

3. *God is the "One who is" and the "One who causes." Why is that important? Because we need a big God. And if God is the "One who is," then he is an unchanging God.*

   A. Why do we need a big God? Why do we need an unchanging God?

   B. What would be different about your life if God were smaller than he is? How would you feel if he changed capriciously?

4. *Unchanging. Uncaused. Ungoverned. These are only a fraction of God's qualities, but aren't they enough to give you a glimpse of your Father? Don't we need this kind of shepherd? Don't we need an unchanging shepherd?*

   A. How do you answer Max's questions?

   B. Give an example of how God has been an unchanging shepherd in your life.

Traveling Up

1. Read Exodus 3:13–17; 6:2–8.

   A. What do you learn about God from his name?

   B. What do you learn about God from his track record?

   C. What do you learn about God's concern for his people?

2. Read Psalm 102:25–27; 139:7–12.

   A. What do you learn about God from these passages? How do these verses affect your view of God?

3. Read 1 Timothy 6:13–16.

   A. What do you learn about God from this text?

   B. How does Paul suggest we respond to this God?

4. Read Isaiah 40:21–31.

   A. What does this text reveal about God?

   B. What does God think of pretenders to his throne?

   C. How does God intend for this majestic picture of him to encourage our weary hearts?

Traveling On

1. Do a study on the false gods described in Scripture. Start with names such as "Chemosh," "Baal," "Asherah," and the generic "gods." Do other research, perhaps in a good Bible dictionary, to discover something about these "lesser gods." How do they compare to the God of Jesus?

2. Spend some time meditating and concentrating on the attributes of the real God of the Bible. Consider using a daily devotional such as *How Great Thou Art* (Sister, Ore.: Multnomah, 1999), which focuses for a full year on the majesty and greatness of God.

3

I'll Do It My Way

The Burden of Self-Reliance

Traveling Back

1. *We humans want to do things our way. Forget the easy way. Forget the common way. Forget the best way. Forget God's way. We want to do things our way.*

   A. What is it about us that causes us to desire our own way?

   B. When we rely on ourselves rather than God, what is the result?

2. *When David, who was a warrior, minstrel, and ambassador for God, searched for an illustration of God, he remembered his days as a shepherd. . . . And the way he cared for the sheep reminded him of the way God cares for us. David rejoiced to say, "The* Lord *is my shepherd," and in so doing he proudly implied, "I am his sheep."*

   A. Why do you think David chose to picture God through the image of a shepherd? Why not use another image?

   B. Do you proudly think of yourself as a sheep? Explain.

3. *Will you humor me and take a simple quiz? See if you succeed in self-reliance. Raise your hand if any of the following describe you.*

   You can control your moods.
   You are at peace with everyone.
   You have no fears.
   You need no forgiveness.

   A. Describe someone you know who believes he or she fits one of the previous four statements.

B. Which of these four areas of life cause you the most struggles? Explain.

C. Why is it that the ones who most need a shepherd resist him so?

Traveling Up

1. Read Jeremiah 17:5–8.

    A. What does the Lord think of someone who relies on himself (v. 5)?

    B. What is the result of relying on yourself (v. 6)?

    C. How does the Lord feel about those who trust in him (v. 7)?

    D. What is the result of trusting in God (v. 8)?

2. Read Deuteronomy 8:10–18.

    A. What are we to do in times of prosperity (v. 10)?

    B. In what way can prosperity create a spiritual threat (vv. 11–14)?

    C. Why is it always foolish to believe that we are self-sufficient (vv. 15–18)?

3. Read 1 Corinthians 4:6–7.

    A. What does it mean to "not go beyond what is written" (v. 6 NIV)? Why does the Bible warn us to "not go beyond what is written"?

    B. How would you answer Paul's three questions in verse 7?

Traveling On

1. Consciously get out of your comfort zone, and do something that requires you to rely on another person. Make it as exotic as a parachute jump or as mundane as asking directions to a place you've never visited.

2. Read the classic *A Shepherd Looks at Psalm 23* by Phillip Keller to gain a better picture of what it means to be a sheep in the fold of God.

4

The Prison of Want

The Burden of Discontent

Traveling Back

1. *The prison of want. You've seen her prisoners. They are "in want." They want something. They want something bigger. Nicer. Faster. Thinner. They want.*

   A. Are you in prison?

   B. What things in life are most likely to send you to this prison? Describe them.

2. *David has found the pasture where discontent goes to die. It's as if he is saying, "What I have in God is greater than what I don't have in life."*

   A. What do you have in God? List the first ten things that come to mind.

   B. Can you say that what you have in God is greater than what you don't have in life? Explain.

3. *Are you hoping that a change in circumstances will bring a change in your attitude? If so, you are in prison, and you need to learn a secret of traveling light.*

   A. Answer the question above and explain your answer.

   B. What is this secret of traveling light? How does one master it?

4. *What is the one thing separating you from joy? How do you fill in this blank: "I will be happy when ____________________"? When I am healed. When I am promoted. When I am married. When I am single. When I am rich. How would you finish that statement?*

   A. Answer the question above.

B. How does this thing separate you from joy? How long has it been doing so? How can you deprive it of its power over you?

Traveling Up

1. Read Luke 12:13–21.
   A. What warning does Jesus give in verse 15? What declaration does he make?
   B. What error did the rich man make in the parable Jesus told?
   C. What does it mean to be "rich toward God" (v. 21)? Are you rich toward God? Explain.
2. Read Philippians 4:10–13.
   A. Why did Paul "rejoice greatly in the Lord" (v. 10 NIV)?
   B. What secret does Paul describe in verse 12? How did he gain access to this secret? Do you know this secret? Explain.
   C. How does verse 13 relate to the context of the passage? How does it relate specifically to contentment?
3. Read 1 Timothy 6:3–10.
   A. How does Paul characterize those who teach that godliness is a means to financial gain (v. 5)?
   B. What does Paul say *is* "great gain" (v. 6 NIV)?
   C. What reason does Paul give for his statement (vv. 7–8)?
   D. What warning does Paul give in verses 9–10? Why do so many people ignore this warning? What do you think of his warning? Explain.

Traveling On

1. Make a list of at least a dozen things you possess, whether spiritual or material, that came to you as a result of your relationship with God.
2. Do a Bible study on contentment. Use a good concordance to look up words such as *content* and *contented,* then study the verses that you find. Also see what a good Bible dictionary or encyclopedia has to say on the topic. What do you learn?

5

I Will Give You Rest

The Burden of Weariness

Traveling Back

1. *People with too much work and too little sleep step over to the baggage claim of life and grab the duffel bag of weariness. You don't carry this one. You don't hoist it onto your shoulder and stride down the street. You drag it as you would a stubborn St. Bernard.*

   A. What sorts of things tend to make you weary?

   B. How do you normally deal with weariness? What did you do the last time weariness struck hard?

2. *In our book, busyness is next to godliness. We idolize Thomas Edison, who claimed he could live on fifteen-minute naps. Somehow we forget to mention Albert Einstein, who averaged eleven hours of sleep a night.*

   A. How often do you tell others, "I'm really busy right now"? What keeps you so busy?

   B. How much sleep do you normally get? Is it sufficient for you to function well? Explain.

3. *God's message is plain: "If creation didn't crash when I rested, it won't crash when you do." Repeat these words after me: It is not my job to run the world.*

   A. Name some of the reasons you have heard (or used yourself) for not getting adequate rest.

   B. Why do you think God so emphasized the fourth commandment, about resting on the Sabbath day?

4. *In a world rocky with human failure, there is a land lush with divine mercy. Your Shepherd invites you there. He wants you to lie down. Nestle*

deeply until you are hidden, buried, in the tall shoots of his love, and there you will find rest.

A. What is your favorite way of nestling deeply "in the tall shoots of his love"? Describe what most refreshes you.

B. What is keeping you from resting in God's love right now?

Traveling Up

1. Read Exodus 20:8–11.

   A. What does it mean to keep the Sabbath day "holy"?

   B. What does God command Israel in verses 9–10?

   C. What reason does God give in verse 11 for his command?

   D. Why do you think God so highly values our rest?

2. Read Isaiah 30:15–18.

   A. According to verse 15, Israel's salvation consisted in what? How did the nation respond to this direction?

   B. What response is described in verse 16? How do we often respond in a similar way?

   C. What is the result of ignoring God's command to rest (v. 17)?

   D. Despite our foolishness, how does the Lord treat us (v. 18)?

3. Read Hebrews 4:1–11.

   A. What does the writer warn us about in verse 1?

   B. What keeps people from entering God's rest (vv. 2–6)?

   C. When is the best time to obey God's command (v. 7)?

   D. What kind of rest is the writer describing in verse 9?

   E. How do we "labour" to enter God's rest (v. 11 KJV)?

Traveling On

1. What activities or events keep you busy? Try an experiment to judge the accuracy of your assumptions. Keep a "busyness journal"

for one week, recording the things that occupy your time. Write down not only what you did but also how long each took. Then at the end of the week evaluate your journal. Are you busy doing the things that matter most? Or do you need to make some changes?

2. How much sleep do you get? Keep a chart for one month, accurately recording the amount and quality of your sleep. Do the results surprise you? What changes, if any, do you need to make?

6

Whaddifs and Howells

The Burden of Worry

Traveling Back

1. *Worry is the burlap bag of burdens. It's overflowing with "whaddifs" and "howells." "Whaddif it rains at my wedding?" "Howell I know when to discipline my kids?" "Whaddif I marry a guy who snores?" "Howell we pay our baby's tuition?"*

   A. What "whaddifs" trouble you the most?

   B. What "howells" give you the most grief?

   C. How do you typically deal with these "whaddifs" and "howells"?

2. *Worry divides the mind. The biblical word for* worry (merimnao) *is a compound of two Greek words,* merizo *("to divide") and* nous *("the mind"). Anxiety splits our energy between today's priorities and tomorrow's problems. Part of our mind is on the now; the rest is on the not yet. The result is half-minded living.*

   A. What practical things can we do to keep from spending today's energies on tomorrow's problems?

   B. What issues are most likely to nudge you toward half-minded living? Why?

3. *God leads us. God will do the right thing at the right time. And what a difference that makes.*

   A. How has God led you in the past? Describe at least one incident.

   B. Do we believe that God will do the right thing at the right time? How would our lives change if we really believed this?

C. What in your life would change *right now* if you believed this fully?

4. *Meet today's problems with today's strength. Don't start tackling tomorrow's problems until tomorrow. You do not have tomorrow's strength yet. You simply have enough for today.*

   A. How many of the things you have worried about actually have come to pass?

   B. What issues that should be dealt with today are you avoiding by trying to tackle tomorrow's problems?

Traveling Up

1. Read Matthew 6:25–34.

   A. What reason does Jesus give for refusing to worry (vv. 25–27)?

   B. Why should worry not trouble Christians in the same way it troubles nonbelievers (vv. 31–32)?

   C. If we are not to worry, what are we to do (v. 33)? What does this mean in practical terms?

   D. What additional reason for not worrying does Jesus give in verse 34?

2. Read Philippians 4:6–8.

   A. How does Paul recommend that we combat worry?

   B. According to Paul, what will we enjoy when we follow his counsel?

   C. Rather than worry, what kinds of things should fill our minds (v. 8)?

3. Read Hebrews 4:14–16.

   A. Describe the high priest pictured in this passage.

   B. How is verse 16 designed to combat our worry?

Traveling On

1. Make a list of the things in life that worry you the most. Then, one by one, commit these items to the Lord in prayer. As you pray for each concern, tear it off your sheet of paper and throw it in the trash.

2. Use a good concordance to do a word study on worry. Look up terms such as *worry, worried, anxious,* and *anxiety,* and study the verses that you find. What do you learn about how to combat worry?

7

It's a Jungle Out There

The Burden of Hopelessness

Traveling Back

1. *Hopelessness is an odd bag. Unlike the others, it isn't full. It is empty, and its emptiness creates the burden. Unzip the top and examine all the pockets. Turn it upside down and shake it hard. The bag of hopelessness is painfully empty.*

   A. Describe a time when you felt hopeless. What made you feel that way?

   B. What in your life right now threatens your hope? How will you deal with it?

2. *If you have only a person but no renewed vision, all you have is company. If he has a vision but no direction, you have a dreamer for company. But if you have a person with direction—who can take you from this place to the right place—ah, then you have one who can restore your hope.*

   A. Why does it take a competent guide to restore hope?

   B. Do you have such a guide? Explain.

3. *God, your rescuer, has the right vision. He also has the right direction. He made the boldest claim in the history of man when he declared, "I am the way."*

   A. What did Jesus mean when he said, "I am the way"?

   B. Why wasn't it arrogant of Jesus to say that he was *the* way? Then what about Muhammad, the Dalai Lama, or spiritual leaders of other faiths?

4. *We ask God, "Where are you taking me? Where is the path?" And he, like the guide, doesn't tell us. Oh, he may give us a hint or two, but that's*

all. If he did, would we understand? Would we comprehend our location? No, like the traveler, we are unacquainted with this jungle. So rather than give us an answer, Jesus gives us a far greater gift. He gives us himself.

A. How does it make you feel that God almost never tells us what lies ahead for us? Do you wish he did things differently? Explain.

B. In what ways has Jesus guided you in the past? How are you depending upon his guidance right now?

Traveling Up

1. Read Psalm 121.

A. From where did the psalmist expect his hope to arrive (v. 2)?

B. How much sleep does God get each night (vv. 3–4)? Why is this important?

C. What kinds of things is the Lord said to watch over in verses 5–8? How can this give you hope?

2. Read Psalm 33:16–22.

A. What *cannot* save a king or a warrior (vv. 16–17)? Why are these things vain hopes?

B. On whom does the Lord fix his eyes (v. 18)? What difference does this make?

C. What does it mean to "wait in hope" (v. 20 NIV)? How can you put your hope in the Lord?

3. Read Romans 8:18–25.

A. Why should we avoid attaching too much importance to our present sufferings (v. 18)?

B. Why do we need hope in the first place (vv. 19–23)?

C. How does Paul define real hope (v. 24)?

D. Why is it always too soon to give up hope (v. 25)?

Traveling On

1. Take a guided tour of a place you've never visited. During the tour, consciously remind yourself of how your Savior desires to guide you through life. What unexpected discoveries or parallels do you uncover?

2. Do a Bible study on hope. Use a good concordance to look up the word *hope* and its derivatives, like *hoping, hoped, hopeful,* etc. What do you learn?

8

A Heavenly Exchange

The Burden of Guilt

Traveling Back

1. *God is never wrong. He has never rendered a wrong decision, experienced the wrong attitude, taken the wrong path, said the wrong thing, or acted the wrong way. He is never too late or too early, too loud or too soft, too fast or too slow. He has always been and always will be right. He is righteous.*

   A. Has it ever felt as if God made a mistake with your life? If so, how did you deal with this feeling?

   B. Who is the most "righteous" person you know? What makes you say this about him or her?

2. *The weight of weariness pulls you down. Self-reliance misleads you. Disappointments discourage you. Anxiety plagues you. But guilt? Guilt consumes you. So what do we do? Our Lord is right, and we are wrong. His party is for the guiltless, and we are anything but. What do we do?*

   A. Answer the question above.

   B. How do you deal with disappointments? With anxiety? Guilt?

3. *It was, at once, history's most beautiful and most horrible moment. Jesus stood in the tribunal of heaven. Sweeping a hand over all creation, he pleaded, "Punish me for their mistakes. See the murderer? Give me his penalty. The adulteress? I'll take her shame. The bigot, the liar, the thief? Do to me what you would do to them. Treat me as you would a sinner." And God did.*

   A. Why did innocent Jesus request to take the punishment due to murderers, adulterers, and other sinners?

B. Have you allowed Jesus to take on himself your own sin? Explain.

4. *The path of righteousness is a narrow, winding trail up a steep hill. At the top of the hill is a cross. At the base of the cross are bags. Countless bags full of innumerable sins. Calvary is the compost pile for guilt.*

   A. In what way is Calvary "the compost pile for guilt"?

   B. If you have set your bag of guilt at the foot of Calvary, describe how this came to be. If you have not already done so, why not?

Traveling Up

1. Read Romans 3:9–18.

   A. What does it mean to be "under sin" (NIV)? Who is "under sin" (v. 9)?

   B. List the characteristics of being "under sin" (vv. 10–17).

   C. How does verse 18 summarize all the characteristics you just listed?

2. Read Isaiah 45:21–25.

   A. How does God describe himself in verse 21?

   B. What command does God give in verse 22?

   C. What prediction does God give in verses 23–24?

   D. What promise does God give in verse 25? To whom is he referring?

3. Read Romans 5:6–11 and 1 Peter 3:18.

   A. According to Romans 5:6, for whom did Christ die?

   B. What drove Christ to die for us (v. 8)?

   C. What is the difference between being "justified" and "saved" (v. 9 NIV)?

   D. What is the normal response of one who has been "reconciled" (v. 11 NIV)? Is this your response? Explain.

Traveling On

1. Read a contemporary book by an author who exchanged his or her guilt for the forgiveness of God. How does this remind you of your own need for forgiveness?

2. Is there someone in your life whom you need to forgive but haven't? Remember Jesus' words: "But if you do not forgive men their sins, your Father will not forgive your sins" (Matthew 6:15 NIV). Commit today to forgive this person—and if possible, let him or her know what you've done.

9

Get Over Yourself

The Burden of Arrogance

Traveling Back

1. *God . . . doesn't dislike arrogance. He doesn't disapprove of arrogance. He's not unfavorably disposed toward arrogance. God hates arrogance. What a meal of maggots does for our stomach, human pride does for God's.*

   A. Why do you think God dislikes human pride?

   B. Would you consider yourself a prideful person? Would others agree with you? Explain.

2. *God . . . hates arrogance because we haven't done anything to be arrogant about. Do art critics give awards to the canvas? Is there a Pulitzer for ink? Can you imagine a scalpel growing smug after a successful heart transplant? Of course not. They are only tools, so they get no credit for the accomplishments.*

   A. In what way are we "tools" in God's hands?

   B. Is there any room at all for taking pride in one's accomplishments? Explain.

3. *Why does God have anything to do with us?* For his name's sake. *No other name on the marquee. No other name up in lights. No other name on the front page. This is all done for God's glory.*

   A. Why isn't it vain of God to associate with us for *his* name's sake?

   B. What is meant by "God's glory"? Why is God's glory so important?

4. Consider several ways to cultivate humility and kill ungodly pride:

- Assess yourself honestly.
- Don't take success too seriously.
- Celebrate the significance of others.
- Don't demand your own parking place.
- Never announce your success before it occurs.
- Speak humbly.
- Live at the foot of the cross.

A. Who can help you assess yourself honestly? What does such an assessment reveal?

B. How can you celebrate the significance of others? Who in your immediate circle do you need to celebrate right now?

C. How can you "live at the foot of the cross"? What does this mean?

Traveling Up

1. Read Proverbs 16:5, 18–19.

   A. What does the Lord think of the proud (v. 5)? How will he respond to them?

   B. What is the outcome of pride (v. 18)?

   C. What contrast is made in verse 19? Why is this true?

2. Read Isaiah 57:15–19; 66:2.

   A. How does the Lord describe himself in verse 15? With whom is he pleased to live?

   B. Why will God not "accuse forever" (v. 16)?

   C. How will the Lord respond to those who turn to him in faith (vv. 18–19)?

   D. Whom does God esteem, according to Isaiah 66:2? Why does the Lord delight in men and women like this?

3. Read Philippians 2:3–11.

   A. What does verse 3 instruct us not to do? What should we do instead?

   B. What overall instruction do we receive in verse 5?

   C. How did Jesus follow this instruction during his earthly ministry (vv. 6–8)?

   D. How will God reward Jesus for his faithfulness (vv. 9–11)?

   E. In what way are we to emulate Jesus' example? How are you doing in this regard? Explain.

Traveling On

1. Watch a classic movie such as *Citizen Kane* to see how even Hollywood sometimes recognizes the deadly poison of human pride. How does pride ultimately destroy the person who lets it control him or her?

2. Do a Bible study on how God does everything for the sake of his name. Look up references to "the name," "my name," "his name," etc. What do you discover?

10

I Will Lead You Home

The Burden of the Grave

Traveling Back

1. *Someday our Shepherd . . . will take us to the mountain by way of the valley. He will guide us to his house through the valley of the shadow of death.*

   A. Do you think of your own death, or do you avoid the thought? Explain.

   B. Has a believer you were close to ever died? If so, describe how the Shepherd guided him or her through the valley of the shadow of death.

2. *David grants us two important reminders that can help us surrender our fear of the grave.* We all have to face it. . . . *And though his first reminder sobers us, his second reminder encourages us:* We don't have to face death alone.

   A. If you were to face your own death tomorrow, would you be ready? Explain.

   B. Do you feel as though you would be facing death alone? Explain.

3. *Don't face death without facing God. Don't even speak of death without speaking to God. He and he alone can guide you through the valley. Others may speculate or aspire, but only God knows the way to get you home. And only God is committed to getting you there safely.*

   A. Name a few ways in which God helps his children face death.

   B. How can we be certain God is committed to getting us to heaven safely?

4. *[Jesus] may send missionaries to teach you, angels to protect you, teachers to guide you, singers to inspire you, and physicians to heal you, but he sends no one to take you. He reserves this job for himself.*

   A. When Jesus comes to take you home, what do you think you might say to him first?

   B. Why do you think Jesus insists on coming in person to get you? How does this make you feel?

Traveling Up

1. Read Psalm 116:15; 139:16.

   A. What does Psalm 116:15 say is "precious" to God? Why is this so?

   B. What claim does Psalm 139:16 make? Does this give you comfort? Explain.

2. Read 1 Thessalonians 4:13–18.

   A. What do you learn from this passage about those who die in Christ?

   B. How are these words intended to "encourage" us? Why are we instructed to repeat these words to others?

3. Read 2 Corinthians 5:1–10.

   A. What does Paul mean by "earthly tent" (v. 1 NIV)? Why use this picture?

   B. What is life like in this "tent"? How does Paul contrast life in the "heavenly dwelling" (v.2 NIV)?

   C. What token has God given us to assure us that what he says will one day happen, will actually happen (v. 5)?

   D. How is the information in this passage supposed to make us "confident" (v. 6 NIV)?

   E. What preference does Paul express in verse 8? Why does he prefer this?

   F. How is verse 10 both a promise and a warning?

Traveling On

1. Visit a nearby cemetery, and spend at least an hour reading the gravestones to remind yourself both of death's reality and of the hope believers can have despite its cold embrace.

2. Read Herbert Lockyer's classic book. *Last Words of Saints and Sinners*. How do the deaths of the two groups compare?

11

When Mourning Comes

The Burden of Grief

Traveling Back

1. *The black bag of sorrow is hard to bear. It's hard to bear because not everyone understands your grief. They did at first. They did at the funeral. They did at the graveside. But they don't now; they don't understand. Grief lingers.*

   A. How do you personally deal with sorrow?

   B. How can we help someone whose grief just won't go away?

2. *Only God knows the reasons behind his actions. But here is a key truth on which we can stand.* Our God is a good God.

   A. Why do you think God seldom "explains" his actions in our lives?

   B. How have you personally experienced that God is a good God?

3. *Death is God's way of taking people away from evil. From what kind of evil? An extended disease? An addiction? A dark season of rebellion? We don't know. But we know that no person lives one day more or less than God intends.*

   A. Have you ever thought about death in this way? That it's God's way of taking people away from evil? How do you respond to this idea?

   B. How can the idea of God's sovereignty bring comfort in a time of death? How can the doctrine be used to increase someone's pain?

4. *God will lead you* through, *not around, the valley of the shadow of death. And, by the way, aren't you glad it's just a shadow?*

A. If God really loves us, why doesn't he lead us *around* the valley of the shadow of death? Why lead us *through* it?

B. Is death merely a shadow for you? Explain.

Traveling Up

1. Read Lamentations 3:31–33.

   A. How can verse 31 give you hope when you find yourself engulfed in grief?

   B. What do you learn about God in verse 32?

   C. Why is it important that God does not "willingly" bring us grief (v. 33 NIV)? Why does he bring us grief at all?

2. Read John 16:20–22.

   A. What two promises did Jesus give his disciples in verse 20?

   B. What illustration did Jesus use in verse 21 to picture his promises of verse 20? What can we learn from this illustration?

   C. What promise does Jesus give in verse 22? How certain is this promise? On what is it based? How can it continue to help you today when you face grief?

3. Read 1 Peter 1:3–9.

   A. What great blessing does Peter describe in verses 3–4? Do you share in this blessing? Explain.

   B. What kind of shield are we promised in verse 5?

   C. Does genuine faith exempt one from grief (v. 6)? Why or why not?

   D. How do trials and the grief they bring fit in with the Christian life (v. 7)?

   E. What blessing comes to those who believe in Christ (v. 8)?

   F. What blessing does faith ultimately bring to those who exercise it (v. 9)?

Traveling On

1. Interview someone you know to be gifted in the art of comforting the grieving. Look for someone whom others seek out in a time of loss. Ask the person what he or she does at these times. What do you learn?

2. Do a Bible study on the words *tear* and *tears.* What do you learn?

12

From Panic to Peace

The Burden of Fear

Traveling Back

1. *Jesus flat on the ground? Face in the dirt? Extended hands gripping grass? Body rising and falling with sobs? Face as twisted as the olive trees that surround him? What do we do with this image of Jesus? Simple. We turn to it when we look the same.*

   A. Describe the last time you felt the way Jesus is described above.

   B. How does it help us to know that Jesus felt this way?

2. *When you feel the panic, don't focus on the people; focus on the opening. Good counsel in golf. Good counsel in life. Rather than focus on the fear, focus on the solution.*

   A. What kind of situations make you most fearful?

   B. When you face one of these frightening events, how can you "focus on the opening"? What "solution" can you call upon?

3. *Don't avoid life's Gardens of Gethsemane. Enter them. Just don't enter them alone. And while there, be honest. Pounding the ground is permitted. Tears are allowed. And if you sweat blood, you won't be the first. Do what Jesus did; open your heart.*

   A. How do we try to avoid life's Gardens of Gethsemane? Describe the last time you tried to avoid one.

   B. Is it easy or hard for you to express your emotions like this? Explain.

4. *Don't measure the size of the mountain; talk to the One who can move it. Instead of carrying the world on your shoulders, talk to the One who holds the universe on his. Hope is a look away.*

   A. How do we often try to "measure the size of the mountain"? Why is this a bad idea?

   B. In what way is hope "a look away"? How can prayer help to restore our hope? Does it help restore yours? Explain.

Traveling Up

1. Read Psalm 56:3–4.

   A. How does the psalmist deal with his own fears? Do you follow his example? Explain.

   B. Why is the psalmist unafraid of "mortal man" (v. 4 NIV)? Is this a statement of ignorance or something else? Explain.

2. Read Isaiah 41:10–14.

   A. Why does God tell Israel not to fear (v. 10)?

   B. What promise does God give in verses 11–12?

   C. What reason does God give for his promise in verse 13?

   D. What command and promise does God give in verse 14? How can his words encourage you today?

3. Read 1 John 4:16–19.

   A. On what should we rely when we are afraid (v. 16)?

   B. How does John describe God in verse 16? What difference does this make?

   C. How can we have "confidence on the day of judgment" (v. 17 NIV)?

   D. What antidote to fear does John give in verse 18? How does this antidote work?

   E. How is this antidote to be shared? How does this show that we really have the antidote?

Traveling On

1. In your journal write about a time you had "garden" experiences. Explain what situation took you there, how you felt, what prayers you prayed, and how God ministered to you.

2. Read *Foxe's Book of Martyrs* to see how many of God's choicest saints overcame their fear even as they faced death.

13

Silent Nights and Solitary Days

The Burden of Loneliness

Traveling Back

1. *By now you've learned that you don't have to be alone to feel lonely.*

   A. What's the difference between being alone and feeling lonely?

   B. Do you avoid being alone? Explain.

   C. How often, in a normal week, would you say you feel lonely?

2. *Loneliness is not the absence of faces. It is the absence of intimacy. Loneliness doesn't come from being alone; it comes from feeling alone.*

   A. How would you define nonsexual intimacy? With how many friends can you speak intimately? Are you satisfied with this number? Explain.

   B. How do you deal with loneliness? When you feel lonely, what do you do?

3. *Could it be that loneliness is not a curse but a gift? A gift from God? . . . I wonder if loneliness is God's way of getting our attention.*

   A. Do you agree that loneliness can be a gift from God? Explain.

   B. Why might God want to get your attention through loneliness? To what might he want to call your attention?

4. *God changes your* n *into a* v. *You go from* lonely *to* lovely. *When you know God loves you, you won't be desperate for the love of others.*

   A. How does assurance of God's love for you, personally, change everything?

   B. Does knowledge of God's love eliminate the need for intimate friends? Explain.

C. What's the difference between desiring the love of others and being desperate for it?

Traveling Up

1. Read Psalm 88.
   - A. How would you describe the man who wrote this psalm?
   - B. Why do you think God included this psalm in the Bible?
   - C. Have you ever felt as the psalmist did in verses 13–14? Explain.
   - D. Most psalms do not end as this one does (v. 18). Why do you think it ends like this? Is this a comfort to you? Explain.
2. Read Deuteronomy 31:6–8.
   - A. What command does God give the Israelites in verse 6? What encouragement does he give them?
   - B. Why do you suppose that Moses repeats to Joshua both the command and the encouragement in verses 7–8? What does this suggest to you about dealing with your own fears?
3. Read John 14:16–18; Matthew 28:16–20.
   - A. What request did Jesus say he would make of the Father in John 14:16?
   - B. What promise did Jesus make in John 14:18? How is he fulfilling this promise today?
   - C. How can we take courage from Jesus' words in Matthew 28:18?
   - D. What encouragement can we get from Jesus' final words in Matthew 28:20? Are you relying on this promise? Why or why not?

Traveling On

1. Examine your schedule, and find an entire day when you can plan to get alone, just you and God. Go to a retreat center, a solitary spot, a place in the woods, any place where you can spend a whole

day in solitude. Bring your Bible, and make no other plans than to spend the day alone with God.

2. Get a group of your believing friends together, and spend a few hours visiting some of your church's shut-ins, whether at their homes or in care centers. Relieve their loneliness for a while.

14

The Crowing Rooster and Me

The Burden of Shame

Traveling Back

1. *Is Peter the only person to do the very thing he swore he'd never do? "Infidelity is behind me!" "From now on, I'm going to bridle my tongue." "No more shady deals. I've learned my lesson." Oh, the volume of our boasting. And, oh, the heartbreak of our shame.*

   A. Describe a time when you followed Peter's example and did the very thing you swore you'd never do. What happened?

   B. Why do you think we engage in such foolish boasting? What do we think we'll gain?

2. *We weep as Peter wept, and we do what Peter did. We go fishing. We go back to our old lives. We return to our pre-Jesus practices. We do what comes naturally, rather than what comes spiritually. And we question whether Jesus has a place for folks like us.*

   A. Have you ever "gone fishing" or returned to your pre-Jesus practices after a spiritual failure? If so, how did you feel at the time?

   B. Why do we question whether Jesus has a place for folks like us? Have you ever felt this way? Explain.

3. *Jesus prepared a table in the presence of the enemy. Judas was allowed to see the supper, but he wasn't allowed to stay there.* You are not welcome here. This table is for my children. You may tempt them. You may trip them. But you will never sit with them. *This is how much he loves us.*

A. Why do you think Jesus allowed Judas to see the supper? Why not banish him before the disciples gathered?

B. What does the Lord's Supper mean to you personally? What goes through your mind during the service?

4. *The same Jesus who'd prepared a meal for Peter had prepared one for me. The same Shepherd who had trumped the devil trumped him again. The same Savior who had built a fire on the shore stirred a few embers in my heart.* "Every one *of you drink this." And so I did. It felt good to be back at the table.*

A. Why do you think Jesus prepared a meal for Peter, who denied him, but not for Judas, who betrayed him? What was the difference?

B. How do the stories of both Peter and Max show true repentance? How does Jesus always respond to true repentance? Why is this important to understand?

Traveling Up

1. Read Joel 2:25–27.

A. What promise does God make to his people who repent (v. 25)?

B. Why do you think God twice says in verses 26–27 that his people will never again be shamed? Why does God care about getting rid of shame?

2. Read 2 Timothy 2:15–16.

A. What instruction is given in verse 15? How can you comply with this command?

B. How can we avoid being ashamed, according to verse 15?

C. How does verse 16 continue to tell us how to avoid being ashamed?

3. Read Hebrews 12:2–3.

A. What are we instructed to do in verse 2? How can this keep us from being ashamed?

B. How did Jesus react to the shame of the cross? Why was there shame at the cross?

C. How are we to benefit from the example of Jesus on the cross?

Traveling On

1. Think of Max's story and how shame kept him from fellowship with God. Be honest with yourself, and ask if you're dealing with anything similar. If so, follow Max's courageous example, and admit this "shameful thing" to a trusted and godly friend. Break its power over you by confessing and forsaking it—and be glad at the Lord's table once more.

2. If you ever have the opportunity, attend a Seder prepared by someone who can explain the Messianic significance of this ancient Jewish meal. Enrich your appreciation of the Lord's Supper.

15

Slippery Sheep and Healed Hurts

The Burden of Disappointment

Traveling Back

1. *A disappointment is a missed appointment. What we hoped would happen, didn't. We wanted health; we got disease. We wanted retirement; we got reassignment. Divorce instead of family. Dismissal instead of promotion.*

   A. What disappointments have you had to face recently?

   B. What do you do with your disappointments?

2. *Just like sheep, we have wounds, but ours are wounds of the heart that come from disappointment after disappointment. If we're not careful, these wounds lead to bitterness. And so just like sheep, we need to be treated.*

   A. How do repeated disappointments lead to bitterness?

   B. What kinds of things have made you bitter? How do you deal with bitterness?

3. *The large portion of our problems are not lion-sized attacks, but rather the day-to-day swarm of frustrations and mishaps and heartaches.*

   A. What little things in life tend to frustrate you the most?

   B. What help can you offer to someone plagued with a swarm of mishaps or heartaches?

4. *Jesus tends to his sheep. And he will tend to you. If you will let him. How? How do you let him? The steps are so simple. First, go to him. Second, assume the right posture. Bow before God. Third, trust in him.*

   A. How can you "go to" Jesus? What does it mean to "go to" him?

   B. Why is it necessary to "bow" before God? What does this mean?

C. What does it mean to "trust" in God? How do we do this, practically speaking?

Traveling Up

1. Read Psalm 22:2–5.

   A. What disappointment did David suffer in verse 2? Have you ever felt like this? Explain.

   B. How did David combat his disappointment in verses 3–5?

   C. What was the result of the ancestors' trust described in verses 4–5? How is this meant to encourage us?

   D. Consider that this is the psalm Jesus quoted while hanging on the cross. What do you think the psalm taught him about disappointment?

2. Read Romans 5:1–5.

   A. How do we gain peace with God (v. 1)?

   B. What benefit does this peace gain us (v. 2)? How should this make us feel?

   C. What relationship does sufferings have to hope (vv. 3–5)?

   D. Why does hope not disappoint us (v. 5)? How does this matter to us on a day-to-day level?

3. Read Psalm 147:1–3.

   A. How did the Israelites deal with their disappointments (v. 1)?

   B. What encouragement does God give his people in verse 3?

   C. How do you think God heals the brokenhearted? What has he done in your own life?

Traveling On

1. Make a list of your biggest disappointments in life. Write them down. Then take each one, in order, to God in prayer. Give them to him explicitly, one by one.

2. Make a new commitment to get involved in regular prayer. Set a time. Set a place. Set a specific period. Prepare a list of concerns and thanks to bring to God. Then do it.

16

Jam Session

The Burden of Envy

Traveling Back

1. *Jealousy sets her cross hairs on the one who has more.*

   A. Describe a time when you felt jealous of someone. What prompted your jealousy?

   B. Why do most of us want "more"? What keeps us from being content with what we have?

2. *If focusing on our diminishing items leads to envy, what would happen if we focused on the unending items? If awareness of what we don't have creates jealousy, is it possible that an awareness of our abundance will lead to contentment?*

   A. Answer both of the preceding questions.

   B. Try to itemize the "unending items" that you possess. What's on your list?

   C. Try to list your "abundance." What does this tell you about God's provision?

3. *God is not a miser with his grace. Your cup may be low on cash or clout, but it is overflowing with mercy. You may not have the prime parking place, but you have sufficient pardon.*

   A. How often do you ponder God's grace to you? His mercy?

   B. How has God been gracious to you this week? This month? This year?

4. *One thing is certain. When the final storm comes and you are safe in your Father's house, you won't regret what he didn't give. You'll be stunned at what he did.*

A. Try to imagine the day you arrive safe in your Father's house. Look around. What has he given you?

B. How can meditating on your eternal future with God help you to deal with what exists today?

Traveling Up

1. Read Proverbs 14:30; 23:17.

   A. With what does Proverbs 14:30 contrast envy? How is this significant?

   B. In what ways do believers sometimes envy "sinners" (Prov. 23:17)?

   C. What does it mean to be "zealous for the fear of the LORD" (NIV)?

2. Read James 3:13–4:5.

   A. What in verse 13 does James contrast with "bitter envy" in verse 14?

   B. Where does envy come from (v. 15)?

   C. What always accompanies envy (v. 16)?

   D. What causes fights and quarrels among spiritual brothers (4:1)?

   F. God himself is said to "envy" in 4:5 (NIV). How does this differ from human envy?

3. Read Titus 3:3–7.

   A. How does Paul describe his pre-Christian life (v. 3)? What do you think he envied?

   B. How did God deliver us from envy (vv. 4–5)?

   C. To what extent did God pour out his Holy Spirit on us (v. 6)? How is this meant to nip envy in the bud?

   D. What was the purpose of God's saving us (v. 7)? How can meditating on this truth destroy envy?

Traveling On

1. Draw a line down a sheet of paper, creating two columns. On the left side, list some of the things you envy in others. On the right side, list what God has supplied you in abundance and, if possible, include a Scripture reference. For example, in the left column you might say "I wish I had better health," and beside it, in the right column, you might list "God will give me a glorious, eternal body (Phil. 3:20–21)."

2. Make a date to serve dinner at a local rescue mission or homeless shelter. Try not to schedule your visit at Thanksgiving or Christmas (since such service organizations usually have more than enough help during those two holidays). And be thankful for what God has given you.

17

God's Loving Pursuit

The Burden of Doubt

Traveling Back

1. *When Jesus found us, we acted like Eric. Our limitations kept us from recognizing the One who came to save us. We even doubted his presence—and sometimes we still do.*

   A. Do you ever doubt God's presence? If so, why?

   B. How do our limitations keep us from recognizing the One who came to save us? How can we overcome these limitations?

2. *If the Lord is the shepherd who leads the flock, goodness and mercy are the two sheepdogs who guard the rear of the flock.*

   A. How does "goodness" differ from "mercy"? How are they the same?

   B. Where in your life do you most need God's goodness and mercy right now? Why don't you take the time to talk to him about your need?

3. *Trust your faith and not your feelings. . . . Measure your value through God's eyes, not your own. . . . See the big picture, not the small.*

   A. How do we sometimes trust our feelings and not our faith? How can we stop making this mistake?

   B. Take a few minutes to describe your value in God's eyes. What has he said about you in the Bible?

   C. How can we see the big picture, not the small?

4. *Most of all, God gives us himself. Even when we choose our hovel over his house and our trash over his grace, still he follows. Never forcing us.*

Never leaving us. Patiently persistent. Faithfully present. Using all of his power to convince us that he is who he is and that he can be trusted to lead us home.

A. How do you know God has given you himself? How can you be sure of this?

B. How has God used his power to convince you he is who he is? What most convinces you that God can be trusted to lead you home?

Traveling Up

1. Read James 1:5–8.

   A. To whom is verse 5 addressed? Do you qualify? Explain.

   B. What promise does verse 5 make?

   C. What condition is placed in verse 6 on the promise of verse 5?

   D. To what does James compare someone who doubts God's promise? Why is this picture appropriate?

   E. What warning is given in verses 7 and 8? In what way are these individuals "double-minded" (NIV)? How can one correct such a serious problem?

2. Read Jude 20–22.

   A. What instruction is given in verse 20? How is this instruction to be carried out?

   B. What instruction is given in verse 21? What future event empowers us to follow this instruction?

   C. What instruction is given in verse 22? Why do you think the command was given? How can we comply with this command?

3. Read Romans 14:19–23.

   A. Describe the command in verse 19. What is the purpose of this command? How well do you fulfill it? Explain.

B. How is it possible to destroy someone for the sake of food (v. 20)?

C. How does verse 21 relate to doubt?

D. What command is given in verse 22? What blessing is available? What does this blessing mean?

E. How is verse 23 an effective guideline for the entire Christian life? What rule is laid out here?

Traveling On

1. Realize that there is a great difference between doubt and questions. Doubt disbelieves in the promises and good character of God; questions merely wonder how God might pull off some incredible feat. To get a "feel" for the difference between doubt and questions, study the vastly different ways God responded to Zechariah in Luke 1:5–20 and Mary in Luke 1:26–38. They asked similar questions ("How can I be sure of this?" versus "How will this be?" [NIV]) regarding miraculous pregnancies, but one was judged and the other blessed. Why?

2. Read Os Guinness's book *God in the Dark* for a clear and helpful discussion on doubt.

18

Almost Heaven

The Burden of Homesickness

Traveling Back

1. *The twists and turns of life have a way of reminding us—we aren't home here. This is not our homeland. We aren't fluent in the languages of disease and death. The culture confuses the heart, the noise disrupts our sleep, and we feel far from home. And, you know what? That's OK.*

   A. Why do we often forget that this is not our real home?

   B. In what ways do you feel like a foreigner on this earth? Are you OK with that? Explain.

2. *Homesickness is one of the burdens God doesn't mind if we carry. We . . . are being prepared for another house. And we . . . know we aren't there yet.*

   A. Do you feel "homesick" for heaven? Explain.

   B. How is God preparing you for "another house"?

3. *The greatest calamity is not to feel far from home when you are, but to feel right at home when you are not.*

   A. Could it be that much of the disappointment we feel in life comes from trying to feel right at home when we're not? Explain.

   B. How can we consciously guard against feeling at home in this world? Name several practical things we can do.

4. *Every wrinkle and every needle take us one step closer to the last step when Jesus will change our simple bodies into forever bodies. No pain. No depression. No sickness. No end.*

   A. How does your own body remind you that this is not your forever home?

B. How would you respond to someone who says this desire for an eternal, painless body is merely wishful thinking and you'd be better off getting all the gusto while you can?

Traveling Up

1. Read Philippians 1:20–23.

   A. Describe Paul's firm expectation in verse 20. What challenge faced him?

   B. In your own words, explain what Paul meant in verse 21.

   C. Describe Paul's dilemma in verse 22. Why was he so torn?

   D. What did Paul mean by "depart" in verse 23 (NIV)? Depart where? Why would this be "better"?

2. Read Philippians 3:17–4:1.

   A. How does Paul describe the enemies of Christ in verses 18–19? What traits characterize them?

   B. Describe the main contrast of these people with believers in Christ (v. 20).

   C. For whom are Christians waiting (vv. 20–21)? What are they waiting for him to do?

   D. What effect should meditating on this truth have on believers (4:1)? Does it have this effect on you? Explain.

3. Read 1 Corinthians 15:50–57.

   A. What two contrasts does Paul make in verse 50? Why should this matter to us? Why is it important?

   B. What "secret" or "mystery" does Paul describe in verses 51–52?

   C. What kind of "clothes" will believers wear in heaven (v. 53)? Why is this important?

   D. Restate the message of verses 54–57 in your own words. Imagine that you are describing this situation to an eight-year-old.

   E. Are you "homesick"? Why or why not?

Traveling On

1. Do a study in the four Gospels and in the Book of Acts on the Lord Jesus' postresurrection body. Describe it. Then realize that our resurrection bodies will look and act similar to his!

2. Read Joni Eareckson Tada's book titled *Heaven*. Joni has lived in a wheelchair for decades since a diving accident at age seventeen, so she expresses a uniquely powerful vision of heaven.

Next Door SAVIOR

MAX LUCADO

Published in Nashville, Tennessee, by Thomas Nelson. Thomas Nelson is a registered trademark of Thomas Nelson, Inc.

Thomas Nelson, Inc., titles may be purchased in bulk for educational, business, fund-raising, or sales promotional use. For information, please e-mail SpecialMarkets@ThomasNelson.com.

Library of Congress Cataloging-in-Publication Data

Lucado, Max.
Next door Savior / by Max Lucado.
p. cm.
Includes bibliographical references.
ISBN 978-0-8499-1336-5 (tp)
1. Christian life. 2. Jesus Christ—Person and offices. I. Title.
BV4501.3.L85 2003
232—dc21 2003008090

For Billy Graham

My voice is among the chorus of grateful millions.
Thank you for your words.
Thank you for your life.

Acknowledgments

I'm giving rambunctious standing ovations to

Liz Heaney and Karen Hill—for clearing junk, tolerating the funks, and doing the work. I can't thank you enough.

Steve and Cheryl Green—for long-term planning, gate guarding, and being the best friends imaginable.

Susan Perry—for bringing joy—and food—into our world.

The Oak Hills Church family—for sending showers of encouragement and a flood of prayer.

Laura Kendall and Carol Bartley—Your editing and insights are X-Acto-knife sharp.

Steve Halliday—Your study guides always help people dig deeper.

Thomas Nelson—for seeing so much more than I ever see. You're the best!

The UpWords team—for your tireless, behind-the-scenes work.

Bill Hybels—Thanks for sharing the secret of Matthew. Thanks even more for living it.

Charles Prince—for jewels of knowledge and a treasure chest of kindness.

Todd Phillips—Thanks for your timely insights and appreciated encouragement.

Larry King and team—Thanks for the seed thoughts.

Michael W., 3D, and the CTAW group—What a ride! Thanks for listening to these messages.

My Jenna, Andrea, and Sara—Should I ever doubt God's goodness, I need only to look at you. Thanks for being the best daughters in the world.

My wife, Denalyn—If love were a mountain, then my love for you would be the Alps. I'll love you forever.

You, the reader—May you find safe living in his neighborhood.

And you, dear Jesus—Eternal thanks for moving in.

Will God really live on earth among people?

—*Solomon*
2 Chronicles 6:18 NLT

I

Our Next Door Savior

Now when Jesus came into the district of Caesarea Philippi, He was asking His disciples, "Who do people say that the Son of Man is?" And they said, "Some say John the Baptist; and others, Elijah; but still others, Jeremiah, or one of the prophets." He said to them, "But who do you say that I am?" Simon Peter answered, "You are the Christ, the Son of the living God."

Matthew 16:13–16

The words hang in the air like a just-rung bell. "Who do you say that I am?" Silence settles on the horseshoe of followers. Nathanael clears his throat. Andrew ducks his eyes. John chews on a fingernail. Judas splits a blade of grass. He won't speak up. Never does. Peter will. Always does.

But he pauses first. Jesus' question is not new to him.

The previous thousand times, however, Peter had kept the question to himself.

That day in Nain? He'd asked it. Most people stand quietly as funeral processions pass. Mouths closed. Hands folded. Reverently silent. Not Jesus. He approached the mother of the dead boy and whispered something in her ear that made her turn and look at her son. She started to object but didn't. Signaling to the pallbearers, she instructed, "Wait."

Jesus walked toward the boy. Eye level with the corpse, he spoke. Not over it, as a prayer, but to it, as a command. "Young man, I say to you, arise!" (Luke 7:14).

With the tone of a teacher telling students to sit or the authority of a mom telling kids to get out of the rain, Jesus commanded the dead boy *not to be dead.* And the boy obeyed. Cold skin warmed. Stiff limbs moved. White cheeks flushed. The men lowered the coffin, and the boy jumped up and into his mother's arms. Jesus "gave him back to his mother" (Luke 7:15).

An hour later Jesus and the guys were eating the evening meal. He laughed at a joke and asked for seconds on bread, and the irony of it all jolted Peter. *Who are you?* he wondered so softly that no one but God could hear. *You just awakened the dead! Should you not be encased in light or encircled by angels or enthroned higher than a thousand Caesars? Yet, look at you—wearing clothes I would wear and laughing at jokes I tell and eating the food we all eat. Is this what death defeaters do? Just who are you?*

And then there was the storm. The tie-yourself-to-the-mast-and-kiss-your-boat-good-bye storm. Ten-foot waves yanked the disciples first forward and then backward, leaving the boat ankle-deep in water. Matthew's face blanched to the shade of spaetzle. Thomas death-gripped the stern. Peter suggested that they pray the Lord's Prayer. Better still, that the Lord lead them in the Lord's Prayer. That's when he heard the Lord.

Snoring.

Jesus was asleep. Back against the bow. Head drooped forward. Chin flopping on sternum as the hull bounced on waves. "Jesus!" Peter shouted.

The carpenter woke up, looked up. He wiped the rain from his eyes, puffed both cheeks with a sigh, and stood. He raised first his hand, then his voice, and as fast as you could say "glassy," the water became just that. Jesus smiled and sat, and Peter stared and wondered, "Who is this? Even the wind and the waves obey him!" (Mark 4:41 NCV).

This time Jesus is the one posing the question: "Who do you say that I am?" (Matt. 16:15).

Perhaps Peter's reply had the tone of an anchorman on the six o'clock news. Arched eyebrow. Half smile. James Bondish baritone voice. "I believe that you are the Son of God." But I doubt it.

I'm seeing Peter kick the dirt a bit. Clear his throat. Less swagger, more swallow. Gulp. More like a first-time parachutist about to jump out of the plane. "Are you ready to jump?" he's asked. "I, uh, I, uh, I, uh . . ."

"Who do you say that I am?"

"I, uh, I, uh . . . I believe . . . that you are the Christ, the Son of the living God" (see Matt. 16:16).

If Peter was hesitant, you can hardly fault him. How many times do you call a callous-handed nail bender from a one-camel town the Son of God?

There was something wrong with the picture.

We used to look at such scenes in elementary school. To keep us occupied, the teacher would pass out drawings with the question at the bottom "What's wrong with this picture?" Remember them? We'd look closely for something that didn't fit. A farmyard scene with a piano near the water trough. A classroom with a pirate seated on the back row. An astronaut on the moon with a pay phone in the background. We'd ponder the picture and point to the piano or pirate or pay phone and say, "This doesn't fit." Something is out of place. Something is absurd. Pianos don't belong in farmyards. Pirates don't sit in classrooms. Pay phones aren't found on the moon, and God doesn't chum with the common folk or snooze in fishing boats.

But according to the Bible he did. "For in Christ there is all of God in a human body" (Col. 2:9 TLB). Jesus was not a godlike man, nor a manlike God. He was God-man.

Midwifed by a carpenter.

Bathed by a peasant girl.

The maker of the world with a bellybutton.

The author of the Torah being taught the Torah.

Heaven's human. And because he was, we are left with scratch-your-head, double-blink, what's-wrong-with-this-picture? moments like these:

Bordeaux instead of H_2O.

A cripple sponsoring the town dance.

A sack lunch satisfying five thousand tummies.

And, most of all, a grave: guarded by soldiers, sealed by a rock, yet vacated by a three-days-dead man.

What do we do with such moments?

What do we do with such a *person?* We applaud men for doing good things. We enshrine God for doing great things. But when a man does God things?

One thing is certain, we can't ignore him.

Why would we want to? If these moments are factual, if the claim of Christ is actual, then he was, at once, man and God.

There he was, the single most significant person who ever lived. Forget MVP; he is the entire league. The head of the parade? Hardly. No one else shares the street. Who comes close? Humanity's best and brightest fade like dime-store rubies next to him.

Dismiss him? We can't.

Resist him? Equally difficult. Don't we need a God-man Savior? A just-God Jesus could make us but not understand us. A just-man Jesus could love us but never save us. But a God-man Jesus? Near enough to touch. Strong enough to trust. A next door Savior.

A Savior found by millions to be irresistible. Nothing compares to "the surpassing worth of knowing Christ Jesus my Lord" (Phil. 3:8 RSV). The reward of Christianity is Christ.

Do you journey to the Grand Canyon for the souvenir T-shirt or the snow globe with the snowflakes that fall when you shake it? No. The reward of the Grand Canyon is the Grand Canyon. The wide-eyed realization that you are part of something ancient, splendid, powerful, and greater than you.

The cache of Christianity is Christ. Not money in the bank or a car in the garage or a healthy body or a better self-image. Secondary and tertiary fruits perhaps. But the Fort Knox of faith is Christ. Fellowship with him. Walking with him. Pondering him. Exploring him. The heart-stopping realization that in him you are part of something ancient, endless, unstoppable, and unfathomable. And that he, who can dig the Grand Canyon with his pinkie, thinks you're worth his death on Roman timber. Christ is the reward of Christianity. Why else would Paul make him his supreme desire? "I want to know Christ" (Phil. 3:10 NCV).

Do you desire the same? My idea is simple. Let's look at some places he went and some people he touched. Join me on a quest for his "God-manness." You may be amazed.

More important, you may be changed. "We all, with unveiled face, beholding the glory of the Lord, are being changed into his likeness from one degree of glory to another; for this comes from the Lord who is the Spirit" (2 Cor. 3:18 RSV).

As we behold him, we become like him.

I experienced this principle firsthand when an opera singer visited our church. We didn't know his voice was trained. You couldn't have known by his corduroy coat and loafers. No tuxedo, cummerbund, or silk tie. His appearance raised no eyebrow, but his voice certainly did. I should know. He was in the pew behind mine.

His vibrato made dentures rattle and rafters shake. He tried to contain himself. But how can a tuba hide in a room of piccolos?

For a moment I was startled. But within a verse, I was inspired. Emboldened by his volume, I lifted mine. Did I sing better? Not even I could hear me. My warbles were lost in his talent. But did I try harder? No doubt. His power brought out the best in me.

Could your world use a little music? If so, invite heaven's baritone to cut loose. He may look as common as the guy next door, but just wait till you see what he can do. Who knows? A few songs with him might change the way you sing.

Forever.

Part One

No Person He Won't Touch

Most of us had a hard time learning to tie our shoes. Squirting toothpaste on a brush was tough enough, but tightening shoes by wrapping strings together? Nothing easy about that. Besides, who needs them? Wear loafers. Go barefoot. Who came up with the idea of shoes anyhow?

And knees don't help. Always in your face. Leaning around them, pushing them away—a person can't concentrate.

And, oh, the advice! Everyone had a different approach. "Make a tree with the loop, and let the squirrel run around it into the hole." "Shape a rabbit ear, and then wrap it with a ribbon." Dad said, "Go fast." Your uncle said to take your time. Can't anyone agree? Only on one thing. You need to know how.

Learning to tie your shoes is a rite of passage. Right in there with first grade and first bike is first shoe tying. But, oh, how dreadful is the process.

Just when you think you've made the loops and circled the tree . . . you get the rabbit ears in either hand and give them a triumphant yank and, voilà!—a knot. Unbeknownst to you, you've just been inducted into reality.

My friend Roy used to sit on a park bench for a few minutes each morning. He liked to watch the kids gather and play at the bus stop. One day he noticed a little fellow, maybe five or six years of age, struggling to board the bus. While others were climbing on, he was leaning down, frantically trying to disentangle a knotted shoestring. He grew more anxious by the moment, frantic eyes darting back and forth between the shoe and the ride.

All of a sudden it was too late. The door closed.

The boy fell back on his haunches and sighed. That's when he saw Roy. With tear-filled eyes he looked at the man on the bench and asked, "Do you untie knots?"

Jesus loves that request.

Life gets tangled. People mess up. You never outgrow the urge to look up and say, "Help!"

Jesus had a way of appearing at such moments. Peter's empty boat. Nicodemus's empty heart. Matthew has a friend issue. A woman has a health issue. Look who shows up.

Jesus, our next door Savior.

"Do you untie knots?"

"Yes."

2

Christ's Theme Song

Every Person

HEBREWS 2:17–18

Most families keep their family secrets a secret. Most don't talk about the swindling uncle or the streetwalking great-aunt. Such stories remain unmentioned at the family reunion and unrecorded in the family Bible.

That is unless you are the God-man. Jesus displays the bad apples of his family tree in the first chapter of the New Testament. You've barely dipped a toe into Matthew's gospel when you realize Jesus hails from the Tilted-Halo Society. Rahab was a Jericho harlot. Grandpa Jacob was slippery enough to warrant an electric ankle bracelet. David had a personality as irregular as a Picasso painting—one day writing psalms, another day seducing his captain's wife. But did Jesus erase his name from the list? Not at all.

You'd think he would have. *Entertainment Tonight* could quarry a season of gossip out of these stories. Why did Jesus hang his family's dirty laundry on the neighborhood clothesline?

Because your family has some too. An uncle with a prison record. The dad who never came home. The grandparent who ran away with the coworker. If your family tree has bruised fruit, then Jesus wants you to know, "I've been there."

The phrase "I've been there" is in the chorus of Christ's theme song. To the lonely, Jesus whispers, "I've been there." To the discouraged, Christ nods his head and sighs, "I've been there."

Just look at his hometown. A sleepy, humble, forgotten hamlet.

To find its parallel in our world, where would we go? We'd leave the United States. We'd bypass Europe and most of Latin America. Israel wasn't a superpower or a commercial force or a vacation resort. The land Joshua settled and Jesus loved barely registered on the Roman Empire radar screen!

But it was there. Caesar's soldiers occupied it. Like Poland in the 1940s or Guatemala in the 1980s, the Judean hills knew the rumbles of a foreign army. Though you've got to wonder if Roman soldiers ever made it as far north as Nazareth.

Envision a dusty, quiet village. A place that would cause people to say, "Does anything good come out of ____________?" In the case of Christ, the blank was filled with the name Nazareth. An unimpressive town in an unimpressive nation.

Where do we go to find such a place today? Iraq? Afghanistan? Burkina Faso? Cambodia? Take your pick. Find a semiarid, agriculturally based region orbiting on the fringe of any social epicenter. Climb into a jeep, and go there looking for a family like Jesus'.

Ignore the nicer homes of the village. Joseph and Mary celebrated the birth of Jesus with a temple offering of two turtledoves, the gift of the poor (Luke 2:22–24). Go to the poorer part of town. Not poverty stricken or destitute, just simple.

And look for a single mom. The absence of Joseph in the adult life of Jesus suggests that Mary may have raised him and the rest of the kids alone. We need a simple home with a single mom and an ordinary laborer. Jesus' neighbors remembered him as a worker. "He's just a carpenter" (Mark 6:3 MSG).

Jesus had dirty hands, sweat-stained shirts, and—this may surprise you—common looks. "No stately form or majesty that we should look upon Him, nor appearance that we should be attracted to Him" (Isa. 53:2).

Drop-dead smile? Steal-your-breath physique? No. Heads didn't turn when Jesus passed. If he was anything like his peers, he had a broad peasant's face, dark olive skin, short curly hair, and a prominent nose. He stood five feet one inch tall and weighed around 110 pounds.[1] Hardly worthy of a *GQ* cover. According to a third-century historian, Origen, "his body was small and ill-shapen and ignoble."[2]

Are your looks run-of-the-mill and your ways simple? So were his. He's been there.

Questionable pedigree. Raised in an overlooked nation among oppressed people in an obscure village. Simple home. Single mom. An ordinary laborer with ordinary looks. Can you spot him? See the adobe house with the thatched roof? Yes, the one with the chickens in the yard and the gangly teenager repairing chairs in the shed. Word has it he can fix your plumbing as well.

He's been there.

"He had to enter into every detail of human life. Then, when he came before God as high priest to get rid of the people's sins, he would have already experienced it all himself—all the pain, all the testing—and would be able to help where help was needed" (Heb. 2:17–18 MSG).

Are you poor? Jesus knows how you feel. Are you on the lowest rung of the social ladder? He understands. Ever feel taken advantage of? Christ paid taxes to a foreign emperor.

He's been there. He understands the meaning of obscurity.

But what if your life is not obscure? What if you have a business to run or crowds to manage or a classroom to lead? Can Jesus relate?

Absolutely. He recruited and oversaw his own organization. Seventy men plus an assortment of women looked to him for leadership. Do you make budgets and lead meetings and hire personnel? Christ knows leadership is not easy. His group included a zealot who hated the Romans and a tax collector who had worked for them. The mother of his key men demanded special treatment for her sons. Jesus understands the stress of leadership.

Ever feel as if you need to get away? So did Jesus. "Early the next morning, while it was still dark, Jesus woke and left the house. He went to a lonely place, where he prayed" (Mark 1:35 NCV).

Ever have so many demands that you can't stop for lunch? He can relate. "Crowds of people were coming and going so that Jesus and his followers did not even have time to eat" (Mark 6:31 NCV).

Do you have too much e-mail to fit in a screen or too many calls to make in a day? Christ has been there. "Great crowds came to Jesus, bringing with them the lame, the blind, the crippled, those who could not speak, and many others. They put them at Jesus' feet, and he healed them" (Matt. 15:30 NCV).

How about family tension? "When his family heard what was happening, they tried to take him home with them. 'He's out of his mind,' they said" (Mark 3:21 NLT).

Have you been falsely accused? Enemies called Jesus a wino and a chowhound (Matt. 11:19). The night before his death people "tried to find something false against Jesus so they could kill him" (Matt. 26:59 NCV).

Do your friends ever let you down? When Christ needed help, his friends dozed off. "You men could not stay awake with me for one hour?" (Matt. 26:40 NCV).

Unsure of the future? Jesus was. Regarding the last day of history, he explained, "No one knows when that day or time will be, not the angels in heaven, not even the Son" (Matt. 24:36 NCV). Can Jesus be the Son of God and not know something? He can if he chooses not to. Knowing you would face the unknown, he chose to face the same.

Jesus has been there. He experienced "all the pain, all the testing" (Heb. 2:18 MSG). Jesus was angry enough to purge the temple, hungry enough to eat raw grain, distraught enough to weep in public, fun loving enough to be called a drunkard, winsome enough to attract kids, weary enough to sleep in a storm-bounced boat, poor enough to sleep on dirt and borrow a coin for a sermon illustration, radical enough to get kicked out of town, responsible enough to care for his mother, tempted enough to know the smell of Satan, and fearful enough to sweat blood.

But why? Why would heaven's finest Son endure earth's toughest pain? So you would know that "he is able . . . to run to the cry of . . . those who are being tempted and tested and tried" (Heb. 2:18 AMP).

Whatever you are facing, he knows how you feel.

A couple of days ago twenty thousand of us ran through the streets of San Antonio, raising money for breast cancer research. Most of us ran out of kindness, happy to log three miles and donate a few dollars to the cause. A few ran in memory of a loved one, others in honor of a cancer survivor. We ran for different reasons. But no runner was more passionate than one I spotted. A bandanna covered her bald head, and dark circles shadowed her eyes. She had cancer. While we ran out of kindness, she ran out of conviction. She knows how cancer victims feel. She's been there.

So has Jesus. "He is able . . . to run to the cry of . . . those who are being tempted and tested and tried."

When you turn to him *for* help, he runs to you *to* help. Why? He knows how you feel. He's been there.

By the way, remember how Jesus was not reluctant to call his ancestors his family? He's not ashamed of you either: "Jesus, who makes people holy, and those who are made holy are from the same family. So he is not ashamed to call them his brothers and sisters" (Heb. 2:11 NCV).

He's not ashamed of you. Nor is he confused by you. Your actions don't bewilder him. Your tilted halo doesn't trouble him. So go to him. After all, you're a part of his family.

3

Friend of Flops

Shady People

MATTHEW 9:9–13

As Jesus was going down the road, he saw Matthew sitting at his tax-collection booth. 'Come, be my disciple,' Jesus said to him. So Matthew got up and followed him" (Matt. 9:9 NLT).

The surprise in this invitation is the one invited—a tax collector. Combine the greed of an embezzling executive with the presumption of a hokey television evangelist. Throw in the audacity of an ambulance-chasing lawyer and the cowardice of a drive-by sniper. Stir in a pinch of a pimp's morality, and finish it off with the drug peddler's code of ethics—and what do you have?

A first-century tax collector.

According to the Jews, these guys ranked barely above plankton on the food chain. Caesar permitted these Jewish citizens to tax almost anything—your boat, the fish you caught, your house, your crops. As long as Caesar got his due, they could keep the rest.

Matthew was a *public* tax collector. Private tax collectors hired other people to do the dirty work. Public publicans, like Matthew, just pulled their stretch limos into the poor side of town and set up shop. As crooked as corkscrews.

His given name was Levi, a priestly name (Mark 2:14; Luke 5:27–28). Did his parents aspire for him to enter the priesthood? If so, he was a flop in the family circle.

You can bet he was shunned. The neighborhood cookouts? Never invited. High-school reunions? Somehow his name was left off the list. The guy was avoided like streptococcus A. Everybody kept his distance from Matthew.

Everyone except Jesus. "'Come, be my disciple,' Jesus said to him. So Matthew got up and followed him" (Matt. 9:9 NLT).

Matthew must have been ripe. Jesus hardly had to tug. Within a punctuation mark, Matthew's shady friends and Jesus' green followers are swapping e-mail addresses. "Then Levi gave a big dinner for Jesus at his house. Many tax collectors and other people were eating there, too" (Luke 5:29 NCV).

What do you suppose led up to that party? Let's try to imagine. I can see Matthew going back to his office and packing up. He removes the Quisling of the Year Award from the wall and boxes up the Shady Business School certificate. His coworkers start asking questions.

"What's up, Matt? Headed on a cruise?"

"Hey, Matthew, the Missus kick you out?"

Matthew doesn't know what to say. He mumbles something about a job change. But as he reaches the door, he pauses. Holding his box full of office supplies, he looks back. They're giving him hangdog looks—kind of sad, puzzled.

He feels a lump in his throat. Oh, these guys aren't much. Parents warn their kids about this sort. Salty language. Mardi Gras morals. They keep the phone number of the bookie on speed dial. The bouncer at the Gentlemen's Club sends them birthday cards. But a friend is a friend. Yet what can he do? Invite them to meet Jesus? Yeah, right. They like preachers the way sheep like butchers. Tell them to tune in to the religious channel on TV? Then they'd think cotton-candy hair is a requirement for following Christ. What if he snuck little Torah tracts in their desks? Nah, they don't read.

So, not knowing what else to do, he shrugs his shoulders and gives them a nod. "These stupid allergies," he says, rubbing the mist from one eye.

Later that day the same thing happens. He goes to the bar to settle up his account. The décor is blue-collar chic: a seedy, smoky place with a Budweiser chandelier over the pool table and a jukebox in the corner. Not the country club, but for Matthew, it's his home on the way home. And when he tells the owner he's moving on, the bartender responds, "Whoa, Matt. What's comin' down?"

Matthew mumbles an excuse about a transfer but leaves with an empty feeling in his gut.

Later on he meets up with Jesus at a diner and shares his problem. "It's my buddies—you know, the guys at the office. And the fellows at the bar."

"What about them?" Jesus asks.

"Well, we kinda run together, you know. I'm gonna miss 'em. Take Josh for instance—as slick as a can of Quaker State, but he visits orphans on Sunday. And Bruno at the gym? Can crunch you like a roach, but I've never had a better friend. He's posted bail for me three times."

Jesus motions for him to go on. "What's the problem?"

"Well, I'm gonna miss those guys. I mean, I've got nothing against Peter and James and John, Jesus . . . but they're Sunday morning, and I'm Saturday night. I've got my own circle, ya know?"

Jesus starts to smile and shake his head. "Matthew, Matthew, you think I came to quarantine you? Following me doesn't mean forgetting your friends. Just the opposite. I want to meet them."

"Are you serious?"

"Is the high priest a Jew?"

"But, Jesus, these guys . . . half of them are on parole. Josh hasn't worn socks since his Bar Mitzvah . . ."

"I'm not talking about a religious service, Matthew. Let me ask you—what do you like to do? Bowl? Play Monopoly? How's your golf game?"

Matthew's eyes brighten. "You ought to see me cook. I get on steaks like a whale on Jonah."

"Perfect." Jesus smiles. "Then throw a little going-away party. A hang-up-the-clipboard bash. Get the gang together."

Matthew's all over it. Calling the caterer, his housekeeper, his secretary. "Get the word out, Thelma. Drinks and dinner at my house tonight. Tell the guys to come and bring a date."

And so Jesus ends up at Matthew's house, a classy split-level with a view of the Sea of Galilee. Parked out front is everything from BMWs to Harleys to limos. And the crowd inside tells you this is anything but a clergy conference.

Earrings on the guys and tattoos on the girls. Moussified hair. Music that rumbles teeth roots. And buzzing around in the middle of the group is Matthew, making more connections than an electrician. He hooks up Peter with the tax collector bass club and Martha with the kitchen staff. Simon the Zealot meets a high-school debate partner. And Jesus? Beaming. What could be better? Sinners and saints in the same room, and no one's trying to determine who is which. But an hour or so into the evening the door opens, and an icy breeze blows in. "The Pharisees and the men who taught the law for the Pharisees began to complain to Jesus' followers, 'Why do you eat and drink with tax collectors and sinners?'" (Luke 5:30 NCV).

Enter the religious police and their thin-lipped piety. Big black books under arms. Cheerful as Siberian prison guards. Clerical collars so tight that veins bulge. They like to grill too. But not steaks.

Matthew is the first to feel the heat. "Some religious fellow you are," one says, practically pulling an eyebrow muscle. "Look at the people you hang out with."

Matthew doesn't know whether to get mad or get out. Before he has time to choose, Jesus intervenes, explaining that Matthew is right where he needs to be. "Healthy people don't need a doctor—sick people do. I have come to call sinners to turn from their sins, not to spend my time with those who think they are already good enough" (vv. 31–32 NLT).

Quite a story. Matthew goes from double-dealer to disciple. He throws a party that makes the religious right uptight, but Christ proud. The good guys look good, and the bad guys hit the road. Some story indeed.

What do we do with it?

That depends on which side of the tax collector's table you find yourself. You and I are Matthew. Don't look at me that way. There's enough hustler in the best of us to qualify for Matthew's table. Maybe you've never taken taxes, but you've taken liberty with the truth, taken credit that wasn't yours, taken advantage of the weak. You and me? Matthew.

If you're still at the table, you receive an invitation. "Follow me." So what if you've got a rube reputation? So did Matthew. You may end up writing your own gospel.

If you've left the table, you receive a clarification. You don't have to be weird to follow Jesus. You don't have to stop liking your friends to follow him. Just the opposite. A few introductions would be nice. Do you know how to grill a steak?

Sometime ago I was asked to play a game of golf. The foursome included two preachers, a church leader, and a "Matthew, B.C." The thought of four hours with three Christians, two of whom were pulpiteers, did not appeal to him. His best friend, a Christ follower and his boss, insisted, so he agreed. I'm happy to report that he proclaimed the experience painless. On the ninth hole he turned to one of us and said, smiling, "I'm so glad you guys are normal." I think he meant this: "I'm glad you didn't get in my face or club me with a King James driver. Thanks for laughing at my jokes and telling a few yourself. Thanks for being normal." We didn't lower standards. But neither did we saddle a high horse. We were nice. Normal and nice.

Discipleship is sometimes defined by being normal.

A woman in a small Arkansas community was a single mom with a frail baby. Her neighbor would stop by every few days and keep the child so she could shop. After some weeks her neighbor shared more than time; she shared her faith, and the woman did what Matthew did. She followed Christ.

The friends of the young mother objected. "Do you know what those people teach?" they contested.

"Here is what I know," she told them. "They held my baby."[1]

I think Jesus likes that kind of answer, don't you?

4

The Hand God Loves to Hold

Desperate People

MARK 5:25–34

To see her hand you need to look low. Look down. That's where she lives. Low to the ground. Low on the priority list. Low on the social scale. She's low.

Can you see it? Her hand? Gnarled. Thin. Diseased. Dirt blackens the nails and stains the skin. Look carefully amid the knees and feet of the crowd. They're scampering after Christ. He walks. She crawls. People bump her, but she doesn't stop. Others complain. She doesn't care. The woman is desperate. Blood won't stay in her body. "There was a woman in the crowd who had had a hemorrhage for twelve years" (Mark 5:25 NLT). Twelve years of clinics. Treatments. Herbs. Prayer meetings. Incantations.

"She had suffered a great deal from many doctors through the years" (v. 26 NLT). Do you smell quackery in those words? Doctors who took, not the disease, but advantage of her? She "had spent everything she had to pay them, but she had gotten no better. In fact, she was worse" (v. 26 NLT).

No health. No money. And no family to help. Unclean, according to the Law of Moses. The Law protected women from aggressive, insensitive men during those times of the month. In this woman's case severe application of the Law left her, not untouched, but untouchable, ceremonially unclean. The hand you see in the crowd? The one reaching for the robe? No one will touch it.

Wasn't always the case. Surely a husband once took it in marriage. The hand looked different in those days: clean, soft skinned, perfumed. A husband once loved this hand.

A family once relied on this hand. To cook, sew. To wipe tears from cheeks, tuck blankets under chins. Are the hands of a mother ever still?

Only if she is diseased.

Maybe the husband tried to stay with her, carting her to doctors and treatment centers. Or maybe he gave up quickly, overwhelmed by her naps, nausea, and anemia. So he put her out. A change of clothes and a handful of change—that's it. Close the door.

So she has nothing. No money. No home. No health. Dilapidated dreams. Deflated faith. Unwelcome in the synagogue. Unwanted by her community. For twelve years she has suffered. She has nothing, and her health is getting worse.

Maybe that's what did it. She "had grown worse" (v. 26). This morning she could scarcely stand. She splashed water on her face and was horrified by the skeletal image in the pool. What you and I see in Auschwitz photos, she saw in her reflection—gaunt cheeks, tired and taut skin, and two full-moon eyes.

She is desperate. And her desperation births an idea.

"She had heard about Jesus" (v. 27 NLT). Every society has a grapevine, even—or especially—the society of the sick. Word among the lepers and the left out is this: Jesus can heal. And Jesus is coming. By invitation of the synagogue ruler, Jesus is coming to Capernaum.

Odd to find the ruler and the woman in the same story. He powerful. She pitiful. He in demand. She insignificant. He is high. She is low. But his daughter is dying. Tragedy levels social topography. So they find themselves on the same path in the village and the same page of the Bible.

As the crowd comes, she thinks, "If I can just touch his clothing, I will be healed" (v. 28 NLT). At the right time, she crab-scurries through the crowd. Knees bump her ribs. "Move out of the way!" someone shouts. She doesn't care and doesn't stop. Twelve years on the streets have toughened her.

Jesus' robe is in sight. Four tassels dangle from blue threads. Ornaments of holiness worn by Jewish men. How long since she has touched anything holy? She extends her hand toward a tassel.

Her sick hand. Her tired hand. The hand the husband no longer wants and the family no longer needs. She touches the robe of Jesus, and "immediately the bleeding stopped, and she could feel that she had been healed!" (v. 29 NLT).

Life rushes in. Pale cheeks turn pink. Shallow breaths become full. Hoover Dam cracks and a river floods. The woman feels power enter. And

Jesus? Jesus feels power exit. "Jesus realized at once that healing power had gone out from him, so he turned around in the crowd and asked, 'Who touched my clothes?'" (v. 30 NLT).

Did Christ surprise even Christ? Has Jesus the divine moved faster than Jesus the human? The Savior outstepped the neighbor? "Who touched my clothes?"

His disciples think the query is odd. "'All this crowd is pressing around you. How can you ask, "Who touched me?"' But he kept on looking around to see who had done it" (vv. 31–32 NLT).

Can we fault this woman's timidity? She doesn't know what to expect. Jesus could berate her, embarrass her. Besides, he was her last choice. She sought the help of a dozen others before she sought his. And the people—what will they do? What will the ruler of the synagogue do? He is upright. She is unclean. And here she is, lunging at the town guest. No wonder she is afraid.

But she has one reason to have courage. She is healed. "The woman, knowing what had happened, knowing she was the one, stepped up in fear and trembling, knelt before him, and gave him the whole story" (v. 33 MSG).

"The whole story." How long had it been since someone put the gear of life in Park, turned off the key, and listened to her story? But when this woman reaches out to Jesus, he does. With the town bishop waiting, a young girl dying, and a crowd pressing, he still makes time for a woman from the fringe. Using a term he gives to no one else, he says, "Daughter, your faith has made you well. Go in peace. You have been healed" (v. 34 NLT).

And Christ moves on.

And she moves on.

But we can't. We can't because we've been there. Been her. Are there. Are her. Desperate. Dirty. Drained.

Illness took her strength. What took yours? Red ink? Hard drink? Late nights in the wrong arms? Long days on the wrong job? Pregnant too soon? Too often? Is her hand your hand? If so, take heart. Your family may shun it. Society may avoid it. But Christ? Christ wants to touch it. When your hand reaches through the masses, he knows.

Yours is the hand he loves to hold.

5

Try Again

Discouraged People

LUKE 5:1–11

There is a look that says, "It's too late." You've seen it. The rolling of the eyes, the shaking of the head, the pursing of the lips.

Your friend is a day from divorce. Over coffee you urge, "Can't you try one more time?"

She shrugs. "Done that."

Your father and brother don't speak to one another. Haven't for years. "Won't you try again?" you ask your dad. He looks away, inhales deeply, and sighs.

Five years this side of retirement the economy Hindenburgs your husband's retirement. You try to make the best of it. "You can go back to school. Learn a new trade." You might as well have told him to swim to London. He shakes his head. "I'm too old . . . It's too late."

Too late to save a marriage.

Too late to reconcile.

Too late for a new career.

Too late to catch any fish. Or so Peter thinks. All night he fished. He witnessed both the setting and the rising of the sun but has nothing to show for it. While other fishermen cleaned their catch, he just cleaned his nets. But now Jesus wants him to try again.

"Now it happened that while the crowd was pressing around Him and listening to the word of God, [Jesus] was standing by the lake of Gennesaret" (Luke 5:1).

The Sea of Gennesaret, or Galilee, is a six-by-thirteen-mile body of water in northern Israel. These days her shore sleeps, attracting only a cluster of tour buses and a handful of fishermen. But in the days of Jesus the area bustled with people. Nine of the seacoast villages boasted populations of fifteen thousand plus. And you get the impression that a good portion of those people was present the morning Christ ministered on the beach. As more people arrived, more people pressed. With every press, Jesus took a step back. Soon he was stepping off the sand and into the water. That's when he had an idea.

> He saw two boats lying at the edge of the lake; but the fishermen had gotten out of them and were washing their nets. And He got into one of the boats, which was Simon's, and asked him to put out a little way from the land. And He sat down and began teaching the people from the boat. When He had finished speaking, He said to Simon, "Put out into the deep water and let down your nets for a catch." (vv. 2–4)

Jesus needs a boat; Peter provides one. Jesus preaches; Peter is content to listen. Jesus suggests a midmorning fishing trip, however, and Peter gives him a look. The it's-too-late look. He runs his fingers through his hair and sighs, "Master, we worked hard all night and caught nothing" (v. 5). Can you feel Peter's futility?

All night the boat floated fishless on the black sheet of the sea. Lanterns of distant vessels bounced like fireflies. The men swung their nets and filled the air with the percussion of their trade.

Swish, slap . . . silence.

Swish, slap . . . silence.

Midnight.

Excited voices from across the lake reached the men. Another boat had found a school. Peter considered moving but decided against it.

Swish, slap . . . silence.

Two o'clock in the morning. Peter rested while his brother fished. Then Andrew rested. James, floating nearby, suggested a move. The others agreed. Wind billowed the sails and blew the boats to a cove. The rhythm resumed.

Swish, slap . . . silence.

Every yank of the net was easy. Too easy. This night the lake was a proper lady. No matter how often the men winked and whistled, she offered nothing.

Golden shafts eventually reclaimed the sky. Most mornings the sunrise inspires the men. Today it only tired them. They didn't want to see it. Who wants to dock an empty boat? Who wants to tie up and clean up, knowing the first question the wife is going to ask? And, most of all, who wants to hear a well-rested carpenter-turned-rabbi say, "Put out into the deep water and let down your nets for a catch" (v. 4)?

Oh, the thoughts Peter might have had. *I'm tired. Bone tired. I want a meal and a bed, not a fishing trip. Am I his tour guide? Besides, half of Galilee is watching. I feel like a loser already. Now he wants to put on a midmorning fishing exhibition? You can't catch fish in the morning. Count me out.*

Whatever thoughts Peter had were distilled to one phrase: "We worked hard all night and caught nothing" (v. 5).

Do you have any worn, wet, empty nets? Do you know the feeling of a sleepless, fishless night? Of course you do. For what have you been casting?

Sobriety? "I've worked so hard to stay sober, but . . ."

Solvency? "My debt is an anvil around my neck . . ."

Faith? "I want to believe, but . . ."

Healing? "I've been sick so long . . ."

A happy marriage? "No matter what I do . . ."

I've worked hard all night and caught nothing.

You've felt what Peter felt. You've sat where Peter sat. And now Jesus is asking you to go fishing. He knows your nets are empty. He knows your heart is weary. He knows you'd like nothing more than to turn your back on the mess and call it a life.

But he urges, "It's not too late to try again."

See if Peter's reply won't help you formulate your own. "I will do as You say and let down the nets" (v. 5).

Not much passion in those words. You might hope for a ten-thousand-candle smile and a fist pumping the air. "I got Jesus in my boat. Momma, warm up the oven!" But Peter shows no excitement. He feels none. Now he has to unfold the nets, pull out the oars, and convince James and John to postpone their rest. He has to work. If faith is measured in seeds, his is an angstrom. Inspired? No. But obedient? Admirably. And an angstrom of obedience is all Jesus wants.

"Put out into the deep water," the God-man instructs.

Why the deep water? You suppose Jesus knew something Peter didn't?

You suppose Jesus is doing with Peter what we parents do with our kids on Easter Sunday? They find most of the eggs on their own. But a couple of treasures inevitably survive the first harvest. "Look," I'd whisper in the ears of my daughters, "behind the tree." A quick search around the trunk, and, what do you know, Dad was right. Spotting treasures is easy for the one who hid them. Finding fish is simple for the God who made them. To Jesus, the Sea of Galilee is a dollar-store fishbowl on a kitchen cabinet.

Peter gives the net a swish, lets it slap, and watches it disappear. Luke doesn't tell us what Peter did while he was waiting for the net to sink, so I will. (I'm glancing heavenward for lightning.)

I like to think that Peter, while holding the net, looks over his shoulder at Jesus. And I like to think that Jesus, knowing Peter is about to be half yanked into the water, starts to smile. A daddy-daughter-Easter-egg smile. Rising cheeks render his eyes half-moons. A dash of white flashes beneath his whiskers. Jesus tries to hold it back but can't.

There is so much to smile about. It's Easter Sunday, and the lawn is crawling with kids. Just wait till they look under the tree.

> When they had done this, they enclosed a great quantity of fish, and their nets began to break; so they signaled to their partners in the other boat for them to come and help them. And they came and filled both of the boats, so that they began to sink. (vv. 6–7)

Peter's arm is yanked into the water. It's all he can do to hang on until the other guys can help. Within moments the four fishermen and the carpenter are up to their knees in flopping silver.

Peter lifts his eyes off the catch and onto the face of Christ. In that moment, for the first time, he sees Jesus. Not Jesus the Fish Finder. Not Jesus the Multitude Magnet. Not Jesus the Rabbi. Peter sees Jesus the Lord.

Peter falls face first among the fish. Their stink doesn't bother him. It is his stink that he's worried about. "Go away from me Lord, for I am a sinful man!" (v. 8).

Christ had no intention of honoring that request. He doesn't abandon self-confessed schlemiels. Quite the contrary, he enlists them. "Do not fear, from now on you will be catching men" (v. 10).

Contrary to what you may have been told, Jesus doesn't limit his recruiting to the stout-hearted. The beat up and worn out are prime prospects in his book, and he's been known to climb into boats, bars, and brothels to tell them, "It's not too late to start over."

Peter learned the lesson. But wouldn't you know it? Peter forgot the lesson. Two short years later this man who confessed Christ in the boat cursed Christ at a fire. The night before Jesus' crucifixion, Peter told people that he'd never heard of Jesus.

He couldn't have made a more tragic mistake. He knew it. The burly fisherman buried his bearded face in thick hands and spent Friday night in tears. All the feelings of that Galilean morning came back to him.

It's too late.

But then Sunday came. Jesus came! Peter saw him. Peter was convinced that Christ had come back from the dead. But apparently Peter wasn't convinced that Christ came back for him.

So he went back to the boat—to the same boat, the same beach, the same sea. He came out of retirement. He and his buddies washed the barnacles off the hull, unpacked the nets, and pushed out. They fished all night, and, honest to Pete, they caught nothing.

Poor Peter. Blew it as a disciple. Now he's blowing it as a fisherman. About the time he wonders if it's too late to take up carpentry, the sky turns orange, and they hear a voice from the coastline. "Had any luck?"

They yell back, "No."

"Try the right side of the boat!"

With nothing to lose and no more pride to protect, they give it a go. "So they cast, and then they were not able to haul it in because of the great number of fish" (John 21:6). It takes a moment for the déjà vu to hit Peter. But when it does, he cannonballs into the water and swims as fast as he can to see the one who loved him enough to *re-create* a miracle. This time the message stuck.

Peter never again fished for fish. He spent the rest of his days telling anyone who would listen, "It's not too late to try again."

Is it too late for you? Before you say yes, before you fold up the nets and head for the house—two questions. Have you given Christ your boat? Your heartache? Your dead-end dilemma? Your struggle? Have you really turned it over to him? And have you gone deep? Have you bypassed the surface-water solutions you can see in search of the deep-channel provisions God can give? Try the other side of the boat. Go deeper than you've gone. You may find what Peter found. The payload of his second effort was not the fish he caught but the God he saw.

The God-man who spots weary fishermen, who cares enough to enter their boats, who will turn his back on the adoration of a crowd to solve the frustration of a friend. The next door Savior who whispers this word to the owners of empty nets, "Let's try again—this time with me on board."

6

Spit Therapy

Suffering People

JOHN 9:1–38

The old guy at the corner hasn't seen him. The woman selling the figs hasn't either. Jesus describes him to the scribes at the gate and the kids in the courtyard. "He's about this tall. Clothes are ragged. Belly-length beard."

No one has a clue.

For the better part of a day Jesus has been searching up and down the Jerusalem streets. He didn't stop for lunch. Hasn't paused to rest. The only time his feet aren't moving is when he is asking, "Pardon me, but have you seen the fellow who used to beg on the corner?"

He searched the horse stable and checked out the roof of a shed. Now Jesus is going door-to-door. "He has a homeless look," Jesus tells people. "Unkempt. Dirty. And he has muddy eyelids."

Finally a boy gives him a lead. Jesus takes a back street toward the temple and spots the man sitting on a stump between two donkeys. Christ approaches from behind and places a hand on his shoulder. "There you are! I've been looking for you." The fellow turns and, for the first time, sees the one who let him see. And what the man does next you may find hard to believe.

Let me catch you up. John introduces him to us with these words. "As [Jesus] passed by, He saw a man blind from birth" (John 9:1). This man has never seen a sunrise. Can't tell purple from pink. The disciples fault the family tree. "Rabbi, who sinned, this man or his parents, that he would be born blind?" (v. 2).

Neither, the God-man replies. Trace this condition back to heaven. The reason the man was born sightless? So "the works of God might be displayed in him" (v. 3).

Talk about a thankless role. Selected to suffer. Some sing to God's glory.

Others teach to God's glory. Who wants to be blind for God's glory? Which is tougher—the condition or discovering it was God's idea?

The cure proves to be as surprising as the cause. "[Jesus] spat on the ground, and made clay of the spittle, and applied the clay to his eyes" (v. 6).

The world abounds with paintings of the God-man: in the arms of Mary, in the Garden of Gethsemane, in the Upper Room, in the darkened tomb. Jesus touching. Jesus weeping, laughing, teaching . . . but I've never seen a painting of Jesus spitting.

Christ smacking his lips a time or two, gathering a mouth of saliva, working up a blob of drool, and letting it go. Down in the dirt. (Kids, next time your mother tells you not to spit, show her this passage.) Then he squats, stirs up a puddle of . . . I don't know, what would you call it?

Holy putty? Spit therapy? Saliva solution? Whatever the name, he places a fingerful in his palm, and then, as calmly as a painter spackles a hole in the wall, Jesus streaks mud-miracle on the blind man's eyes. "Go, wash in the pool of Siloam" (v. 7).

The beggar feels his way to the pool, splashes water on his mud-streaked face, and rubs away the clay. The result is the first chapter of Genesis, just for him. Light where there was darkness. Virgin eyes focus, fuzzy figures become human beings, and John receives the Understatement of the Bible Award when he writes: "He . . . came back seeing" (v. 7).

Come on, John! Running short of verbs? How about "he *raced* back seeing"? "He *danced* back seeing"? "He *roared* back whooping and hollering and kissing everything he could, for the first time, see"? The guy had to be thrilled.

We would love to leave him that way, but if this man's life were a cafeteria line, he would have just stepped from the sirloin to the boiled Brussels sprouts. Look at the reaction of the neighbors: "'Is not this the one who used to sit and beg?' Others were saying, 'This is he,' still others were saying, 'No, but he is like him.' He kept saying, 'I am the one'" (vv. 8–9).

These folks don't celebrate; they debate! They have watched this man grope and trip since he was a kid (v. 20). You'd think they would rejoice. But they don't. They march him down to the church to have him kosher tested. When the Pharisees ask for an explanation, the was-blind beggar says, "He applied clay to my eyes, and I washed, and I see" (v. 15).

Again we pause for the applause, but none comes. No recognition. No celebration. Apparently Jesus failed to consult the healing handbook. "Now it was a Sabbath on the day when Jesus made the clay and opened his eyes. . . . The Pharisees were saying, 'This man is not from God, because He does not keep the Sabbath'" (vv. 14,16).

That noise you hear is the beeping of the absurdity Geiger counter. The religious leaders' verdict bounces the needle. Here is a parallel response. Suppose the swimming pool where you recreate has a sign on the fence that reads Rescues Performed by Certified Lifeguards Only. You never think good or bad about the rule until one day you bang your head on the bottom. You black out, ten feet under.

Next thing you know you're belly down on the side of the pool, coughing up water. Someone rescued you. And when the lifeguards appear, the fellow who pulled you out of the deep disappears. As you come to your senses, you tell the story. But rather than rejoice, people recoil. "Doesn't count! Doesn't count!" they shout like referees waving off a basketball that cleared the net after the clock had expired. "It wasn't official. Wasn't legal. Since the rescuer wasn't certified, consider yourself drowned."

Duh? You bet. Will no one rejoice with this man? The neighbors didn't. The preachers didn't. Wait, here come the parents. But the reaction of the formerly blind man's parents is even worse.

> They called the parents of the very one who had received his sight, and questioned them, saying, "Is this your son, who you say was born blind? Then how does he now see?" His parents answered them and said, "We know that this is our son, and that he was born blind; but how he now sees, we do not know; or who opened his eyes, we do not know. Ask him; he is of age, he will speak for himself." His parents said this because they were afraid of the Jews; for the Jews had already agreed that if anyone confessed Him to be Christ, he was to be put out of the synagogue. (vv. 18–22)

How can they do this? Granted, to be put out of the synagogue is serious. But isn't refusing to help your child even more so?

Who was really blind that day? The neighbors didn't see the man; they saw a novelty. The church leaders didn't see the man; they saw a technicality. The parents didn't see their son; they saw a social difficulty. In the end, no one saw him. "So they put him out" (v. 34).

And now, here he is, on a back street of Jerusalem. The fellow has to be bewildered. Born blind only to be healed. Healed only to be kicked out. Kicked out only to be left alone. The peak of Everest and the heat of Sahara, all in one Sabbath. Now he can't even beg anymore. How would that feel?

You may know all too well. I know of a man who has buried four children. A single mother in our church is raising two autistic sons. We buried a neighbor whose cancer led to heart trouble, which created pneumonia. Her health record was as thick as a phone book. Do some people seem to be dealt more than their share of bad hands?

If so, Jesus knows. He knows how they feel, and he knows where they are. "Jesus heard that they had thrown him out, and went and found him" (v. 35 MSG). In case the stable birth wasn't enough. If three decades of earth walking and miracle working are insufficient. If there be any doubt regarding God's full-bore devotion, he does things like this. He tracks down a troubled pauper.

The beggar lifts his eyes to look into the face of the One who started all this. Is he going to criticize Christ? Complain to Christ? You couldn't blame him for doing both. After all, he didn't volunteer for the disease or the deliverance. But he does neither. No, "he worshiped Him" (v. 38). Don't you know he knelt? Don't you think he wept? And how could he keep from wrapping his arms around the waist of the One who gave him sight? He worshiped him.

And when you see him, you will too.

How dare I make such a statement? This book will be held by arthritic hands. These chapters will be read by tear-filled eyes. Some of your legs are wheelchaired, and your hearts are hope starved. But "these hard times are small potatoes compared to the coming good times, the lavish celebration prepared for us" (2 Cor. 4:17 MSG).

The day you see your Savior you will experience a million times over what Joni Eareckson Tada experienced on her wedding day. Are you acquainted with her story? A diving accident left her paralyzed at the age of seventeen. Nearly all of her fifty-plus years have been spent in a wheelchair. Her handicap doesn't keep her from writing or painting or speaking about her Savior. Nor did her handicap keep her from marrying Ken. But it almost kept her from the joy of the wedding.

She'd done her best. Her gown was draped over a thin wire mesh covering the wheels of her wheelchair. With flowers in her lap and a sparkle in her eye, she felt a "little like a float in the Rose Parade."

A ramp had been constructed, connecting the foyer to the altar. While waiting her turn to motorize over it, Joni made a discovery. Across her dress was a big, black grease mark courtesy of the chair. And the chair, though "spiffed up . . . was still the big, clunky thing it always was." Then the bouquet of daisies on her lap slid off center; her paralyzed hands were unable to rearrange them. She felt far from the picture-perfect bride of *Bride's Magazine.*

She inched her chair forward and looked down the aisle. That's when she saw her groom.

> I spotted him way down front, standing at attention and looking tall and elegant in his formal attire. My face grew hot. My heart began to pound. Our eyes met and, amazingly, from that point everything changed.
>
> How I looked no longer mattered. I forgot all about my wheelchair. Grease stains? Flowers out of place? Who cares? No longer did I feel ugly or unworthy; the love in Ken's eyes washed it all away. I was the pure and perfect bride. That's what he saw, and that's what changed me. It took great restraint not to jam my "power stick" into high gear and race down the aisle to be with my groom.[1]

When she saw him, she forgot about herself.

When you see him, you will too.

I'm sorry about your greasy gown. And your flowers—they tend to slide, don't they? Who has an answer for the diseases, drudgeries, and darkness of this life? I don't. But we do know this. Everything changes when you look at your groom.

And yours is coming. Just as he came for the blind man, Jesus is coming for you. The hand that touched the blind man's shoulder will touch your cheeks. The face that changed his life will change yours.

And when you see Jesus, you will bow in worship.

7

What Jesus Says at Funerals

Grieving People

JOHN 11:1–44

You never know what to say at funerals. This one is no exception. The chapel is library quiet. People acknowledge each other with soft smiles and nods. You say nothing.

What's to be said? There's a dead body in the place, for crying out loud! Just last month you took the guy out to lunch. You and Lazarus told jokes over nachos. Aside from a bad cough, you thought he was healthy.

Within a week you learned of the diagnosis. The doctor gave him sixty days. He didn't make it that long. Now you're both at his funeral. He in the casket. You in the pew. Death has silenced you both.

The church is full, so you stand at the back. Stained glass prisms the afternoon sun, streaking faces with shafts of purple and gold. You recognize many of them. Bethany is a small town. The two women on the front pew you know well. Martha and Mary are the sisters of Lazarus. Quiet, pensive Mary. Bustling, busy Martha. Even now she can't sit still. She keeps looking over her shoulder. *Who for?* you wonder.

In a matter of moments the answer enters. And when he does, she rushes up the aisle to meet him. Had you not known his name, the many whispers would have informed you. "It's Jesus." Every head turns.

He's wearing a tie, though you get the impression he rarely does. His collar seems tight and his jacket dated. A dozen or so men follow him; some stand in the aisle, others in the foyer. They have a well-traveled, wrinkled look, as if they rode all night.

Jesus embraces Martha, and she weeps. As she weeps, you wonder. You wonder what Jesus is going to do. You wonder what Jesus is going to say. He spoke to the winds and the demons. Remarkable. But death? Does he have anything to say about death? Your thoughts are interrupted by

Martha's accusation: "Lord, if You had been here, my brother would not have died" (John 11:21).

You can't fault her frustration. Are she and Jesus not friends? When Jesus and his followers had nowhere else to go, "Martha welcomed them into her home" (Luke 10:38 TLB). Mary and Martha know Jesus. They know Jesus loves Lazarus. "Lord," they told the courier to tell him, "the one you love is very sick" (John 11:3 NLT). This is no fan-mail request. This is a friend needing help.

Desperately needing help. The Greek language has two principle words to express sickness: one describes the presence of a disease, the other its effects. Martha uses the latter. A fair translation of her appeal would be, "Lord, the one you love is sinking fast."

Friends send Christ an urgent appeal in a humble fashion, and what does he do? "He stayed where he was for the next two days and did not go to them" (v. 6 NLT). By the time he arrives, Martha is so broken up she hardly knows what to say. With one breath she rebukes: "Lord, if You had been here, my brother would not have died" (v. 21). With the next she resolves: "But even now I know that whatever You ask of God, God will give You" (v. 22 NKJV).

Every funeral has its Marthas. Sprinkled among the bereaved are the bewildered. "Help me understand this one, Jesus."

This has been the prayer of Karen Burris Davis ever since that November morning when her son—and, consequently, her sun—failed to rise. Jacob was thirteen. The picture of health. Four medical examiners have found no cause of death. Her answer, she says, is no answer.

> I miss Jacob so much that I am not sure I can do this. I stand at the cemetery, knowing his body is down there, and think how insane it is to feel like if I start digging, I could see him just one more time. I just so much want to smell his hair and touch him. . . . How quickly the scent of someone goes away. I would have thought it would have lingered forever, that sour boy smell and those stinky tennis shoes. Of course, sometimes he actually did smell of soap and shampoo. The house is so empty without all his noise and plans.[1]

Grief fogs in the heart like a Maine-coast morning. The mourner hears the waves but sees no water. Detects voices but no faces. The life of the brokenhearted becomes that of a "footwatcher, walking through airports or the grocery store staring at feet, methodically moving through a misty world. One foot, then the other."[2]

Martha sat in a damp world, cloudy, tearful. And Jesus sat in it with her. "I am the resurrection and the life. Those who believe in me, even though they die like everyone else, will live again" (v. 25 NLT). Hear those words in a Superman tone, if you like. Clark Kent descending from nowhere, ripping shirt and popping buttons to reveal the *S* beneath. "I AM THE RESURRECTION AND THE LIFE!!!" Do you see a Savior with Terminator tenderness bypassing the tears of Martha and Mary and, in doing so, telling them and all grievers to buck up and trust?

I don't. I don't because of what Jesus does next. He weeps. He sits on the pew between Mary and Martha, puts an arm around each, and sobs. Among the three, a tsunami of sorrow is stirred; a monsoon of tears is released. Tears that reduce to streaks the watercolor conceptions of a cavalier Christ. Jesus weeps.

He weeps with them.

He weeps for them.

He weeps with you.

He weeps for you.

He weeps so we will know: Mourning is not disbelieving. Flooded eyes don't represent a faithless heart. A person can enter a cemetery Jesus-certain of life after death and still have a Twin Tower crater in the heart. Christ did. He wept, and he knew he was ten minutes from seeing a living Lazarus!

And his tears give you permission to shed your own. Grief does not mean you don't trust; it simply means you can't stand the thought of another day without the Jacob or Lazarus of your life. If Jesus gave the love, he understands the tears. So grieve, but don't grieve like those who don't know the rest of this story.

Jesus touches Martha's cheek, gives Mary a hug, stands, and turns to face the corpse. The casket lid is closed. He tells Martha to have it opened. She shakes her head and starts to refuse but then pauses. Turning to the funeral home director, she says, "Open it."

Since you are standing, you can see the face of Lazarus. It's waxy and white. You think Jesus is going to weep again. You never expect him to speak to his friend.

But he does. A few feet from the casket Jesus yells, "Lazarus, come out!" (v. 43 NCV).

Preachers always address the living. But the dead? One thing is sure. There better be a rumble in that casket, or this preacher is going to therapy. You and everyone else hear the rumble. There is movement in the coffin. "He who had died came out" (v. 44 NKJV).

Dead men don't do that—do they? Dead men don't come out. Dead men don't wake up. Dead hearts don't beat. Dried blood doesn't rush. Empty lungs don't inhale. No, dead men don't come out—unless they hear the voice of the Lord of life.

The ears of the dead may be deaf to your voice and mine but not to his. Christ is "Lord of both the dead and the living" (Rom. 14:9 NIV). When Christ speaks to the dead, the dead listen. Indeed, had Jesus not addressed Lazarus by name, the tenant of every tomb on earth would have stepped forth.

Lazarus jolts up in the coffin, blinks, and looks around the room as if someone carted him there during a nap. A woman screams. Another faints. Everyone shouts. And you? You learned something. You learned what to say at funerals.

You learned there is a time to say nothing. Your words can't dispel a fog, but your presence can warm it. And your words can't give a Lazarus back to his sisters. But God's can. And it's just a matter of time before he speaks. "The Lord himself will come down from heaven with a commanding shout. . . . All the Christians who have died will rise from their graves" (1 Thess. 4:16 NLT).

Till then, we grieve, but not like those who have no hope.

And we listen. We listen for his voice. For we know who has the final say about death.

8

Getting the Hell Out

Tormented People

MARK 5:2–20

> When He got out of the boat, immediately a man from the tombs with an unclean spirit met Him, and he had his dwelling among the tombs. And no one was able to bind him anymore, even with a chain; because he had often been bound with shackles and chains, and the chains had been torn apart by him and the shackles broken in pieces, and no one was strong enough to subdue him. Constantly, night and day, he was screaming among the tombs and in the mountains, and gashing himself with stones. (Mark 5:2–5)

Wiry, clumpy hair. A beard to the chest, ribboned with blood. Furtive eyes, darting in all directions, refusing to fix. Naked. No sandals to protect feet from the rocks of the ground or clothing to protect skin from the rocks of his hand. He beats himself with stones. Bruises blotch his skin like ink stains. Open sores and gashes attract flies.

His home is a limestone mausoleum, a graveyard of Galilean shoreline caves cut out of the cliffs. Apparently he feels more secure among the dead than the living.

Which pleases the living. He baffles them. See the cracked shackles on his legs and broken chains on his wrists? They can't control the guy. Nothing holds him. How do you manage chaos? Travelers skirt the area out of fear (Matt. 8:28). The villagers were left with a problem, and we are left with a picture—a picture of the work of Satan.

How else do we explain our bizarre behavior? The violent rages of a father. The secret binges of a mother. The sudden rebellion of a teenager. Maxed-out credit cards, Internet pornography. Satan does not sit still. A glimpse of the wild man reveals Satan's goal for you and me.

Self-imposed pain. The demoniac used rocks. We are more sophisticated; we use drugs, sex, work, violence, and food. (Hell makes us hurt ourselves.)

Obsession with death and darkness. Even unchained, the wild man loitered among the dead. Evil feels at home there. Communing with the deceased, sacrificing the living, a morbid fascination with death and dying—this is not the work of God.

Endless restlessness. The man on the eastern shore screamed day and night (Mark 5:5). Satan begets raging frenzy. "The evil spirit . . . wanders . . . ," Jesus says, "looking for rest" (Matt. 12:43 PHILLIPS).

Isolation. The man is all alone in his suffering. Such is Satan's plan. "The devil prowls around like a roaring lion, seeking some *one* to devour" (1 Pet. 5:8 RSV, emphasis mine). Fellowship foils his work.

And Jesus?

Jesus wrecks his work. Christ steps out of the boat with both pistols blasting. "Come out of the man, unclean spirit!" (Mark 5:8 NKJV).

No chitchat. No niceties. No salutations. Demons deserve no tolerance. They throw themselves at the feet and mercy of Christ. The leader of the horde begs for the others:

> "What have you to do with me, Jesus, Son of the Most High God? I adjure you by God, do not torment me." . . . Jesus asked him, "What is your name?" He replied, "My name is Legion; for we are many." He begged him earnestly not to send them out of the country. (vv. 7, 9–10 NRSV)

Legion is a Roman military term. A Roman legion involved six thousand soldiers. To envision that many demons inhabiting this man is frightening but not unrealistic. What bats are to a cave, demons are to hell—too many to number.

The demons are not only numerous, they are equipped. A legion is a battalion in arms. Satan and his friends come to fight. Hence, we are urged to "take up the full armor of God, so that you will be able to resist in the evil day, and having done everything, to stand firm" (Eph. 6:13).

Well we should, for they are organized. "We are fighting against forces and authorities and against rulers of darkness and powers in the spiritual world" (Eph. 6:12 CEV). Jesus spoke of the "gates of hell" (Matt. 16:18 KJV), a phrase that suggests the "council of hell." Our enemy has a complex and conniving spiritual army. Dismiss any image of a red-suited Satan with pitchfork and pointy tail. The devil is a strong devil.

But, and this is the point of the passage, in God's presence, the devil is a wimp. Satan is to God what a mosquito is to an atomic bomb.

> Now a large herd of swine was feeding there near the mountains. So all the demons begged Him, saying, "Send us to the swine, that we may enter them." And at once Jesus gave them permission. Then the unclean spirits went out and entered the swine (there were about two thousand); and the herd ran violently down the steep place into the sea, and drowned in the sea. (Mark 5:11–13 NKJV)

How hell's court cowers in Christ's presence! Demons bow before him, solicit him, and obey him. They can't even lease a pig without his permission. Then how do we explain Satan's influence?

Natalie[1] must have asked that question a thousand times. In the list of characters for a modern-day Gerasenes story, her name is near the top. She was raised in a tormented world.

The community suspected nothing. Her parents cast a friendly façade. Each Sunday they paraded Natalie and her sisters down the church aisle. Her father served as an elder. Her mom played the organ. The congregation respected them. Natalie despised them. To this day she refuses to call her parents "Mom" and "Dad." A "warlock" and "witch" don't deserve the distinction.

When she was six months old, they sexually sacrificed Natalie on hell's altar, tagging her as a sex object to be exploited by men in any place, anytime. Cultists bipolarized her world: dressing her in white for Sunday service and, hours later, stripping her at the coven. If she didn't scream or vomit during the attack, Natalie was rewarded with an ice-cream cone. Only by "crawling down deep" inside herself could she survive.

Natalie miraculously escaped the cult but not the memories. Well into her adult years, she wore six pairs of underpants as a wall of protection. Dresses created vulnerability; she avoided them. She hated being a woman; she hated seeing men; she hated being alive. Only God could know the legion of terrors that dogged her. But God did know.

Hidden within the swampland of her soul was an untouched island.

Small but safe. Built, she believes, by her heavenly Father during the hours the little girl sat on a church pew. Words of his love, hymns of his mercy—they left their mark. She learned to retreat to this island and pray. God heard her prayers. Counselors came. Hope began to offset horror. Her faith increasingly outweighed her fears. The healing process was lengthy and tedious but victorious, culminating in her marriage to a godly man.[2]

Her deliverance didn't include cliffs and pigs, but, make no mistake, she was delivered. And we are reminded. Satan can disturb us, but he cannot defeat us. The head of the serpent is crushed.

I saw a literal picture of this in a prairie ditch. A petroleum company was hiring strong backs and weak minds to lay a pipeline. Since I qualified, much of a high-school summer was spent shoveling in a shoulder-high, multimile West Texas trough. A large digging machine trenched ahead of us. We followed, scooping out the excess dirt and rocks.

One afternoon the machine dislodged more than dirt. "Snake!" shouted the foreman. We popped out of that hole faster than a jack-in-the-box and looked down at the rattlesnake nest. Big momma hissed, and her little kids squirmed. Reentering the trench was not an option. One worker launched his shovel and beheaded the rattler. We stood on the higher ground and watched as she—now headless—writhed and twisted in the soft dirt below. Though defanged, the snake still spooked us.

Gee, Max, thanks for the inspirational image.

Inspirational? Maybe not. But hopeful? I think so. That scene in the West Texas summer is a parable of where we are in life. Is the devil not a snake? John calls him "that old snake who is the devil" (Rev. 20:2 NCV).

Has he not been decapitated? Not with a shovel, but with a cross. "God disarmed the evil rulers and authorities. He shamed them publicly by his victory over them on the cross of Christ" (Col. 2:15 NLT).

So how does that leave us? *Confident.* The punch line of the passage is Jesus' power over Satan. One word from Christ, and the demons are swimming with the swine, and the wild man is "clothed and in his right mind" (Mark 5:15). Just one command! No séance needed. No hocus-pocus. No chants were heard or candles lit. Hell is an anthill against heaven's steamroller. Jesus "commands . . . evil spirits, and they obey him" (Mark 1:27 NCV). The snake in the ditch and Lucifer in the pit—both have met their match.

And, yet, both stir up dust long after their defeat. For that reason, though confident, we are still *careful.* For a toothless ol' varmint, Satan sure has some bite! He spooks our work, disrupts our activities, and leaves us thinking twice about where we step. Which we need to do. "Be self-controlled and alert. Your enemy the devil prowls around like a roaring lion looking for someone to devour" (1 Pet. 5:8 NIV). Alertness is needed. Panic is not. The serpent still wiggles and intimidates, but he has no poison. He is defeated, and he knows it! "He knows his time is short" (Rev. 12:12 CEV).

"Greater is He who is in you than he who is in the world" (1 John 4:4). Believe it. Trust the work of your Savior. "Resist the devil and he will flee from you" (James 4:7). In the meantime, the best he can do is squirm.

9

It's Not Up to You

Spiritually Weary People

JOHN 3:1–6

My dog Molly and I aren't getting along. The problem is not her personality. A sweeter mutt you will not find. She sees every person as a friend and every day as a holiday. I have no problem with Molly's attitude. I have a problem with her habits.

Eating scraps out of the trash. Licking dirty plates in the dishwasher. Dropping dead birds on our sidewalk and stealing bones from the neighbor's dog. Shameful! Molly rolls in the grass, chews on her paw, does her business in the wrong places, and, I'm embarrassed to admit, quenches her thirst in the toilet.

Now what kind of behavior is that?

Dog behavior, you reply.

You are right. So right. Molly's problem is not a Molly problem. Molly has a dog problem. It is a dog's nature to do such things. And it is her nature that I wish to change. Not just her behavior, mind you. A canine obedience school can change what she does; I want to go deeper. I want to change who she is.

Here is my idea: a me-to-her transfusion. The deposit of a Max seed in Molly. I want to give her a kernel of human character. As it grew, would she not change? Her human nature would develop, and her dog nature would diminish. We would witness, not just a change of habits, but a change of essence. In time Molly would be less like Molly and more like me, sharing my disgust for trash snacking, potty slurping, and dish licking. She would have a new nature. Why, Denalyn might even let her eat at the table.

You think the plan is crazy? Then take it up with God. The idea is his.

What I would like to do with Molly, God does with us. He changes our nature from the inside out! "I will put a new way of thinking inside you.

I will take out the stubborn hearts of stone from your bodies, and I will give you obedient hearts of flesh. I will put my Spirit inside you and help you live by my rules and carefully obey my laws" (Ezek. 36:26–27 NCV).

God doesn't send us to obedience school to learn new habits; he sends us to the hospital to be given a new heart. Forget training; he gives transplants.

Sound bizarre? Imagine how it sounded to Nicodemus.

> There was a man of the Pharisees, named Nicodemus, a ruler of the Jews; this man came to Jesus by night and said to Him, "Rabbi, we know that You have come from God as a teacher; for no one can do these signs that You do unless God is with him." (John 3:1–2)

Nicodemus is impressive. Not only is he one of the six thousand Pharisees, he is a ruler, one of seventy men who serve on the high council. Think of him as a religious blue blood. What the justices are to the Supreme Court, he is to the Law of Moses. Expert. Credentials trail his name like a robe behind a king. Nicodemus, Ph.D., Th.D., M.S., M.Div. Universities want him on their board. Conferences want him on their platform. When it comes to religion, he's loaded. When it comes to life, he's tired.

As a good Jew, he's trying to obey the Talmud. No small endeavor. He has twenty-four chapters of laws regarding the Sabbath alone. Just a sampling:

- Don't eat anything larger than an olive. And if you bite an olive and find it to be rotten, what you spit out is still a part of your allowance.
- You can carry enough ink to draw two letters, but baths aren't allowed for fear of splashing the floor and washing it.
- Tailors can carry no needles.
- Kids can toss no balls. No one can carry a load heavier than a fig, but anything half the weight of a fig can be carried twice.[1]

Whew!

Can a scientist study stars and never weep at their splendor? Dissect a rose and never notice its perfume? Can a theologian study the Law until he decodes the shoe size of Moses but still lack the peace needed for a good night's sleep?

Maybe that's why Nicodemus comes at night. He is tired but can't sleep. Tired of rules and regulations but no rest. Nicodemus is looking for a change. And he has a hunch Jesus can give it.

Though Nicodemus asks no question, Jesus offers him an answer. "Truly, truly, I say to you, unless one is born again he cannot see the kingdom of God" (v. 3).

This is radical language. To see the kingdom of God you need an unprecedented rebirth from God. Nicodemus staggers at the elephantine thought. "How can a man be born when he is old? He cannot enter a second time into his mother's womb and be born, can he?" (v. 4).

Don't you love those last two words? *Can he?* Nicodemus knows that a grown man doesn't reenter the birth canal. There is no Rewind button on the VCR of life . . . is there? We don't get to start over . . . do we? A man can't be born again . . . can he? What causes the question? What makes Nicodemus add those two words? Old Nick should know better. He wasn't born yesterday.

But maybe he wishes he had been. Maybe he wishes he could be born today. Maybe those last two words—"can he?"—emerge from that part of Nicodemus that longs for strength. Youthful vigor. Fresh wind. New legs.

Nicodemus seems to be saying, "Jesus, I've got the spiritual energy of an old mule. How do you expect me to be born again when I can't even remember if figs can be eaten on the Sabbath? I'm an old man. How can a man be born when he is old?" According to Christ, the new birth must come from a new place. "The truth is, no one can enter the Kingdom of God without being born of water and the Spirit. Humans can reproduce only human life, but the Holy Spirit gives new life from heaven" (vv. 5–6 NLT).

Could Jesus be more direct? "*No one* can enter the Kingdom of God without being born of water and the Spirit." You want to go to heaven? Doesn't matter how religious you are or how many rules you keep. You need a new birth; you need to be "born of water and the Spirit."

God gives no sponge baths. He washes us from head to toe. Paul reflected on his conversion and wrote: "He gave us a good bath, and we came out of it new people, washed inside and out by the Holy Spirit" (Titus 3:5 MSG). Your sins stand no chance against the fire hydrant of God's grace.

But more is needed. God is not content to clean you; he indwells you. God deposits within you "His power, which mightily works" (Col. 1:29).

He does not do with you what my dad did with my brother and me. Our high-school car was a '65 Rambler station wagon. The clunker had as much glamour as Forrest Gump: three speed, shift on the column, bench seats covered with plastic, no air conditioning.

And, oh, the engine. Our lawn mower had more power. The car's highest speed, downhill with a tailwind, was fifty miles per hour. To this day I'm convinced that my father (a trained mechanic) searched for the slowest possible car and bought it for us.

When we complained about her pitiful shape, he just smiled and said, "Fix it up." We did the best we could. We cleaned the carpets, sprayed air freshener on the seats, stuck a peace symbol on the back window, and hung Styrofoam dice from the rearview mirror. We removed the hubcaps and spray-painted the rims black. The car looked better, smelled better, but ran the same. Still a clunker—a clean clunker, to be sure—but still a clunker.

Don't for a microsecond think God does this with you. Washing the outside isn't enough for him. He places power on the inside. Better stated, he places *himself* on the inside. This is the part that stunned Nicodemus. Working for God was not new. But God working in him? *I need to chew on that a bit.*

Maybe you do, as well. Are you a Nicodemus? Religious as Saint Peter's Square, but feeling just as old? Pious, but powerless? If so, may I remind you of something?

When you believe in Christ, Christ works a miracle in you. "When you believed in Christ, he identified you as his own by giving you the Holy Spirit" (Eph. 1:13 NLT). You are permanently purified and empowered by God himself. The message of Jesus to the religious person is simple: It's not what you do. It's what I do. I have moved in. And in time you can say with Paul, "I myself no longer live, but Christ lives in me" (Gal. 2:20 NLT). You are no longer a clunker, not even a clean clunker. You are a sleek Indianapolis Motor Speedway racing machine.

If that is true, Max, why do I still sputter? If I'm born again, why do I fall so often?

Why did you fall so often after your first birth? Did you exit the womb wearing cross-trainers? Did you do the two-step on the day of your delivery?

Of course not. And when you started to walk, you fell more than you stood. Should we expect anything different from our spiritual walk?

But I fall so often, I question my salvation. Again, we return to your first birth. Didn't you stumble as you were learning to walk? And when you stumbled, did you question the validity of your physical birth? Did you, as a one-year-old fresh flopped on the floor, shake your head and think, *I have fallen again. I must not be human*?

Of course not. The stumbles of a toddler do not invalidate the act of birth. And the stumbles of a Christian do not annul his spiritual birth.

Do you understand what God has done? He has deposited a Christ seed in you. As it grows, you will change. It's not that sin has no more presence in your life, but rather that sin has no more power over your life. Temptation will pester you, but temptation will not master you. What hope this brings!

Nicodemuses of the world, hear this. It's not up to you! Within you abides a budding power. Trust him!

Think of it this way. Suppose you, for most of your life, have had a heart condition. Your frail pumper restricts your activities. Each morning at work when the healthy employees take the stairs, you wait for the elevator.

But then comes the transplant. A healthy heart is placed within you. After recovery, you return to work and encounter the flight of stairs—the same flight of stairs you earlier avoided. By habit, you start for the elevator. But then you remember. You aren't the same person. You have a new heart. Within you dwells a new power.

Do you live like the old person or the new? Do you count yourself as having a new heart or old? You have a choice to make.

You might say, "I can't climb stairs; I'm too weak." Does your choice negate the presence of a new heart? Dismiss the work of the surgeon? No. Choosing the elevator would suggest only one fact—you haven't learned to trust your new power.

It takes time. But at some point you've got to try those stairs. You've got to test the new ticker. You've got to experiment with the new you. For if you don't, you will run out of steam.

Religious rule keeping can sap your strength. It's endless. There is always another class to attend, Sabbath to obey, Ramadan to observe. No prison is as endless as the prison of perfection. Her inmates find work but never find peace. How could they? They never know when they are finished.

Christ, however, gifts you with a finished work. He fulfilled the law for you. Bid farewell to the burden of religion. Gone is the fear that having done everything, you might not have done enough. You climb the stairs, not by your strength, but his. God pledges to help those who stop trying to help themselves.

"He who began a good work in you will carry it on to completion until the day of Christ Jesus" (Phil. 1:6 NIV). God will do with you what I only dream of doing with Molly. Change you from the inside out. When he is finished, he'll even let you sit at his table.

10

The Trashman

Imperfect People

JOHN 1:29

The woman flops down on the bench and drops her trash bag between her feet. With elbows on knees and cheeks in hands, she stares at the sidewalk. Everything aches. Back. Legs. Neck. Her shoulder is stiff and her hands raw. All because of the sack.

Oh, to be rid of this garbage.

Unbroken clouds form a gray ceiling, gray with a thousand sorrows. Soot-stained buildings cast long shadows, darkening passageways and the people in them. Drizzle chills the air and muddies the rivulets of the street gutters. The woman collects her jacket. A passing car drenches the sack and splashes her jeans. She doesn't move. Too tired.

Her memories of life without the trash are fuzzy. As a child maybe? Her back was straighter, her walk quicker . . . or was it a dream? She doesn't know for sure.

A second car. This one stops and parks. A man steps out. She watches his shoes sink in the slush. From the car he pulls out a trash bag, lumpy with litter. He drapes it over his shoulder and curses the weight.

Neither of them speaks. Who knows if he noticed her. His face seems young, younger than his stooped back. In moments he is gone. Her gaze returns to the pavement.

She never looks at her trash. Early on she did. But what she saw repulsed her, so she's kept the sack closed ever since.

What else can she do? Give it to someone? All have their own.

Here comes a young mother. With one hand she leads a child; with the other she drags her load, bumpy and heavy.

Here comes an old man, face ravined with wrinkles. His trash sack is so long it hits the back of his legs as he walks. He glances at the woman and tries to smile.

What weight would he be carrying? she wonders as he passes.

"Regrets."

She turns to see who spoke. Beside her on the bench sits a man. Tall, with angular cheeks and bright, kind eyes. Like hers, his jeans are mud stained. Unlike hers, his shoulders are straight. He wears a T-shirt and baseball cap. She looks around for his trash but doesn't see it.

He watches the old man disappear as he explains, "As a young father, he worked many hours and neglected his family. His children don't love him. His sack is full, full of regrets."

She doesn't respond. And when she doesn't, he does.

"And yours?"

"Mine?" she asks, looking at him.

"Shame." His voice is gentle, compassionate.

She still doesn't speak, but neither does she turn away.

"Too many hours in the wrong arms. Last year. Last night . . . shame."

She stiffens, steeling herself against the scorn she has learned to expect. As if she needed more shame. Stop him. But how? She awaits his judgment.

But it never comes. His voice is warm and his question honest. "Will you give me your trash?"

Her head draws back. *What can he mean?*

"Give it to me. Tomorrow. At the landfill. Will you bring it?" He rubs a moist smudge from her cheek with his thumb and stands. "Friday. The landfill."

Long after he leaves, she sits, replaying the scene, retouching her cheek. His voice lingers; his invitation hovers. She tries to dismiss his words but can't. How could he know what he knew? And how could he know and still be so kind? The memory sits on the couch of her soul, an uninvited but welcome guest.

That night's sleep brings her summer dreams. A young girl under blue skies and puffy clouds, playing amid wildflowers, skirt twirling. She dreams of running with hands wide open, brushing the tops of sunflowers. She dreams of happy people filling a meadow with laughter and hope.

But when she wakes, the sky is dark, the clouds billowed, and the streets shadowed. At the foot of her bed lies her sack of trash. Hoisting it over her shoulder, she walks out of the apartment and down the stairs and onto the street, still slushy.

It's Friday.

For a time she stands, thinking. First wondering what he meant, then if he really meant it. She sighs. With hope just barely outweighing hopelessness, she turns toward the edge of town. Others are walking in the same direction. The man beside her smells of alcohol. He's slept many nights in his suit. A teenage girl walks a few feet ahead. The woman of shame hurries to catch up. The girl volunteers an answer before the question can be asked: "Rage. Rage at my father. Rage at my mother. I'm tired of anger. He said he'd take it." She motions to the sack. "I'm going to give it to him."

The woman nods, and the two walk together.

The landfill is tall with trash—papers and broken brooms and old beds and rusty cars. By the time they reach the hill, the line to the top is long. Hundreds walk ahead of them. All wait in silence, stunned by what they hear—a scream, a pain-pierced roar that hangs in the air for moments, interrupted only by a groan. Then the scream again.

His.

As they draw nearer, they know why. He kneels before each, gesturing toward the sack, offering a request, then a prayer. "May I have it? And may you never feel it again." Then he bows his head and lifts the sack, emptying its contents upon himself. The selfishness of the glutton, the bitterness of the angry, the possessiveness of the insecure. He feels what they felt. It is as if he'd lied or cheated or cursed his Maker.

Upon her turn, the woman pauses. Hesitates. His eyes compel her to step forward. He reaches for her trash and takes it from her. "You can't live with this," he explains. "You weren't made to." With head down, he empties her shame upon his shoulders. Then looking toward the heavens with tear-flooded eyes, he screams, "I'm sorry!"

"But you did nothing!" she cries.

Still, he sobs as she has sobbed into her pillow a hundred nights. That's when she realizes that his cry is hers. Her shame his.

With her thumb she touches his cheek, and for the first step in a long nighttime, she has no trash to carry.

With the others she stands at the base of the hill and watches as he is buried under a mound of misery. For some time he moans. Then nothing. Just silence.

The people sit among the wrecked cars and papers and discarded stoves and wonder who this man is and what he has done. Like mourners at a wake, they linger. Some share stories. Others say nothing. All cast occasional glances at the landfill. It feels odd, loitering near the heap. But it feels even stranger to think of leaving.

So they stay. Through the night and into the next day. Darkness comes again. A kinship connects them, a kinship through the trashman. Some doze. Others build fires in the metal drums and speak of the sudden abundance of stars in the night sky. By early morning most are asleep.

They almost miss the moment. It is the young girl who sees it. The girl with the rage. She doesn't trust her eyes at first, but when she looks again, she knows.

Her words are soft, intended for no one. "He's standing."

Then aloud, for her friend, "He's standing."

And louder for all, "He's standing!"

She turns; all turn. They see him silhouetted against a golden sun.

Standing. Indeed.

Part Two

No Place He Won't Go

Charlie was ten. School was out for Christmas, and the family had chosen to spend the holiday in the country. The boy pressed his nose against the bay window of the vacation home and marveled at the British winter. He was happy to trade the blackened streets of London for the cotton-white freshness of snow-covered hills.

His mom invited him to go for a drive, and he quickly accepted. A halcyon moment was in the making. She snaked the car down the twisty road. The tires crunched the snow, and the boy puffed his breath on the window. He was thrilled. The mother, however, was anxious.

Heavy snow began to fall. Visibility lessened. As she took a curve, the car started to slide and didn't stop until it was in a ditch. She tried to drive out. The tires just spun. Little Charlie pushed, and his mom pressed the gas. But no luck. They were stuck. They needed help.

A mile down the road sat a house. Off they went and knocked on the door. "Of course," the woman told them. "Come in; warm yourselves. The phone is yours." She offered tea and cookies and urged them to stay until help arrived.

An ordinary event? Don't suggest that to the woman who opened the door. She has never forgotten that day. She's retold the story a thousand times. And who could blame her? It's not often that royalty appears on your porch.

For the two travelers stranded by the England winter were no less than Queen Elizabeth and the heir to the throne, ten-year-old Charles.[1]

The word on the streets of heaven and the lips of Christians is that something far grander has happened to our world. Royalty has walked down our streets. Heaven's prince has knocked on our door.

His visit, however, was no accident. And he did much more than stay for tea. Wood shops. Wildernesses. Under the water of Jordan. On the water of Galilee. He kept popping up in the oddest places. Places where you'd never expect to spot God.

But, then again, who would have expected to see him at all?

II

He Loves to Be with the Ones He Loves

Every Place
PHILIPPIANS 2:6–7

Holiday time is highway time. Ever since Joseph and Mary packed their bags for Bethlehem, the birth of Jesus has caused people to hit the road. Interestingly, the Christmas trips we take have a lot in common with the maiden voyage of Jesus' folks. We don't see shepherds in the middle of the night, but we have been known to bump into an in-law on the way to the bathroom. We don't sleep in stables, but a living room full of sleeping-bagged cousins might smell like one. And we don't ride donkeys, but six hours in a minivan with four kids might make some moms wish they had one.

"'Tis the season to be traveling." Nothing reveals the true character of family members like a long road trip.

We dads, for example, discover our real identities on the interstate. In the spirit of our Mayflower and Conestoga forefathers, we don't want to stop. Did Lewis and Clark ask for directions? Did the pioneers spend the night at a Holiday Inn? Did Joseph allow Mary to stroll through a souvenir shop in Bethlehem to buy an ornament for the tree?

By no means. We men have a biblical mandate to travel far and fast, stopping only for gasoline.

Wives, however, know the real reason we husbands love to drive: the civil war in the backseat.

Did you know sociologists have proven that backseats have a wolfman impact on kids? Fangs, growls, claws. Social skills disappear into the same black hole as dropped French fries. Sojourning siblings are simply incapable of normal human conversation. If one child says, "I like that song," you might expect the other to say, "That's nice." He won't. Instead, he will reply, "It stinks, and so do your shoes."

The best advice for traveling with children is to be thankful they aren't teenagers. Teens are crawl-under-the-car humiliated by their dads. They are embarrassed by what we say, think, wear, eat, and sing. So, dads, if you seek peaceful passage (and if you ever want to see your unborn grandchildren), don't smile in a restaurant, don't breathe, and don't sing with the window down or up.

Holiday travel. It isn't easy. Then why do we do it? Why cram the trunks and endure the airports? You know the answer. We love to be with the ones we love.

The four-year-old running up the sidewalk into the arms of Grandpa.

The cup of coffee with Mom before the rest of the house awakes.

That moment when, for a moment, everyone is quiet as we hold hands around the table and thank God for family and friends and pumpkin pie.

We love to be with the ones we love.

May I remind you? So does God. He loves to be with the ones he loves. How else do you explain what he did? Between him and us there was a distance—a great span. And he couldn't bear it. He couldn't stand it. So he did something about it.

Before coming to the earth, "Christ himself was like God in everything. . . . But he gave up his place with God and made himself nothing. He was born to be a man and became like a servant" (Phil. 2:6–7 NCV).

Why? Why did Jesus travel so far?

I was asking myself that question when I spotted the squirrels outside my window. A family of black-tailed squirrels has made its home amid the roots of the tree north of my office. We've been neighbors for three years now. They watch me peck the keyboard. I watch them store their nuts and climb the trunk. We're mutually amused. I could watch them all day. Sometimes I do.

But I've never considered becoming one of them. The squirrel world holds no appeal to me. Who wants to sleep next to a hairy rodent with beady eyes? (No comments from you wives who feel you already do.) Give up the Rocky Mountains, bass fishing, weddings, and laughter for a hole in the ground and a diet of dirty nuts? Count me out.

But count Jesus in. What a world he left. Our classiest mansion would be a tree trunk to him. Earth's finest cuisine would be walnuts on heaven's table. And the idea of becoming a squirrel with claws and tiny teeth and a furry tail? It's nothing compared to God becoming a one-celled embryo and entering the womb of Mary.

But he did. The God of the universe kicked against the wall of a womb, was born into the poverty of a peasant, and spent his first night in the feed trough of a cow. "The Word became flesh and lived among us" (John 1:14 NRSV). The God of the universe left the glory of heaven and moved into the neighborhood. Our neighborhood! Who could have imagined he would do such a thing.

Why? He loves to be with the ones he loves.

Dr. Maxwell Maltz tells a remarkable story of a love like this. A man had been injured in a fire while attempting to save his parents from a burning house. He couldn't get to them. They perished. His face was burned and disfigured. He mistakenly interpreted his pain as God's punishment. The man wouldn't let anyone see him—not even his wife.

She went to Dr. Maltz, a plastic surgeon, for help. He told the woman not to worry. "I can restore his face."

The wife was unenthused. Her husband had repeatedly refused any help. She knew he would again.

Then why her visit? "I want you to disfigure my face so I can be like him! If I can share in his pain, then maybe he will let me back into his life."

Dr. Maltz was shocked. He denied her request but was so moved by this woman's love that he went to speak with her husband. Knocking on the man's bedroom door, he called loudly, "I'm a plastic surgeon, and I want you to know that I can restore your face."

No response.

"Please come out."

Again there was no answer.

Still speaking through the door, Dr. Maltz told the man of his wife's proposal. "She wants me to disfigure her face, to make her face like yours in the hope that you will let her back into your life. That's how much she loves you."

There was a brief moment of silence, and then, ever so slowly, the doorknob began to turn.[1]

The way the woman felt for her husband is the way God feels about us. But he did more than make the offer. He took on our face, our disfigurement. He became like us. Just look at the places he was willing to go: feed troughs, carpentry shops, badlands, and cemeteries. The places he went to reach us show how far he will go to touch us.

He loves to be with the ones he loves.

12

What's It Like?

Inward Places

LUKE 1:38

Some things only a mom can do.

Only a mother can powder a baby's behind with one hand and hold the phone with the other. Only a mom can discern which teen is entering the door just by the sound of the key in the lock. Only a mom can spend a day wiping noses, laundering enough socks for the Yankees, balancing a checkbook down to $1.27, and still mean it when she thanks God for her kids. Only a mom.

Some things only a mom can fix. Like Hamburger Helper without the hamburger. Like the cabinet door her husband couldn't and his bruised ego when he found out that she could. Broken shoelace? Broken heart? Breaking out on your face? Breaking up with your sweetheart? Moms can handle that. Some things only a mom can fix.

Some things only a mom can know. The time it takes to drive from piano lesson to Little League practice? She knows. How many pizzas you need for a middle school sleepover? Mom knows. How many Weight Watcher points are left in the day and days are left in the semester? Mom can tell you. She knows.

We men usually don't. The kids are usually clueless. Moms are a breed apart. The rest of us can only wonder, only ponder. We can only ask,

Mom, What's It Like?

When you felt the foot within your womb,
    when the infant cry first filled the room . . .
    to think that you and heaven just circled the moon . . .
What's that like?

And the day the bus pulled to a stop
    and you zipped the jacket up to the top
    and placed a kiss on a five-year-old's cheek
    and waved good-bye, then saw the trike—
    silent and still—
What's it like?

The first time you noticed his voice was deep.
The first time she asked if you were asleep
    and wanted to know when love was real.
And you told her. How did you feel?

Then the candles were lit.
She came down the aisle.
Did you weep? Did you smile?
And when your child with child told you the news,
    and in the quiet of the corner asked for clues.
"Mom," she whispered, "what's it like?"

What you told her would you tell us? Indeed, what is it like?

If we've ever wondered such thoughts about mothers, how much more have we wondered them about the most famous mother of all: Mary. To bear a baby is one thing, but to carry God? What is that like?

The virgin birth is more, much more, than a Christmas story; it is a picture of how close Christ will come to you. The first stop on his itinerary was a womb. Where will God go to touch the world? Look deep within Mary for an answer.

Better still, look deep within yourself. What he did with Mary, he offers to us! He issues a Mary-level invitation to all his children. "If you'll let me, I'll move in!"

Proliferating throughout Scripture is a preposition that leaves no doubt—the preposition *in.* Jesus lives *in* his children.

To his apostles, Christ declared, "I am *in* you" (John 14:20 NCV, emphasis mine).

Paul's prayer for the Ephesians was "that Christ may dwell *in* your hearts through faith" (Eph. 3:17 NIV, emphasis mine).

What is the mystery of the gospel? "Christ *in* you, the hope of glory" (Col. 1:27 NIV, emphasis mine).

John was clear, "Those who obey his commands live *in* him, and he *in* them" (1 John 3:24 NIV, emphasis mine).

And the sweetest invitation from Christ? "Here I am! I stand at the door and knock. If anyone hears my voice and opens the door, I will come *in* and eat with him, and he with me" (Rev. 3:20 NIV, emphasis mine).

Christ grew in Mary until he had to come out. Christ will grow in you until the same occurs. He will come out in your speech, in your actions, in your decisions. Every place you live will be a Bethlehem, and every day you live will be a Christmas. You, like Mary, will deliver Christ into the world.

God *in* us! Have we sounded the depth of this promise?

God was *with* Adam and Eve, walking with them in the cool of the evening.

God was *with* Abraham, even calling the patriarch his friend.

God was *with* Moses and the children of Israel. Parents could point their children to the fire by night and cloud by day; *God is with us,* they could assure.

Between the cherubim of the ark, in the glory of the temple, God was *with* his people. He was *with* the apostles. Peter could touch God's beard. John could watch God sleep. Multitudes could hear his voice. God was *with* them!

But he is *in* you. You are a modern-day Mary. Even more so. He was a fetus in her, but he is a force in you. He will do what you cannot. Imagine a million dollars being deposited into your checking account. To any observer you look the same, except for the goofy smile, but are you? Not at all! With God *in* you, you have a million resources that you did not have before!

Can't stop drinking? Christ can. And he lives within you.

Can't stop worrying? Christ can. And he lives within you.

Can't forgive the jerk, forget the past, or forsake your bad habits? Christ can! And he lives within you.

Paul knew this. "For this purpose also I labor, striving according to His power, which mightily works with*in* me" (Col. 1:29, emphasis mine).

Like Mary, you and I are indwelt by Christ.

Find that hard to believe? How much more did Mary? The line beneath her picture in the high-school annual did not read, "Aspires to be the mother of God." No. No one was more surprised by this miracle than she was.

And no one was more passive than she was. God did everything. Mary didn't volunteer to help. What did she have to offer? Advice? "From my perspective, a heavenly choir would add a nice touch." Yeah, right. She offered no assistance.

And she offered no resistance. She could have. "Who am I to have God in my womb? I'm not good enough," she could have said. Or, "I've got other plans. I don't have time for God in my life."

But Mary didn't say such words. Instead, she said, "Behold, the bond-slave of the Lord; may it be done to me according to your word" (Luke 1:38). If Mary is our measure, God seems less interested in talent and more interested in trust.

Unlike her, we tend to assist God, assuming our part is as important as his. Or we resist, thinking we are too bad or too busy. Yet when we assist or resist, we miss God's great grace. We miss out on the reason we were placed on earth—to be so pregnant with heaven's child that he lives through us. To be so full of him that we could say with Paul, "It is no longer I who live, but Christ lives in me" (Gal. 2:20).

What would *that* be like? To have a child within is a miracle, but to have Christ within?

To have my voice, but him speaking.
My steps, but Christ leading.
My heart, but his love beating
in me, through me, with me.
What's it like to have Christ on the inside?

To tap his strength when mine expires
or feel the force of heaven's fires
raging, purging wrong desires.
Could Christ become my self entire?

So much him, so little me
that in my eyes it's him they see.
What's it like to a Mary be?
No longer I, but Christ in me.

13

A Cure for the Common Life

Ordinary Places

MARK 6:3

You awoke today to a common day. No butler drew your bath. No maid laid out your clothes. Your eggs weren't Benedict, and your orange juice wasn't fresh squeezed. But that's OK; there's nothing special about the day. It's not your birthday or Christmas; it's like every other day. A common day.

So you went to the garage and climbed into your common car. You once read that children of the queen never need to drive. You've been told of executives and sheiks who are helicoptered to their offices. As for you, a stretch limo took you to your wedding reception, but since then it's been sedans and minivans. Common cars.

Common cars that take you to your common job. You take it seriously, but you would never call it extraordinary. You're not clearing your calendar for Jay Leno or making time to appear before Congress. You're just making sure you get your work done before the six o'clock rush turns the Loop into a parking lot.

Get caught in the evening traffic, and be ready to wait in line. The line at the freeway on-ramp. The line at the grocery or the line at the gas station. If you were the governor or had an Oscar on your mantel, you might bypass the crowds. But you aren't. You are common.

You lead a common life. Punctuated by occasional weddings, job transfers, bowling trophies, and graduations—a few highlights—but mainly the day-to-day rhythm that you share with the majority of humanity.

And, as a result, you could use a few tips. You need to know how to succeed at being common. Commonhood has its perils, you know. A face in the crowd can feel lost in the crowd. You tend to think you are unproductive, wondering if you'll leave any lasting contribution. And you can feel insignificant. Do commoners rate in heaven? Does God love common people?

God answers these questions in a most uncommon fashion. If the word *common* describes you, take heart—you're in fine company. It also describes Christ.

Christ common? Come on. Since when is walking on water "common"? Speaking to the dead "common"? Being raised from the dead "common"? Can we call the life of Christ "common"?

Nine-tenths of it we can. When you list the places Christ lived, draw a circle around the town named Nazareth—a single-camel map dot on the edge of boredom. For thirty of his thirty-three years, Jesus lived a common life. Aside from that one incident in the temple at the age of twelve, we have no record of what he said or did for the first thirty years he walked on this earth.

Were it not for a statement in Mark's gospel, we would not know anything about Jesus' early adult life. It's not much, but just enough thread to weave a thought or two for those who suffer from the common life. If you chum with NBA stars and subscribe to *Yachting Monthly*, you can tune out. If you wouldn't know what to say to NBA stars and have never heard of *Yachting Monthly*, then perk up. Here is the verse:

"Is not this the carpenter?" (Mark 6:3).

(Told you it wasn't much.) Jesus' neighbors spoke those words. Amazed at his latter-life popularity, they asked, "Is this the same guy who fixed my roof?"

Note what his neighbors did not say:

"Is not this the carpenter who owes me money?"

"Is not this the carpenter who swindled my father?"

"Is not this the carpenter who never finished my table?"

No, these words were never said. The lazy have a hard time hiding in a small town. Hucksters move from city to city to survive. Jesus didn't need to. Need a plow repaired? Christ could do it. In need of a new yoke? "My neighbor is a carpenter, and he will give you a fair price." The job may have been common, but his diligence was not. Jesus took his work seriously.

And the town may have been common, but his attention to it was not. The city of Nazareth sits on a summit. Certainly no Nazarene boy could resist an occasional hike to the crest to look out over the valley beneath. Sitting six hundred feet above the level of the sea, the young Jesus could examine this world he had made. Mountain flowers in the spring. Cool sunsets. Pelicans winging their way along the streams of Kishon to the Sea of Galilee. Thyme-besprinkled turf at his feet. Fields and fig trees in the distance. Do you suppose moments here inspired these words later? "Observe how the lilies of the field grow" (Matt. 6:28) or "Look at the birds of the air" (Matt. 6:26). The words of Jesus the rabbi were born in the thoughts of Jesus the boy.

To the north of Nazareth lie the wood-crowned hills of Naphtali. Conspicuous on one of them was the village of Safed, known in the region as "the city set upon the hill."[1] Was Jesus thinking of Safed when he said, "A city set on a hill cannot be hidden" (Matt. 5:14)?

The maker of yokes later explained, "My yoke is easy" (Matt. 11:30). The one who brushed his share of sawdust from his eyes would say, "Why do you look at the speck that is in your brother's eye, but do not notice the log that is in your own eye?" (Matt. 7:3).

He saw how a seed on the path took no root (Luke 8:5) and how a mustard seed produced a great tree (Matt. 13:31–32). He remembered the red sky at morning (Matt. 16:2) and the lightning in the eastern sky (Matt. 24:27). Jesus listened to his common life.

Are you listening to yours? Rain pattering against the window. Silent snow in April. The giggle of a baby on a crowded plane. Seeing a sunrise while the world sleeps. Are these not personal epistles? Can't God speak through a Monday commute or a midnight diaper change? Take notes on your life.

> There is no event so commonplace but that God is present within it, always hiddenly, always leaving you room to recognize him or not recognize him. . . . See [your life] for the fathomless mystery that it is. In the boredom and pain of it no less than in the excitement and gladness: touch, taste, and smell your way to the holy and hidden heart of it because in the last analysis all moments are key moments, and life itself is grace.[2]

Next time your life feels ordinary, take your cue from Christ. Pay attention to your work and your world. Jesus' obedience began in a small town carpentry shop. His uncommon approach to his common life groomed him for his uncommon call. "When Jesus entered public life he was about thirty years old" (Luke 3:23 MSG). In order to enter public life, you have to leave private life. In order for Jesus to change the world, he had to say good-bye to *his* world.

He had to give Mary a kiss. Have a final meal in the kitchen, a final walk through the streets. Did he ascend one of the hills of Nazareth and think of the day he would ascend the hill near Jerusalem?

He knew what was going to happen. "God chose him for this purpose long before the world began" (1 Pet. 1:20 NLT). Every ounce of suffering had been scripted—it just fell to him to play the part.

Not that he had to. Nazareth was a cozy town. Why not build a carpentry business? Keep his identity a secret? Return in the era of guillotines or electric chairs, and pass on the cross. To be forced to die is one thing, but to willingly take up your own cross is something else.

Alan and Penny McIlroy can tell you. The fact that they have two adopted children is commendable but not uncommon. The fact that they have adopted special needs children is significant but not unique. It's the severity of the health problems that sets this story apart.

Saleena is a cocaine baby. Her birth mother's overdose left Saleena unable to hear, see, speak, or move. Penny and Alan adopted her at seven weeks. The doctor gave her a year. She's lived for six.

As Penny introduced me to Saleena, she ruffled her hair and squeezed her cheeks, but Saleena didn't respond. She never does. Barring a miracle, she never will. Neither will her sister. "This is Destiny," Penny told me. In the adjacent bed one-year-old Destiny lay, motionless and vegetative. Penny will never hear Destiny's voice. Alan will never know Saleena's kiss. They'll never hear their daughters sing in a choir, never see them walk across the stage. They'll bathe them, change them, adjust their feeding tubes, and rub their limp limbs, but barring God's intervention, this mom and dad will never hear more than we heard that afternoon—gurgled breathing. "I need to suction Saleena's nose," Penny said to me. "You might want to leave."[3]

I did, and as I did, I wondered, what kind of love is this? What kind of love adopts disaster? What kind of love looks into the face of children, knowing full well the weight of their calamity, and says, "I'll take them"?

When you come up with a word for such a love, give it to Christ. For the day he left Nazareth is the day he declared his devotion for you and me. We were just as helpless, in a spiritually vegetative state from sin. According to Peter, our lives were "dead-end, empty-headed" (1 Pet. 1:18 MSG). But God, "immense in mercy and with an incredible love . . . embraced us. He took our sin-dead lives and made us alive in Christ. He did all this on his own, with no help from us!" (Eph. 2:4–5 MSG).

Jesus left Nazareth in pursuit of the spiritual Saleenas and Destinys of the world and brought us to life.

Perhaps we aren't so common after all.

14

Oh, to Be DTP-Free!

Religious Places

LUKE 2:41–49

Remember when only people contracted viruses? Remember when terms like *parasite* and *worm* were applied to living organisms and little brothers? Remember when viral infections were treated by doctors and *quarantine* meant the isolation of diseased people and pets?

No longer. Nowadays computers get sick. Preparation of this chapter would have begun several hours earlier had not a biohazardous, chemical-warfare-type warning put a freeze on my keyboard. "Open nothing! Your computer may have a virus!" I half expected Centers for Disease Control agents wearing radioactive gear to rush in, cover me, and run out with my laptop.

They didn't, but a computer doctor did. He installed an antivirus program that protects the machine against 60,959 viruses.

I started to ask if Ebola was one, but I didn't. I did learn that hundreds of thousands of viruses have been created, I'm assuming by the same folks who spray graffiti on buildings and loosen salt shakers at restaurants. Troublemakers who Trojan horse their way into your computer and gobble your data like a Pac-Man. I told the computer guy I'd never seen anything like it.

Later I realized I had. Indeed, a computer virus is a common cold compared to the Chernobyl-level attack you and I must face. Think of your mind as a computer made to store and process massive amounts of data (no comments about your neighbor's hard-drive capacity, please). Think of your strengths as software. Pianists are loaded with music programs. Accountants seem to be born with spreadsheet capacity. Fun lovers come with games installed. We are different, but we each have a computer and software, and, sadly, we have viruses. You and I are infected by destructive thoughts.

Computer viruses have names like Klez, Anna Kournikova, and ILOVEYOU. Mental viruses are known as anxiety, bitterness, anger, guilt, shame, greed, and insecurity. They worm their way into your system and diminish, even disable, your mind. We call these DTPs: destructive thought patterns. (Actually, I'm the only one to call them DTPs.)

Do you have any DTPs?

When you see the successful, are you jealous?

When you see the struggler, are you pompous?

If someone gets on your bad side, is that person as likely to get on your good side as I am to win the Tour-de-France?

Ever argue with someone in your mind? Rehash or rehearse your hurts? Do you assume the worst about the future?

If so, you suffer from DTPs.

What would your world be like without them? Had no dark or destructive thought ever entered your mind, how would you be different? Suppose you could relive your life sans any guilt, lust, vengeance, insecurity, or fear. Never wasting mental energy on gossip or scheming. Would you be different?

What would you have that you don't have? (Suggested answers found on page 567.)

What would you have done that you haven't done? (Suggested answers found on page 567.)

Oh, to be DTP-free. No energy lost, no time wasted. Wouldn't such a person be energetic and wise? A lifetime of healthy and holy thoughts would render anyone a joyful genius.

But where would you find such an individual? An uninfected computer can be bought—but an uninfected person? Impossible. Trace a computer virus back to a hacker. Trace our mental viruses back to the fall of the first man, Adam. Because of sin, our minds are full of dark thoughts. "Although they knew God, they neither glorified him as God nor gave thanks to him, but their thinking became futile and their foolish hearts were darkened. Although they claimed to be wise, they became fools" (Rom. 1:21–22 NIV).

Blame DTPs on sin. Sin messes with the mind. But what if the virus never entered? Suppose a person never opened Satan's e-mails? What would that person be like?

A lot like the twelve-year-old boy seated in the temple of Jerusalem. Though he was beardless and unadorned, this boy's thoughts were profound. Just ask the theologians with whom he conversed. Luke gives this account:

> [His parents] found Him in the temple, sitting in the midst of the teachers, both listening to them and asking them questions. And all who heard Him were amazed at His understanding and His answers. (Luke 2:46–47)

For three days Joseph and Mary were separated from Jesus. The temple was the last place they thought to search. But it was the first place Jesus went. He didn't go to a cousin's house or a buddy's playground. Jesus sought the place of godly thinking and, in doing so, inspires us to do the same. By the time Joseph and Mary located their son, he had confounded the most learned men in the temple. This boy did not think like a boy.

Why? What made Jesus different? The Bible is silent about his IQ. When it comes to the RAM size of his mental computer, we are told nothing. But when it comes to his purity of mind, we are given this astounding claim: Christ "knew no sin" (2 Cor. 5:21). Peter says Jesus "did no sin, neither was guile found in his mouth" (1 Pet. 2:22 KJV). John lived next to him for three years and concluded, "In Him there is no sin" (1 John 3:5).

Spotless was his soul, and striking was the witness of those who knew him. His fleshly brother James called Christ "the righteous man" (James 5:6). Pilate could find no fault in him (John 18:38). Judas confessed that he, in betraying Christ, betrayed innocent blood (Matt. 27:4). Even the demons declared his unique status: "I know who you are—the Holy One of God!" (Luke 4:34 NIV).

The loudest testimony to his perfection was the silence that followed this question. When his accusers called him a servant of Satan, Jesus demanded to see their evidence. "Which one of you convicts Me of sin?" he dared (John 8:46). Ask my circle of friends to point out my sin, and watch the hands shoot up. When those who knew Jesus were asked this same question, no one spoke. Christ was followed by disciples, analyzed by crowds, criticized by family, and scrutinized by enemies, yet not one person would remember him committing even one sin. He was never found in the wrong place. Never said the wrong word. Never acted the wrong way. He never sinned. Not that he wasn't tempted, mind you. He was "tempted in all things as we are, yet without sin" (Heb. 4:15).

Lust wooed him. Greed lured him. Power called him. Jesus—the human—was tempted. But Jesus—the holy God—resisted. Contaminated e-mail came his way, but he resisted the urge to open it.

The word *sinless* has never survived cohabitation with another person. Those who knew Christ best, however, spoke of his purity in unison and with conviction. And because he was sinless, his mind was stainless. DTP-less. No wonder people were "amazed at his teaching" (Mark 1:22 NCV). His mind was virus-free.

But does this matter? Does the perfection of Christ affect me? If he were a distant Creator, the answer would be no. But since he is a next door Savior, the reply is a supersized yes!

Remember the twelve-year-old boy in the temple? The one with sterling thoughts and a Teflon mind? Guess what. That is God's goal for you! You are made to be like Christ! God's priority is that you be "transformed by the renewing of your mind" (Rom. 12:2 NIV). You may have been born virus-prone, but you don't have to live that way. There is hope for your head! Are you a worrywart? Don't have to be one forever. Guilt plagued and shame stained? Prone to anger? Jealousy? God can take care of that. God can change your mind.

If ever there was a DTP candidate, it was George. Abandoned by his father, orphaned by his mother, the little boy was shuffled from foster parent to homelessness and back several times. A sitting duck for bitterness and anger, George could have spent his life getting even. But he didn't. He didn't because Mariah Watkins taught him to think good thoughts.

The needs of each attracted the other—Mariah, a childless washerwoman, and George, a homeless orphan. When Mariah discovered the young boy sleeping in her barn, she took him in. Not only that, she took care of him, took him to church, and helped him find his way to God. When George left Mariah's home, among his few possessions was a Bible she'd given him. By the time he left her home, she had left her mark.[1]

And by the time George left this world, he had left his.

George—George Washington Carver—is a father of modern agriculture.

History credits him with more than three hundred products extracted from peanuts alone. The once-orphaned houseguest of Mariah Watkins became the friend of Henry Ford, Mahatma Gandhi, and three presidents. He entered his laboratory every morning with the prayer "Open thou mine eyes, that I may behold wondrous things out of thy law."[2]

God answers such prayers. He changes the man by changing the mind. And how does it happen? By doing what you are doing right now. Considering the glory of Christ. "But we all, with unveiled face, beholding as in a mirror the glory of the Lord, are being transformed into the same image from glory to glory, just as from the Lord, the Spirit" (2 Cor. 3:18).

To behold him is to become like him. As Christ dominates your thoughts, he changes you from one degree of glory to another until—hang on!—you are ready to live with him.

Heaven is the land of sinless minds. Virus-free thinking. Absolute trust. No fear or anger. Shame and second-guessing are practices of a prior life. Heaven will be wonderful, not because the streets are gold, but because our thoughts will be pure.

So what are you waiting on? Apply God's antivirus. "Set your mind on the things above, not on the things that are on earth" (Col. 3:2). Give him your best thoughts, and see if he doesn't change your mind.

Answers to questions on page 564:

More sleep, joy, and peace

Hugged kids more, loved spouse better, invented computer-virus killer, and traveled to Paris to watch Max win the Tour-de-France

15

Tire Kicker to Car Buyer

Unexpected Places

MATTHEW 3:13–17

No one pays him special attention. Not that they should. Nothing in his appearance separates him from the crowd. Like the rest, he is standing in line, waiting his turn. The coolness of the mud feels nice between his toes, and the occasional lap of water is welcome on his feet. He, like the others, can hear the voice of the preacher in the distance.

Between baptisms, John the Baptist is prone to preach. Impetuous. Fiery. Ferocious. Fearless. Bronzed face, unshorn locks. His eyes are as wild as the countryside from which he came. His whole presence is a sermon—a voice, "a voice of one calling in the desert, 'Prepare the way for the Lord'" (Luke 3:4 NIV).

He stands waist-deep in the cobalt-colored Jordan. He makes a wardrobe out of camel's hair, a meal out of bugs, and, most important, he makes a point of calling all people to the water. "He went into all the country around the Jordan, preaching a baptism of repentance for the forgiveness of sins" (Luke 3:3 NIV).

Baptism wasn't a new practice. It was a required rite for any Gentile seeking to become a Jew. Baptism was for the moldy, second-class, unchosen people, not the clean, top-of-the-line class favorites—the Jews. Herein lies the rub. John refuses to delineate between Jew and Gentile. In his book, every heart needs a detail job.

Every heart, that is, except one. That's why John is stunned when that one wades into the river.

> But John didn't want to baptize him. "I am the one who needs to be baptized by you," he said, "so why are you coming to me?"

> But Jesus said, "It must be done, because we must do everything that is right." So then John baptized him.
>
> After his baptism, as Jesus came up out of the water, the heavens were opened and he saw the Spirit of God descending like a dove and settling on him. And a voice from heaven said, "This is my beloved Son, and I am fully pleased with him." (Matt. 3:14–17 NLT)

John's reluctance is understandable. A baptismal ceremony is an odd place to find the Son of God. He should be the baptizer not the baptizee. Why would Christ want to be baptized? If baptism was, and is, for the confessed sinner, how do we explain the immersion of history's only sinless soul?

You'll find the answer in the pronouns: "Jesus answered, 'For now this is how it should be, because *we* must do all that God wants *us* to do'" (Matt. 3:15 CEV, emphasis mine).

Who is "we"? Jesus and us. Why does Jesus include himself? It's easy to understand why you and I and John the Baptist and the crowds at the creek have to do what God says. But Jesus? Why would he need to be baptized?

Here's why: He did for us what I did for one of my daughters in the shop at New York's La Guardia Airport. The sign above the ceramic pieces read Do Not Touch. But the wanting was stronger than the warning, and she touched. And it fell. By the time I looked up, ten-year-old Sara was holding the two pieces of a New York City skyline. Next to her was an unhappy store manager. Over them both was the written rule. Between them hung a nervous silence. My daughter had no money. He had no mercy. So I did what dads do. I stepped in. "How much do *we* owe you?" I asked.

How was it that I owed anything? Simple. She was my daughter. And since she could not pay, I did.

Since you and I cannot pay, Christ did. We've broken so much more than souvenirs. We've broken commandments, promises, and, worst of all, we've broken God's heart.

But Christ sees our plight. With the law on the wall and shattered commandments on the floor, he steps near (like a neighbor) and offers a gift (like a Savior).

What do we owe? We owe God a perfect life. Perfect obedience to every command. Not just the command of baptism, but the commands of humility, honesty, integrity. We can't deliver. Might as well charge us for the property of Manhattan. But Christ can and he did. His plunge into the Jordan is a picture of his plunge into our sin. His baptism announces, "Let me pay."

Your baptism responds, "You bet I will." He publicly offers. We publicly accept. We "became part of Christ when we were baptized" (Rom. 6:3 NCV). In baptism we identify with Christ. We go from tire kicker to car buyer. We step out of the shadows, point in his direction, and announce, "I'm with him."

I used to do this at the drive-in movie theater.

Remember drive-in movies? (Kids, ask a grownup.) The one in Andrews, Texas, had a Friday night special—a carload for the price of the driver. Whether the car carried one passenger or a dozen, the price was the same. We often opted for the dozen route. The law would not allow us to do today what we did then. Shoulders squished. Little guy on the big guy's lap. The ride was miserable, but the price was right. When the person at the ticket window looked in, we pointed to the driver and said, "We're with him."

God doesn't tell you to climb into Christ's car; he tells you to climb into Christ! "There is now no condemnation for those who are in Christ Jesus" (Rom. 8:1 NIV). He is your vehicle! Baptism celebrates your decision to take a seat. "For all of you who were baptized *into* Christ have clothed yourselves with Christ" (Gal. 3:27, emphasis mine). We are not saved by the act, but the act demonstrates the way we are saved. We are given credit for a perfect life we did not lead—indeed, a life we could never lead.

We are given a gift similar to the one Billy Joel gave his daughter. On her twelfth birthday she was in New York City, and the pop musician was in Los Angeles. He phoned her that morning, apologizing for his absence, but told her to expect the delivery of a large package before the end of the day. The daughter answered the doorbell that evening to find a seven-foot-tall, brightly wrapped box. She tore it open, and out stepped her father, fresh off the plane from the West Coast.

Can you imagine her surprise?[1]

Perhaps you can. Your gift came in the flesh too.

16

The Long, Lonely Winter

Wilderness Places

LUKE 4:1–13

The wilderness of the desert. Parched ground. Sharp rocks. Shifting sand. Burning sun. Thorns that cut. A miraging oasis. Wavy horizons ever beyond reach. This is the wilderness of the desert.

The wilderness of the soul. Parched promises. Sharp words. Shifting commitments. Burning anger. Rejections that cut. Miraging hope. Distant solutions ever beyond reach. This is the wilderness of the soul.

Some of you know the first. All of you know the second. Jesus, however, knew both.

With skin still moist with Jordan water, he turned away from food and friends and entered the country of hyenas, lizards, and vultures. He was "led around by the Spirit in the wilderness for forty days, being tempted by the devil. And He ate nothing during those days, and when they had ended, He became hungry" (Luke 4:1–2).

The wilderness was not a typical time for Jesus. Normalcy was left at the Jordan and would be rediscovered in Galilee. The wilderness was and is atypical. A dark parenthesis in the story of life. A fierce season of face-to-face encounters with the devil.

You needn't journey to Israel to experience the wilderness. A cemetery will do just fine. So will a hospital. Grief can lead you into the desert. So can divorce or debt or depression.

Received word this morning of a friend who, thinking he was cancer-free, is going back for chemotherapy. Wilderness. Ran into a fellow at lunch who once talked to me about his tough marriage. Asked him how it was going. "It's going," he shrugged. Wilderness. Opened an e-mail from an acquaintance who is spending her summer at the house of her dying mother. She and hospice and death. Waiting. In the wilderness.

You can often chalk up wilderness wanderings to transition. Jesus entered the Jordan River a carpenter and exited a Messiah. His baptism flipped a breaker switch.

Been through any transitions lately? A transfer? Job promotion? Job demotion? A new house? If so, be wary. The wilderness might be near.

How do you know when you're in one?

You are lonely. Whether in fact or in feeling, no one can help, understand, or rescue you.

And your struggle seems endless. In the Bible the number forty is associated with lengthy battles. Noah faced rain for forty days. Moses faced the desert for forty years. Jesus faced temptation for forty nights. Please note, he didn't face temptation for one day out of forty. Jesus was "in the wilderness for forty days, being tempted by the devil" (vv. 1–2). The battle wasn't limited to three questions. Jesus spent a month and ten days slugging it out with Satan. The wilderness is a long, lonely winter.

Doctor after doctor. Résumé after résumé. Diaper after diaper. Zoloft after Zoloft. Heartache after heartache. The calendar is stuck in February, and you're stuck in South Dakota, and you can't even remember what spring smells like.

One more symptom of the badlands: You think the unthinkable. Jesus did. Wild possibilities crossed his mind. Teaming up with Satan? Opting to be a dictator and not a Savior? Torching Earth and starting over on Pluto? We don't know what he thought. We just know this. He was tempted. And "one is tempted when he is carried away and enticed by his own lust" (James 1:14). Temptation "carries" you and "entices" you. What was unimaginable prior to the wilderness becomes possible in it. A tough marriage can make a good man look twice at the wrong woman. Extended sickness makes even the stoutest soul consider suicide. Stress makes the smokiest nightclub smell sweet. The wilderness weakens resolve.

For that reason, the wilderness is the maternity ward for addictions. Binge eating, budget-busting gambling, excessive drinking, pornography—all short-term solutions to deep-seated problems. Typically they have no appeal, but in the wilderness you give thought to the unthinkable.

Jesus did. Jesus was "tempted by the devil" (Luke 4:2). Satan's words, if for but a moment, gave him pause. He may not have eaten the bread, but he stopped long enough in front of the bakery to smell it. Christ knows the wilderness. More than you might imagine. After all, going there was his idea.

Don't blame this episode on Satan. He didn't come to the desert looking for Jesus. Jesus went to the badlands looking for him. "The Spirit led Jesus into the desert *to be tempted* by the devil" (Matt. 4:1 NCV, emphasis mine). Heaven orchestrated this date. How do we explain this? The list of surprising places grows again. If Jesus in the womb and the Jordan waters doesn't stun you, Jesus in the wilderness will. Why did Jesus go to the desert?

Does the word *rematch* mean anything to you? For the second time in history an unfallen mind will be challenged by the fallen angel. The Second Adam has come to succeed where the first Adam failed. Jesus, however, faces a test far more severe. Adam was tested in a garden; Christ is in a stark wasteland. Adam faced Satan on a full stomach; Christ is in the midst of a fast. Adam had a companion: Eve. Christ has no one. Adam was challenged to remain sinless in a sinless world. Christ, on the other hand, is challenged to remain sinless in a sin-ridden world.

Stripped of any aid or excuses, Christ dares the devil to climb into the ring. "You've been haunting my children since the beginning. See what you can do with me." And Satan does. For forty days the two go toe-to-toe. The Son of heaven is tempted but never wavers, struck but never struck down. He succeeds where Adam failed. This victory, according to Paul, is a huge victory for us all. "Here it is in a nutshell: Just as one person did it wrong and got us in all this trouble with sin and death, another person did it right and got us out of it" (Rom. 5:18 MSG).

Christ continues his role as your proxy, your stand-in, your substitute. He did for you what my friend Bobby Aycock did for David. The two were in boot camp in 1959. David was a very likable, yet physically disadvantaged soldier. He had the desire but not the strength. There was simply no way he would pass the fitness test. Too weak for the pull-ups.

But Bobby had such a fondness for David that he came up with a plan. He donned his friend's T-shirt. The shirt bore David's last name, two initials, and service serial number. The superiors didn't know faces; they just read the names and numbers off the shirts and marked scores on a list of names. So Bobby did David's pull-ups. David came out looking pretty good and never even broke a sweat.

Neither did you. Listen, you and I are no match for Satan. Jesus knows this. So he donned our jersey. Better still, he put on our flesh. He was "tempted in every way, just as we are—yet was without sin" (Heb. 4:15 NIV). And because he did, we pass with flying colors.

God gives you Jesus' wilderness grade. Believe that. If you don't, the desert days will give you a one-two punch. The right hook is the struggle. The left jab is the shame for not prevailing against it. Trust his work.

And trust his Word. Don't trust your emotions. Don't trust your opinions. Don't even trust your friends. In the wilderness heed only the voice of God.

Again, Jesus is our model. Remember how Satan teased him? "If you are the Son of God . . ." (Luke 4:3, 9 NCV). Why would Satan say this? Because he knew what Christ had heard at the baptism. "This is My beloved Son, in whom I am well-pleased" (Matt. 3:17).

"Are you really God's Son?" Satan is asking. Then comes the dare—"Prove it!" Prove it by doing something:

"Tell this stone to become bread" (Luke 4:3).

"If You worship before me, it shall all be Yours" (v. 7).

"Throw Yourself down from here" (v. 9).

What subtle seduction! Satan doesn't denounce God; he simply raises doubts about God. Is his work enough? Earthly works—like bread changing or temple jumping—are given equal billing with heavenly works. He attempts to shift, ever so gradually, our source of confidence away from God's promise and toward our performance.

Jesus doesn't bite the bait. No heavenly sign is requested. He doesn't solicit a lightning bolt; he simply quotes the Bible. Three temptations. Three declarations.

"It is written . . ." (v. 4 NCV).

"It is written . . ." (v. 8 NCV).

"It is said . . ." (v. 12).

Jesus' survival weapon of choice is Scripture. If the Bible was enough for his wilderness, shouldn't it be enough for ours? Don't miss the point here. Everything you and I need for desert survival is in the Book. We simply need to heed it.

On a trip to the United Kingdom, our family visited a castle. In the center of the garden sat a maze. Row after row of shoulder-high hedges, leading to one dead end after another. Successfully navigate the labyrinth, and discover the door to a tall tower in the center of the garden. Were you to look at our family pictures of the trip, you'd see four of our five family members standing on the top of the tower. Hmmm, someone is still on the ground. Guess who? I was stuck in the foliage. I just couldn't figure out which way to go.

Ah, but then I heard a voice from above. "Hey, Dad." I looked up to see Sara, peering through the turret at the top. "You're going the wrong way," she explained. "Back up and turn right."

Do you think I trusted her? I didn't have to. I could have trusted my own instincts, consulted other confused tourists, sat and pouted and wondered why God would let this happen to me. But do you know what I did? I listened. Her vantage point was better than mine. She was above the maze. She could see what I couldn't.

Don't you think we should do the same with God? "God is . . . higher than the heavens" (Job 22:12 TLB). "The LORD is high above all nations" (Ps. 113:4). Can he not see what eludes us? Doesn't he want to get us out and bring us home? Then we should do what Jesus did.

Rely on Scripture. Doubt your doubts before you doubt your beliefs. Jesus told Satan, "Man shall not live on bread alone, but on every word that proceeds out of the mouth of God" (Matt. 4:4). The verb *proceeds* is literally "pouring out." Its tense suggests that God is constantly and aggressively communicating with the world through his Word. God is speaking still!

Hang in there. Your time in the desert will pass. Jesus' did. "The devil left Him; and behold, angels came and began to minister to Him" (Matt. 4:11).

Till angels come to you:

Trust his Word. Just like me in the maze, you need a voice to lead you out.

Trust his work. Like David at boot camp, you need a friend to take your place.

Thank God you have One who will.

17

God Gets into Things

Stormy Places

MATTHEW 14:22–33

On a September morning in 2001, Frank Silecchia laced up his boots, pulled on his hat, and headed out the door of his New Jersey house. As a construction worker, he made a living making things. But as a volunteer at the World Trade Center wreckage, he just tried to make sense of it all. He hoped to find a live body. He did not. He found forty-seven dead ones.

Amid the carnage, however, he stumbled upon a symbol—a twenty-foot-tall steel-beam cross. The collapse of Tower One on Building Six created a crude chamber in the clutter. In the chamber, through the dusty sunrise, Frank spotted the cross.

No winch had hoisted it; no cement secured it. The iron beams stood independent of human help. Standing alone, but not alone. Other crosses rested randomly at the base of the large one. Different sizes, different angles, but all crosses.

Several days later engineers realized the beams of the large cross came from two different buildings. When one crashed into another, the two girders bonded into one, forged by the fire.[1]

A symbol in the shards. A cross found in the crisis. "Where is God in all this?" we asked. The discovery dared us to hope, "Right in the middle of it all."

Can the same be said about our tragedies? When the ambulance takes our child or the disease takes our friend, when the economy takes our retirement or the two-timer takes our heart—can we, like Frank, find Christ in the crisis? The presence of troubles doesn't surprise us. The absence of God, however, undoes us.

We can deal with the ambulance if God is in it.

We can stomach the ICU if God is in it.

We can face the empty house if God is in it.

Is he?

Matthew would like to answer that question for you. The walls falling around him were made of water. No roof collapsed, but it seemed as though the sky had.

A storm on the Sea of Galilee was akin to a sumo wrestler's belly flop on a kiddy pool. The northern valley acted like a wind tunnel, compressing and hosing squalls onto the lake. Waves as tall as ten feet were common.

The account begins at nightfall. Jesus is on the mountain in prayer, and the disciples are in the boat in fear. They are "far away from land . . . fighting heavy waves" (Matt. 14:24 NLT). When does Christ come to them? At three o'clock in the morning (v. 25 NLT)! If "evening" began at six o'clock and Christ came at three in the morning, the disciples were alone in the storm for nine hours! Nine tempestuous hours. Long enough for more than one disciple to ask, "Where is Jesus? He knows we are in the boat. For heaven's sake, it was his idea. Is God anywhere near?"

And from within the storm comes an unmistakable voice: "I am."

Wet robe, soaked hair. Waves slapping his waist and rain stinging his face. Jesus speaks to them at once. "Courage! I am! Don't be afraid!" (v. 27).[2]

That wording sounds odd, doesn't it? If you've read the story, you're accustomed to a different shout from Christ. Something like, "Take courage! It is I" (NIV) or "It's all right. . . . I am here!" (NLT) or "Courage, it's me" (MSG).

A literal translation of his announcement results in "Courage! I am! Don't be afraid." Translators tinker with his words for obvious reasons. "I am" sounds truncated. "I am here" or "It is I" feels more complete. But what Jesus shouted in the storm was simply the magisterial: "I am."

The words ring like the cymbal clash in the *1812 Overture.* We've heard them before.

Speaking from a burning bush to a knee-knocking Moses, God announced, "I AM WHO I AM" (Exod. 3:14).

Double-dog daring his enemies to prove him otherwise, Jesus declared, "Before Abraham was born, I am" (John 8:58).

Determined to say it often enough and loud enough to get our attention, Christ chorused:

- "I am the bread of life" (John 6:48).
- "I am the Light of the world" (John 8:12).
- "I am the gate; whoever enters through me will be saved" (John 10:9 NIV).
- "I am the good shepherd" (John 10:11).
- "I am God's Son" (John 10:36 NCV).
- "I am the resurrection and the life" (John 11:25).
- "I am the way, and the truth, and the life" (John 14:6).
- "I am the true vine" (John 15:1).

The present-tense Christ. He never says, "I was." We do. We do because "we were." We were younger, faster, prettier. Prone to be people of the past tense, we reminisce. Not God. Unwavering in strength, he need never say, "I was." Heaven has no rearview mirrors.

Or crystal balls. Our "I am" God never yearns, "Someday I will be."

Again, we do. Dream-fueled, we reach for horizons. "Someday I will . . ." Not God. Can water be wetter? Could wind be windless? Can God be more God? No. He does not change. He is the "I am" God. "Jesus Christ is the same yesterday, today, and forever" (Heb. 13:8 NLT).

From the center of the storm, the unwavering Jesus shouts, "I am." Tall in the Trade Tower wreckage. Bold against the Galilean waves. ICU, battlefield, boardroom, prison cell, or maternity ward—whatever your storm, "I am."

The construction of this passage echoes this point. The narrative is made up of two acts, each six verses long. The first, verses 22–27, centers on the power walk of Jesus. The second, verses 28–33, centers on the faith walk of Peter.

In the first act, Christ comes astride the waves and declares the words engraved on every wise heart: "Courage! I am! Don't be afraid!" In the second act, a desperate disciple takes a step of faith and—for a moment—does what Christ does. He waterwalks. Then he takes his eyes away from Christ and does what we do. He falls.

Two acts. Each with six verses. Each set of six verses contains 90 Greek words. And right in between the two acts, the two sets of verses, and the 180 words is this two-word declaration: "I am."

Matthew, who is good with numbers, reinforces his point. It comes layered like a sub sandwich:

Graphically: Jesus—soaked but strong.

Linguistically: Jesus—the "I am" God.

Mathematically: whether in the words or the weathered world, Jesus—in the midst of it all.

God gets into things! Red Seas. Big fish. Lions' dens and furnaces. Bankrupt businesses and jail cells. Judean wildernesses, weddings, funerals, and Galilean tempests. Look and you'll find what everyone from Moses to Martha discovered. God in the middle of our storms.

That includes yours.

During the days this book was written, a young woman died in our city. She was recently married, the mother of an eighteen-month-old. Her life felt abbreviated. The shelves of help and hope go barren at such times. But at the funeral the officiating priest shared a memory in his eulogy that gave both.

For several years she had lived and worked in New York City. Due to their long friendship, he stayed in constant touch with her via e-mail. Late one night he received a message indicative of God's persistent presence.

She had missed her station on the subway. By the time she realized her mistake, she didn't know what to do. She prayed for safety and some sign of God's presence. This was no hour or place for a young, attractive woman to be passing through a rough neighborhood alone. At that moment the doors opened, and a homeless, disheveled man came on board and plopped down next to her. *God? Are you near?* she prayed. The answer came in a song. The man pulled out a harmonica and played, "Be Thou My Vision"—her mother's favorite hymn.

The song was enough to convince her. Christ was there, in the midst of it all.

Silecchia saw him in the rubble. Matthew saw him in the waves. And you? Look closer. He's there. Right in the middle of it all.

18

Hope or Hype?

The Highest Place

LUKE 9:28–36

Texas State Fair, 1963. A big place and a big night for a wide-eyed eight-year-old boy whose week peaked out at the Dairy Queen on Saturday. The sights and lights of the midway left me quoting Dorothy, "Toto, we're not in Kansas anymore."

The carnival rumbled with excitement. Roller coasters. Ferris wheels. Candied apples, cotton candy, and the Cotton Bowl. And, most of all, the voices.

"Step right up and try your luck!"

"This way, young man. Three shots for a dollar."

"Come on, fellow. Win your mom a teddy bear."

Odysseus and his men never heard sweeter sirens. Do I cut the cards with the lanky fellow at the stand-up booth? Or heed the call of the hefty lady and heave a ball at the dairy bottles? The guy in the top hat and tails dares me to explore the haunted house. "Come in. What's wrong? Afraid?"

A gauntlet of barkers—each taking his turn. Dad had warned me about them. He knew the way of the midway. I can't recall his exact instructions, but I remember the impact. I stuck next to him, my little hand lost in his big one. And every time I heard the voices, I turned to his face. He gave either protection or permission. A roll of the eyes meant "Move on." He smelled a huckster. A smile and a nod said, "Go on—no harm here."

My father helped me handle the voices.

Could you use a little help yourself? When it comes to faith, you likely could. Ever feel as if you are walking through a religious midway?

The Torah sends you to Moses. The Koran sends you to Muhammad. Buddhists invite you to meditate; spiritists, to levitate. A palm reader wants your hand. The TV evangelist wants your money. One neighbor consults her stars. Another reads the cards. The agnostic believes no one can know. The hedonist doesn't care to know. Atheists believe there is nothing to know.

"Step right up. Try my witchcraft."

"Psssst! Over here. Interested in some New Age channels?"

"Hey, you! Ever tried Scientology?"

What do you do? Where's a person to go? Mecca? Salt Lake City? Rome? Therapy? Aromatherapy?

Oh, the voices.

"Father, help me out! Please, modulate one and relegate the others." If that's your prayer, then Luke 9 is your chapter—the day God isolated the authoritative voice of history and declared, "Listen to him."

It's the first scene of the final act in the earthly life of Christ. Jesus has taken three followers on a prayer retreat.

"He took along Peter and John and James, and went up on the mountain to pray. And while He was praying, the appearance of His face became different, and His clothing became white and gleaming" (Luke 9:28–29).

Oh, to have heard that prayer. What words so lifted Christ that his face was altered? Did he see his home? Hear his home?

As a college sophomore, I took a summer job far from home. Too far. My courage melted with each mile I drove. One night I was so homesick I thought my bones would melt. But my parents were traveling, and cell phones were uninvented. Though I knew no one would answer, I called home anyway. Not once or twice, but half a dozen times. The familiar ring of the home phone brought comfort.

Maybe Jesus needed comfort. Knowing that his road home will pass through Calvary, he puts in a call. God is quick to answer. "And behold, two men were talking with Him; and they were Moses and Elijah" (v. 30).

The two were perfect comfort givers. Moses understood tough journeys. Elijah could relate to an unusual exit. So Jesus and Moses and Elijah discuss "His departure which He was about to accomplish at Jerusalem" (v. 31).

Peter, James, and John, meanwhile, take a good nap.

> All at once they woke up and saw how glorious Jesus was. They also saw the two men who were with him.

> Moses and Elijah were about to leave, when Peter said to Jesus, "Master, it is good for us to be here! Let us make three shelters, one for you, one for Moses, and one for Elijah." But Peter did not know what he was talking about. (vv. 32–33 CEV)

What would we do without Peter? The guy has no idea what he is saying, but that doesn't keep him from speaking. He has no clue what he is doing but offers to do it anyway. This is his idea: three monuments for the three heroes. Great plan? Not in God's book. Even as Peter is speaking, God starts clearing his throat.

> While he was saying this, a cloud formed and began to overshadow them; and they were afraid as they entered the cloud. Then a voice came out of the cloud, saying, "This is My Son, My Chosen One; listen to Him!" (vv. 34–35)

Peter's error is not that he spoke, but that he spoke heresy. Three monuments would equate Moses and Elijah with Jesus. No one shares the platform with Christ. God comes with the suddenness of a blue norther and leaves Peter gulping. "This is My Son." Not "a son" as if he were clumped in with the rest of us. Not "the best son" as if he were valedictorian of the human race. Jesus is, according to God, "My Son, My Chosen One," absolutely unique and unlike anyone else.[1] So:

"Listen to Him!"

In the synoptic Gospels, God speaks only twice—at the baptism and then here at the Transfiguration. In both cases he begins with "This is My beloved Son." But at the river he concludes with affirmation: "in whom I am well pleased" (Matt. 3:17 NKJV). On the hill he concludes with clarification: "Listen to Him."

He does not command, "Listen to *them.*" He could have. Has a more austere group ever assembled? Moses, the lawgiver. Elijah, the prophet. Peter, the Pentecost preacher. James, the apostle. John, the gospel writer and revelator. The Bible's first and final authors in one place. (Talk about a writers' conference!) God could have said, "These are my priceless servants; listen to them."

But he doesn't. Whereas Moses and Elijah comfort Christ, God crowns

Christ. "Listen to Him . . ." The definitive voice in the universe is Jesus. He is not one among many voices; he is the One Voice over all voices.

You cross a line with that claim. Many people recoil at such a distinction. Call Jesus godly, godlike, God inspired. Call him "a voice" but not "the voice"; a good man but not God-man.

But *good man* is precisely the terminology we cannot use. A good man would not say what he said or claim what he claimed. A liar would. Or a God would. Call him anything in between, and you have a dilemma. No one believed that Jesus was equal with God more than Jesus did.

His followers worshiped him, and he didn't tell them to stop.

Peter and Thomas and Martha called him the Son of God, and he didn't tell them they were wrong.

At his own death trial, his accusers asked, "'Are You the Son of God, then?' And He said to them, 'Yes, I am'" (Luke 22:70).

His purpose, in his words, was to "give his life as a ransom for many" (Matt. 20:28 NIV).

According to Jesus, no one could kill him. Speaking of his life, he said, "I lay it down on My own initiative. I have authority to lay it down, and I have authority to take it up again" (John 10:18).

Could he speak with more aplomb than he did in John 14:9? "He who has seen Me has seen the Father."

And could words be more blasphemous than John 8:58? "Before Abraham was, I AM" (NKJV). The claim infuriated the Jews. "They picked up stones to throw at Him" (v. 59). Why? Because only God is the great I AM. And in calling himself I AM, Christ was equating himself with God. "I am the way, and the truth, and the life; no one comes to the Father but through Me" (John 14:6).

Make no mistake, Jesus saw himself as God. He leaves us with two options. Accept him as God, or reject him as a megalomaniac. There is no third alternative.

Oh, but we try to create one. Suppose I did the same? Suppose you came across me standing on the side of the road. I can go north or south. You ask me which way I'm going. My reply? "I'm going sorth."

Thinking you didn't hear correctly, you ask me to repeat the answer.

"I'm going sorth. I can't choose between north and south, so I'm going both. I'm going sorth."

"You can't do that," you reply. "You have to choose."

"OK," I concede, "I'll head nouth."

"Nouth is not an option!" you insist. "It's either north or south. One way or the other. To the right or to the left. When it comes to this road, you gotta pick."

When it comes to Christ, you've got to do the same. Call him crazy, or crown him as king. Dismiss him as a fraud, or declare him to be God. Walk away from him, or bow before him, but don't play games with him. Don't call him a great man. Don't list him among decent folk. Don't clump him with Moses, Elijah, Buddha, Joseph Smith, Muhammad, or Confucius. He didn't leave that option. He is either God or godless. Heaven sent or hell born. All hope or all hype. But nothing in between.

C. S. Lewis summarized it classically when he wrote:

> A man who was merely a man and said the sort of things Jesus said would not be a great moral teacher. He would either be a lunatic—on a level with the man who says he is a poached egg—or else he would be the Devil of Hell. . . . You can shut Him up for a fool, you can spit at Him and kill Him as a demon; or you can fall at His feet and call Him Lord and God. But let us not come with any patronising nonsense about His being a great human teacher. He has not left that open to us. He did not intend to.[2]

Jesus won't be diminished. Besides, do you want him to be? Don't you need a distinctive voice in your noisy world? Of course you do. Don't walk the midway alone. Keep your hand in his and your eyes on him, and when he speaks:

"Listen to him."

19

Abandoned!

Godforsaken Places

MATTHEW 27:45–46

Abandon. *Such a haunting word.*

On the edge of the small town sits a decrepit house. Weeds higher than the porch. Boarded windows and a screen door bouncing with the wind. To the front gate is nailed a sign: *Abandoned.* No one wants the place. Even the poor and desperate pass it by.

A social worker appears at the door of an orphanage. In her big hand is the small, dirty one of a six-year-old girl. As the adults speak, the wide eyes of the child explore the office of the director. She hears the worker whisper, "Abandoned. She was abandoned."

An elderly woman in a convalescent home rocks alone in her room on Christmas. No cards, no calls, no carols.

A young wife discovers romantic e-mails sent by her husband to another woman.

After thirty years on the factory line, a worker finds a termination notice taped to his locker.

Abandoned by family.

Abandoned by a spouse.

Abandoned by big business.

But nothing compares to being abandoned by God.

> At noon the whole country was covered with darkness, which lasted for three hours. At about three o'clock Jesus cried out with a loud shout, *"Eli, Eli, lema sabachthani?"* which means, "My God, my God, why did you abandon me?" (Matt. 27:45–46 TEV)

By the time Christ screams these words, he has hung on the cross for six hours. Around nine o'clock that morning, he stumbled to the cleft of Skull Hill. A soldier pressed a knee on his forearm and drove a spike through one hand, then the other, then both feet. As the Romans lifted the cross, they unwittingly placed Christ in the very position in which he came to die—between man and God.

A priest on his own altar.

Noises intermingle on the hill: Pharisees mocking, swords clanging, and dying men groaning. Jesus scarcely speaks. When he does, diamonds sparkle against velvet. He gives his killers grace and his mother a son. He answers the prayer of a thief and asks for a drink from a soldier.

Then, at midday, darkness falls like a curtain. "At noon the whole country was covered with darkness, which lasted for three hours" (v. 45 TEV).

This is a supernatural darkness. Not a casual gathering of clouds or a brief eclipse of the sun. This is a three-hour blanket of blackness. Merchants in Jerusalem light candles. Soldiers ignite torches. Parents worry. People everywhere ask questions. From whence comes this noonday night? As far away as Egypt, the historian Dionysius takes notice of the black sky and writes, "Either the God of nature is suffering, or the machine of the world is tumbling into ruin."[1]

Of course the sky is dark; people are killing the Light of the World.

The universe grieves. God said it would. "On that day . . . I will make the sun go down at noon, and darken the earth in broad daylight. . . . I will make it like the mourning for an only son, and the end of it like a bitter day" (Amos 8:9–10 RSV).

The sky weeps. And a lamb bleats. Remember the time of the scream? "At about three o'clock Jesus cried out." Three o'clock in the afternoon, the hour of the temple sacrifice. Less than a mile to the east, a finely clothed priest leads a lamb to the slaughter, unaware that his work is futile. Heaven is not looking at the lamb of man but at "the Lamb of God, who takes away the sin of the world" (John 1:29 RSV).

A weeping sky. A bleating lamb. But more than anything, a screaming Savior. "Jesus cried out with a loud voice" (Matt. 27:46). Note the sturdy words here. Other writers employed the Greek word for "loud voice" to describe a "roar."[2] Soldiers aren't cupping an ear asking him to speak up. The Lamb roars. "The sun and the moon shall be darkened. . . . The LORD also shall roar out of Zion, and utter his voice from Jerusalem" (Joel 3:15–16 KJV).

Christ lifts his heavy head and eyelids toward the heavens and spends his final energy crying out toward the ducking stars. " '*Eli, Eli, lema sabachthani?*' which means, 'My God, my God, why did you abandon me?'" (Matt. 27:46 TEV).

We would ask the same. Why him? Why forsake your Son? Forsake the murderers. Desert the evildoers. Turn your back on perverts and peddlers of pain. Abandon them, not him. Why would you abandon earth's only sinless soul?

Ah, there is the hardest word. *Abandon.* The house no one wants. The child no one claims. The parent no one remembers. The Savior no one understands. He pierces the darkness with heaven's loneliest question: "My God, my God, why did you abandon me?"

Paul used the same Greek word when he urged Timothy: "Be diligent to come to me quickly; for Demas has *forsaken* me, having loved this present world, and has departed for Thessalonica" (2 Tim. 4:9–10 NKJV, emphasis mine).

As Paul looks for Demas, can he find him? No. Forsaken.

As Jesus looks for God, can he find him? No. Forsaken.

Wait a second. Doesn't David tell us, "I have never seen the righteous forsaken" (Ps. 37:25 NIV)? Did David misspeak? Did Jesus misstep? Neither. In this hour Jesus is anything but righteous. But his mistakes aren't his own. "Christ carried our sins in his body on the cross so we would stop living for sin and start living for what is right" (1 Pet. 2:24 NCV).

Christ carried all our sins in his body . . .

May I get specific for a moment? May I talk about sin? Dare I remind you and me that our past is laced with outbursts of anger, stained with nights of godless passion, and spotted with undiluted greed?

Suppose your past was made public? Suppose you were to stand on a stage while a film of every secret and selfish second was projected on the screen behind you?

Would you not crawl beneath the rug? Would you not scream for the heavens to have mercy? And would you not feel just a fraction . . . just a fraction of what Christ felt on the cross? The icy displeasure of a sin-hating God?

I tasted something similar at the age of sixteen with my own father. He and I were close, best friends. I never feared his abuse or absence. Near the top of my list of blessings is the name Jack Lucado. Near the top of my toughest days is the day I let him down.

Dad had one unbendable rule. No alcohol. He saw liquor dismantle the lives of several of his siblings. If he had his way, it wouldn't touch his family. None was allowed.

Wouldn't you know it? I decided I was smarter than he. A weekend party left me stumbling into the bathroom at midnight and vomiting a belly full of beer. Dad appeared at the door—so angry. He threw a washrag in my direction and walked away.

The next morning I awoke with a headache and the horrible awareness that I had sickened my father's heart. Walking into the kitchen (to this day I could retrace those steps), I saw him seated at the table. His paper was open, but he wasn't reading. Coffee cup was full, but he wasn't drinking. He stared at me, eyes wide with hurt, lips downturned with disbelief. More than any other time in my life, I felt the displeasure of a loving father.

I came undone. How could I survive my father's disgust?

Jesus, enduring a million times more, wondered the same.

Christ carried all our sins in his body . . .

See Christ on the cross? That's a gossiper hanging there. See Jesus? Embezzler. Liar. Bigot. See the crucified carpenter? He's a wife beater. Porn addict and murderer. See Bethlehem's boy? Call him by his other names—Adolf Hitler, Osama bin Laden, and Jeffrey Dahmer.

Hold it, Max. Don't you lump Christ with those evildoers. Don't you place his name in the same sentence with theirs!

I didn't. *He* did. Indeed he did more. More than place his name in the same sentence, he placed himself in their place. And yours.

With hands nailed open, he invited God, "Treat me as you would treat them!" And God did. In an act that broke the heart of the Father, yet honored the holiness of heaven, sin-purging judgment flowed over the sinless Son of the ages.

And heaven gave earth her finest gift. The Lamb of God who took away the sin of the world.

"My God, my God, why did you abandon me?" Why did Christ scream those words?

So you'll never have to.

20

Christ's *Coup de Grâce*

God-Ordained Places

LUKE 22:37

A man and his dog are in the same car. The dog howls bright-moon-in-the-middle-of-the-night caterwauling howls. The man pleads, promising a daily delivery of dog biscuit bouquets if only the hound will hush. After all, it's only a car wash.

Never occurred to him—ahem, to me—that the car wash would scare my dog. But it did. Placing myself in her paws, I can see why. A huge, noisy machine presses toward us, pounding our window with water, banging against the door with brushes. *Duck! We're under attack.*

"Don't panic. The car wash was my idea." "I've done this before." "It's for our own good." Ever tried to explain a car wash to a canine? Dog dictionaries are minus the words *brush* and *detail job.* My words fell on fallen flaps. Nothing helped. She just did what dogs do; she wailed.

Actually, she did what *we* do. Don't we howl? Not at car washes perhaps but at hospital stays and job transfers. Let the economy go south or the kids move north, and we have a wail of a time. And when our Master explains what's happening, we react as if he's speaking Yalunka. We don't understand a word he says.

Is your world wet and wild?

God's greatest blessings often come costumed as disasters. Any doubters need to do nothing more than ascend the hill of Calvary.

Jerusalem's collective opinion that Friday was this: Jesus is finished. What other conclusion made sense? The religious leaders had turned him in. Rome had refused to bail him out. His followers had tucked their tails and scattered. He was nailed to a cross and left to die, which he did. They silenced his lips, sealed his tomb, and, as any priest worth the price of a phylactery would tell you, Jesus is history. Three years of power and promises are decomposing in a borrowed grave. Search the crucifixion sky for one ray of hope, and you won't find it.

Such is the view of the disciples, the opinion of the friends, and the outlook of the enemies. Label it the dog-in-the-passenger-seat view.

The Master who sits behind the wheel thinks differently. God is not surprised. His plan is right on schedule. Even in—*especially* in—death, Christ is still the king, the king over his own crucifixion.

Want proof?

During his final twenty-four hours on earth, what one word did Jesus speak the most? Search these verses for a recurring phrase:

- "I, the Son of Man, must die, as the Scriptures declared long ago" (Matt. 26:24 NLT).
- "Tonight all of you will desert me," Jesus told them. "For the Scriptures say, 'God will strike the Shepherd, and the sheep of the flock will be scattered'" (Matt. 26:31 NLT).
- He could have called thousands of angels to help him but didn't, for this reason. "If I did, how would the Scriptures be fulfilled that describe what must happen now?" (Matt. 26:54 NLT).
- Rather than fault the soldiers who arrested him, he explained that they were players in a drama they didn't write. "But this is all happening to fulfill the words of the prophets as recorded in the Scriptures" (Matt. 26:56 NLT).
- "The Scriptures declare, 'The one who shares my food has turned against me,' and this will soon come true" (John 13:18 NLT).
- To his heavenly Father he prayed: "I guarded them so that not one was lost, except the one headed for destruction, as the Scriptures foretold" (John 17:12 NLT).
- He said to them, "The Scripture says, 'He was treated like a criminal,' and I tell you this scripture must have its full meaning. It was written about me, and it is happening now" (Luke 22:37 NCV).

Did you detect it? *Scripture. Love, sacrifice,* and *devotion* are terms we might expect. But *Scripture* leads the list and reveals this truth: Jesus orchestrated his final days to fulfill Old Testament prophecies. As if he was following a mental list, Jesus checked them off one by one.

Why did Scripture matter to Christ? And why does it matter to us that it mattered to him? Because he loves the Thomases among us. While others kneel and worship, you stroke your chin and wonder if you could see some proof. "How can I know the death of Christ is anything more than the death of a man?"

Begin with the fulfilled prophecy. More Old Testament foretellings were realized during the crucifixion than on any other day. Twenty-nine different prophecies, the youngest of which was five hundred years old, were completed on the day of Christ's death.

What are the odds of such a constellation? The answer staggers the statisticians. Mathematician Peter Stoner estimates the probability of just eight prophecies being fulfilled in one lifetime this way:

> Cover the state of Texas two feet deep in silver dollars. On one dollar place one mark. What is the probability that a person could, on the first attempt, select the marked dollar? Those are the same odds that eight prophecies would be satisfied in the life of one man.[1]

But Christ fulfilled twenty-nine in one day! Want some examples?

> But He was wounded for our transgressions, He was bruised for our iniquities; the chastisement for our peace was upon Him, and by His stripes we are healed. (Isa. 53:5 NKJV)

> They pierced My hands and My feet. (Ps. 22:16 NKJV)

> They divide My garments among them,
>   And for My clothing they cast lots. (Ps. 22:18 NKJV)

> "And it shall come to pass in that day," says the Lord GOD, "that I will make the sun go down at noon, and I will darken the earth in broad daylight." (Amos 8:9 NKJV)[2]

Don't call Jesus a victim of circumstances. Call him an orchestrator of circumstances! He engineered the action of his enemies to fulfill prophecy. And he commandeered the tongues of his enemies to declare truth.

Christ rarely spoke on that Friday. He didn't need to. His accusers provided accurate play-by-play. Remember the sign nailed to the cross?

> And Pilate posted a sign over him that read, "Jesus of Nazareth, the King of the Jews." The place where Jesus was crucified was near the city; and the sign was written in Hebrew, Latin, and Greek, so that many people could read it. (John 19:19–20 NLT)

Trilingual truth. Thank you, Pilate, for funding the first advertising campaign of the cross and introducing Jesus as the King of the Jews.

And thanks to the Pharisees for the sermon:

> He saved others; himself he cannot save. (Matt. 27:42 KJV)

Could words be more dead-center? Jesus could not, at the same time, save others and save himself. So he saved others.

The award for the most unlikely spokesman goes to the high priest. Caiaphas said, "It is better for one man to die for the people than for the whole nation to be destroyed" (John 11:50 NCV).

Was Caiaphas a believer? Sure sounds like one. Indeed, it *was* better for Christ to die than for all of us to perish. Heaven gets no argument from him. You'd almost think heaven caused him to say what he said. If that's what you think, you are right.

> Caiaphas did not think of this himself. As high priest that year, he was really prophesying that Jesus would die for [the Jewish] nation and for God's scattered children to bring them all together and make them one. (vv. 51–52 NCV)

What's going on here? Caiaphas preaching for Christ? The Pharisees explaining the cross? Pilate painting evangelistic billboards? Out of tragedy emerges triumph. Every disaster proves to be a victory.

This turn of events reminds me of the mule in the well. A mule tumbled down a water shaft. The villagers compared the effort of a rescue with the value of the animal and decided to bury him. They started shoveling dirt. The mule had other ideas. As the clods hit his back, he shook them off and stomped them down. Each spade of earth lifted him higher. He reached the top of the well and walked out. What his would-be killers thought would bury him actually delivered him.

The men who murdered Jesus did the same. Their actions elevated Jesus. Everything—the bad and the good, the evil and the decent—worked together for the *coup de grâce* of Christ.

Should we be surprised? Didn't he promise this would happen? "We know that in everything God works for the good of those who love him" (Rom. 8:28 NCV).

Everything? Everything. Chicken-hearted disciples. A two-timing Judas. A pierced side. Spineless Pharisees. A hardhearted high priest. In everything God worked. I dare you to find one element of the cross that he did not manage for good or recycle for symbolism. Give it a go. I think you'll find what I found—every dark detail was actually a golden moment in the cause of Christ.

Can't he do the same for you? Can't he turn your Friday into a Sunday?

Some of you doubt it. How can God use cancer or death or divorce? Simple.

He's smarter than we are. He is to you what I was to four-year-old Amy. I met her at a bookstore. She asked me if I would sign her children's book. When I asked her name, she watched as I began to write, "To Amy . . ."

She stopped me right there. With wide eyes and open mouth, she asked, "How did you know how to spell my name?"

She was awed. You aren't. You know the difference between the knowledge of a child and an adult. Can you imagine the difference between the wisdom of a human and the wisdom of God? What is impossible to us is like spelling "Amy" to him. "For as the heavens are higher than the earth, so are My ways higher than your ways and My thoughts than your thoughts" (Isa. 55:9).

I keep taking Molly to the car wash. She's howling less. I don't think she understands the machinery. She's just learning to trust her master.

Maybe we'll learn the same.

21

Christ's Crazy Claim

Incredible Places

MATTHEW 28:1–10

What's the wildest announcement you've ever heard? I'm wondering because I'm about to hear one. Any second now an airlines agent is going to pick up his microphone and . . . wait a minute . . . he's about to talk. I can see him. The guy acts sane. Appears normal. Looks like the kind of fellow who bowls and loves his kids. But what he is about to say qualifies him for a free night in a padded cell. "Ladies and gentlemen, the airplane is now ready. Flight 806 to Chicago will be departing soon. Please listen as we call you to board . . ."

Think about what he just said. He's inviting us to ascend seven miles into the sky in a plane the size of a modern-day ranch house and be hurled through the air at three times the speed of the fastest NASCAR racer in history.

Can you believe what he is asking us to do? Of course you can. But what if you'd never heard such an invitation? Wouldn't you be stunned? Wouldn't you feel like the women who heard this announcement three days after Christ had died on the cross? "He is not here. He has risen from the dead as he said he would" (Matt. 28:6 NCV).

This is what happened:

> Early on Sunday morning, as the new day was dawning, Mary Magdalene and the other Mary went out to see the tomb. Suddenly there was a great earthquake, because an angel of the Lord came down from heaven and rolled aside the stone and sat on it. His face shone like lightning, and his clothing was as white as snow. The guards shook with fear when they saw him, and they fell into a dead faint. (Matt. 28:1–4 NLT)

How conditions have changed since Friday. The crucifixion was marked by sudden darkness, silent angels, and mocking soldiers. At the empty tomb the soldiers are silent, an angel speaks, and light erupts like Vesuvius. The one who was dead is said to be alive, and the soldiers, who are alive, look as if they are dead. The women can tell something is up. What they don't know is Someone is up. So the angel informs them: "Don't be afraid! . . . I know you are looking for Jesus, who was crucified. He isn't here! He has been raised from the dead, just as he said would happen. Come, see where his body was lying" (vv. 5–6 NLT).

Such words mess with you. They cause you either to leave the airport or get on the plane. Be they false, the body of Jesus lay like John Brown's, a-moldering in a borrowed grave. Be they false, then we have no good news. An occupied tomb on Sunday takes the good out of Good Friday.

Be they true, however—if the rock is rolled and the Lord is living—then pull out the fiddle and don your dancing shoes. Heaven unplugged the grave's power cord, and you and I have nothing to fear. Death is disabled. Get on board, and let a pilot you've never seen and a power you can't understand take you home.

Can we trust the proclamation? The invitation of the angel is "Come and see . . ."

The empty tomb never resists honest investigation. A lobotomy is not a prerequisite of discipleship. Following Christ demands faith, but not blind faith. "Come and see," the angel invites. Shall we?

Take a look at the vacated tomb. Did you know the opponents of Christ never challenged its vacancy? No Pharisee or Roman soldier ever led a contingent back to the burial site and declared, "The angel was wrong. The body is here. It was all a rumor."

They would have if they could have. Within weeks disciples occupied every Jerusalem street corner, announcing a risen Christ. What quicker way for the enemies of the church to shut them up than to produce a cold and lifeless body? Display the cadaver, and Christianity is stillborn. But they had no cadaver to display.

Helps explain the Jerusalem revival. When the apostles argued for the empty tomb, the people looked to the Pharisees for a rebuttal. But they had none to give. As A. M. Fairbairn put it long ago, "The silence of the Jews is as eloquent as the speech of the Christians!"[1]

Speaking of the Christians, remember the followers' fear at the crucifixion? They ran. Scared as cats in a dog pound. Peter cursed Christ at the fire. Emmaus-bound disciples bemoaned the death of Christ on the trail. After the crucifixion, "the disciples were meeting behind locked doors because they were afraid of the Jewish leaders" (John 20:19 NLT).

These guys were so chicken we could call the Upper Room a henhouse.

But fast-forward forty days. Bankrupt traitors have become a force of life-changing fury. Peter is preaching in the very precinct where Christ was arrested. Followers of Christ defy the enemies of Christ. Whip them and they'll worship. Lock them up and they'll launch a jailhouse ministry. As bold after the Resurrection as they were cowardly before it.

Explanation:

Greed? They made no money.

Power? They gave all the credit to Christ.

Popularity? Most were killed for their beliefs.

Only one explanation remains—a resurrected Christ and his Holy Spirit. The courage of these men and women was forged in the fire of the empty tomb. The disciples did not dream up a resurrection. The Resurrection fired up the disciples. Have doubts about the empty tomb? Come and see the disciples.

While you're searching, come and see the alternatives. If Christ is not raised, if his body is decayed into dust, what are you left with?

How about Eastern mysticism? Let's travel back in time and around the globe to India. It's 490 B.C., and Buddha is willing to see us. Here is our question: "Can you defeat death?" He never opens his eyes, just shakes his head. "You are disillusioned, dear child. Seek enlightenment."

So we do. By virtue of a vigorous imagination, we travel to Greece to meet with the father of logic, Socrates. He offers a sip of hemlock, but we pass, explaining that we have only one question. "Do you have power over the grave? Are you the Son of Zeus?" He scratches his bald head and calls us *raca* (Greek for turkey brains).

Undeterred, we advance a thousand years and locate the ancient village of Mecca. A bearded Muhammad sits in the midst of followers. From the back of the crowd we cry out, "We are looking for Allah incarnate. Are you he?" He stands and rips his robe and demands that we be banished for such heresy.

But we escape. We escape back in time to Jerusalem. We ascend the stairs of a simple house where the King of the Jews is holding court. The room is crowded with earnest disciples. As we find a seat, we look into the radiant face of the resurrected Christ. The love in his eyes is as real as the wounds on his body.

If we ask the question of him—"Are you raised from the dead? Are you the Son of God?"—we know his answer.

Jesus might well personalize the words he gave to the angel. "I am raised from the dead as I said I would be. Come and see the place where my body was."

Quite a claim. Just like passengers in the airport about to board a plane, we get to choose how we respond. Either board and trust the pilot—or try to get home on our own.

I know which choice I prefer.

Conclusion

Still in the Neighborhood

In the aftermath of September 11, 2001, a group of religious leaders was invited by the White House to come to Washington and pray with the president. How my name got on the list, who knows. But I was happy to oblige. Thirty or so of us were seated in a room.

The group was well frocked and well known. Several Catholic cardinals. The president of the Mormon Church and a leader of the B'hai faith. Esteemed Jewish and Muslim spokesmen. Quite ecclesiastically eclectic. Had Christ chosen to return at that moment, a lot of questions would have been answered by who was left standing in the room.

You might wonder if I felt out of place. I lead no denomination. The only time I wear a robe is when I step out of the shower. No one calls me "The Right Most Reverend Lucado." (Although Denalyn promises me she will. Once. Someday. Before I die.)

Did I feel like a minnow in a whale's world? Hardly. I was special among them. And when my turn came to meet George W. Bush, I had to mention why. After giving my name, I added, "And, Mr. President, I was raised in Andrews, Texas." For those of you whose subscription to *National Geographic* has expired, Andrews is only a half-hour drive from Midland, his hometown. Upon learning that we are neighbors, he hitched his britches and smiled that lopsided smile and let his accent drawl ever so slightly. "Why, I know your town. I've walked those streets. I've even played your golf course."

I stood a tad taller. It's nice to know that the most powerful man in the world has walked my streets.

How much nicer to know the same about God.

Yes, he is in heaven. Yes, he rules the universe. But, yes, he has walked your streets. He's still the next door Savior. Near enough to touch. Strong enough to trust. Paul merges these truths into one promise: "Christ Jesus is He who died, yes, rather who was raised, who is at the right hand of God, who also intercedes for us" (Rom. 8:34).

See his divinity? He is "at the right hand of God."

"Right hand of God" equals the highest honor. Is Jesus above all powers? You bet he is:

> He is *far above* any ruler or authority or power or leader or anything else in this world or in the world to come. And God has put all things under the authority of Christ, and he gave him this authority for the benefit of the church. And the church is his body; it is filled by Christ, who fills everything everywhere with his presence. (Eph. 1:21–23 NLT, emphasis mine)

Christ is running the show. Right now. A leaf just fell from a tree in the Alps. Christ caused it to do so. A newborn baby in India inhaled for the first time. Jesus measured the breath. The migration of the belugas through the oceans? Christ dictates their itinerary. He is

> the firstborn of all creation. For by Him all things were created, both in the heavens and on earth, visible and invisible, whether thrones or dominions or rulers or authorities—all things have been created through Him and for Him. (Col. 1:15–16)

What a phenomenal list! Heavens and earth. Visible and invisible. Thrones, dominions, rulers, and authorities. No thing, place, or person omitted. The scale on the sea urchin. The hair on the elephant hide. The hurricane that wrecks the coast, the rain that nourishes the desert, the infant's first heartbeat, the elderly person's final breath—all can be traced back to the hand of Christ, the firstborn of creation.

Firstborn in Paul's vernacular has nothing to do with birth order. *Firstborn* refers to order of rank. As one translation states: "He ranks higher than everything that has been made" (v. 15 NCV). Everything? Find an exception. Peter's mother-in-law has a fever; Jesus rebukes it. A tax needs to be paid; Jesus pays it by sending first a coin and then a fisherman's hook into the mouth of a fish. When five thousand stomachs growl, Jesus renders a boy's basket a bottomless buffet. Jesus exudes authority. He bats an eyelash, and nature jumps. No one argues when, at the end of his earthly life, the God-man declares, "All authority has been given to Me in heaven and on earth" (Matt. 28:18).

> Out of the south comes the storm. . . .
> [God] disperses the cloud of His lightning.
> It changes direction, turning around by His guidance,
> That it may do whatever He commands it
> On the face of the inhabited earth.
> Whether for correction . . .
> Or for lovingkindness, He causes it to happen. . . .
> Stand and consider the wonders of God.
>
> (Job 37:9, 11–14)

Stand and consider, indeed.

- The Hubble Space Telescope sends back infrared images of faint galaxies that are perhaps twelve billion light-years away (twelve billion times six trillion miles).[1]
- Astronomers venture a feeble estimate that the number of stars in the universe equals the number of grains of sand on all the beaches of the world.[2] The star Eta Carinae outshines our sun, in the same way Yankee Stadium outshines a cigarette lighter. Five million times brighter![3]
- The star Betelgeuse has a diameter of 100 million miles, which is larger than the earth's orbit around the sun.[4]

Why the immensity? Why such vast, unmeasured, unexplored, "unused" space? So that you and I, freshly stunned, could be stirred by this resolve: "I can do all things through Christ who strengthens me" (Phil. 4:13 NKJV).

The Christ of the galaxies is the Christ of your Mondays. The Starmaker manages your travel schedule. Relax. You have a friend in high places. Does the child of Arnold Schwarzenegger worry about tight pickle-jar lids? Does the son of Nike founder Phil Knight sweat a broken shoestring? If the daughter of Bill Gates can't turn on her computer, does she panic?

No. Nor should you. The universe's Commander in Chief knows your name. He has walked your streets.

Even in heaven, Christ remains our next door Savior. Even in heaven, he is still "Christ Jesus . . . who died." The King of the universe commands comets with a human tongue and directs celestial traffic with a human hand. Still human. Still divine. Living forever through his two natures. As Peter Lewis states:

> Go to the spiritual heart of this created universe, and you will find a man! Go to the place where angels bow who never fell, and you will find a man! Go to the very center of the manifested glory of the invisible God, and you will find a man: true human nature, one of our own race, mediating the glory of God![5]

Wait a second, Max. Are you saying that Jesus is still in his fleshly body? That angels worship what Galileans touched? Yes, indeed. Jesus appeared to the followers in a flesh-and-bone body: "A spirit does not have flesh and bones as you see that I have" (Luke 24:39). His resurrected body was a real body, real enough to walk on the road to Emmaus, to be mistaken for that of a gardener, to swallow fish at breakfast.

In the same breath, Jesus' real body was *really* different. The Emmaus disciples didn't recognize him, and walls didn't stop him. Mark tried to describe the new look and settled for "[Jesus] appeared in another form" (Mark 16:12 NKJV). While his body was the same, it was better; it was glorified. It was a heavenly body.

And I can't find the passage that says he shed it. He ascended in it. "He was lifted up while they were looking on, and a cloud received Him out of their sight" (Acts 1:9). He will return in it. The angel told the followers, "This Jesus, who has been taken up from you into heaven, will come in just the same way as you have watched Him go into heaven" (Acts 1:11).

The God-man is still both. The hands that blessed the bread of the boy now bless the prayers of the millions. And the mouth that commissions angels is the mouth that kissed children.

You know what this means? The greatest force in the cosmos understands and intercedes for you. "We have an Advocate with the Father, Jesus Christ the righteous" (1 John 2:1).

Sir John Clarke dedicated many years to Bible translation in the Belgian Congo. He had difficulty translating the word *advocate.* For two years he searched for a suitable translation. His search ended the day he visited the king of the Mulongo people. During the time with the king, an aide appeared, received his instructions, and left. The king told Clarke that the aide was his Nsenga Mukwashi, which was not a name, but a title.

The king explained that the servant represented the people to the king. Clarke immediately asked for permission to watch the man at work. He went to the edge of the village where he found him talking with three women. The husband of one of the women had died, and she was being evicted from her hut. She needed help.

"I will take you to the king," the Nsenga Mukwashi told her.

"Do not do that," she objected. "I am old and timid and would become speechless in his presence."

"There will be no need for you to speak," he assured her. "I shall speak for you."

And he did. Succinctly and clearly and passionately. Clarke noted the flash of anger in the king's eyes. The sovereign ordered his court to care for the widow and seize the culprits. The widow found justice, and Clarke found his word—*Nsenga Mukwashi.*[6]

You, too, have an advocate with the Father. When you are weak, he is strong. When you are timid, he speaks. Your next door Savior is your Nsenga Mukwashi.

> Jesus understands every weakness of ours, because he was tempted in every way that we are. But he did not sin! So whenever we are in need, we should come bravely before the throne of our merciful God. There we will be treated with undeserved kindness, and we will find help. (Heb. 4:15–16 CEV)

Alas, my illustration of the president falls short. Can I call him? Even if I had the number, he's too busy. Yet can I call God? Anytime. He is not too busy for me—or you. Endowed with sleepless attention and endless devotion, he listens. The fact that we can't imagine how he hears a million requests as if they were only one doesn't mean he can't or doesn't. For he can and he does.

And among the requests he hears and heeds is yours. For even though he is in heaven, he never left the neighborhood.

Next Door SAVIOR

DISCUSSION GUIDE

Prepared by Steve Halliday

CHAPTER ONE
OUR NEXT DOOR SAVIOR

TOURING THE NEIGHBORHOOD

1. *Who are you?* he wondered so softly that no one but God could hear. *You just awakened the dead! Should you not be encased in light or encircled by angels or enthroned higher than a thousand Caesars? Yet, look at you—wearing clothes I would wear and laughing at jokes I tell and eating the food we all eat. Is this what death defeaters do? Just who are you?*

   A. When you first learned of Jesus, who did you think he was? Who do you now think he is?

   B. What most amazes you about Jesus? Why?

2. A just-God Jesus could make us but not understand us. A just-man Jesus could love us but never save us. But a God-man Jesus? Near enough to touch. Strong enough to trust. A next door Savior.

   A. What is a "just-God Jesus"? A "just-man Jesus"?

   B. Why would a "just-man Jesus" have no power to save us?

   C. Explain what Max means by a "next door Savior."

3. The cache of Christianity is Christ. Not money in the bank or a car in the garage or a healthy body or a better self-image. . . . Christ is the reward of Christianity.

   A. In what way is Christ the reward of Christianity?

   B. How does our pursuit of Christ affect our everyday actions?

4. Could your world use a little music? If so, invite heaven's baritone to cut loose. He may look as common as the guy next door, but just wait till you see what he can do. Who knows? A few songs with him might change the way you sing. Forever.

   A. In what way could your world use "a little music"?

   B. How could you invite "heaven's baritone to cut loose" in your life?

   C. How does life with Jesus change the way you "sing"?

City Center

1. Read Luke 7:11–17.
   A. What happened when Jesus saw the funeral procession described in this passage? What did he immediately do (vv. 13–15)?
   B. How did the people react to this incident? What conclusion did they reach (v. 16)?
   C. How did this event demonstrate Jesus' humanity? How did it reveal his divinity?
2. Read Mark 4:35–41.
   A. Why did the storm disturb the disciples' trust?
   B. What reply did Jesus make to the disciples' question (vv. 39–40)?
   C. Given all the disciples had seen Jesus do, why do you think they questioned who Jesus was?
3. Read Colossians 1:15–20; 2:9.
   A. What do these verses teach us about the identity of Jesus? Why is this important?
   B. How do these verses describe a "next door Savior"? What makes him the Savior? In what way is he next door?

Community Improvement

To help you think of Jesus as your "next door Savior," take a walk through your neighborhood, praying for those who live around you. Ask the Lord to make himself real to them, to show his true nature to them—and ask him how you might help in the process.

CHAPTER TWO
Christ's Theme Song

Touring the Neighborhood

1. Why did Jesus hang his family's dirty laundry on the neighborhood clothesline? Because your family has some too.

   A. What kind of "dirty laundry" did Jesus mention? Why was it important for him to do so?
   B. Based on Jesus' example, what should be our attitude toward our families' past?

2. The phrase "I've been there" is in the chorus of Christ's theme song. To the lonely, Jesus whispers, "I've been there." To the discouraged, Christ nods his head and sighs, "I've been there."
   A. Does it help you to know that Christ has experienced the disappointments and hardships of being human? How?
   B. In what area of your life is it especially comforting to know that Christ has "been there"? Why?

3. He's not ashamed of you. Nor is he confused by you. Your actions don't bewilder him. Your tilted halo doesn't trouble him. So go to him. After all, you're a part of his family.
   A. Do you truly believe Christ is not ashamed of you? How does accepting or rejecting this fact affect your attitude? Your behavior?
   B. Do your actions ever bewilder yourself? Explain.
   C. In what way are you a part of Christ's family?
   D. How do you go to Jesus during times of difficulty? What do you do?

City Center

1. Read Isaiah 53:2–3.
   A. Why do you suppose God chose not to make Christ extraordinary in appearance?
   B. What does it mean that Christ grew up as "a root out of parched ground"? What is the "parched ground"? How did this enable him to identify with us?

2. Read Mark 3:20–22.
   A. How did Jesus' own family respond to his early ministry (v. 21)? Why do you think they reacted like this?
   B. How did the teachers of the law respond to Jesus' teaching (v. 22)? Why do you think they reacted like this?

C. How do you respond to Jesus' teaching? Explain.

3. Read Hebrews 2:10–18.

   A. What does it mean that Jesus was made perfect through sufferings (v. 10)?

   B. Why is Jesus not ashamed to call us his brothers (v. 11)?

   C. Why did the Son of God become human, according to verse 14?

   D. How did Jesus' earthly experience qualify him to become our "high priest" (v. 17)? According to Hebrews 5:1–10, what does Jesus do for us as our high priest?

   E. In what way did Jesus suffer when he was tempted? How did his painful experience benefit us (v. 18)?

Community Improvement

Jesus went out of his way to identify with us. How do you identify with your neighbors? If you haven't met your next door neighbors yet, determine to do so this week. Invite them over for coffee or out to a movie. Start the process of getting to know them and identifying with their struggles and concerns.

CHAPTER THREE
Friend of Flops

Touring the Neighborhood

1. Jesus starts to smile and shake his head. "Matthew, Matthew, you think I came to quarantine you? Following me doesn't mean forgetting your friends. Just the opposite. I want to meet them."

   A. Why do some people like Matthew think that Jesus came to quarantine them?

   B. Why does Jesus want to meet "flops"—and their friends?

2. What could be better? Sinners and saints in the same room, and no one's trying to determine who is which.

   A. What's good about having saints and sinners in the same room?

   B. What's good about not trying to figure out who belongs to which group?

3. Quite a story. Matthew goes from double-dealer to disciple. He throws a party that makes the religious right uptight, but Christ proud. The good guys look good, and the bad guys hit the road. Some story indeed. What do we do with it?

   A. Why did Matthew's party make the religious right uptight?

   B. What parallel situations do you see today? Do you generally respond to them like Christ or like the religious leaders? Why?

4. You don't have to be weird to follow Jesus. You don't have to stop liking your friends to follow him. Just the opposite. A few introductions would be nice. Do you know how to grill a steak?

   A. Do you know someone who thinks "weirdness" is essential to discipleship?

   B. What are some effective ways you have introduced your friends to Jesus?

   C. What does Max really mean when he asks, "Do you know how to grill a steak?" How would you answer his question?

City Center

1. Read Matthew 9:9–13.

   A. What problem did the Pharisees have with Jesus' attending Matthew's party (vv. 10–11)? To whom did they direct their question? Why didn't they ask Jesus directly?

   B. Who responded to the Pharisees' question? What reply was given (v. 12)?

   C. Who were the "healthy" in this incident? Who were the "sick"? Did everyone know their true condition? Explain.

   D. What did Jesus tell the Pharisees to go and learn (v. 13)? How could a correct answer begin leading them to spiritual health?

2. Read 1 Corinthians 1:26–31.

   A. What point does Paul make in verse 26? Why is this significant?

   B. How does Paul explain God's actions (vv. 27–29)?

   C. How does Paul describe Jesus' role (v. 30)?

   D. What conclusion does Paul reach (v. 31)?

3. Read Revelation 5:9–10.
   A. How does this song to Jesus describe the people for whom he died? What is their makeup?
   B. What will Jesus do for these people for whom he died? What is their destiny?

Community Improvement

To become a friend, you have to do more than learn a name; you have to learn a *person.* Be a friend to someone in your area, preferably an older person who could use your help and friendship. Demonstrate your offer of friendship by a creative kindness: Mow a lawn, walk a pet, help with a needed repair, run an errand, or just give your neighbor your phone number, saying "Call me if I can ever help you."

CHAPTER FOUR
The Hand God Loves to Hold

Touring the Neighborhood

1. Life rushes in. Pale cheeks turn pink. Shallow breaths become full. Hoover Dam cracks and a river floods. The woman feels power enter. And Jesus? Jesus feels power exit.
   A. Try to put yourself in the woman's sandals. How do you think you would have felt at that moment of healing? Surprised? Elated? Astonished? Fearful? Explain.
   B. Why do you think Jesus wanted to know who had touched him? Why was this so important for him, especially since his demand frightened the woman?

2. "The whole story." How long had it been since someone put the gear of life in Park, turned off the key, and listened to her story? But when this woman reaches out to Jesus, he does. With the town bishop waiting, a young girl dying, and a crowd pressing, he still makes time for a woman from the fringe.
   A. Why do you think Jesus wanted to hear the woman's whole story? What did he hope to accomplish?

   B. How do you think it benefited the woman to tell her whole story?

   C. How does Jesus still make time for "people on the fringe"? How have you personally seen him do this?

3. Illness took her strength. What took yours? Red ink? Hard drink? Late nights in the wrong arms? Long days on the wrong job? Pregnant too soon? Too often? Is her hand your hand? If so, take heart. Your family may shun it. Society may avoid it. But Christ? Christ wants to touch it.

   A. Answer Max's question. What took your strength?

   B. In what way has this separated you from others? From Christ?

4. Yours is the hand he loves to hold.

   A. Do you believe this statement? Explain.

   B. How does Jesus "hold" our hands today? In what instances of your life has he held your hand?

City Center

1. Read Mark 5:21–34.

   A. What request did the synagogue ruler make of Jesus (v. 23)? How did Jesus respond (v. 24)?

   B. Describe the woman's problem (vv. 25–26). What would be comparable today to her situation?

   C. How was her touch different from the touch of all the others around Jesus? How did the disciples react to his question about who touched him (v. 31)?

   D. How did Jesus respond to the woman's confession (v. 34)?

2. Read Mark 10:13–16.

   A. Why did the disciples rebuke certain people? To what did the disciples object (v. 13)?

   B. How did Jesus react to the disciples' action (v. 14)? What reason did he give for his reaction (vv. 14–15)?

   C. What did Jesus do to emphasize his point (v. 16)?

3. Read Isaiah 42:1, 5–7.
   - A. Who is speaking in this passage? How does the prophet describe him (v. 5)?
   - B. What does God promise to do for his "Servant" (v. 6)? To whom is he sending this Servant?
   - C. How does the touch of God affect the Servant, and then how does the touch of the Servant affect us (v. 7)?

Community Improvement

It has been said that the hands of his disciples are the hands of Christ to the world. As his follower, you can "touch" the people in your world for him. Do a little research to see where a "helping hand" might be needed in your own neighborhood or community. Can you volunteer at a food bank, serve as a story reader at a local grade school, offer to serve a meal at a homeless shelter? Find out what the opportunities are, and then take advantage of one. Be the hands of Christ.

Chapter Five
Try Again

Touring the Neighborhood

1. There is a look that says, "It's too late."
   - A. What kind of look says, "It's too late"? Have you seen this look? Explain.
   - B. Have you ever worn this kind of look? Explain.
2. You've felt what Peter felt. You've sat where Peter sat. And now Jesus is asking you to go fishing. He knows your nets are empty. He knows your heart is weary. He knows you'd like nothing more than to turn your back on the mess and call it a life. But he urges, "It's not too late to try again."
   - A. What is making you feel weary right now?
   - B. In what way might Jesus be asking you to "go fishing"?

3. Spotting treasures is easy for the one who hid them. Finding fish is simple for the God who made them. To Jesus, the Sea of Galilee is a dollar-store fishbowl on a kitchen cabinet.
   A. If Jesus could so easily find hard-to-find fish on the Sea of Galilee, what kind of hard-to-find "fish" would you like him to point out in your own sea?
   B. How would your life change if you consciously remembered all of the time that Jesus was (and is) God in the flesh?

4. Contrary to what you may have been told, Jesus doesn't limit his recruiting to the stout-hearted. The beat up and worn out are prime prospects in his book, and he's been known to climb into boats, bars, and brothels to tell them, "It's not too late to start over."
   A. In what ways do we sometimes think that Jesus *does* limit his recruiting to the stout-hearted? Why do we believe this myth?
   B. Who have you known that started over? How far did Jesus go to reach them? How did they respond?
   C. Has Jesus ever told you, "It's not too late to start over"? Explain.

City Center

1. Read Luke 5:1–11.
   A. What request did Jesus make of Simon Peter in verse 3? Why did he make the request?
   B. What request did Jesus make of Simon in verse 4?
   C. How did Simon respond to Jesus' request (v. 5)? What did he do anyway?
   D. What happened when Simon complied with Jesus' request (vv. 6–7)?
   E. Why did Simon respond as he did to the miracle (vv. 8–10)?
   F. How did Jesus respond to Simon's reaction (v. 10)?
   G. Why do you think Simon and his partners left everything to follow Jesus?

2. Read Romans 7:14–25.
   A. How does Paul characterize himself in verse 14? Why is this significant?
   B. What personal problem does Paul describe in verses 15–23? Can you identify with this problem? Explain.
   C. How does this problem make the apostle feel (v. 24)? Can you identify with this? Explain.
   D. What question does Paul ask in verse 24? What answer does he give in verse 25? What does all this have to do with "trying again"?

Community Improvement

Most of us have a neighbor or friend or family member with whom we've had a disagreement or conflict. Perhaps you've already tried, unsuccessfully, to mend fences. Why not try again? What's keeping you from making another attempt? Before you approach this person, commit to spending at least an hour in prayer about your attitude, your fears, and your goal. Then . . . try again!

Chapter Six
Spit Therapy

Touring the Neighborhood

1. Talk about a thankless role. Selected to suffer. Some sing to God's glory. Others teach to God's glory. Who wants to be blind for God's glory? Which is tougher—the condition or discovering it was God's idea?
   A. Would you like to sing for God's glory? Teach to God's glory? Be blind for God's glory? Explain.
   B. Which do you think would be tougher, to be blind or to learn your condition was God's idea? Explain.
   C. How would you explain this story to someone outside the faith? How would you explain that God allowed someone to be born blind—and live in that condition for many years—so others could see his glory when he healed him?

2. Who was really blind that day? The neighbors didn't see the man; they saw a novelty. The church leaders didn't see the man; they saw a technicality. The parents didn't see their son; they saw a social difficulty. In the end, no one saw him.
    - A. What people in our culture does no one "see"?
    - B. Have you ever felt invisible to others? Explain.
    - C. What examples can you think of where we daily overlook the miracles occurring around us and perhaps instead focus on the negative?
3. Do some people seem to be dealt more than their share of bad hands? If so, Jesus knows. He knows how they feel, and he knows where they are.
    - A. Answer Max's question.
    - B. Who in your life seems to have been dealt more than his or her share of bad hands? Describe the person's situation. How have you seen people respond differently to great difficulties? What was the result in each case?
    - C. Why do you think God allows this uneven sharing of life's hands?
4. I'm sorry about your greasy gown. And your flowers—they tend to slide, don't they? Who has an answer for the diseases, drudgeries, and darkness of this life? I don't. But we do know this. Everything changes when you look at your groom.
    - A. How do you respond to the diseases, drudgeries, and darkness of this life?
    - B. What changes when you look at your groom?

City Center

1. Read John 9:1–41.
    - A. What question began this whole incident (v. 2)? How are some forms of this question still being asked today?
    - B. How did the man's neighbors react to his healing (vv. 8–10)? Why do you think they responded like this?

C. How did the Pharisees react to the man's healing (vv. 13–16)? Why did they react like this?

D. How did the man's parents react to their son's healing (vv. 18–23)? Why did they react like this?

E. In what way did the man show courage the second time the religious leaders summoned him (vv. 24–33)? How did the leaders react to his courage (v. 34)?

F. How did Jesus react to the ill treatment of the man (vv. 35–37)? How did the man react to Jesus, once he heard the truth (v. 38)?

2. Read 2 Corinthians 4:16–18.

A. How can we keep from losing heart, according to verse 16?

B. How does verse 17 help us to keep moving ahead spiritually, despite unexplained suffering?

C. What strategy for living does verse 18 develop? How do you fix your eyes on the unseen? What are some practical ways to do this?

Community Improvement

Who in your life needs a little encouragement right now? What can you do to brighten an otherwise gloomy day? Don't let another day go by without doing what you can to bring some cheer into that person's life, whether through a phone call, a thoughtfully written letter, a personal visit, or something else more appropriate.

CHAPTER SEVEN
What Jesus Says at Funerals

Touring the Neighborhood

1. Every funeral has its Marthas. Sprinkled among the bereaved are the bewildered. "Help me understand this one, Jesus."

A. Have you ever been a "Martha" at a funeral? If so, describe how you felt.

B. Whose death has most bewildered you? Why?

2. Jesus weeps. He weeps with them. He weeps for them. He weeps with you. He weeps for you.
   A. How does it make you feel to know that Jesus weeps over human tragedy?
   B. What does it mean that Jesus weeps "with" us?
   C. What does it mean that Jesus weeps "for" us?
3. Grief does not mean you don't trust; it simply means you can't stand the thought of another day without the Jacob or Lazarus of your life.
   A. Why do we sometimes think that grieving *does* mean we're not trusting?
   B. Does there come a point where grieving crosses over into a failure to trust? Explain.
4. When Christ speaks to the dead, the dead listen. Indeed, had Jesus not addressed Lazarus by name, the tenant of every tomb on earth would have stepped forth.
   A. Do you agree with Max's statements? What does this say about Christ's power over the dead? Over the living?
   B. Is there someone you have given up on, thinking he or she would never "hear" Christ's voice? How does this encourage you?

City Center

1. Read John 11:1–44.
   A. Why does verse 4 seem to contradict verse 14? In what way was the contradiction resolved?
   B. Why did Jesus stay where he was for three days before going to see his friend Lazarus? What was Jesus' priority?
   C. Why do you think Jesus did not tell the sisters what he was about to do? Why did he keep it a secret until he did it?
   D. How did the sisters show both trust and doubt in this story? How do we often do the same?

2. Read Romans 14:8–10.
   - A. What kinds of people belong to the Lord, according to verse 8? Why is this significant?
   - B. Why did Christ die and rise again, according to verse 9?
   - C. How does Paul apply this theological truth to a very practical problem in verse 10?
3. Read 1 Thessalonians 4:13–18.
   - A. What prompted Paul to write this passage, according to verse 13?
   - B. How did Paul intend to encourage his friends who had lost believing loved ones (vv. 14–17)?
   - C. What did Paul want his friends to do with the instruction he gave them (v. 18)? Why did he make this request?

Community Improvement

Read a compassionate and well-written work on grief or caring for the grieving, such as C. S. Lewis's *A Grief Observed* or Charles Swindoll's *For Those Who Hurt.* Make it a goal to learn something new about how you can help in the grieving process, and then look for ways to put your new knowledge to work.

CHAPTER EIGHT
Getting the Hell Out

Touring the Neighborhood

1. Satan does not sit still. A glimpse of the wild man reveals Satan's goal for you and me. *Self-imposed pain.* The demoniac used rocks. We are more sophisticated; we use drugs, sex, work, violence, and food. (Hell makes us hurt ourselves.)
   - A. How have you seen people around you suffer from self-imposed pain?
   - B. In what way(s) has hell made you hurt yourself?
   - C. How did you deal with this self-imposed pain?

2. Satan can disturb us, but he cannot defeat us. The head of the serpent is crushed.

   A. What does it mean that Satan cannot "defeat" us?

   B. What does it mean that the head of the serpent is crushed?

   C. How is Satan disturbing you or your family at this moment?

3. One word from Christ, and the demons are swimming with the swine, and the wild man is "clothed and in his right mind." Just one command! No séance needed. No hocus-pocus. No chants were heard or candles lit. Hell is an anthill against heaven's steamroller.

   A. Why could Christ control the demons with a single command?

   B. What does it mean for you that Christ has such power over hell?

4. The snake in the ditch and Lucifer in the pit—both have met their match. And, yet, both stir up dust long after their defeat. For that reason, though confident, we are still *careful.* For a toothless ol' varmint, Satan sure has some bite!

   A. How are you "careful" in dealing with Satan and his forces?

   B. Describe some recent examples of Satan's "bite."

City Center

1. Read Mark 5:1–20.

   A. Why do you think the demon-possessed man came out to meet Jesus when the Lord got out of the boat (v. 2)? Why wouldn't he just run away?

   B. What request did the man make of Jesus (v. 7)? Why do you think he made this request?

   C. Why do you think the demons wanted to enter the pigs (v. 12)?

   D. How did the townspeople respond to this divine show of force (vv. 14–17)?

   E. What did the cured man request of Jesus (v. 18)? What answer did Jesus give (v. 19)? Why do you think he gave this answer?

2. Read 1 Peter 5:8–10.
   - A. How does this passage picture the devil (v. 8)? Why is this an apt description?
   - B. How are you to "resist" Satan (v. 9)?
   - C. How do you steady yourself so that you stand "firm in your faith"?
   - D. Why does it help to remember that you are not alone in suffering and temptation (v. 9)?
   - E. From where does all spiritual strength ultimately come (v. 10)?
3. Read Ephesians 6:10–18.
   - A. Why does a Christian need spiritual armor and spiritual weapons (vv. 11–12)?
   - B. What sort of armor does Paul describe here? What sort of weaponry?
   - C. Name each of the items listed here. Which ones do you think you have a good grip on? Which ones need more of your attention? Why?

Community Improvement

The topic of spiritual warfare can scare off a lot of people and bring out the kookiness in others, but Scripture makes it clear that we are in a very real spiritual battle. Read 2 Corinthians 10:3–5, and make a list of what you need to improve in this area. Share your list with a trusted friend, and ask him or her to keep you accountable to work on it.

CHAPTER NINE
It's Not Up to You

Touring the Neighborhood

1. God doesn't send us to obedience school to learn new habits; he sends us to the hospital to be given a new heart. Forget training; he gives transplants.
   - A. Why do we need new hearts rather than mere obedience?
   - B. Do you have a new heart? Explain.
   - C. What are the indications of a new heart? How do they contrast with acts of mere obedience?

2. There is no Rewind button on the VCR of life . . . is there? We don't get to start over . . . do we? A man can't be born again . . . can he?
   - A. Have you ever wanted to hit the Rewind button on the VCR of life? What would you like to go back and change? Since you can't change the past, how could you use it for good?
   - B. How does God allow us to "start over"? What does this look like?
   - C. What does it mean to you to be "born again"?
3. The stumbles of a toddler do not invalidate the act of birth. And the stumbles of a Christian do not annul his spiritual birth.
   - A. Why do we sometimes think that stumbles invalidate spiritual birth?
   - B. How do you feel when you stumble? Does it bother you? Explain.
   - C. What kind of stumbles are you most prone to take?
4. He has deposited a Christ seed in you. As it grows, you will change. It's not that sin has no more presence in your life, but rather that sin has no power over your life. Temptation will pester you, but temptation will not master you.
   - A. What is the "Christ seed" that God deposits in his children?
   - B. How have you changed since you first became a Christian?
   - C. Does temptation have a tendency more often to pester or master you? Explain.

City Center

1. Read John 3:1–16.
   - A. Why do you think Nicodemus came to see Jesus at night?
   - B. Name some similarities and differences between physical and spiritual birth.
   - C. Who takes the lead role in spiritual birth (v. 8)? Why is this important?
   - D. What role does belief or trust play in spiritual birth (v. 15)?
   - E. What is promised to those who place their trust in Christ (v. 16)?

2. Read Titus 3:3–6.
   - A. How does Paul characterize his life and that of his friends before their conversion (v. 3)?
   - B. Who took the lead role in their conversions (vv. 4–5)?
   - C. How does Paul picture his salvation (v. 5)?
   - D. What part did Jesus Christ play in this accomplishment (v. 6)?

3. Read Philippians 1:3–6.
   - A. Why does Paul say he prays for the Philippians (vv. 3–5)?
   - B. Who "began a good work" in Paul's friends (v. 6)? What does this mean?
   - C. Who will bring to completion this work in Paul's friends? How will he do this?

Community Improvement

Believers who stumble in their walk of faith often feel like failures and sometimes wonder whether God can even stand them anymore. Think of someone you know who has taken a nasty stumble in the past few days or weeks. What could you do to help this person recover from the fall and get on with life in Christ? Make a plan and then put it into action.

CHAPTER TEN
The Trashman

Touring the Neighborhood

1. His voice is warm and his question honest. "Will you give me your trash?"
   - A. What is the "trash" mentioned here?
   - B. What sort of "trash" do you carry around?
   - C. Do you tend to hand over or hang on to your trash? Explain.

2. By the time they reach the hill, the line to the top is long. Hundreds walk ahead of them. All wait in silence, stunned by what they hear—a scream, a pain-pierced roar that hangs in the air for moments, interrupted only by a groan. Then the scream again. His.

A. Why did the Trashman scream?

B. Why did the Trashman subject himself to such pain?

3. Her words are soft, intended for no one. "He's standing." Then aloud, for her friend, "He's standing." And louder for all, "He's standing!" She turns; all turn. They see him silhouetted against a golden sun. Standing. Indeed.

   A. What does this image of the Trashman standing represent in our world?

   B. How does it make you feel to know that a risen Christ is standing?

City Center

1. Read John 1:29–31.

   A. Why did John the Baptist call Jesus "the Lamb of God"?

   B. Given their culture, how would John's audience have interpreted the reference to a lamb?

   C. Since Jesus was born several months after John, in what way was Jesus "before" John (v. 30)?

   D. Using a Bible concordance, look up several different types of references to "lambs." In what ways was Jesus like a lamb?

2. Read 2 Corinthians 5:17–6:2.

   A. How does being a "new creature" in Christ relate to the picture of laying one's trash before the Trashman?

   B. When God redeems us (and takes away our trash), what does he ask us to do in return (vv. 18–20)?

   C. When is the best time to give God your trash (v. 2)?

Community Improvement

What "trash" do you tend to carry around with you? How is it weighing you down? What keeps you from placing this garbage at the feet of Jesus? Set aside a good chunk of time today, and bring all of this trash to your Savior. Spend at least a half-hour in prayer, confessing whatever you need to confess and asking the Lord to carry your burden for you. Make sure to close your prayer time with healthy praise for the One who offers to carry your burdens.

CHAPTER ELEVEN
He Loves to Be with the Ones He Loves

Touring the Neighborhood

1. Holiday travel. It isn't easy. Then why do we do it? Why cram the trunks and endure the airports? You know the answer. We love to be with the ones we love.
   A. Describe the last time you took a holiday trip. What challenges did it present?
   B. If we love to be with the ones we love, then why are we so often separated from them?
2. What a world he left. Our classiest mansion would be a tree trunk to him. Earth's finest cuisine would be walnuts on heaven's table.
   A. What, to you, is the most remarkable thing about Jesus' leaving heaven to come to earth?
   B. Why do you think Jesus left heaven to live among us on earth?
3. Speaking through the door, Dr. Maltz told the man of his wife's proposal. "She wants me to disfigure her face, to make her face like yours in the hope that you will let her back into your life. That's how much she loves you." There was a brief moment of silence, and then, ever so slowly, the doorknob began to turn.
   A. What finally got through to the man? What force drove him to change his mind?
   B. Have you ever experienced human love as great as that of the wife in the story? Explain.
4. God took on our face, our disfigurement. He became like us. Just look at the places he was willing to go: feed troughs, carpentry shops, badlands, and cemeteries. The places he went to reach us show how far he will go to touch us.

A. How did Jesus take on our disfigurement? Why did he do so?

B. What nasty places have you seen Jesus go to? What did he do there?

C. Where did Jesus find you? Describe what happened.

City Center

1. Read Philippians 2:4–11.

   A. What command are we given in verse 4? What's hard and what's easy about following this command?

   B. What kind of example did Jesus set for us? Name some specific areas.

   C. How will God reward Jesus for his obedience (vv. 9–11)? How is this meant to encourage us?

2. Read John 1:14.

   A. Who is "the Word" in this verse? How do you know?

   B. From where did this Word come?

   C. What does it mean that he was "full" of truth?

   D. What does it mean that he was "full" of grace?

3. Read John 14:15–18.

   A. How do we prove our love for Jesus, according to verse 15?

   B. To whom will Jesus send another "Helper" or "Counselor" or "Comforter," according to verse 16? Who is this Helper?

   C. Where can we find this Helper (v. 17)?

   D. What promise did Jesus make in verse 18? How is he keeping it today? How does this show that he loves to be with the ones he loves?

Community Improvement

The book of Hebrews talks about sympathizing with those in prison (10:34) and remembering them as if we were there with them (13:3). Have you ever considered visiting someone in prison? Do a little research to see what local ministries reach out to prisoners, or check out www.pfm.org (Prison Fellowship's Web site) to get some helpful direction. And then plan a trip!

CHAPTER TWELVE
WHAT'S IT LIKE?

TOURING THE NEIGHBORHOOD

1. The first stop on Christ's itinerary was a womb. Where will God go to touch the world? Look deep within Mary for an answer.
   - A. Why do you think God bothered with a human birth? If he did an "end around" a human father, why not do another "end around" a human mother?
   - B. What is most remarkable to you about Mary? According to human wisdom, why might she seem an unlikely choice?
2. Christ grew in Mary until he had to come out. Christ will grow in you until the same occurs. He will come out in your speech, in your actions, in your decisions. Every place you live will be a Bethlehem, and every day you live will be a Christmas.
   - A. How is Christ coming out in your speech, your actions, your decisions?
   - B. Can you say that everywhere you live is a Bethlehem? Explain.
3. You are a modern-day Mary. Even more so. He was a fetus in her, but he is a force in you. He will do what you cannot.
   - A. Do you have trouble thinking of yourself as a "modern-day Mary"? Explain.
   - B. Describe some things that Jesus has done through you that you couldn't have done on your own.
4. If Mary is our measure, God seems less interested in talent and more interested in trust.
   - A. Why would God be more interested in trust than in talent?
   - B. Is this good news for you or bad? Explain.

CITY CENTER

1. Read Luke 1:26–38.
   - A. How did the angel greet Mary (v. 28)? How did Mary react (v. 29)? Why?

B. What promise did the angel give to Mary (vv. 30–33)? What important details did he seem to leave out (v. 34)?

C. How did the angel answer Mary's lone question (v. 35)? In what way did this answer really not give many answers?

D. How did Mary respond to the whole announcement (v. 38)? What does this show about her?

2. Read Acts 26:9–24.

   A. How did Paul describe himself before he met Jesus on the road to Damascus (vv. 9–11)?

   B. According to 2 Corinthians 6:4–10, how did Paul describe his life after he met Jesus?

   C. According to Galatians 2:20, to what did Paul attribute the remarkable change in his life?

3. Read Ephesians 3:16–19.

   A. What prayer did Paul offer for the Ephesians in verse 16? Name the various elements of this prayer.

   B. What does it mean for Christ to "dwell" in a person's heart "through faith"?

   C. What further prayer did Paul offer in verse 18? How does this prayer build upon his previous one?

   D. What did Paul see as the final answer of this prayer (v. 19)?

Community Improvement

What are you currently doing in your Christian life that you absolutely could *not* do if Christ were not working through you? Make a list of these things. If your list seems short, make a one-month commitment to God to pray for his instruction and leading in this area. Ask God to show you how to let Christ live through you in everyday, "normal" kinds of activities—and then note what changes start to come.

CHAPTER THIRTEEN
A Cure for the Common Life

Touring the Neighborhood

1. You lead a common life. Punctuated by occasional weddings, job transfers, bowling trophies, and graduations—a few highlights—but mainly the day-to-day rhythm that you share with the majority of humanity.

   A. What is "common" about your life?

   B. What is extraordinary about your life?

2. For thirty of his thirty-three years, Jesus lived a common life. Aside from that one incident in the temple at the age of twelve, we have no record of what he said or did for the first thirty years he walked on this earth.

   A. Why do you think Jesus waited until about the age of thirty to begin his public ministry?

   B. What value was there in Jesus' thirty years of "common life"?

3. Next time your life feels ordinary, take your cue from Christ. Pay attention to your work and your world.

   A. Do you like feeling "ordinary"? Explain.

   B. How could you make "ordinary" experiences extraordinary?

4. What kind of love adopts disaster? What kind of love looks into the face of children, knowing full well the weight of their calamity, and says, "I'll take them"?

   A. Answer these questions.

   B. Why would God say these things about us? Why would he adopt us?

City Center

1. Read Mark 6:1–6.

   A. Why did the preaching of Jesus astonish his hometown neighbors (vv. 2–3)?

   B. How did Jesus respond to the comments of his neighbors (vv. 4–6)?
   C. Why was Jesus amazed at his neighbors?

2. Read 1 Peter 1:17–21.
   A. What does it mean to live in "reverent fear" (v. 17 NIV)? What does this look like?
   B. How does Peter describe the kind of life handed down to us (v. 18)?
   C. How does Peter describe the one who redeemed us (v. 19)?
   D. What are the human and divine elements in Jesus' life described in verse 20?
   E. In whom do we place our faith, according to verse 21? Through whom do we exercise this faith? What is significant about this?

Community Improvement

Some Christians get off on an unhealthy track because they desperately want to be seen as anything but ordinary. But read 1 Thessalonians 4:11–12. What does Paul say here about an ordinary Christian life? To what does it lead? What might you have to do, if anything, to get more in step with this instruction? Commit these two verses to memory, and meditate on them for the next week or two. Look for an unheralded, "ordinary" opportunity to serve.

Chapter Fourteen
Oh, to Be DTP-Free!

Touring the Neighborhood

1. Do you have any DTPs? When you see the successful, are you jealous? When you see the struggler, are you pompous? If someone gets on your bad side, is that person as likely to get on your good side as I am to win the Tour-de-France?
   A. Describe what Max means by a Destructive Thought Pattern (DTP).
   B. Answer his questions. What other DTPs come to mind?

2. Lust wooed him. Greed lured him. Power called him. Jesus—the human—was tempted. But Jesus—the holy God—resisted. Contaminated e-mail came his way, but he resisted the urge to open it.
   - A. How could a sinless Son of God actually be tempted? What would it mean for us if he couldn't be tempted?
   - B. How did Jesus resist the urge to open the "contaminated e-mail"? How can we do the same?

3. Remember the twelve-year-old boy in the temple? The one with sterling thoughts and a Teflon mind? Guess what. That is God's goal for you! You are made to be like Christ!
   - A. In what ways do you wish you were more like Christ? Be specific.
   - B. Describe someone whose faith you respect. In what ways does this person model Christ to you?

4. He changes the man by changing the mind. And how does it happen? By doing what you are doing right now. Considering the glory of Christ.
   - A. What does it mean to consider "the glory of Christ"?
   - B. How often do you let your mind ponder the person and work of Jesus? What is most effective in helping you to do this?

City Center

1. Read Luke 2:41–50.
   - A. Why do you think Jesus neglected to tell his parents that he was going to stay behind in Jerusalem?
   - B. What sort of questions do you imagine Jesus asked the teachers in the temple?
   - C. Why do you think Jesus asked his parents the questions he raised in verse 49?
   - D. Why do you think Jesus' parents did not understand what he said to them?
   - E. Luke tells us that Jesus was obedient to his parents, even though they misunderstood him (v. 50). How is this significant?

2. Read Romans 8:5–11.
   - A. What test does Paul give in verse 5 for telling whether we are pursuing God or our own selfish interests?
   - B. What does the sinful mind produce (v. 6)? What does the godly mind produce?
   - C. How can we make sure that our minds experience peace and life (v. 9)? What does this require, practically speaking?
   - D. What promise are we given in verse 11?
3. Read Colossians 3:1–17.
   - A. What instruction does Paul give us in verses 1–2? What does this mean in practical terms?
   - B. How does Paul "flesh out" his command in the verses that follow? How can you tell if you are complying with his instructions or not?
   - C. Create a two-column list. On the right side, put the "good" qualities Paul says we are to pursue; on the left, put the "bad" qualities we are to avoid. How does striving for the mind of Christ lead naturally to this way of life?

Community Improvement

Up for a challenge? It's not an "easy" book, but John Piper's *Future Grace* has some terrific guidance and insights into conquering specific temptations that everyone faces. He demonstrates how to use particular Scripture verses to combat several besetting sins, such as anxiety, pride, shame, impatience, bitterness, lust, and despondency. Get a copy of the book and start reading the section on the temptation that causes you the most trouble.

Chapter Fifteen
Tire Kicker to Car Buyer

Touring the Neighborhood

1. Baptism wasn't a new practice. It was a required rite for any Gentile seeking to become a Jew. Baptism was for the moldy, second-class,

unchosen people, not the clean, top-of-the-line class favorites—the Jews. Herein lies the rub. John refuses to delineate between Jew and Gentile. In his book, every heart needs a detail job.

A. Why did John believe that "every heart needs a detail job"?

B. In what way does *your* heart need a detail job? Explain.

2. What do we owe? We owe God a perfect life. Perfect obedience to every command.

   A. Do you agree with these statements? Why or why not?

   B. If you stopped at the requirement, how would you feel? Why?

3. Baptism celebrates your decision to take a seat. . . . We are not saved by the act, but the act demonstrates the way we are saved. We are given credit for a perfect life we did not lead— indeed, a life we could never lead.

   A. How does the act of baptism celebrate and demonstrate the way we are saved?

   B. Why do you think God uses physical acts to serve as spiritual markers?

4. The daughter answered the doorbell that evening to find a seven-foot-tall, brightly wrapped box. She tore it open, and out stepped her father, fresh off the plane from the West Coast. Can you imagine her surprise? Perhaps you can. Your gift came in the flesh too.

   A. How did your Father become a gift?

   B. What have you done with this gift? What are you doing with this gift?

City Center

1. Read Matthew 3:13–17.

   A. Why do you think Jesus wanted to be baptized by John?

   B. How did John react to Jesus' wish to be baptized (v. 14)?

   C. In what way did Jesus' baptism "fulfill all righteousness" (v. 15)?

   D. How did God demonstrate his approval of Jesus at this event (vv. 16–17)?

2. Read Romans 6:3–7.
   A. What does Paul mean that Christians are "baptized" into the death of Christ (v. 3)?
   B. How does baptism symbolize the beginning of a new way of life (v. 4)?
   C. If we are "buried" with Christ in baptism, to what are we "raised" (v. 5)?
3. Read Galatians 3:26–29.
   A. How does one become a son of God, according to verse 26?
   B. What does it mean to be "clothed with Christ" (v. 27)?
   C. How does this "clothing" lead to Paul's statement in verse 28?
   D. What promise does Paul reiterate in verse 29?

Community Improvement

Have you followed the Lord in baptism? If you have made a commitment of faith to Christ, why not? If this is a step of obedience which you're ready to take, then get it on the schedule. Make an appointment with your pastor to talk about what's involved in baptism and what it means, and then prepare yourself for the event. Invite family and friends—hey, why not neighbors too?—and make it the celebration God means it to be. If you already have been baptized, find out when a friend or loved one is scheduled to be baptized, and have your special celebration then.

Chapter Sixteen
The Long, Lonely Winter

Touring the Neighborhood

1. How do you know when you're in the wilderness? You are lonely. Whether in fact or in feeling, no one can help, understand, or rescue you.
   A. Describe the last time you were in the wilderness of loneliness. What put you there?
   B. When you feel lonely, why does it seem no one can help, understand, or rescue you?
   C. How do you deal with times of loneliness?

2. Listen, you and I are no match for Satan. Jesus knows this. So he donned our jersey. Better still, he put on our flesh. . . . And because he did, we pass with flying colors.
   - A. How do we sometimes demonstrate that we think we *are* a match for Satan? What inevitably happens?
   - B. How did Jesus deal with the temptations posed by Satan?

3. Satan doesn't denounce God; he simply raises doubts about God. . . . He attempts to shift, ever so gradually, our source of confidence away from God's promise and toward our performance.
   - A. How does Satan most often raise doubts about God in your life?
   - B. Describe the last time your confidence started shifting away from God's promise and toward your performance. What happened?

4. Jesus' survival weapon of choice is Scripture. If the Bible was enough for his wilderness, shouldn't it be enough for ours? . . . Doubt your doubts before you doubt your beliefs.
   - A. Why do you think Jesus chose Scripture as his "weapon of choice"?
   - B. How do you use Scripture when you feel under spiritual attack?
   - C. What does it mean to doubt your doubts before you doubt your beliefs?

City Center

1. Read Luke 4:1–13.
   - A. Jesus didn't just wander into the desert; the Spirit *led* him there (v. 1). Why?
   - B. When did Satan tempt Jesus with bread? When he was full or empty, strong or weak? What does this suggest about Satan's temptation of us (v. 2)?
   - C. What three temptations are recorded in Scripture? How did Jesus respond to all three?
   - D. What does it mean to put the Lord to the test (v. 12)?
   - E. Verse 13 says Satan left Jesus "until an opportune time." What does this suggest to us about our own temptations?

2. Read James 1:13–15.
   A. What is the source of our temptations? What is *never* the source?
   B. Describe the "life cycle" of temptation and sin. Why is this life cycle important to grasp?

3. Read Hebrews 4:14–16.
   A. How does verse 14 describe the risen Christ? Why is this important to us?
   B. How does verse 15 describe Jesus? Why is this important to us?
   C. What application of these truths does verse 16 make? Have you applied the truth in this way? Explain.

Community Improvement

Many studies have shown that loneliness has become a national epidemic. Think about your neighbors for a moment. Who among them appears lonely? In a gentle and sensitive way, be alert to the lonely in your neighborhood, and then see what you can do to lessen that loneliness. Invite the person to join you for a game or a movie or a family outing. Try *something*. You don't have to be a doctor to help cure loneliness.

Chapter Seventeen
God Gets into Things

Touring the Neighborhood

1. The presence of troubles doesn't surprise us. The absence of God, however, undoes us. We can deal with the ambulance if God is in it. We can stomach the ICU if God is in it. We can face the empty house if God is in it. Is he?
   A. Describe the last time you faced a major trial. Did it feel as though God was there with you? Explain.
   B. When is it most difficult to believe that God is with you?

2. The present-tense Christ. He never says, "I was." We do. We do because "we were." We were younger, faster, prettier. Prone to be people of the past tense, we reminisce. Not God. Unwavering in

strength, he need never say, "I was." Heaven has no rearview mirrors.

A. What does it mean for us that Christ is always "present tense"?

B. Do you think God has any regrets? Explain.

3. God gets into things! Red Seas. Big fish. Lions' dens and furnaces. Bankrupt businesses and jail cells. Judean wildernesses, weddings, funerals, and Galilean tempests. Look and you'll find what everyone from Moses to Martha discovered. God in the middle of our storms. That includes yours.

A. How has God gotten into things in your life? Describe a couple of incidents.

B. How do you look for God in the middle of your personal storms?

C. How can you help others find God in the middle of their own tempests?

City Center

1. Read Matthew 14:22–33.

A. Whose idea was it for the disciples to cross to the other side of the lake (v. 22)? Why is this important to remember?

B. What did Jesus do after dismissing the crowd (v. 23)? What example does he give us?

C. Why did the disciples think Jesus was a ghost (v. 26)? How often do we mistake Jesus for something or someone else?

D. How did Jesus respond to his disciples' fear (v. 27)?

E. Do you applaud or disapprove of Peter's request (v. 28)? Why?

F. What caused Peter to sink (v. 30)? How is this very much like us?

G. How does verse 33 give an appropriate end to the story? Why would this be an appropriate end to our stories as well?

2. Read John 6:48; 8:12, 58; 10:9, 11, 36; 11:25; 14:6; 15:1.

A. Spend some time discussing each of the "I am" statements of Christ in the gospel of John. What does each one signify? How is each one meant to give you hope and a future?

B. Substitute "I was" or "I will be" for these statements. How does that affect the hope they provide?

Community Improvement

Teachable moments for children can be found in reaching out to those in our communities who are less fortunate. If you have children, consider taking them on a church-sponsored family missions trip to an underprivileged culture. Or you might take them to help serve for an afternoon or a day at a downtown rescue mission. Teens can help with city-sponsored literacy courses. Investigate your opportunities for service to the underprivileged, and then get the whole family involved.

Chapter Eighteen
Hope or Hype?

Touring the Neighborhood

1. Ever feel as if you are walking through a religious midway?

   A. Answer this question.

   B. Describe some of the religious come-ons you've heard in the past year.

   C. How can you tell when you're hearing a religious "carnival barker"?

2. Peter's error is not that he spoke, but that he spoke heresy. Three monuments would equate Moses and Elijah with Jesus. No one shares the platform with Christ.

   A. Why shouldn't Moses and Elijah share the platform with Christ?

   B. How does Jesus far outstrip any spiritual hero of the past?

   C. Why do you think God had Moses and Elijah meet with Jesus on the mountain?

3. In the synoptic Gospels, God speaks only twice—at the baptism and then here at the Transfiguration. In both cases he begins with "This is My beloved Son." But at the river he concludes with affirmation: "in whom I am well pleased." On the hill he concludes with clarification: "Listen to Him."

A. Why do you think God spoke audibly from heaven only twice in the Gospels? Why not speak more often?

B. For what reason do you think God would say of Jesus on the first occasion, "in whom I am well pleased," while on the second he said, "Listen to Him"?

C. How do you actively listen to Jesus?

4. Make no mistake, Jesus saw himself as God. He leaves us with two options. Accept him as God, or reject him as a megalomaniac. There is no third alternative.

   A. Why do you think so many people insist that Jesus never claimed to be God?

   B. How would you show someone that Jesus truly did claim to be divine?

   C. What decision have you made about the identity of Christ? Why did you make this decision?

City Center

1. Read Luke 9:27–36.

   A. In what way was the Transfiguration a fulfillment of prophecy (v. 27)?

   B. How do you think the disciples recognized Moses and Elijah (v. 33)?

   C. Why do you think the disciples grew afraid as a cloud from God covered them (v. 34)?

   D. Why do you think the disciples for a time kept to themselves the story of the Transfiguration (v. 36)?

2. Read Matthew 24:30.

   A. What connection does this verse have with the Transfiguration story?

   B. How can the truth declared by this verse give you hope and strength to continue, even in hard circumstances?

Community Improvement

Many religious cults claim some connection to Jesus Christ while at the same time flatly denying his divinity. Get a copy of a good resource on non-Christian cults (*Dictionary of Cults, Sects, Religions and the Occult,* for example, or Walter Martin's classic *Kingdom of the Cults*), and bone up on the reasons why Christians believe in the deity of Christ, as well as why these cultic groups deny it.

CHAPTER NINETEEN
Abandoned!

Touring the Neighborhood

1. This is a supernatural darkness. Not a casual gathering of clouds or a brief eclipse of the sun. This is a three-hour blanket of blackness.
   - A. Imagine how the witnesses of this event might have reacted to the darkness.
   - B. Why would God cause such a darkness?
   - C. Have you experienced a sudden, dramatic act of nature? How did you react?
2. Ah, there is the hardest word. *Abandon.* The house no one wants. The child no one claims. The parent no one remembers. The Savior no one understands. He pierces the darkness with heaven's loneliest question: "My God, my God, why did you abandon me?"
   - A. Describe a time when you felt abandoned.
   - B. Do you ever fear being abandoned? Explain.
   - C. Why would God abandon his only Son, "in whom I am well pleased"?
3. See Christ on the cross? That's a gossiper hanging there. See Jesus? Embezzler. Liar. Bigot. See the crucified carpenter? He's a wife beater. Porn addict and murderer. See Bethlehem's boy? Call him by his other names—Adolf Hitler, Osama bin Laden, and Jeffrey Dahmer.

A. Was it unfair of God to place the sin of the world on his perfectly obedient Son? Explain.

B. Does Jesus' hesitation in the Garden of Gethsemane make more sense to you when you ponder the sin he "became" on the cross? Explain.

City Center

1. Read Matthew 27:45–54.

   A. Why do you think Matthew tells us about the darkness that covered the land for three hours (v. 45)?

   B. What do you think was going through Jesus' mind as he cried out the words recorded in verse 46?

   C. What happened at the moment that Jesus died (vv. 51–53)? Why are these things significant?

   D. How did the Roman soldiers react to what they saw (v. 54)?

2. Read Psalm 22:1–18.

   A. Read carefully through these verses, and see how many prophetic fulfillments you can find in the crucifixion of Christ.

   B. When you are fearful, what scripture gives you strength?

3. Read 2 Timothy 4:9–18.

   A. Briefly describe Paul's personal situation as he speaks of it in this passage.

   B. How did the apostle react to being abandoned (vv. 10, 16)?

   C. How did the apostle find strength in God even in his abandonment (vv. 17–18)? How can we do the same?

Community Improvement

A popular worship song says Jesus was abandoned so we didn't have to be. But some people—including Christians—feel abandoned nonetheless. You can help break the chains of abandonment by demonstrating your care and concern for someone in your world. From a small beginning, such as an invitation to dinner, you can show someone that he or she has not been abandoned. If a personal invitation might be overwhelming to the person, try a group event, such as a neighborhood party. Call it a "get-acquainted" party, implying that there will be others in the group who are new to the neighborhood, thereby making the event more welcoming and less intimidating.

CHAPTER TWENTY
CHRIST'S *COUP DE GRÂCE*

TOURING THE NEIGHBORHOOD

1. Don't we howl? Not at car washes perhaps but at hospital stays and job transfers. Let the economy go south or the kids move north, and we have a wail of a time. And when our Master explains what's happening, we react as if he's speaking Yalunka. We don't understand a word he says.
   A. How do you normally react when unexpected difficulties hit? Do you wail? Explain.
   B. Describe a time when you just couldn't understand what God was doing in your life. In hindsight, what do you now think God might have been doing?
   C. Is your present world "wet and wild"? Explain. What have you learned that can help you weather this time?
2. More Old Testament foretellings were realized during the crucifixion than on any other day. Twenty-nine different prophecies, the youngest of which was five hundred years old, were completed on the day of Christ's death.
   A. Does it encourage you or inspire you in your faith to realize how many ancient prophecies Christ fulfilled while on the cross? Why or why not?
   B. Have you ever done a study on fulfilled prophecy? If not, why not?
3. Don't call Jesus a victim of circumstances. Call him an orchestrator of circumstances! He engineered the action of his enemies to fulfill prophecy. And he commandeered the tongues of his enemies to declare truth.

A. Think through the gospel story. How did God appear to arrange circumstances to orchestrate the result he desired?

B. If God really does orchestrate even what appear to be tragic circumstances for the benefit of his people, how should that affect the way you live? Does it so affect your life? Explain.

4. I dare you to find one element of the cross that he did not manage for good or recycle for symbolism. Give it a go. I think you'll find what I found—every dark detail was actually a golden moment in the cause of Christ.

A. Take Max's challenge. What do you discover?

B. How do you think God can take "every dark detail" of your own life and use it for your ultimate good?

City Center

1. Read Matthew 26:24, 31, 54, 56; John 12:20–27; 13:18; 17:12.

A. What do all of these texts have in common?

B. Why is it important for us to realize that Jesus knew exactly what was happening as the time of his arrest drew near?

C. What confidence can it give you in your faith to realize that God has history under control?

2. Read John 11:49–52.

A. Who spoke prophetically in this passage (v. 49)? Why is that unusual?

B. What do you think the speaker meant to convey through his statement? What did God intend for his words to convey (vv. 51–52)?

C. How does this incident demonstrate God's shepherding of history—yours included?

3. Read Acts 4:23–31.

A. How did their knowledge of prophecy frame the apostles' interpretation of Jesus' crucifixion?

B. Did the fulfillment of prophecy encourage the apostles or make them fearful? What did they do as a result?

Community Improvement

If you'd like a gripping, journalistic-style account of what happened when Jesus went to the cross, get a copy of Jim Bishop's *The Day Christ Died.* Bishop uses modern reportorial techniques and up-to-date historical information to paint a fascinating picture of what happened on the day Jesus gave his life for humankind.

CHAPTER TWENTY-ONE
Christ's Crazy Claim

Touring the Neighborhood

1. An occupied tomb on Sunday takes the good out of Good Friday.
   A. Why would an occupied tomb on Sunday take the good out of Good Friday?
   B. What was good about the death of Christ? Why couldn't the disciples see this ahead of time?
2. The empty tomb never resists honest investigation. A lobotomy is not a prerequisite of discipleship. Following Christ demands faith, but not blind faith.
   A. How is it possible to investigate the Crucifixion and Resurrection two millenniums after the Gospels say they occurred?
   B. Give some examples of intelligent questions regarding the truth of Christianity.
   C. What is the difference between faith and blind faith? Why is one legitimate and the other not?
3. The courage of these men and women was forged in the fire of the empty tomb. The disciples did not dream up a resurrection. The Resurrection fired up the disciples. Have doubts about the empty tomb? Come and see the disciples.
   A. Compare the actions and demeanor of the disciples before and after Resurrection Sunday. What differences do you note?
   B. Why is it harder to believe that the disciples dreamed up the Resurrection than that the Resurrection fired up the disciples?

4. Just like passengers in the airport about to board a plane, we get to choose how we respond. Either board and trust the pilot—or try to get home on our own.
   - A. How do some people try to get home on their own?
   - B. How do you demonstrate your trust in the "Pilot"? Could observers see this trust? Explain.

City Center

1. Read Matthew 28:1–10.
   - A. To whom did the angel direct his comments in this passage (v. 5)? Why do you think he didn't speak to the guards?
   - B. What did the angel tell the women? What did he direct them to do (vv. 5–7)?
   - C. Why do you think the women were both afraid and filled with joy at the angel's words (v. 8)?
   - D. Why do you think the risen Christ would tell his disciples to go to Galilee, where he would appear to them? Why not appear to them where they already were?
2. Read Acts 2:22–41.
   - A. How does Peter begin his comments on Jesus in this passage (v. 22)? Why start out this way?
   - B. How does Peter interpret the arrest and crucifixion of Christ (v. 23)?
   - C. What event does Peter highlight in his sermon (vv. 24–32)?
   - D. How does Peter connect this event to what has just happened in Jerusalem (v. 33)?
   - E. What conclusion does Peter state in verse 36?
   - F. What solution does Peter suggest in verses 38–40?
3. Read 1 Corinthians 15:1–8, 12–20.
   - A. Name the main points of the "gospel" Paul said he preached.
   - B. What personal connection did the apostle have to these events (v. 8)?
   - C. Why is the resurrection of Christ central to the message of Christianity (vv. 12–20)? What happens without it?

Community Improvement

The resurrection of Jesus Christ forms the cornerstone of our entire faith—but that cornerstone does people no good if they don't know about it. When was the last time you told someone else about the great Savior you have? Who in your sphere of influence still needs to hear about Jesus? Make a list of the five people in your life who first come to mind. Commit to praying for them, that they might invite Jesus to become their Savior—and pray specifically for how you might fit into the introduction.

CONCLUSION
Still in the Neighborhood

Touring the Neighborhood

1. Why the immensity? Why such vast, unmeasured, unexplored, "unused" space? So that you and I, freshly stunned, could be stirred by this resolve: "I can do all things through Christ who strengthens me."

   A. How does the vastness of space make you feel? Awed? Miniscule? Explain.

   B. How does the immensity of space encourage us to believe that we can do all things through Christ, who strengthens us?

2. The Christ of the galaxies is the Christ of your Mondays. The Starmaker manages your travel schedule. Relax. You have a friend in high places.

   A. Does knowing that Christ both runs the universe and watches over you help you to relax? Explain.

   B. How close are you to your friend Jesus? Could you call him a best friend? Why or why not?

3. Even in heaven, Christ remains our next door Savior. Even in heaven, he is still "Christ Jesus . . . who died." The King of the universe commands comets with a human tongue and directs celestial traffic with a human hand. Still human. Still divine. Living forever through his two natures.

A. Why is it important for us to remember that Jesus forever remains both human and divine?

B. Do you look forward to shaking the very real hand of your very real Savior? Explain.

4. Even though he is in heaven, he never left the neighborhood.

A. How could Jesus be both in heaven and in your neighborhood?

B. Does it help you to think of Jesus as a next door Savior? Explain.

City Center

1. Read Romans 8:34.

A. What current role does this verse assign to Jesus Christ?

B. How does this role encourage you to keep moving ahead in your faith?

2. Read Ephesians 1:15–23.

A. What requests did Paul make of God on behalf of the Ephesians (vv. 17–19)?

B. What do you learn about Christ's resurrection (vv. 19–20)?

C. What do you learn about Christ's current activities (vv. 20–22)?

D. How do these truths affect you?

3. Read Matthew 28:16–20.

A. Why do you think that when the disciples saw Jesus after his resurrection, most worshiped him but some doubted (v. 17). What was there to doubt?

B. How did Jesus describe his status in verse 18? What significance does this have for us?

C. What commands does Jesus give his disciples in verses 19–20? How are you complying with these directions?

D. What promise does Jesus give in verse 20? How is this designed to encourage and strengthen us?

Community Improvement

Spend some time in prayer thanking God for sending his Son, Jesus Christ, to be your next door Savior. Thank him for the specific benefits he has granted you. Praise him for his kindness in providing such a wonderful Savior. And ask him how you might be able to share your Savior's love with others, whether under your own roof or in your own neighborhood.

Notes

Chapter 2: Christ's Theme Song

1. Jeordan Legon, "From Science and Computers, a New Face of Jesus," 25 December 2002. Found at www.cnn.com/2002/TECH/science/12/25/face.jesus.
2. Dean Farrar, *The Life of Christ* (London, England: Cassell & Company, Ltd., n.d.), 84.

Chapter 3: Friend of Flops

1. Thanks to Landon Saunders for sharing this story with me.

Chapter 6: Spit Therapy

1. Joni Eareckson Tada et al., *When Morning Gilds the Skies: Hymns of Heaven and Our Eternal Hope* (Wheaton, Ill.: Crossway Books, 2002), 23–24. Used by permission.

Chapter 7: What Jesus Says at Funerals

1. Used by permission of Karen and Bill Davis.
2. Billy Sprague, *Letter to a Grieving Heart: Comfort and Hope for Those Who Hurt* (Eugene, Oreg.: Harvest House, 2001), 9.

Chapter 8: Getting the Hell Out

1. Not her real name.
2. Linda Dillow and Lorraine Pintus, *Gift-Wrapped by God: Secret Answers to the Question, "Why Wait?"* (Colorado Springs, Colo.: WaterBrook Press, 2002), 59–64. Used by permission.

Chapter 9: It's Not Up to You

1. John MacArthur, Jr., *The MacArthur New Testament Commentary: Matthew 8–15* (Chicago: Moody Press, 1987), 281–283.

Part Two: No Place He Won't Go

1. Paul Aurandt, *Destiny and 102 Other Real-Life Mysteries* (New York: Bantam Books, 1983), 225.

Chapter 11: He Loves to Be with the Ones He Loves

1. Maxie Dunnam, *This Is Christianity* (Nashville: Abingdon Press, 1994), 60–61.

Chapter 13: A Cure for the Common Life

1. Dean Farrar, *The Life of Christ* (London: Cassell and Co., Ltd., 1906), 57.
2. George Connor, comp., *Listening to Your Life: Daily Meditations with Frederick Buechner* (San Francisco: Harper & Row Publishers, 1992), 2.
3. Destiny went to be with Jesus on December 3, 2002.

Chapter 14: Oh, to Be DTP-Free!

1. Taken from Don Stephens, "Of Mercy—and Peanut Butter," The Mercy Minute, at www.mercyships.org/mercyminute/vol5/mmv5–32.htm, and Harold S. McNabb Jr., "Inspirational Thoughts from the Legacy of George Washington Carver," speech at Iowa State University.
2. Psalm 119:18 KJV.

Chapter 15: Tire Kicker to Car Buyer

1. My thanks to Bob Russell for sharing this story.

Chapter 17: God Gets into Things

1. Ann Coulter, "Dressing for Distress," 24 October 2001. Found at www.worldnetdaily.com.
2. Frederick Dale Bruner, *The Churchbook: Matthew 13–28,* vol. 2 of *Matthew: A Commentary by Frederick Dale Bruner* (Dallas: Word Publishing, 1990), 534.

Chapter 18: Hope or Hype?

1. "Chosen" is the translation of *agapetos,* "the absolutely unique and solitary one." "Son" is preceded by a definite article: "*the* Son of mine," *ho huios mou.* Ibid., 606.
2. C. S. Lewis, *Mere Christianity* (New York: MacMillan, 1952), 56.

Chapter 19: Abandoned!

1. Matthew Henry, *Matthew to John,* vol. 5 of *Matthew Henry's Commentary on the Whole Bible* (Old Tappan, N.J.: Fleming H. Revell Company, 1985), 428.
2. Walter Bauer, *A Greek-English Lexicon of the New Testament,* trans. William F. Arndt and F. Wilbur Gingrich (Chicago: University of Chicago Press, 1979), 50.

Chapter 20: Christ's Coup de Grâce

1. Josh McDowell, *The New Evidence That Demands a Verdict* (Nashville: Thomas Nelson, 1999), 193.
2. Ibid., 186, 189, 192.

Chapter 21: Christ's Crazy Claim

1. Peter Lewis, *The Glory of Christ* (London, England: Hodder & Stoughton, 1992), 342.

Conclusion: Still in the Neighborhood

1. John Piper, *Seeing and Savoring Jesus Christ* (Wheaton, Ill.: Crossway Books, 2001), 19.
2. John MacArthur, Jr., *The MacArthur New Testament Commentary: Colossians and Philemon* (Chicago: Moody Press, 1992), 48.
3. Piper, *Seeing and Savoring Jesus Christ,* 19.
4. MacArthur, Jr., *MacArthur New Testament Commentary: Colossians and Philemon,* 47.
5. Lewis, *Glory of Christ,* 135.
6. Charles J. Rolls, *Time's Noblest Name: The Names and Titles of Jesus Christ* (Neptune, N.J.: Loizeaux Brothers, 1985), 84–86.

God's Great Big Love for Me

With colored beads built right in, this board book is the perfect book to teach the verse and meaning behind John 3:16 to preschool children.
Available February 2008

3:16 – The Numbers of Hope Teen Edition

Max offers his unique and simple storytelling for this important message while Tricia Goyer writes teen responses to Max's message, guiding teens to fully understand how this verse can impact their lives. From confession to praise, these responses are sure to bring an insightful look into the personal faith of teens.
Available February 2008

A DVD for Small Group Study

This is a kit designed and priced specifically for small groups. It will include a copy of the study guide for small groups, an evangelism booklet, the Indelible DVD, and a CD-ROM with facilitator's guide information and promotional material.

MAX LUCADO
3:16
THE NUMBERS OF HOPE
A DVD STUDY FOR SMALL GROUPS

The Teaching Ministry of Max Lucado

You're invited to partner with UpWords to bring radio and the Internet a message of hope, pure and simple, in Jesus Christ!

Visit www.maxlucado.com to find FREE valuable resources for spiritual growth and encouragement, such as:

- Archives of UpWords, Max's daily radio program. You will also find a listing of radio stations and broadcast times in your area.
- Daily devotionals
- Book excerpts
- Exclusive features and presentations
- Subscription information on how you can receive email messages from Max
- Downloads of audio, video, and printed material

You will also find an online store and special offers.

Call toll-free,

1-800-822-9673

for more information and to order by phone.

UpWords Ministries
P.O. Box 692170
San Antonio, TX 78269-2170
1-800-822-9673
www.maxlucado.com